Tamalpais Trails

Barry Spitz

Potrero Meadow Publishing

Copyright © 1998 by Barry Spitz

Design, Layout, Cover, and Cartography: Dewey Livingston
Photographs: Brad Rippe
Front Cover: *Mt. Tamalpais from King Mountain*, painting by Kathleen Lipinski
Back Cover: Kerri Hogue in Muir Woods, photograph by Randy Hogue

Library of Congress Cataloging-in-Publication Data
Spitz, Barry, 1948-
Tamalpais Trails / by Barry Spitz.
p. 312
Includes index.
ISBN 0-9620715-2-8 : $18.95
1. Hiking—California—Tamalpais, Mount—Guide-books.
2. Trails—California—Tamalpais, Mount—Guide-books.
3. Tamalpais, Mount (Calif.)—Description and travel-Guide-books.
I. Title.
GV199.42.C22T367 1989
917.94'62 — dc20   89-8739 CIP

Published by: Potrero Meadow Publishing Co.,
P.O. Box 3007,
San Anselmo, CA 94979

Printed in Canada

Printing history:
First edition, 1990; second printing, 1990
Second edition, 1992
Third edition, 1995
Fourth edition, 1998

THIS BOOK IS DEDICATED TO THE MEMORY
OF MY SISTER, SYDELLE (1941-1981),
WHO WAS GRANTED BUT ONE VISIT
TO THE TOP OF MT. TAMALPAIS

"I only went out for a walk and finally concluded to stay out till sundown, for going out, I found, was really going in."

— John Muir

Acknowledgments

I wish to thank the following people, who, along with many others, helped make this book possible:

JIM VITEK, the grand old man of the Mountain's north side;
DEWEY LIVINGSTON, the best mapmaker and designer;
MIKE HOY, jack of all trades;
FRED SANDROCK, dean of Tam's historians;
BRAD RIPPE, brilliant photographer, and Tam lover;
NANCY SKINNER, Tam's unofficial archivist
BEN SCHMIDT, who perhaps knows Mt. Tamalpais better than anyone;
KEN WILSON, with his passion for measurement;;
LARRY BRAUER, computer guru;
LINCOLN FAIRLEY, who walked these paths before me;

JOHN ARANSON, PATTI BREITMAN, FAITH DUNCAN,
WILMA FOLLETTE, JAY GALLOWAY, RANDY HOGUE,
BOB LETHBRIDGE, DICK and BRUN LIEBES, CASEY MAY,
MIA MONROE, SALEM RICE, BRIAN SANDFORD,
BOND SHANDS, TY STEFAN, and DAVID WIMPFHEIMER
all contributed in significant ways.

A special thank you goes to the thousands of volunteers who built, maintained, and still work on Tamalpais' trails.

And thank you, PAMELA, SALLY, and LILY, for everything.

Errors that remain are entirely my own.

Tamalpais

Out our house windows,
or coming home from the cardinal points,
it waits like a welcome lamp
set against the sky.

Fog hides it,
seduces it,
tickles it,
rain puts it behind a scrim
but it remains steadfast—yes.

Large enough for awe,
small enough for an afternoon hike,
covered with evergreen
and a seasonal blush of wildflowers,
it catches rain clouds
and shakes them loose of their harvest
and its creeks and rivers churn with water.

Evening throws it into purple,
sunlight casts it green and blue.
While lower hills turn summer-gold
it stays viridian and needled.

And yet despite this familiarity,
it rises sacred against the sky
holding something back,
something for the gods in us.

—CB Follett

As published in *BESIDE THE SLEEPING MAIDEN, Poets of Marin*,
edited by CB Follett (Arctos Press, Sausalito, 1997)

Table of Contents

Giant madrone, Pilot Knob Trail.

Mount Tamalpais

IT WOULD BE DIFFICULT to overstate the importance of Mount Tamalpais to the quality of life in the San Francisco Bay Area. Tamalpais' presence—immutable, ever green, pristine, its famous profile visible from so vast an area—provides an assurance of nature's timelessness in a world rapidly changing. Millions of visitors come each year to hike or run, to ride bikes or horses, to look at plants and birds, to fly kites or hang glide, to walk through Muir Woods, to see the Mountain Play, to simply escape the pressures of urban life and modern times. Many couples marry on Tam, others have chosen it as their final resting place. Few mountains anywhere are more beloved or zealously guarded or have inspired more legends, poems or paintings. Just why is Mount Tamalpais, but 2,571 feet high and not even the tallest peak in the Bay Area, so special?

One reason is Tamalpais' stunning setting. Straddling the Marin Peninsula, Tam overlooks the Pacific Ocean to the west, the Marin Headlands and the Golden Gate to the south, San Francisco Bay to the east, and seemingly limitless open rolling hills to the north. The famous "Sleeping Maiden" profile of Tam's summit ridge is a quintessential natural feature of the Bay Area.

Another factor is Tamalpais' accessibility. Generations of San Franciscans have used the Mountain as their playground; Tam lies barely ten miles from the City's downtown. Once a railroad rose to near its summit; now a road does. Most of the Mountain is publicly owned. It is open every day, without charge, to all.

The Mountain retains a natural environment. True, nearly all Tam's old growth redwoods have been logged; its bears and elk gone; its largest creek dammed several times; and countless structures built on it. Still, much of the Mountain's setting remains wild, with forests, streams, grassy slopes, marshes, meadows, chaparral, and rock outcroppings. An abundant, diverse flora and fauna remains. Even coyotes and mountain lions have returned.

Unmeasurable but no less real is a special quality long associated with the Mountain. The native Americans who lived beside it revered Tam, perhaps unwilling to tred on its summit. Many who regularly visit Tamalpais develop a similar veneration. For example, the Dalai Lama, spiritual leader of Tibetan Buddhists, chose to hold a service on Tam's West Peak in 1989.

Another factor is that Mt. Tamalpais does hold several impressive physical honors. It is the tallest mountain bordering San Francisco Bay. It is the highest point directly on the California coast from Big Sur north into Mendocino County, a distance of more than 250 miles. There is no other peak above 2,000 feet in a 30 mile radius of Tamalpais, making it the most prominent feature in a circle of nearly 3,000 square miles.

And then, of course, there are the trails. Perhaps no parkland of comparable size in the nation has a greater number of, or more richly diversified, or consistently lovelier, trails than Mt. Tamalpais. You can spend your whole life on the Mountain and still discover new trails and new treasures on familiar routes.

This book is about Mt. Tamalpais and those trails that help open its pleasures, its secrets. All of the Mountain's some 170 reasonably maintained longer trails and fire roads, totaling more than 210 miles in length, are described in detail. (Though I don't doubt that, despite my years of research, a few other hidden trails exist on Tamalpais.) Presented are the distances, elevations, intersecting trails, flowers and trees and creeks and rocks and other natural features passed along the way, the man-made changes, the story of each trail's name. Each description is intended to be interesting in its own right and, more, an invitation and a guide for exploration. Hopefully all Mountain users; hikers, runners, cyclists, horse riders, historians, and naturalists, plus armchair mountaineers, will find the book of value.

The thought that I could play some role in helping open, even to one person, the rich experiences that Mt. Tamalpais has to offer is what motivated me to write and to update this book. I describe some of the things I've seen and that you might see. If you give it the chance, the Mountain will work its special magic, and your experiences and discoveries will be like no one else's.

The Name "Tamalpais"

The origin of the word "Tamalpais" has been much debated. Many hold that the name is of Coast Miwok Indian origin. "Tamal" meant either "coast," "bay," or "west," and "pa" meant "mountain" or "near." Others believe the name is entirely of Spanish origin, stemming either from: "country ("pais") of the Tamals," a name for the local Indians; "mal pais," a common Spanish term for barren, rocky terrain; the Aztec place name "Tamaulipas," transferred from Mexico; or even the dish "tamales." The name Tamalpais was officially applied to the Mountain around 1860. Some earlier survey maps referred to it as Table Mountain, but other names were used as well.

Notes On The Fourth Edition

I am happy to report that changes on Mt. Tamalpais' trails have been relatively minor since concluding research on the previous (third) edition in 1994, reassurance of an eternal quality so many seek on the Mountain. Still, there was enough new information to warrant this revision.

All trails have been revisited and all descriptions contain at least some new material. Four trails have been added—King Mountain Loop, Three Wells, Tucker Cutoff, and Van Wyck Creek. There are significant updates, such as the new fees at Muir Woods, expanded signage on Water District trails, and some route closures. Insights passed on by readers have been incorporated. Errors, such as a faulty description of the crest of Benstein Trail, have been amended. Dewey Livingston has made revisions to his wonderful map, which is now enlarged and printed on higher quality paper stock. Brad Rippe has contributed several never before published photographs. The renowned artist Kathleen Lipinski offered a new painting for the cover. Internal changes make the book easier to read and use.

Should owners of *Tamalpais Trails* buy the fourth edition? The majority of even occasional Tam visitors who have only a first or second edition would probably find the updates since sufficient to consider the investment. Most third edition owners, save for hard core Tam lovers, would find the latest changes rather subtle. You decide!

—*Barry Spitz, January 1998*

How To Use This Book

EACH OF THE 167 trails and fire roads in this book are presented in a standardized format. First, they are grouped into twelve major trailheads, then described alphabetically. Below each trail's heading are five to seven subheading lines.

Line one: The trail's start and end points, and total mileage.
Line two: The type of terrain the trail traverses, and the managing jurisdiction.
Line three: The elevation of the start and end points, and the steepness.
Line four: Distances to all intersecting trails.
Line five: Directions to the trail's start.
Line six: Any special amenities at the start, end, or along the trail.
Line seven: Any spurs or short branches.

Each of these elements is explained later in this section. Beneath the capsule summary is the full trail description. To find a particular trail, use the alphabetical Index in the back of the book or the Table of Contents, grouped by trailhead, in the front. After the trail descriptions are chapters on Tamalpais' creeks, lakes, rocks, weather, flora, fauna, history, key trail junctions, jurisdictions, and recreational opportunities.

The Boundaries Of Mt. Tamalpais

Mt. Tamalpais can be described as an L-shaped ridge running east-west from East Peak to Bolinas Ridge, then northwest. The three-mile long, east-west summit ridge (sometimes called Tamalpa Ridge) has three distinct peaks; East (2,571 feet), Middle (2,490 feet), and West (2,567 feet), separated by saddles. Bolinas Ridge in turn runs some 15 miles northwest to the Olema Valley. There are also many prominent subsidiary ridges; the longest, Throckmorton, runs four miles.

Except on the southwest, where the Mountain drops to the Pacific Ocean, Tamalpais' physical boundaries are not clear-cut. The boundaries used in this book are based on drops to sea level, creek drainages, public open space boundaries, roads (which usually follow natural contours), traditional maps, and popular conceptions. These boundaries are given below.

North: Fairfax-Bolinas Road, north of which is a separate watershed (also with much public land) from Mt. Tamalpais.
Northeast: The borders of Marin Municipal Water District lands.
East: The Magnolia Ave.-Camino Alto corridor (the original route of Highway 101).
Southeast: The Dipsea Trail.
South: Highway 1 as it passes through Green Gulch.
Southwest: The Pacific Ocean.
West: Highway 1 bordering Bolinas Lagoon.
Northwest: The lands of Audubon Canyon Ranch, which are open to the public only seasonally.

This is a roughly 64 square mile area, stretching some eight miles both east-west and north-south, and covering 13% of Marin County. Since some 210 miles of trails are described in this book, Mt. Tamalpais can be said to average 3.3 miles of trails and fire roads per square mile.

The complete area covered by this book is shown on the foldout map, drawn by long-time Tam cartographer Dewey Livingston, included in the back.

Trail Standards

The trails and fire roads on Mt. Tamalpais described in this book all meet a minimum set of standards. Each trail and fire road is:

- Unpaved all, or most, its length;
- Closed to motor vehicles;
- At least 2-3 feet wide;
- Reasonably clear to follow;
- Entirely on public land, or has an easement through privately owned sections;
- At least occasionally maintained;
- At least a quarter-mile (.25 miles) long;
- Reasonably safe regarding such hazards as steepness, poison oak, sharp-pointed shrubs, and the like;
- Not specifically posted as closed by the managing jurisdiction.

Trailheads

All trails are grouped into twelve major trailheads. Trailheads may be a single place (Deer Park, Mountain Home, Muir Woods, Phoenix Lake, Pantoll, Rock Spring) or an area (East Ridgecrest Boulevard, Highway One, Old Highway 101, Mill Valley, Sky Oaks, West Ridgecrest Boulevard). Each is accessible by automobile, all have parking. Some have amenities such as outhouses, fountains, telephones, and informational displays; others no more than a signpost. The Muir Woods trailhead is always staffed, the Sky Oaks and Pantoll trailheads often.

Each trailhead introduction has directions from Highway 101, Marin's main artery. Each introduction also presents a number of suggested classic loop walks, arranged by distance, from the trailhead. Loop descriptions are very concise; refer to the individual trail sections for detail.

Trail Names

Trail names are colorful features of Mt. Tamalpais. While most trails have one generally agreed upon name, many carry multiple names and some have no name at all. There is no central naming authority for the trails; given the several jurisdictions into which the Mountain is divided, and the cherished place of alternate names, standardization is not likely soon.

Trail names used by those managing Mountain lands—Marin Municipal Water District (MMWD), Mount Tamalpais State Park (MTSP), Marin County Open Space District (MCOSD), Muir Woods National Monument (MWNM), Golden Gate National Recreation Area (GGNRA), and some Marin towns— on their own maps and signs generally take precedence. The excellent Tamalpais maps published by The Olmsted Bros. Map Co. and by Eureka Cartography (formerly Freese Bros.) are also key sources. For unnamed trails, I sought tags used by local visitors or Mountain old-timers. In a handful of cases, I coined a name based on a characteristic feature of the trail.

For some trails, the origin of the name is obscure. This too is part of the Mountain's lore and appeal. I talked with Mountain veterans, and read published and unpublished references, but I've no doubt others can expand upon my stories.

There are also variations in the "surnames" of trails. The terms "trail," "road," "fire road," "protection road," "fire trail," and "grade" have been attached to names without standardization, and often vary on different maps. Following is a summary of the surname conventions used in this book.

Trail: This is the standard surname. If no surname is given for a route, "trail" is assumed.

Fire Road: Trails wide enough to accommodate vehicles are called fire roads, whether or not they were built to help in fire control. Many are labeled "protection roads" on signs at their entry gates.

Grade: Four fire roads have traditionally been, and continue to be, called "grades." They are Old Railroad, Eldridge, Fish, and Shaver.

Road: Three fire roads that are partly paved are called roads. They are Old Stage Road, Camp Eastwood Road, and Rocky Point Road.

Fire Trail: Some of these were originally broad, ridge line cuts to help block the spread of fires. They are now classified either as a trail if advancing vegetation has narrowed them, or as a fire road if still wide.

Spur: A few trails have shorter, unnamed branches, which are here called "spurs." They are cited in the trail summaries.

Connector: A trail or fire road that meets minimum standards but is not described separately, usually because it is too short (under .25 miles), is called a connector. Connectors are described with a "from" or "to," or with both.

Path: Any route beneath this book's standards of safety, steepness, or ease of following is considered a path. These include deer paths, abandoned trails, improperly worn in shortcuts, etc. Paths are only mentioned when they are prominent enough to cause confusion. Their use is discouraged because of the environmental damage that can be caused (one goes right by the only known Marin location of the wildflower *Sidalcea hickmanii*).

For clarity, the words "trail," "fire road," "grade," "road," and "fire trail" are capitalized when referring to the specific route of the chapter heading.

From ....To

A trail can, obviously, be followed in either direction. Still, the given "start" and "end" points were not selected arbitrarily. Generally, the end at or nearer an auto-access trailhead is considered the "from" of the heading. When both ends of a trail are auto-accessible, or both are remote, the trail is generally described going uphill. A few exceptions to these rules were made when one end of a trail was much easier to spot than the other, when one direction was deemed unsafe, or when the trail formed a likely loop partner with another trail.

Distance

Nearly all the trails in this book were personally measured with a surveyor's wheel. For the handful of others (generally too rocky), distances are estimated.

Distances are expressed in hundredths of a mile (e.g., 1.03m) or tenths (e.g., .4 miles or .4m). Distances of less than .1 mile are sometimes given in feet or yards, rounded off. Admittedly vague terms, such as "immediately," "directly," and "shortly," are used for variety. They imply distances of less than 25 yards or so, and indicate the reader should be alert for the noted intersection or point of interest.

Terrain

The "terrain" line contains very brief descriptions of the trail's nature. The vegetation summary is based on the plant communities as presented in the "Flora" chapter in the back of the book. "Woodland" and "forest" imply shade, "chaparral" and "grassland" connote openness. "Riparian" means the trail passes beside a creek or lake. "Unmaintained" means that the trail is not recognized by the governing jurisdiction, so is not officially maintained and is probably unmarked. Some "unmaintained" trails remain in reasonable condition due to steady use or occasional clearings by volunteers. Those trails that are in poor condition, on the edge of this book's standards for inclusion, are designated "MARGINAL."

If horses or bicycles are permitted on the trail (both are presumed allowed on fire roads), that is noted here. Also, for those who want (or don't want!) to encounter others, the most visited trails and fire roads are described as "heavily used." At the end of the terrain line is an abbreviation for the jurisdiction(s) through which the trail passes. See the "Jurisdictions" chapter in the back for greater detail. Those routes that are part of the new Bay Area Ridge Trail (which is not a separate jurisdiction) are so noted.

Elevation

For each trail, the elevation in feet is given for the start and end point, and for any significantly higher or lower places passed in between. These elevations come largely from the United States Geological Survey topographic map of the Mt. Tamalpais 15' quadrangle (1954, photorevised 1980). Most elevations are given to the nearest 40 feet, the Survey map's contour line interval.

Along with the elevation is a word or two on the trail's steepness. Since what, for example, is "very steep" to some may be no problem to others, the following rather conservative guidelines are used. They apply to the general nature of the trail; significant sections that differ are noted.

Extremely steep: Elevation changes greater than 850 feet per mile. Stretches may require using hands for safety, with risk of falling if attempted downhill. Trails with "extremely steep" sections should be avoided by all but fit and nimble users.
Very steep: Elevation changes of 600-850 feet per mile. These trails might be a problem for those with concerns about their fitness or sureness of foot.
Steep: Elevation changes of 350-600 feet per mile. When taken slowly, these trails can be comfortably handled by almost all Mountain users.
Gradual: Elevation changes of 100-350feet per mile. These trails would be con-

sidered easy by almost all users.

Almost level: Elevation changes of under 100 feet per mile.While no trail on Mt. Tamalpais is truly flat, these come closest.

Rolling: The route has significantly more uphill and downhill than the net change in elevation indicates.

Intersecting Trails

Each intersecting trail, fire road, and connector, with its mileage from the starting point, is given. With this feature, readers can design for themselves an all but infinite number of fully described and measured trip possibilities.

Directions

This is the shortest or easiest-to-follow route to the trail's starting point from the sectional trailhead. "Limited or no parking" means there are no, or very few, legal spaces by the trail's start. Try to carpool.

Amenities

If there are unexpected amenities on the trail or at its start or end, they are noted. These include water fountains, telephones, outhouses or bathrooms (flush toilets and running water), picnic areas, and wheelchair accessibility.

Abbreviations

Below are abbreviations commonly used in this book. Mount Tamalpais itself is interchangeably referred to as "Mt. Tamalpais," "Tamalpais," "Tam," and "the Mountain." All phone numbers cited are area code "415," unless otherwise stated.

FAA: The Federal Aviation Administration facility at West Peak

F.R.: Fire Road

GGNRA: Golden Gate National Recreation Area

m: mile

MCOSD: Marin County Open Space District

MMWD: Marin Municipal Water District (also called "the Water District")

MTIA: Mount Tamalpais Interpretive Association

MTSP: Mount Tamalpais State Park (also called "the State Park")

MWNM: Muir Woods National Monument.

A Note On Creek Banks

Most Tam trails cross or run along a creek or two. Throughout the text, the terms left and right bank are used to remove any ambiguity about where the trail is in relation to the creek. When facing in the direction of a creek's flow, which should be obvious even in summer when the bed may be dry, the left bank is on the left and the right bank is to the right. For example, if a trail skirts a creek's left bank, the creek will be to your right when you are traveling downhill and to your left when traveling uphill.

Douglas iris, slope above Deer Park Fire Road.

Deer Park Trailhead

Deer Park Trailhead

Directions to Deer Park:

Highway 101 — Sir Francis Drake Blvd. (exit) west, Greenbrae, to San Anselmo — left on Center Blvd. to Broadway, Fairfax — left on Bolinas Road — left on Porteous Ave. to end (or to Wood Lane and end)

DEER PARK, a delightful picnic area beside both banks of Deer Park Creek, serves as access to the northernmost trails in this book. The picnic area is maintained by Marin County but is on, and surrounded by, Water District land. The adjacent Deer Park School, owned by the Ross Valley School District, is leased to the Fairfax-San Anselmo Children's Center. Pass to the left of the school to enter the trail network. There are outhouses and fountains by the parking lot. (Please leave the nearest parking spaces for school use. If the lot is full, there is parking on adjacent residential streets; Meernaa Avenue may be a better choice than narrow Porteous.)

Deer Park Fire Road and Deer Park and Ridge trails leave from near the parking area. Deer Park F.R. is the most used route. It leads, in 1/3 mile, to four-way Oak Tree Junction and, in 2/3 miles, to seven-way Boy Scout Junction.

A second, nearby public access to the Mountain is through the Marin Stables at the end of Wood Lane, off Porteous on the way to Deer Park. Be quiet when passing through the stables, so as not to startle the horses.

There is a completely separate Deer Park, and fire road, on the southwest side of Tamalpais.

Suggested loops from Deer Park (elevation 190 feet)

• Deer Park Trail, .8m, to Worn Spring F.R. — right, .4m to Yolanda Trail — right, .9m, to Six Points Junction — right, .4m, on Bald Hill Trail and fire road connector to Five Corners — right, 1.1m, on Deer Park F.R. to start **3.6 miles.**

• Deer Park F.R., .4m, to Junction Trail — right, .3m, to Moore Trail — right, .5m, to Canyon Trail — left, .7m, to Concrete Pipeline F.R. — left, .6m, to Five Corners — left on Deer Park F.R., 1.1m, to start **3.6 miles.**

• Deer Park F.R., 1.1m, to Five Corners — left on Concrete Pipeline F.R., 1.4m, to Fish Gulch Trail — left, .4m, to Phoenix Junction — left on Shaver Grade, .4m, to Hidden Meadow Trail — right, .8m, to Six Points Junction — left on Bald Hill Trail, .7m, to Boy Scout Junction — right on Deer Park F.R., .7m, to start **5.5 miles.**

BALD HILL TRAIL
FROM BOY SCOUT JUNCTION TO SIX POINTS JUNCTION / .71 miles

Terrain: Mostly madrone woodland, parts through redwoods and grassland; horses permitted / MMWD
Elevation: From 380' to 550' / gradual, short part very steep
Intersecting Trails: Connector fire road to Five Corners (.4m)
Directions: Deer Park trailhead—Deer Park F.R., .7 miles

BALD HILL TRAIL begins at a seven-way intersection, passes a connector to Five Corners (which has six options), and ends at a five way junction called Six Points! We'll try to untangle things.

When arriving at Boy Scout Junction on Deer Park F.R. from Deer Park, Bald Hill Trail is the first fork left. The others, in order clockwise, are: Deer Park F.R. continuing to Five Corners, a connector fire road dropping to Canyon Trail, Moore Trail, Ridge Trail, and Junction Trail.

Bald Hill Trail starts steeply uphill on the western flank of Bald Hill. This opening section is particularly rich with wildflowers in spring. The iris, wonderfully variable, is one star. Note that early on the irises are mostly deep blues and purples. Further along the Trail the shadings are more pink and white.

In just under .4 miles, the Trail hits a ridge line at a T-intersection. To the right, a connector fire road drops .1 mile to Five Corners. There are magnificent views of Mt. Tam.

Bald Hill Trail continues left, along the spine of what is sometimes called Kentucky Ridge. It skirts an area closed for erosion control, then veers left into a redwood forest at another rerouting. Bald Hill Trail re-emerges onto the ridge top. A spur of Hidden Meadow Trail here has been closed for erosion control.

In another .1 mile, the Trail ends at Six Points on the western flank of Bald Hill. The four other trails are, clockwise: Six Points dropping to Deer Park F.R., Yolanda going to Worn Spring F.R., Yolanda towards Phoenix Lake, and Hidden Meadow Trail dropping to Hidden Meadow. The now overgrown sixth option out of Six Points ascended Bald Hill.

BUCKEYE TRAIL
BETWEEN WORN SPRING FIRE ROAD / .25 miles

Terrain: Grassy hillside; unmaintained and narrow / MMWD
Elevation: Around 540' / almost level
Intersecting Trails: None
Directions: Deer Park Trail to top

THIS QUARTER-MILE Trail cuts off a stiff up and down section on Worn Spring Fire Road.

Buckeye's northern end is 100 feet above the top of Deer Park Trail. The Trail, only recently marked by the MMWD, is quite narrow. Pause to enjoy the views of Bald Hill and of many miles of open space. In fall, the Trail remains colored by late blooming wildflowers, pink from willow-herbs and yellow from madias.

Except for an oak or two, all the trees passed along the way are buckeyes. Several nearly uprooted ones cling to life. The buckeye's fragrant candle-like blossoms and palmate leaves in spring and summer, the buckeye seed pods in fall, and the bare limbs in winter are all highly distinctive.

Aptly named Buckeye Trail ends at Worn Spring Fire Road in a saddle. To the right, the fire road passes the north end of Yolanda Trail and continues up Bald Hill. Left returns to Buckeye's start.

CANYON TRAIL
FROM MARIN STABLES TO CONCRETE PIPELINE F.R. / .69 miles

Terrain: Riparian; woodland; muddy in winter; horses permitted / MMWD
Elevation: 190' to 480' / gradual, last part very steep
Intersecting Trails: Moore (.1m), connector fire road to Boy Scout Junction (.6m)
Directions: Wood Lane, Fairfax, to end—through Marin Stables

CANYON TRAIL begins directly behind Fairfax' Marin Stables, to the left of the last stall when entering from Wood Lane. The stables, although on MMWD land, are privately run. This arrangement, unique in the watershed, provokes some opposition whenever the stables' lease comes up for renewal. Be quiet as you walk through the area, so as not to disturb the horses housed there. Canyon Trail is used principally by horseback riders to and from the stables, which keeps it among the muddiest of Tam's trails in winter.

The opening half-mile parallels a usually placid stream through a peaceful, tree-lined canyon. One hundred yards past the stables, (Ethel and Harry) Moore Trail forks left while Canyon continues right, beside the stream. The main stream is crossed once, to the left bank, at around .2 miles. Just after, a feeder stream is also crossed. The trees are mostly laurels, with some madrones. Farther in, redwoods dominate.

In .5 miles, a connector fire road to Boy Scout Junction rises to the left across the stream. Canyon Trail continues straight. It now climbs very steeply via switchbacks.

Canyon Trail ends at Concrete Pipeline F.R. To the right is Taylor Trail and Fairfax-Bolinas Road. To the left, it is .8 miles to Five Corners.

The canyon and stream that this Trail follows are unnamed. The Trail itself dates at least to the 1930's, when it was simply known as "Horse Trail."

DEER PARK FIRE ROAD
FROM DEER PARK TO FIVE CORNERS / 1.13 miles

Terrain: Wooded; riparian; heavily used / Marin County & MMWD
Elevation: From 190' to 520' / first half level, second half very steep
Intersecting Trails: Six Points (.3m), Junction (.3m), Bald Hill (.7m), connector fire road to Canyon (.7m), Moore (.7m), Junction (.7m), Ridge (.7m)
Directions: Deer Park trailhead—left of school, across field to gate

DEER PARK FIRE ROAD is the principal route out of the Deer Park trailhead. It is popular both for short out and back jaunts and as an entry to many other trails.

The Fire Road begins at a gate across the playing field behind the old Deer Park School (now the Fairfax-San Anselmo Children's Center). The separate Deer Park Trail goes left from the near side of the field.

The Fire Road is level at first, through a lovely oak woodland. Deep rows of poison-oak, among the densest on Tam, line the margins. An MMWD display board once stood (briefly) in the first clearing. Here too, a path comes in from the right; it crosses Deer Park Creek and connects to Ridge Trail.

In just over .3 miles is four-way Oak Tree Junction, presided over by a huge, old oak. To the left is Six Points Trail, rising to Six Points. To the right, beside the landmark oak, is Junction Trail, a pedestrian-only alternate route up to Boy Scout Junction.

Deer Park F.R. then begins climbing steeply under a lovely madrone-laurel canopy. After a stiff rise, the Fire Road briefly levels and opens as it meets seven-way Boy Scout Junction. The intersecting trails, clockwise, are: Bald Hill rising to Six Points, Deer Park F.R. continuing, a connector fire road down to Canyon Trail, Ridge Trail and Moore Trail, and the top of Junction Trail.

Deer Park F.R. continues to climb, but less steeply, through woodland. The Fire Road ends at *six*-way Five Corners. The trails meeting here are, clockwise: a connector fire road uphill to Bald Hill Trail, the combined Shaver Grade and Concrete Pipeline F.R. going downhill, Elliott going uphill, Shaver Grade going uphill, and Concrete Pipeline towards Fairfax-Bolinas Road.

The Fire Road was built by the Marin County Fire Department in 1948. There is a second, longer Deer Park Fire Road on Tam, running between Muir Woods Road and Coastal Fire Road.

DEER PARK TRAIL
FROM DEER PARK SCHOOL TO WORN SPRING FIRE ROAD / .84 miles

Terrain: Lower part riparian and wooded, upper part grassland; horses permitted / MMWD
Elevation: From 190' to 520' / steep
Intersecting Trails: None
Directions: Deer Park trailhead—left behind school—left in meadow

DEER PARK TRAIL offers serenity within minutes of the Deer Park trailhead. Its warm southern exposure makes it outstanding for wildflowers. It is also part of the main Deer Park-Bald Hill summit route.

To reach the Trail from Deer Park, pass the school, which is now a day care center, on the left. You enter an open playing field. Deer Park Trail rises from it, signed, to the left, by a black oak. Directly across the field, behind the gate, is the start of Deer Park Fire Road.

The Trail winds its way steadily up the northwest flank of Bald Hill. The area is pretty and peaceful. A stream runs alongside in the lower part.

Wildflowers are particularly abundant in the open area just above. You can count on milk-maids and hound's-tongue to lead the annual parade, beginning in January. Dozens more species follow. Several deer paths cut through the area. Views open. Look down to see the Trail snaking up the hill.

Deer Park Trail ends at Worn Spring Fire Road. To the left, an extremely steep path drops back to the Deer Park parking lot. Another path straight across leads (over private property) to Fairfax. To the right, Worn Spring Fire Road rises past Buckeye Trail (30 yards uphill), then continues to the top of Bald Hill.

ELLIOTT TRAIL
FROM FIVE CORNERS TO SKY OAKS-LAGUNITAS TRAIL / .48 miles

Terrain: Madrone woodland; horses permitted / MMWD
Elevation: 520' to 700' / gradual, short part steep
Intersecting Trails: Shaver Grade (.3m)
Directions: Deer Park F.R. to Five Corners OR Sky Oaks Road-Shaver Grade, .2 miles

ELLIOTT IS THE ONLY Trail option at the Five Corners junction; the other spokes are fire roads. It winds its way uphill as an equestrian and pedestrian bypass of Shaver Grade.

Elliott starts up a few wooden steps, between the two arms of Shaver Grade. It ascends through a madrone-dominated woodland, becoming very steep for a stretch. Shaver Grade, running roughly parallel to the right, is visible.

In one-third mile, Elliott crosses Shaver Grade at a marked junction. The Trail continues climbing, unsigned, through a quintessential California oak woodland. At a crest, a path forks right to a lovely, isolated grassy knoll. Elliott continues to the left, descending to again meet Shaver Grade.

Until the early 1990's, Elliott continued up the other side of Shaver, around the bend where Logging Trail descends. But the uphill on Elliott have been posted as closed for erosion control, blocking the former link to Sky Oaks-Lagunitas Trail.

R. Walter and Harriet Elliott built the nearby Marin Stables, and were guiding forces among the Tamalpais Trail Riders. Walter Elliott died while riding in 1962; the Trail was built soon after.

JUNCTION TRAIL
BETWEEN DEER PARK F.R. AT OAK TREE JUNCTION TO DEER PARK F.R. AT BOY SCOUT JUNCTION / .25 miles

Terrain: Lightly wooded hillside; narrow and rocky / MMWD
Elevation: From 200' to 380' / steep
Intersecting Trails: None
Directions: Deer Park F.R., .3 miles

THIS QUARTER-MILE TRAIL connects two junctions; Oak Tree and Boy Scout. It provides a pedestrian alternative to heavily-used Deer Park Fire Road.

Junction Trail begins at Oak Tree Junction, the four-way intersection on Deer Park F.R. just before the uphill when coming from Deer Park. Junction Trail sets off to the right. Across the fire road is the base of Six Points Trail.

Junction Trail immediately passes the huge, and apparently dying, oak that gives the junction its name. It then rises steeply, with some rocky sections. The Trail's southern exposure helps spring wildflowers, including a mass of baby-blue-eyes near the top, to bloom early. The Trail is particularly lovely on warm summer evenings, when it catches the last sunlight in the canyon.

The Trail ends at Boy Scout Junction. The other six spokes here are, clockwise: Deer Park F.R. from Deer Park, Bald Hill Trail, Deer Park F.R. continuing on to Five Corners, a connector fire road down to Canyon Trail, Moore Trail, and Ridge Trail.

MOORE TRAIL
FROM CANYON TRAIL TO BOY SCOUT JUNCTION / .40 miles

Terrain: Laurel-dominated woodland; muddy in winter; horses permitted / MMWD
Elevation: 220' to 380' / gradual
Intersecting Trails: Ridge Trail, .4m
Directions: End of Wood Lane, Fairfax, to Marin Stables — Canyon Trail, .1m

ONE HUNDRED YARDS beyond the Marin Stables, Canyon Trail meets a fork. Canyon continues to the right, along the stream. Moore Trail sets off left and uphill. Signs here name it for Ethel and Harry Moore.

Moore Trail climbs steadily through a forest of mostly laurels, with occasional madrones. In winter, the Trail can be muddy from the many horses that use it; in summer, dusty. At a short uphill, the Trail splits, then quickly reunites.

Moore Trail ascends gradually. A few yards before its end, with the first views of Bald Hill and beyond, a sign reads "Ethel Moore Trail." The "Harry Moore" mate here has been missing here for years. Ridge Trail, signed, joins from the left. The final yards down to Boy Scout Junction can be considered part of either Ridge or Moore Trail; I'll opt for the latter.

The other intersecting trails at Boy Scout Junction are, clockwise: Junction to Deer Park F.R., Deer Park F.R. down to Deer Park, Bald Hill, Deer Park F.R. up to Five Corners, and a connector fire road back down to Canyon Trail for a short loop.

The Moores were horse lovers closely associated with Marin Stables, and were charter members of the Tamalpais Trail Riders. Harry Moore died in 1944. The Trail was built a few years later and named for him. Ethel Moore, then 86, was present during the dedication ceremony.

RIDGE TRAIL
FROM DEER PARK TO BOY SCOUT JUNCTION / 1.09 miles

Terrain: Oak-madrone woodland; unmaintained; narrow, with poison oak; MARGINAL; horses permitted / MMWD
Elevation: From 200' to 560' to 380' / very steep
Intersecting Trails: None
Directions: Deer Park trailhead

RIDGE TRAIL is at this book's northern limit. It had also long been at or below the book's minimum standard for conclusion, as it had not been maintained since the mid-1970's, become overgrown with broom, and passed several tricky, unmarked forks. But its proximity to the popular Deer Park trailhead, and now a new trail sign at the upper end, will likely continue to bring enough foot traffic to keep the route passable.

The Trail can be said to begin at the entrance to Deer Park, on the left bank of Deer Park Creek. It quickly passes a picnic area with several tables and a water fountain by a bridge over the creek (don't cross).

Ridge Trail continues on the redwood-lined creek's left bank. Beware of poison oak here and all the rest of the way. Opposite the far end of the school playground, veer right up the first fork. The creekside path straight ahead has other, rougher entries that connect up to Ridge Trail.

Ridge Trail rises steeply. Irises dot the hillside in spring. The school children can usually still be heard playing. The other entries come in from the left. Keep climbing on what appears the most-used route.

The Trail reaches Deer Park Ridge and the uphill eases. In clearings, there are extraordinary Tam views, among the best in Marin. There appears nary a sign of human presence in the heavily-wooded vista.

Broom, French and Scotch, presses against both sides of the Trail. The Trail rolls over several oak-studded knolls along the ridge spine.

Almost a mile in, Ridge Trail begins a final descent. It ends at its junction with Moore Trail, although the remaining few yards down to Boy Scout Junction can be considered part of either trail. A new MMWD signpost here is the only Ridge Trail marking.

Ridge Trail was built during World War II by the Tamalpais Trail Riders. They wanted to provide additional equestrian routes to replace the many that were closed off by the military. The Trail was originally called Harry Scott Trail, for the man who built nearby Crest Farm. Scott was a founder, and the first president, of the Trail Riders.

SIX POINTS TRAIL
FROM DEER PARK F.R. AT OAK TREE JUNCTION TO SIX POINTS JUNCTION / .57 miles

Terrain: Deeply wooded; riparian; horses permitted / MMWD
Elevation: From 220′ to 550′ / steep
Intersecting Trails: None
Directions: Deer Park Fire Road, .3 miles

SIX POINTS TRAIL plays a role in many loops out of Deer Park. It is a lovely Trail, alongside a stream through deep woods.

The Trail rises to the left (south) of Deer Park F.R., .3 miles from the fire road's start. On the opposite side of the four-way intersection, called Oak Tree Junction for the ancient oak to the right, is Junction Trail.

Six Points Trail heads off into a quiet, creekside woodland, lined with redwoods, madrones and laurels. It quickly begins ascending steeply alongside Deer Park Creek. Switchbacks ease the climb.

The cool, wet forest—which barely ever sees the sun in mid-winter—supports a lush vegetation. Ferns are abundant. In summer, you may be lucky enough to spot the small greenish-white flowers of rein-orchis, in the always special orchid family.

Near the top, the Trail veers right, away from and above the headwaters of the creek. It ends at *five*-way Six Points Junction, on a ridge with striking Mt. Tam views. The other four trails are, clockwise: Yolanda heading to Worn Spring Fire Road, Yolanda towards Phoenix Lake, Hidden Meadow downhill, and Bald Hill Trail on to Boy Scout Junction. The missing sixth point is a now overgrown path up Bald Hill.

The Trail has also been known as Redwood Trail, particularly among equestrians.

The hard-to-find "Pioneers of Aviation" plaque, below East Peak lookout.

*Northern panorama to Mt. St. Helena, with Pilot Knob (nearest)
and Bald Hill in foreground, from Verna Dunshee Trail.*

East Ridgecrest Trailhead

East Ridgecrest Trailhead

Directions to East Ridgecrest Boulevard:
1) Highway 101 — Highway 1 — Panoramic Highway — Southside (Pantoll) Road to Rock Spring; 2) Fairfax-Bolinas Road, from Fairfax (where it is called Bolinas Road) or from Highway 1 at Bolinas cutoff — West Ridgecrest Boulevard to Rock Spring

RIDGECREST BOULEVARD runs 6.6 miles from Fairfax-Bolinas Road to the East Peak parking area. Some 20 trails branch off it. The road was built during the 1920's, although the stretch between Fairfax-Bolinas Road and Rock Spring (West Ridgecrest) was not paved until 1939. A toll was collected at the Fairfax-Bolinas Road junction, a site called Ridgecrest. A sign there proclaimed the road the most beautiful in the world. The military closed the boulevard soon after America's entrance into World War II. It reopened after the war as a free, public road.

Ridgecrest Boulevard can be divided into two halves centered at Rock Spring; West Ridgecrest (3.7 miles) to Fairfax-Bolinas Road and East Ridgecrest (2.9 miles), the highest road in Marin County, to the East Peak parking lot. West Ridgecrest and Rock Spring are treated as separate trailheads.

The East Peak parking area, from which the summit is a short (but steep) walk, has long been a popular destination, and remains so despite the new $5 parking fee ($4 for seniors). Nearby are bathrooms, fountains, picnic tables, snack bar, telephone, even a pay view scope.

The Mt. Tam Visitor Center there, a one-time restroom refurbished by the Mt. Tamalpais Interpretive Association, is staffed by volunteers and open every weekend. Inside are informative displays, and books, maps and Tam t-shirts are sold.

The East Peak Snack Bar has been run by Sharon Worlund since 1993. She replaced the Beckers, who had managed it since 1965. Worlund signed a new 10-year lease with the State Park in 1997, besting many other contenders. The stand is open daily, 10 a.m. to 6 p.m., from June 15 through Labor Day, and on weekends and holidays from 10 a.m. to 5 p.m. the rest of the year.

The trails that intersect East Ridgecrest are, in order eastward from Rock Spring: Rock Spring, Mountain Top, Rock Spring-Lagunitas F.R., Arturo, Eastwood, International, Miller, Lakeview, Middle Peak F.R., Old Railroad Grade, Eldridge Grade and Fern Creek. There are a few parking spots near each of these junctions.

Gates at Fairfax-Bolinas Road and Pantoll bar vehicular access to Ridgecrest Road at night (usually between sunset and 9 a.m.); call Pantoll Ranger Station at 388-2070 to check closing and opening times.

Suggested loops from East Peak parking area (elevation 2,360'):

• Verna Dunshee Trail *.7 miles.*

• Redwood Spring Trail, .4m, to Northside Trail — right, .6m, to East Peak Fire Trail — right, .1m, to Eldridge Grade — right, .7m, to Ridgecrest Blvd. and up to start **1.8 miles**.

• Fern Creek Trail, .7m, to Old Railroad Grade — right, .1m, to Miller Trail — right, .7m, to across Ridgecrest Blvd. — right on Lakeview Trail, .2m, to Middle Peak F.R. — left, .7m, to Ridgecrest Boulevard and up to start **2.4 miles.**

• Eldridge Grade, 1.2m, to Northside Trail — left, 1.6m, to Colier Trail — left (uphill), .4m, to International Trail — left, .1m, to across Ridgecrest Blvd. — Miller Trail, .3m, to Old Railroad Grade — left, .8m, to Ridgecrest Boulevard and up to start **4.4 miles.**

ARTURO TRAIL
FROM FAA GATE OFF EAST RIDGECREST BOULEVARD TO RIFLE CAMP / .49 miles

Terrain: Deep woodland / GGNRA & MMWD
Elevation: From 2,360' to 2,000' / very steep
Intersecting Trails: None
Directions: Rock Spring — East Ridgecrest Road 1.2 miles to FAA gate

THE REOPENING of Arturo Trail in 1985 was a source of joy to Mountain veterans. The Trail was long part of a popular route between Tam's north and south sides. But it was closed in 1951, after the construction of the Mill Valley Air Force Station on Tamalpa (West Peak) Ridge. It is now again a key north-south link.

To reach the upper end of Arturo, enter the main Federal Aviation Administration (FAA) entry gate off Ridgecrest Road. Veer left (right, toward the domes, is off limits), through a gap in the gate. Follow the hiker symbol sign down the left fork of the paved road. Another hiker sign, to the right, marks the trailhead. A yellow "Trail" arrow has also been painted on the asphalt.

In World War II, the military secured long-term leases to Water District lands here. In 1983, the remaining leases, save for the parcel on the very top of West Peak, were turned over to the Golden Gate National Recreation Area. After a spirited debate, a decision was made to remove the structures and return the area to open space. The work started, was halted for years when high levels of asbestos were found, then finally resumed and all but completed in 1997.

Arturo drops sharply at its start. At the first bend left, a short path leads to still-standing building #307. Arturo passes through the Air Force base's old fence, then spends a few yards besides it before veering off downhill into a haunting forest of laurels. A small grove of rare bitter-cherry trees (*Prunus emarginata*) is dedicated to the late Tam historian Lincoln Fairley.

But dominating are Douglas-firs. Some 100 years ago, this area was rather open, probably in the aftermath of a fire. Manzanitas came in, enjoying the full sunlight. Then Douglas-firs invaded, crowding out the manzanita, whose "skeletons" remain. Some of the huge, older firs, which grew here without competition for sunlight, have sizable lower limbs. These monarchs are called "wolf trees" because they supposedly choke out competing plant growth. An impressive pair beside the Trail have been named Romulus and Remus. Near them, a path, the old Potrero Cutoff, sets off for Potrero Meadow.

Quiet is assured in this delightful woodland. Lower down, bays, tanbark oaks, and madrones resist the Douglas-fir's ascendancy.

Arturo Trail ends when it hits Rock Spring-Lagunitas Fire Road at Rifle Camp. Also at this junction, Northside Trail departs right on its 2.7-mile journey to Eldridge Grade and, across the fire road, Azalea Meadow Trail begins its descent to Kent Trail. Potrero Meadow, a must visit, is a few yards up to the left.

Arthur, or Arturo, Oettl, a member of the Cross-Country Boys Club, built the Trail in the 1920's. It was a partial reroute of the old Coyote Trail, the first ever constructed by the Tamalpais Conservation Club. The Marin Conservation Corps, the GGNRA, the MMWD, and the Mt. Tamalpais History Project all played key roles in Arturo's reopening.

AZALEA MEADOW TRAIL
FROM ROCK SPRING-LAGUNITAS F.R. AT RIFLE CAMP TO JUNCTION OF KENT AND HIGH MARSH TRAILS / .85 miles

Terrain: Riparian; heavily wooded; passes two meadows / MMWD
Elevation: 2,000' to 1,500' / steep, short parts very steep
Intersecting Trails: Cross Country Boys (.3m)
Directions: East Ridgecrest Blvd. — Rock Spring-Lagunitas F.R. 1.1 miles, or Arturo Trail to lower end

Azalea Meadow Trail has only recently appeared on Tam maps, and even more recently, been signed. It is a thoroughly delightful Trail, isolated in deep forest, beside a roaring, azalea-laden creek.

The Trail begins off Rock Spring-Lagunitas F.R. at Rifle Camp, directly across from the signed Arturo-Northside trail junction. The Trail descends through a deep woodland of mostly Douglas-fir and madrone. The nearby stream, followed closely throughout but not crossed (though there is one rivulet fording), is the East Fork of Swede George Creek.

The wonderful clearing known as Azalea Meadow (Azalea Flat on Olmsted) suddenly appears. But be aware of two tricky (but now finally signed) three-way intersections just above it. At the first, Cross Country Boys Trail forks left to Kent Trail. Cross Country Boys and Azalea Meadow then run down the steps together for 15 yards to a second junction. Cross Country departs to the right, to Lagoon Fire Road.

Western azaleas are usually in full bloom here in May and June. Their creamy white flowers exude an intoxicatingly sweet nectar. Bees swarm above the meadow, creating a steady hum as they pollinate the next generation of azaleas.

Continue left, downhill, besides the creek. Swede George flows all year. Azaleas line the creek and Trail. This little-traveled part of the Mountain charms all visitors. Boulders offer places to rest. About .3 miles down from Azalea Meadow is a second, larger clearing, Willow Meadow. It too has many azalea bushes. Blue elderberry (*Sambucus mexicana*) is abundant in summer but beware, the berries are toxic.

The Trail runs left, along the clearing's perimeter. It then drops another .1 mile to its end at a four-way intersection. Left (up to Potrero) and right (down to Serpentine Knoll) is Kent Trail. Straight across is the eastern end of High Marsh Trail, with High Marsh itself some 200 yards ahead.

EASTWOOD TRAIL
FROM EAST RIDGECREST BLVD. TO ROCK SPRING TRAIL / .50 miles

Terrain: Chaparral; rocky; unmaintained and MARGINAL / MMWD
Elevation: From 2,400' to 1,920' / extremely steep
Intersecting Trails: None
Directions: Rock Spring — East Ridgecrest Blvd., 1.2 miles

THIS IS ONE OF THE HIGHEST trails on Tam, and has some of the most spectacular views. However, you may find yourself watching only your footing as the Trail is extremely steep, narrow, and rocky.

The upper end of Eastwood (or Alice Eastwood) Trail is 25 yards above, and across Ridgecrest Boulevard from, the gate into the Federal Aviation Administration tracking facility. There is no sign; the former hiking figure symbol marking the top is now gone. Look for it leaving a small dirt turnout.

Eastwood Trail enters a small grove of isolated Sargent cypress trees. It then meets an open area of reddish rock amid blue-green serpentine. The views here — of ocean, Marin Headlands, San Francisco skyline, East Bay — are breathtaking. The distant Farallon Islands, for example, are not even on the horizon.

The Trail bends right (a path rises left back to the road) and begins its precipitous descent through chaparral. Manzanitas are, appropriately, dominant; they were Alice Eastwood's botanical specialty,

Lack of maintenance is causing the route to be overgrown with shrubs, some of them, particularly manazanita and chaparral pea, sharp-pointed. A smoother shrub to grip for safety on the steepest sections is chamise.

The Trail ends when it meets Rock Spring Trail. It is .4 miles left to West Point Inn and 1.1 miles right to the Mountain Theater. In 1993, the MMWD covered the "Eastwood" name side of the junction's signpost. It was only six years earlier that the signpost was placed and the Trail reopened after years of neglect.

Alice Eastwood was one of the most beloved of all people associated with Mt. Tamalpais. She was an outstanding botanist, Curator of Botany at the California Academy of Sciences in San Francisco for 47 years. She did much of her field research on Tamalpais, from 1891 to her death, at 94, in 1953. She described and named five of the Mountain's six manzanita species. The MTIA recently reprinted her 1944 *A Collection of Popular Articles on the Flora of Mount Tamalpais.* The 32-page pamphlet is sold at the East Peak Visitor Center.

Eastwood also walked with the swiftest and ruggedest of the Mountain's male hikers, often over 30 miles a day (while carrying plant presses!). She was accepted as an equal in their fraternity. Alice Eastwood is honored on Tamalpais by this Trail, by Camp Eastwood, and by Camp Eastwood Road.

Eastwood wrote in 1923: "The Eastwood Trail is so named because I recognized it as a short cut to the Potrero [Meadow] from West Point and open most of the way though very steep. It was cleared by John Colier." The Trail dates from around 1914.

FERN CREEK TRAIL
FROM RIDGECREST BOULEVARD TO OLD RAILROAD GRADE / .74 miles

Terrain: Upper half through chaparral, loose rock; lower part riparian and wooded / MMWD
Elevation: From 2,340' to 1,580' / extremely steep
Intersecting Trails: Tavern Pump (.5m)
Directions: East Peak parking lot

FERN CREEK DESCENDS some 2,000 feet in elevation as it flows to Redwood Creek in Muir Woods. Fern Creek Trail follows the creek's upper reaches, high on Tam's south face. A separate trail, Fern Canyon (also sometimes called Fern Creek Trail), borders the creek much lower, in Muir Woods.

Fern Creek Trail is important, and well-used, as a shortcut to and from the top of the Mountain, bypassing three miles of Old Railroad Grade. Since its upper end is accessible by car, the Trail will be described downhill. The MMWD has recently worked on the Trail to improve safety, for example adding several sets of stairs over the steepest sections. Still, be careful. Some of the many stumbles on the Trail are due to weariness of the hikers descending after a trip to the summit.

Fern Creek Trail starts southbound from just below the East Peak parking lot. The topmost 125-yard section, between the one-way upper and lower arms of Ridgecrest Road, is little used. The crossing of lower Ridgecrest is marked by white lines and a State Park sign.

Fern Creek then descends very steeply through chaparral. There are fine southern views over the canyon. After a plunging bend left, the drop becomes somewhat more gradual. The Trail passes beneath a telephone line, and a water pipeline joins on the left.

In .4 miles, the Trail meets a water tank and the building that houses the Tavern Pump. The pump sends water through the pipeline, on a narrow sliver of State Park property in the midst of MMWD lands, to the East Peak area. Steps lead down left to the pump (and to a stand of azaleas.) Tavern Pump Trail, rising to Old Railroad Grade, sets off, signed, to the right. Fern Creek Trail continues straight. From the middle of the next bend left, a path (now blocked) once set off straight ahead. Around the bend, the Trail drops to cross Fern Creek. A new bridge carries the Trail to the creek's left bank, where it remains.

Framing the bridge is a stand of chain (woodwardia) ferns, one of the several fern species encountered along the creek. Chain ferns are Marin's largest ferns, reaching nine feet in height elsewhere on the Mountain. Look on the undersides of the fronds (leaves) and you might see the spore clusters (called sori) lined in the chain-like formation that gives the fern its name.

The Trail follows the creek down through the lovely, forested, creek canyon. Several short but tricky drops over boulders and roots must be negotiated. Loose dirt and slippery tanbark oak acorns also slow the descent.

Fern Creek Trail ends at a bend in Old Railroad Grade, amidst some huge redwoods. Hogback F.R. is .4 miles to the left. Right leads to Miller Trail (.1m) and the West Point Inn (one mile). Fern Creek itself continues under the Grade through a culvert.

INTERNATIONAL TRAIL
FROM EAST RIDGECREST BLVD. TO NORTHSIDE TRAIL / .52 miles

Terrain: Forest; lowest yards open serpentine / MMWD
Elevation: From 2,300' to 2,060' / gradual, parts steep
Intersecting Trails: Colier (.1m)
Directions: East Ridgecrest Blvd., 1.9 miles to saddle between West and Middle peaks

INTERNATIONAL TRAIL starts at one of Tamalpais' best view spots, and ends at another. The signed trailhead is on the north side of Ridgecrest Road at a turnout. Here, in the dip between West and Middle peaks, is a rare vista to both the north and south of Tam. A few yards up Ridgecrest is the west end of Lakeview Trail. Across the pavement (south) is the upper end of Miller Trail.

International Trail immediately enters woodland. In 100 yards the top of extremely steep Colier Trail, which drops all the way to Lake Lagunitas, enters on the right.

After a short uphill, International begins its long descent. Parts are steep, including a haunting stretch through a stand of dead manzanita. At the base of this main downhill, 20 yards before a huge Douglas-fir, a path goes left. Called Birthday Trail by some, it rises one-sixth mile to Rocky Ridge Fire Trail.

International continues down, less steeply. It leaves the forest, replaced by serpentine rock and chaparral. There are again excellent views.

International ends at Northside Trail. Some 100 yards to the left, Northside crosses broad Rocky Ridge Fire Trail. To the right, Northside heads to Colier Spring and Trail, offering a nice loop option.

International was built in the 1940's as a replacement north-south route over the Mountain's summit ridge for Arturo Trail, which was closed during World War II. One story relates that it was named in a spirit of harmony to reflect the many ethnic backgrounds of those who worked on it. Another story has it that MMWD patrolman Joe Zapella remarked, when planning to talk to those responsible for the Trail's unauthorized construction, there would be an "international situation" because of the many nationalities of the builders.

LAKEVIEW TRAIL
FROM EAST RIDGECREST BOULEVARD TO MIDDLE PEAK F.R. / .25 miles

Terrain: Light woodland and chaparral / MMWD
Elevation: From 2,300' to 2,400' / gradual
Intersecting Trails: None
Directions: East Ridgecrest Blvd., 1.9 miles to saddle between West and Middle peaks

LAKEVIEW TRAIL (completely separate from Lakeview Fire Road, which connects Lake Lagunitas to Eldridge Grade) is one of Tamalpais' oldest trails. It once ran from Old Railroad Grade, over today's upper Miller Trail, to the saddle between Middle and East Peak.

Lakeview sets off on the north side of Ridgecrest Road at the splendid vista point of the West-Middle Peak saddle. The top of International Trail is a few yards below off Ridgecrest. Miller Trail descends from the opposite, south side of the road. Lakeview gently rises along the northern face of Middle Peak. Between the shrubs and trees are splendid views, but not as sweeping as years ago, when fires and trimming kept the foliage lower. Lake Lagunitas, the closest of the three visible lakes and the "view lake" that gave the Trail its name, can now just barely be glimpsed. Bon Tempe Lake is more prominent, with a bit of Alpine Lake visible beyond Bon Tempe Dam.

Lakeview Trail ends (actually a bit under a quarter-mile) at its junction with Middle Peak Fire Road. Straight ahead, the fire road, over the original Lakeview Trail route, descends to Ridgecrest Road by the tops of both Old Railroad and Eldridge grades. To the right, the fire road rises .2 miles to Middle Peak's summit.

LOWER NORTHSIDE TRAIL
FROM COLIER SPRING TO ROCK SPRING-LAGUNITAS F.R. / .91 miles

Terrain: Heavily wooded; parts open and rocky / MMWD
Elevation: From 1,840' to 1,800' / almost level
Intersecting Trails: None
Directions: East Ridgecrest Blvd. — International Trail — Colier Trail to Colier
Spring

Lower Northside Trail runs, nearly level, through a remote area high on the
Mountain's north face. To reach the trailhead, follow Colier Trail down to the
delightful, traditional hiker's resting spot of Colier Spring. The other intersect-
ing trails here are, clockwise: Northside (or Upper Northside) heading west to
Rifle Camp, Lower Northside, Colier Trail descending to Lake Lagunitas, and
Northside going east to Eldridge Grade. The classic old sign pointing the way to
Lower Northside disappeared in 1992.

Lower Northside begins amidst towering redwoods. There is a brief opening, another redwood grove, then a somewhat rocky stretch. The Trail gently
rises to a view site, with Pilot Knob and Bald Hill framed between the trees. A
short rise brings Lower Northside to another stand of redwoods, and the crossing
of the upper reaches of the West Fork of Lagunitas Creek.

Just about all the most common trees of Tam are to be found in the woodland ahead: huge Douglas-firs and redwoods along with bay, madrone, live oak,
tanbark oak and California nutmeg. The Trail leaves the forest to enter an open
area of serpentine rock. Here only shrubs and stunted Sargent cypress trees grow.
The views to the north and west are outstanding.

Lower Northside meets Rocky Ridge Fire Trail. One-third mile uphill (left),
Northside Trail intersects Rocky Ridge, offering a loop opportunity. In 1997,
Lower Northside was cleared the additional 100 yards to Rock Spring-Lagunitas
Fire Road.

This Trail, often spelled Lower North Side, was built in the 1930's.

MIDDLE PEAK FIRE ROAD
FROM RIDGECREST BOULEVARD TO MIDDLE PEAK / .62 miles

Terrain: Mostly chaparral; short part paved / MMWD
Elevation: From 2,240' to 2,480' / gradual
Intersecting Trails: Lagunitas Fire (.2m), Lakeview (.4m)
Directions: East Ridgecrest 2.5 miles to saddle between Middle and East peaks

Middle Peak Fire Road starts on the north side of Ridgecrest Road, in the
saddle between Middle Peak and East Peak. This saddle and the trees that stand
in it are quite visible from the Ross Valley miles below. The area was once known

as Pieville. A funicular from here to Middle Peak was built in 1905; its route up the peak's face is now overgrown. Opposite the trailhead is the top of Old Railroad Grade. Just uphill is the top of Eldridge Grade.

Middle Peak F.R. begins rising gradually beyond the gate. There are fine views to the north between gaps in the foliage; be patient, the vistas will soon open completely. In .2 miles, the unsigned, easy-to-miss Lagunitas Fire Trail comes in on the right. A gray, rectangular, metal cover, utility pole, and a boulder stand at the junction. The fire trail drops extremely steeply to Lake Lagunitas.

The Fire Road, paved for a short stretch, bends sharply to the left. Lakeview Trail sets off straight ahead, to Ridgecrest Road at the saddle between Middle and West peaks. Middle Peak Fire Road continues uphill.

The Fire Road ends at Middle Peak's flattened crest. The true summit, off limits behind a fence to the left, is 2,490 feet in elevation. The nearly 360-degree panorama, only partially blocked by East and West peaks (taller by 91 and 87 feet, respectively) is stunning. On clear days, there is a unique vista of both Mt. Tamalpais (East Peak) and Mt. Diablo.

The futuristic-looking, green, geodesic-shaped building left was built in 1981. It is the hub of a privately run microwave communications network used by several government agencies and private firms. To the right, also not to be disturbed, is an array of Federal Aviation Administration equipment. Use of Middle Peak for communication purposes has a long history. In 1905, two 300-foot tall wooden radio transmission towers were erected, using the funicular. They blew over the next year.

Middle Peak Fire Road was built over the eastern half of the older Lakeview Trail to access the new facilities on the summit.

MILLER TRAIL
FROM EAST RIDGECREST BLVD. TO OLD RAILROAD GRADE / .68 miles

Terrain: Upper half chaparral, lower half riparian and wooded; parts rocky / MMWD
Elevation: From 2,300' to 1,580' / very steep
Intersecting Trails: Old Railroad Grade (.3m)
Directions: East Ridgecrest Boulevard, 1.9 miles to saddle between West and Middle peaks

MILLER TRAIL has two completely different characters. Its upper half is through chaparral, with excellent views from high on the Mountain. Its lower half is heavily wooded, alongside a stream in a deep canyon. Each part contributes to make Miller one of Tamalpais' lovelier trails.

East Ridgecrest Road drops to a saddle, or dip, between West and Middle peaks. There are paved parking turnouts, and splendid views, on both sides of the road. To the north is the top of International Trail, with Lakeview Trail just to its right. On the south side is the signed top of Miller Trail.

Miller starts with a few downhill steps over a pipe, and continues dropping very steeply. The canyon of the headwaters of the West Fork of Fern Creek is to the right. Chaparral shrubs line the Trail as it passes over serpentine rock. A couple of pioneeering Douglas-firs stand out; they may one day cover the canyon.

In 1/3 mile, Miller hits Old Railroad Grade; the last few yards before the junction are quite rocky and steep. A wooden signpost, and the remains of an older metal one, mark the intersection. West Point Inn is .7 miles to the right.

Miller continues across the Grade. It offers a one-mile shortcut downhill compared to the less steep Grade. Miller again is steep and rocky. In summer, the highly fragrant pink-purple flowers of western pennyroyal (*Monardella* spp.), in the mint family, dot the serpentine rocks. In .1 mile, the Trail enters woodland. Miller crosses a feeder creek, to its left bank.

The Tiail plunges deeper into the forest as it meets the West Fork of Fern Creek. Keep a sharp eye to spot where the Trail crosses the creek, to the right bank. Chain ferns and elk clover mark the site. Rocks help with the fording.

Miller Trail continues down at the edge of the lively creek. This is a lovely, quiet, haunting area. Soon after the Trail recrosses back to the creek's left bank over a newly constructed bridge.

The Trail encounters a slide from the great storm of January 1982. Redwoods lie fallen across the creek, other huge ones still tower above. The Trail was repaired in 1989 with dozens of steps added to ease the remaining descent. A pipe, which carried water from a dam on the creek, lays broken off at both ends.

Miller ends at its second junction with Old Railroad Grade. The junction is easy to spot as Old Railroad Grade rises on both sides of the redwood-lined bend. This rarity on the Grade also dates from January 1982. The raging creek tore off 40 feet of the Grade, which was then refilled. Note a redwood stump spouting young trees from its top. Fern Creek Trail is .1 mile to the left and West Point a mile to the right.

John Miller was a native of Canada who came to San Francisco in 1895 at age 29. He joined the Tamalpais Conservation Club in 1921, and worked tirelessly on the Mountain's trails until his death in 1951. When he was 80, he badly injured his back while prying a boulder on this Trail. The accident left him bedridden for most of the final three years of his life, and the Trail was named in his honor. He left a sizable bequest to the TCC, which helped toward purchase of additions to the State Park, notably the Scott property around O'Rourke's Bench. To Miller is attributed the wonderful quote, "Why should I deserve praise? Hasn't the Mountain always repaid whatever work I did on it, giving me health, happiness and friendships?"

MOUNTAIN TOP TRAIL
FROM EAST RIDGECREST BLVD. TO THE FORMER AIR FORCE BASE ON TAMALPA
RIDGE / .54 miles

Terrain: Lightly wooded; unmaintained / MMWD & GGNRA
Elevation: From 2,100' to 2,400' / steep
Intersecting Trails: None
Directions: East Ridgecrest Blvd., .4m to Rock Spring-Lagunitas F.R. gate

MOUNTAIN TOP TRAIL originally did go to the highest point on Tam, the 2,604-foot summit of West Peak. But in 1951, West Peak was bulldozed and leveled to 2,567 feet, four feet below East Peak, during construction of the now-abandoned Mill Valley Air Force Station. (A California Alpine Club World War I memorial cairn at the summit was plowed under.) Mountain Top Trail was left an "orphan." Only a half-mile of its westernmost section remains today.

The Trail begins at a gate on the north side of Ridgecrest Road, across from a parking area for the Mountain Theater. Rock Spring-Lagunitas Fire Road also begins here. Unsigned Mountain Top climbs parallel to, and above, East Ridgecrest Boulevard.

Cross a log barrier. The first tree on the right, requiring a bit of ducking, is a Sargent cypress. Beyond, Douglas-firs form most of the low canopy. Between the foliage are outstanding views out to the San Francisco skyline.

At .4 miles, the Trail passes through the base's old fence line. The route becomes narrower and rougher. The Trail peters out just below the ridge, which is known as West Peak Ridge, Tamalpa Ridge, or, earlier, Bill Williams Ridge. A scramble up leads to the old base site and an off-limits communications building. The base bowling alley and movie theater stood directly atop the Trail but, like most all other Air Force station structures, were torn down in 1997.

If you venture right, you'll see the foundations of the former base housing — up to 300 servicemen and their families enjoyed the best residential views in the Bay Area. Look left for a unique view down to Potrero Meadow. Beyond you can still see the old tennis court; the net was only recently removed. There will undoubtedly be many more changes here — one of the most spectacular sites on the Mountain — over the coming years. Continue in the direction of the West Peak domes to pick up the top of Arturo Trail, which descends to Rifle Camp.

A trail, called Bill Williams (separate from the Bill Williams Trail that connects Phoenix Lake to Tucker Trail), ran along Tamalpa Ridge to West Peak since the late 1800's. A parallel fire trail, just to the south of Bill Williams, appears on the 1914 map published by the Tamalpais Fire Association. It is apparently this fire trail that survives as Mountain Top Trail.

NORTHSIDE TRAIL
FROM RIFLE CAMP TO ELDRIDGE GRADE / 2.66 miles

Terrain: Mostly wooded; parts in chaparral, rocky; horses permitted / MMWD
Elevation: Around 2,000' / almost level
Intersecting Trails: Rocky Ridge (.5m), International (.6m), Lower Northside (1.1m), Colier (1.1m), Lagunitas Fire (1.6m), Redwood Spring (2.1m), East Peak Fire (2.7m)
Directions: East Ridgecrest Blvd. — Rock Spring-Lagunitas F.R., 1.1m, or Arturo Trail to lower end

No trail in Marin runs longer above 1,800 feet than Northside. It also plays a role in most circuit routes of Tam.

Northside Trail departs from Rock Spring-Lagunitas F.R. at Rifle Camp, adjacent to the base of Arturo Trail. This western section of Northside, to Colier Spring, is sometimes called Upper Northside.

Douglas-fir dominates in the deep woodland. Soon laurel become the principal forest tree. In 1/3 mile, the Trail enters an open serpentine rock area. The views from this short section, just above 2,000 feet, are spectacular. They sweep from Point Reyes across Marin into Sonoma and Napa Counties. The only trees that grow in this calcium-poor, heavy metal-rich soil are Sargent cypress, and even they are shrub-like.

Northside crosses broad Rocky Ridge Trail beneath a telephone line. Rocky Ridge goes uphill to the old Air Force base and downhill to Lower Northside Trail and Rock Spring-Lagunitas F.R.

Northside continues across at a wood signpost. In 120 yards, still on the open serpentine, International Trail comes in from the right. It rises to Ridgecrest Road.

Northside returns to woodland. It passes through a grove of short redwoods. In the next grove, near Colier Spring, the redwoods are towering. Colier Spring was once a reliable source of water. Since a storm shifted its underground source away from the outlet pipe, it is usually dry. Still, it is one of the best loved resting spots on the Mountain. Five routes converge. Clockwise from Northside, they are: Lower Northside, dropping to Rock Spring-Lagunitas F.R.; Colier, descending extremely steeply to Lake Lagunitas; Northside, continuing; and Colier, uphill to International Trail.

Northside Trail rises slightly as it leaves the redwood forest. At 1/4 mile past Colier is another pipe, tapping a more reliable spring. Chain ferns mark the damp site. Shortly past are azalea bushes, on both sides of the Trail. Their striking, and fragrant, pinkish-white flowers bloom in late spring. Earlier, irises abound here.

Back in the chaparral, the unsigned, extremely steep Lagunitas Fire Trail crosses Northside. Left leads down to Lake Lagunitas, right up to Middle Peak Fire Road.

The last mile of Northside offers many outstanding vista points. Attention to footing also becomes important as the Trail passes through a 1/4-mile band of loose, broken rocks. Two hundred yards past the end of the rock scree is the unsigned, easy-to-miss, lower end of Redwood Spring Trail. It rises on the right to Redwood Spring, Eldridge Grade, and the East Peak parking area.

Northside crosses the East Fork of Lagunitas Creek. The Trail has now passed all three forks of the Mountain's most important creek, the one that is dammed to form, in order, Lakes Lagunitas, Bon Tempe, Alpine, and Kent. Madrone and California nutmeg become the most common trees. A clearing offers a fine view down the canyon to Pilot Knob and beyond.

Northside then hits Inspiration Point, a rock ledge with a splendid northern panorama. Here the precipitous East Peak Fire Trail crosses, left down to Lakeview F.R., right to high on Eldridge Grade.

Northside goes on, wider, for another 100 yards. It ends at a bend in Eldridge Grade roughly halfway between the Wheeler Trail intersection below and the top of East Peak Fire Trail above. A classic old sign marks the spot.

Mountain veterans Ted Abeel and Earl Parks began working on Northside in 1926 to improve the hiking possibilites over the Mountain's less visited north face. Other sources credit the Sierra Club and the Civilian Conservation Corps as playing key roles. The Trail's name is often spelled North Side.

PLANKWALK TRAIL
FROM EAST PEAK PARKING AREA TO EAST PEAK / .29 miles

Terrain: Chaparral; loose rock; heavily used / MTSP
Elevation: From 2,390′ to 2,571′ / very steep
Intersecting Trails: None
Directions: Upper end of East Ridgecrest Boulevard

PLANKWALK TRAIL rises to the highest point in Marin County, Tam's 2,571-foot East Peak. The lure of reaching the summit makes Plankwalk one of the most used trails on the Mountain.

Planks now again carry Plankwalk up from the Verna Dunshee Trail loop behind the refreshment stand. In 150 yards there is a bend to the right, a shortcut route to the top that the State Park closed in 1989. They were reacting to a lawsuit by a visitor, in inappropriate footwear, who had slipped on the rocky terrain. The somewhat safer route to the left narrows.

Plankwalk continues upward on the north, then the east side, of the peak. The views are splendid, unsurpassed. The Trail bends right. At the next bend left, an overgrown and precipitous "path" continues straight. It leads, in a few yards beside a pipe, to one of the Mountain's hidden treasures. Just yards below the northwest corner of the lookout tower is an old bench and plaque. The well preserved plaque reads:

BENEATH THIS PLATE ARE THE NAMES OF THOSE HEROES OF THE AIR WHO HAVE FALLEN IN THE PURSUIT OF THE SCIENCE OF AVIATION, ERECTED BY THE CITIZENS OF MILL VALLEY, MAY 30, 1915.

Return to the stone steps for the final yards up Plankwalk, to the door of Gardner Lookout atop the Mountain. Strong winds are common, but there are perfectly calm days as well; you'll want to stay a while in any case.

The panorama is now complete. It is interesting to compare what the surveyor George Davidson recorded as visible from here during his visits, dating from 1858. (The list is reproduced in Lincoln Fairley's *Mount Tamalpais, A History*.)

Many natural landmarks he observed are still often, or occasionally, visible. They include (with his marginally overstated distances in parenthesis), proceeding clockwise: Point Reyes Head (24-3/4 miles); Bodega Head (37-1/2 miles); Mount St. Helena (51-2/3 miles); Mt. Diablo (36-2/3 miles); Mt. Hamilton (65-1/2 miles); San Bruno Mountain (17-2/3 miles); and Montara Mountain (26 miles). The 56-mile long chain of Sierra peaks he saw, at a distance of 158 miles, are only partially visible now on the clearest of winter days. Davidson also notes that the ocean horizon is 67 miles distant, with the Farallon Islands some 28 miles away. Other landmarks that Davidson recorded can now never be seen, such as the golden dome of the State Capitol building in Sacramento.

The Gardner Lookout atop the East Peak summit was built by the Civilian Conservation Corps in 1935-36. Its resident lookout (since the early 1990's, it has been staffed by volunteers) plays an important role in spotting fires on the Mountain and elsehere in the County. An earlier structure here, built in 1901 through financing by the *San Francisco Examiner*, was used for marine communications until 1919 and as a fire lookout from 1921. It was blown down by high winds in the early 1930's. Edwin Burroughs Gardner (1880-1935) was the first chief warden of the Tamalpais Fire District.

East Peak itself is an erosion-resistant block of the metamorphic rock quartz tourmaline. Plankwalk Trail was once indeed lined with wood planks to provide surer footing to the summit.

REDWOOD SPRING TRAIL
FROM MT. TAM VISITOR CENTER TO NORTHSIDE TRAIL / .43 miles

Terrain: Woodland; parts rocky / MMWD
Elevation: From 2,380' to 2,000' / very steep, parts extremely steep
Intersecting Trails: None
Directions: Upper end of East Ridgecrest Boulevard
Amenities: Fountain, picnic tables

FOR MANY YEARS only the upper section of Redwood Spring Trail was open, serving as a shortcut between the East Peak parking area and Eldridge Grade. In 1989, the Trail's lower half was re-cleared, again opening the route to Redwood Spring itself, and on to Northside Trail for loop possibilities.

The Trail sets off below the two water fountains by the refreshment stand. It immediately passes the Mt. Tam Visitor Center, a one-time bathroom that the Mount Tamalpais Interpretive Association (MTIA) has been renovating. The center is presently open on weekends, staffed by cheerful and knowledgeable MTIA volunteers. Inside are several well-done displays. Proceeds from sales of books, clothing, and maps help support the State Park.

The Trail continues below the small, shaded picnic area. It then drops steeply. The few feet just above Eldridge Grade have been covered by a slide, making them dangerous to descend. The crossing of Eldridge Grade is unsigned.

The lower section of Redwood Spring Trail is little-known, and delightful. It drops through a woodland of California nutmegs, madrones, and oaks. Then, almost magically, is a stand of redwoods, the highest on Mt. Tamalpais. Watering the redwoods is Redwood Spring, seeping from the earth and from old, broken pipes. A downed redwood will likely remain for years. This is one of Tam's special places.

The Trail's remaining .1 mile descent is extremely steep; be cautious. Redwood Spring Trail ends at Northside Trail. The unsigned junction is hard to spot. A young California nutmeg and a mature madrone frame the entrance. Lagunitas Fire Trail and East Peak Fire Trail are each about a half-mile away on Northside, to the left and right, respectively.

ROCKY RIDGE FIRE TRAIL
FROM ROCK SPRING-LAGUNITAS FIRE ROAD TO NEAR WEST PEAK / .8 miles

Terrain: Lightly wooded, parts open; loose rock; unmaintained / MMWD
Elevation: From 1,760' to 2,260' / very steep
Intersecting Trails: Lower Northside (.1m), Northside (.3m)
Directions: East Ridgecrest Blvd. to West-Middle peak saddle — International Trail — left on Northside Trail

ROCKY RIDGE Fire Trail was once cleared as a broad, continuous fire break from Alpine Lake to West Peak. Construction of Rock Spring-Lagunitas F.R. then cut the Fire Trail in two, with the two sections separated by a half-mile. The lower section survives as Rocky Ridge F. R. The upper section, here called Rocky Ridge Fire Trail, became a deadend when the Air Force fenced off their new base in 1951, and was little used. Erosion problems are now prompting the MMWD to consider closing the Fire Trail altogether, or at least the section below Northside Trail.

Rocky Ridge Fire Trail can be reached by climbing 1.7 miles up Rock Spring-Lagunitas Fire Road from Lake Lagunitas. Easier is to descend International Trail from East Ridgecrest Boulevard, then go left 100 yards on Northside Trail. Northside meets Rocky Ridge Fire Trail halfway up, but it will be described from its base, .3 miles right.

Directly across Rock Spring-Lagunitas F.R. at the start is Upper Berry Trail, with an overgrown remnant of Berry setting off just left. Seventy-five yards up Rocky Ridge, at a signpost, Lower Northside Trail goes left to Colier Spring and right, over a section only built in 1997, to Rock Spring-Lagunitas F.R. Continue climbing over the rocks and gullies. The views open ever more dramatically behind, including Point Reyes and Mt. St. Helena.

In .3 miles, Northside Trail crosses. It goes left to International Trail, Colier Spring and Eldridge Grade, and right to Rifle Camp.

The remaining upper section of Rocky Ridge Fire Trail is little visited. Water pipelines, laid from Lake Lagunitas to the former Air Force station on West Peak, are visible to the left of the Trail. Beside the pipeline is a row of Sargent cypress trees, in their element on these serpentine outcrops high on the Mountain. Higher, Douglas-fir becomes the dominant tree. Turn around for the spectacular views, and to catch your breath!

Rocky Ridge meets a once-formidable, barbed wire-topped fence. A fading sign to the right (along a path to Arturo Trail) warns that further climbing is in violation of the Internal Security Act of 1950. As the base itself is now closed and part of Golden Gate National Recreation Area (under lease from the MMWD until 2005), hikers may proceed though the hole in the fence.

Rocky Ridge Fire Trail climbs another 250 yards to end at a paved road. Left, 100 yards beyond the gate, is the base's old heliport. The main road is still in use for access up to the prominent white tracking domes atop West Peak; that fenced area remains strictly off-limits. Plans by the Federal Aviation Administration and the Air Force to replace the two domes with a single but larger dome met with opposition from environmental groups and the MMWD. Right on the paved road leads to the top of Arturo Trail and, farther, to Mountain Top Trail.

The prominent rib of Rocky Ridge itself is one of the oldest summit routes on the Mountain. Noted early California surveyor and diarist William Brewer climbed it in 1862.

TAVERN PUMP TRAIL
FROM OLD RAILROAD GRADE (BELOW MILEPOST 8) TO FERN CREEK TRAIL / .33 miles

Terrain: Chaparral and light woodland / MMWD
Elevation: From 2,080' to 1,920' / steep
Intersecting Trails: None
Directions: East Ridgecrest Blvd. — Old Railroad Grade, .5 miles

TAVERN PUMP Trail is little used; most visitors opt for the nearby, easier to reach Fern Creek Trail. Still, Tavern Pump is attractive and opens some loop options.

Tavern Pump Trail sets off from Old Railroad Grade about .1 mile below the mile 8 post and one-quarter mile above Miller Trail. An MMWD signpost marks the top.

The opening 15 yards are extremely steep; the rest of the way is well-graded. The Trail begins in a forest of laurels and tanbark oaks. A bit lower, manzanita, forming a canopy, lines the way.

Around half-way down, Tavern Pump Trail crosses a pair of seeps supporting giant chain ferns. Just below, a new bridge carries the Trail over a creek.

The Trail drops toward a water tank and building. It ends there, at a signed junction with Fern Creek Trail, which rises left to the East Peak parking lot and drops right to Old Railroad Grade. Azaleas impart a fragrance here in late spring and early summer.

Steps lead down to the water tank and the blue building which houses the "tavern pump." Water from Fern Creek was once pumped up to the Tavern of Tamalpais, which stood at the terminus of the Mt. Tamalpais Railway by the present East Peak parking area. The renowned tavern was built in 1896 as part of the railway project, and rebuilt in 1923 after a fire. In 1950, twenty years after the railway ceased operations, park officials deliberately burned the tavern down because it had fallen into total disrepair. The pump, meanwhile, still delivers water via a pipeline, on a sliver of State Park property amidst Water District land, up to the East Peak area.

UPPER BERRY TRAIL
BETWEEN ROCK SPRING-LAGUNITAS FIRE ROAD / .45 miles

Terrain: Deep forest / MMWD
Elevation: From 1,920′ to 1,760′ / gradual, parts steep
Intersecting Trails: Lagoon F.R. (.3m), Cross Country Boys (.4m)
Directions: East Ridgecrest Blvd. — Arturo Trail — right on Rock Spring-Lagunitas F.R., .1m

UPPER BERRY is the surviving top section of the old Berry Trail (see Lower Berry Trail), an historic route up the north side of Tamalpais.

Upper Berry, newly re-signed by the MMWD, sets off north from Rock Spring-Lagunitas F.R. about 100 yards below Rifle Camp and the base of Arturo Trail. Opposite is a concrete water tank.

Upper Berry plunges down through the deep woodland. It meets and crosses the East Fork of Swede George Creek at a new bridge. A wood plaque affixed to a laurel here identifies this as the former site of Ted Cooper's Bridge, originally built in 1928. (The "D.&O.C." refers to the Down & Outer's Club, a small group of Tam hikers who frequented the area.) Two plaques below read:

TED COOPER BRIDGE
RECONSTRUCTED APRIL 25, 1992

IN HONOR OF ROBERT AND JEANNIE FOR THEIR MANY
CONTRIBUTIONS TO THIS BEAUTIFUL MOUNTAIN.

The earlier replacement of Cooper's original bridge was itself a victim of a fallen tree.

Just to the right is a remnant of a now murky old swimming hole, fed by an underground spring. Cooper (originally named Coopana) lived in a camp just downstream from here, and did significant work on the Trail. He died in an auto accident on the Mountain in 1932, on the way to a vacation in Steep Ravine. His ashes were scattered by his camp.

Over a short rise, a connector to Cross Country Boys Trail and Azalea Meadow forks left. Look left to see a massive madrone, perhaps second in size on Tam only to the "Giant Madrone" of Pilot Knob Trail.

Upper Berry then meets and crosses Lagoon Fire Road. Rock Spring-Lagunitas Fire Road is visible just uphill. Left leads to Cross Country Trail's crossing of Lagoon, and lower to Serpentine Knoll.

Across Lagoon F.R., Upper Berry Trail may be overgrown. It drops to meet Cross Country Boys Trail. The two continue together (as Upper Berry here).

Upper Berry ends at a signed junction when it again meets Rock Spring-Lagunitas Fire Road. It was the building of the Fire Road that split Berry Trail and led to the abandonment of the middle section. That former continuation downhill is still clearly evident across the Fire Road. Just to the right of that continuation, Rocky Ridge Fire Trail begins climbing toward West Peak.

S. Lucien Berry and Emil Barth cleared the route around 1900. Berry's ashes were also scattered on the Trail.

VERNA DUNSHEE TRAIL
LOOP AROUND EAST PEAK / .68 miles

Terrain: Chaparral and rock; asphalt; heavily used / MMWD & MTSP
Elevation: Around 2,400' / almost level
Intersecting Trails: Temelpa (.3m)
Directions: East Ridgecrest Blvd. to upper (east) end
Amenities: Parts wheelchair accessible

MILLIONS OF VISITORS have taken this loop Trail over the decades, and been rewarded with its unsurpassed views. The East Peak snack shack and Visitor Center both sell, for 25 cents, a State Park *Self-Guided Trail Walk* brochure keyed to 11 numbered stops along the loop. The late Otto Reutinger wrote an earlier guide to the Trail (1986, reprinted by the MTIA in 1992). The MTIA also conducts guided loop walks on weekends.

We'll follow the Verna Dunshee loop counterclockwise from the bathrooms. This level clearing was the terminus of the famed Mt. Tamalpais & Muir Woods Railway, in operation from 1896 to 1929. Here too stood, its foundations still evident, the railroad's Tavern of Tamalpais. After falling into extreme disrepair, it was razed by the Water District in 1950. A plaque at the start of the loop names Verna Dunshee "The First Lady of the State Park System, She Did So Much For So Many."

Stop #1 is by an interpretive sign noting what can be seen to the southeast on clear, fogless days. Distant landmarks include the Diablo Range east of Hollister (120 miles and now only rarely visible), Sutro Tower in San Francisco (14 miles), Montara Mountain on the San Mateo coast (26 miles), and the ocean horizon (58 miles). A pay telescope was recently added here.

Shrubs have been cleared to open the views at stops #2 and #3. At .2 miles (stop #4), a railing surrounds Sunrise Point. At this famous site was the Tamalpais

Locator, a spotting scope helping visitors identify distant landmarks. A stone bench carved with the words "Sunrise Point" offers a place to sit and enjoy the views. Three Bay Area peaks taller than Tam — Mount St. Helena to the north, Mt. Diablo to the east, and Mt. Hamilton to the south — are often visible. On the clearest of winter days, the snow-covered Sierra, 160 miles away, can be discerned.

A few feet beyond Sunrise Point the Trail edges beneath "Profile Rock" (#5), named for its resemblance to a face in profile. Unfortunately, the wood boards under the rock are presently posted with a "no wheelchairs" sign, barring a loop.

At .3 miles, Dunshee meets the signed top of Temelpa Trail. After a rerouted gradual start, Temelpa drops precipitously to Hoo-Koo-E-Koo Fire Road and Mill Valley's Summit Avenue. Only the nimblest of hikers should attempt its full length.

Some hundred feet beyond is a bench and stop #6. Just past, a slide is shored by railroad ties dubbed, on a small signpost, "the great wall of Mt. Tamalpais." The "wall" was built in February 1982, a month after a massive slide (which stopped only in a redwood grove just above Hoo-Koo-E-Koo Fire Road) triggered by Marin's heaviest rainstorm in decades.

Next, no longer signed, is the upper end of Indian Fire Trail. This extremely steep trail is closed from entry points below (so not described in this book) for erosion and safety reasons, and to give vegetation a chance to cover it. The overgrown section here follows the ridge top to the quartz tourmaline rock outcropping known as North Knee.

Views open north (stops #7-10), to Mendocino County on clear days. Much nearer are Lakes Lagunitas (visible from only a handful of Tam trails) and Bon Tempe. Enjoy the well-placed benches.

At .6 miles (stop #11), a plaque on a rock to the right carries the inscription:

BACK TO THE MOUNTAIN IN THE FULLNESS OF LIFE.

It is dedicated to George Grant, who died at age 72 in 1914, and his wife, Grace Adelaide, who passed away the following year. George Grant was a former "Cariboo" gold miner who came to be called the "old man of the Mountain." There was once a Grant Trail up from West Point; it is now overgrown.

Beyond the plaque are steps, another barrier for wheelchair users. The original, more level, dirt trail (still evident to the left) ran up to 16 feet higher but was rerouted after a slide. There has been talk of improving this section for wheelchair users. Back on level terrain, is a section of track. It was laid in conjunction with the 1996 centennial celebration of the Mountain Railway. At the end of the loop, Plankwalk Trail rises a quarter-mile to the lookout tower atop East Peak.

Verna Dunshee first hiked on Tam in 1913 while a student at the University of California, Berkeley. She and her husband Bertram moved to Ross in 1920. Both became leading activists in preserving Marin's open space for State and County parks. Mrs. Dunshee was president of the Tamalpais Conservation Club in 1950-51. The Trail was dedicated to her by the California State Parks Rangers Association in 1973, the year she died, at age 80. The loop is sometimes called "Twenty Minute Trail," for the length of the walk (the brochure now suggests 30 minutes). It was also once known as Race Track Trail.

Ocean view from Dias Ridge Fire Road.

Highway One Trailhead

Highway One Trailhead

Directions to Highway One:
Highway 101 — Highway 1 exit (between Sausalito and Mill Valley)

CALIFORNIA STATE HIGHWAY 1 is among the world's most scenic roads, and an engineering marvel. It hugs the Golden State's rugged coastline for more than 500 miles. The section across Tamalpais, which is also known as Shoreline Highway, is particularly dramatic, winding along the Mountain's western edge with a precipitous drop to the ocean just beyond the shoulder.

Many Tam trails and fire roads meet, or come within yards of, Highway 1. These trails are, in order from Highway 1's eastern junction with Panoramic Highway: Miwok, Ranch M, Redwood Creek, Owl, Coastal, Heather Cutoff, Lone Tree Fire Road, Rocky Point Trail, Rocky Point Road, Steep Ravine, Red Rock, the Dipsea, Matt Davis, Willow Camp Fire Road, McKennan Trail and, at the book's northern boundary, Morse's Gulch Trail. Dias Ridge Fire Road and Dias Trail run near Highway 1, so are included here as well. Some of these trails, such as the Dipsea, Steep Ravine and Matt Davis, are far more commonly joined from trailheads to the east and so are described in other sections.

Trailheads are noted with the nearest Highway 1 mileage marker sign. None have amenities other than some off-road parking. The town of Muir Beach has no commercial establishments except for the renown Pelican Inn, which is definitely worth a visit or stay. The town of Stinson Beach has a full range of visitor services, except for a gasoline station; there are presently none on Highway 1 between Tam Junction and Olema.

Because of the steep terrain of Tam's west slope, all loop options involve strenuous climbs.

Suggested loops from Highway 1:
• Lone Tree Fire Road (elevation 420'), 1.0m, to first Dipsea Trail junction — left, .9m, to second Steep Ravine Trail junction — left, .4m, to Highway 1 — Rocky Point Road, .5m, to Rocky Point Trail — left, .4m, to start **3.2 miles.**
• Matt Davis Trail (elevation 60'), 2.4m, to Coastal Trail — left, 1.4m, to Willow Camp F.R. — left, 1.8m, to Avenida Farralone — .1m to Belvedere Avenue — left, .4m (streets and trail) to start **6.1 miles.**
• Miwok Trail (elevation 620'), 2.2m, to Redwood Creek Trail — left, 1.7m, to end — left on Highway 1, .4m, to Ranch M Trail — 1.0m to Dias Ridge F.R. — right, 1.0m, to second Miwok Trail junction — right, .4m, to start **6.7 miles.**

DIAS RIDGE FIRE ROAD
FROM PANORAMIC HIGHWAY TO RANCH M TRAIL / 1.24 miles

Terrain: Coastal scrub and grassland / MTSP; part of Bay Area Ridge Trail
Elevation: From 620' to 700' / gradual to steep; rolling
Intersecting Trails: Miwok (.2m-.3m)
Directions: Panoramic Highway to milepost 0.18

DIAS RIDGE, topped by this Fire Road, is a spur off Tam's long Throckmorton Ridge, which descends all the way from East Peak. There are splendid views en route, including perhaps the most striking anywhere of Mt. Tamalpais' southern wall. The Fire Road opens several route options between Mill Valley and the coast.

The signed Fire Road trailhead is beside Panoramic Highway, near milepost 0.18 (measured from the Panoramic-Highway 1 junction). This is also one-third mile south from Four Corners (where Panoramic Highway, Sequoia Valley Road, and the Muir Woods Road join), beside the Mt. Tamalpais State Park boundary sign. There is some off-road parking.

In 200 feet, Dias Ridge F.R. meets a connector path, which runs parallel to the highway to the north. In another 500 feet, the Fire Road is joined on the left by an alternate Panoramic Highway entry path. Just beyond are massive stumps of cut eucalyptus trees. Baccharis (coyote brush) lines the Fire Road margin.

At 1/4 mile, Miwok Trail, from Highway 1 (Shoreline Highway), enters on the left. Miwok carries Bay Area Ridge Trail hikers, equestrians, and mountain bikers from the south onto Dias Ridge. At present, cyclists wishing to continue on the Bay Area Ridge Trail face a deadend here; there is no connection with the next part of the route, Deer Park Fire Road. In .1 miles, Miwok departs, with the hiking and equestrian routes of the Bay Area Ridge Trail, right, down to Redwood Creek Trail.

There are stunning views, except when the area's notorious summer fog is pouring in off the ocean. On the right is an almost unobstructed panorama of the entire south face of Mt. Tamalpais. To the left, beyond Green Gulch, is Fox Ridge with the GGNRA trails and fire roads that traverse it clearly beckoning.

At .4 miles is a large rock outcropping, covered with poison oak. Shortly past, the Fire Road briefly levels and there are Pacific Ocean views.

At .6 miles, the Fire Road dips, only to quickly climb again to its high point. Just a few trees — oaks, wind-sculpted laurels, Douglas-firs — dot the coastal scrub. Views south over Fox Ridge, past the mouth of the Golden Gate to Montara Mountain on the San Mateo shore, open.

The Fire Road crests at an intersection. Old Freese maps show the road as ending here, and I will too. The continuation straight ahead, fire road-width but later narrowing, is described in this book as the separate Dias Trail.

On the right, atop the hill, is the highest point on the ridge (864'). To the left, through an old gate (re-close it if passing through) and fence line, is Ranch M Trail. It descends, through GGNRA lands, to Highway 1 opposite Green Gulch Farm near Muir Beach.

Dias Ridge Fire Road was once a ranch road. Dias Ranch was one of several dairy ranches, originally designated A through Z, carved out of the 19,000-acre Mexican land grant called Rancho Sausalito. Most of the grant lands, including what became Dias Ranch, were leased to, then acquired by, settlers from Portugal's Azores Islands, then renamed. George Dias operated the ranch and the Sausalito Creamery in the early 1900's. Cows continued to graze the slopes for decades. In 1960, the State purchased 376 acres of the Dias Ranch and made it the southern-most part of Mt. Tamalpais State Park.

DIAS TRAIL
FROM DIAS RIDGE F.R. TO REDWOOD CREEK TRAIL / .93 miles

Terrain: Grassland; unmaintained and MARGINAL / MTSP
Elevation: From 700' to 60' / extremely steep
Intersecting Trails: None
Directions: Panoramic Highway — Dias Ridge F.R., 1.2 miles

THE ROUTE described below may be replaced. The State Park began work in 1992 on a longer, more gradual, safer trail. (It is designated as "proposed" on the 1994 MTSP map.) But as work is halted at press-time, I'll still describe the old route.

At the crest of Dias Ridge Fire Road, 1.2 miles from Panoramic Highway, there is a junction. Ranch M Trail departs to the left, onto GGNRA land, be-yond the gate. Dias Trail, still fire road-width in its upper section, continues straight ahead.

The broad, upper section of the Trail commands panoramic Pacific, Tam, and Marin Headlands views. In .3 miles, an old fence line is crossed. A few old cow paths lace the scrub.

The Trail drops to a level area overlooking the farm houses and horse camps of Franks Valley. The present continuation down from here is markedly narrower, and quite steep, eroded, and slippery. A planned rerouting, actually staked out in 1992, has been delayed over environmental concerns. It would cut through un-spoiled habitat in which endangered spotted owls nest. There is a splendid mini-forest of low, wind-sculpted laurel trees.

The route ends, unmarked, at Redwood Creek Trail; a high voltage utility pole, bearing the carved numbers "71" and "5-40" is 25 yards to the right. Two hundred fifty yards to the right is signed Heather Trail, where any re-route of Dias Trail would likely end.

See Dias Ridge Fire Road for background on the Dias name.

LONE TREE FIRE ROAD
FROM HIGHWAY 1 TO COASTAL FIRE ROAD / 1.68 miles

Terrain: Grassland / MTSP
Elevation: From 420' to 1,380' / very steep
Intersecting Trails: Dipsea (1.1m, 1.2m, 1.3m, 1.4m, 1.5m, 1.6m)
Directions: Highway 1 by south side of mileage marker 10.67

THOUGH THE OCEAN VIEWS are continuous and spectacular when following Lone Tree F. R. downhill, it is described uphill because the bottom is accessible by car. Climbing Lone Tree also permits a descent on either of its close loop partners, the Dipsea or Steep Ravine trails. And the views going uphill are outstanding as well. Given the route's steepness, there will be plenty of reason to rest and enjoy them.

Lone Tree F.R. starts from a gate on the east side of Highway 1 by mile sign-post 10.67. Across the highway is a parking turnout and the top of Rocky Point Trail, which goes to the Steep Ravine cabins. The State Park trailhead signs at both ends (but not the new State Park map) still call the Fire Road "Dipsea Fire Trail"; the Dipsea and Lone Tree routes have long been closely tied. Indeed, much of today's Dipsea Trail of race fame was originally called Lone Tree Trail.

The climb begins very steeply and rarely relents the whole way. Baccharis is the common shrub alongside the entire route of the Fire Road, having taken over the formerly grazed grassland. No trails cross the large area to the right (south), across the canyons of Lone Tree Gulch and Cold Stream, until Coastal Fire Road. This whole southwest face of Tamalpais remains little visited.

Older maps show now-overgrown paths heading left to Webb Creek. At one mile, a sign marks where the Dipsea Trail departs left to Stinson Beach. The Dipsea Trail then criss-crosses and runs together with Lone Tree F.R. the rest of the ascent. Several young colonizing Douglas-firs have rooted.

There is a brief downhill, a welcome respite from the steady grind. Lone Tree F.R. rises to the edge of a hill covered with Douglas-firs. The Dipsea Trail goes right, bypassing an uphill. The hill above was bare — even called Bald Hill around the turn of the century — save for a single redwood, the famous "Lone Tree" or, incorrectly, "Lone Pine." That redwood is still alive and visible on the lower, right edge of the tree line.

A short path to the left of Lone Tree F.R. circles behind the redwood and passes the Lone Tree fountain. The fountain was built by the Tamalpais Conservation Club in 1917 by tapping Lone Tree Spring. It is the only water on the Dipsea Trail and runners (and others) have been using it ever since. A storm in the winter of 1989 narrowed the flow to a trickle; it is now restored. The fountain area offers a lovely, sheltered picnic site on hot or windy days. Note the old fence behind the fountain, which kept horses from the spring's source.

The Dipsea Trail departs right at its last intersection with Lone Tree F.R. The Fire Road ends just above, when it meets Coastal Fire Road at a three-way intersection. The MTSP signs here can be a bit confusing. Left leads to Old Mine Trail, the separate Lone Tree Hill F.R., and to Pantoll. Right on Coastal leads to the Dipsea Trail at Cardiac Hill, the top of Deer Park Fire Road and Highway 1.

The lower section of Lone Tree Fire Road, below the first Dipsea junction, has been known as Warm Spring Trail because it once continued (before construction of Highway 1) to the hot spring at the mouth of Webb Creek. The whole historic route was widened to a fire road, separate from the Dipsea, in the 1950's.

MIWOK TRAIL
FROM HIGHWAY 1 TO REDWOOD CREEK TRAIL / 2.17 miles

Terrain: Upper part grassland, lower part oak-laurel woodland; horses permitted full length, bicycles south of Dias Ridge F.R. only / MTSP
Elevation: From 620' to 730' to 110' / gradual
Intersecting Trails: Dias Ridge F.R. (.4m-.5m)
Directions: Highway 1 (Shoreline Highway) to .4 miles west of Panoramic Highway

MIWOK IS ONE OF THE LONGEST trails in Marin County. Beginning at Bobcat Trail in Rodeo Valley, it rises north over Wolf Ridge, drops to Tennessee Valley, climbs Fox Ridge, which it then follows, drops again to the head of Green Gulch, crosses Highway 1, climbs over Dias Ridge, then descends to Franks Valley and its end at Redwood Creek. There are spectacular views almost the whole route. Only this last 2.17-mile section, between Highway 1 and Redwood Creek, is part of Mt. Tamalpais State Park and described here.

Our Miwok trailhead is by a pullout on Highway 1 (Shoreline Highway), .4 miles west of the Panoramic Highway junction. Miwok Trail runs on both sides of the paved road; we take it north. Signs mark the route as a multi-use — hikers, horses, and bikes (but not dogs) — part of the Bay Area Ridge Trail.

There is a gradual climb through the often windswept grassland. Within 250 yards, views of San Francisco Bay open. In another 100 yards, East Peak, then Middle Peak, then West Peak come into view. The huge yellow flowers of wyethia are conspicuous in early summer.

In one-third mile, Miwok Trail meets Dias Ridge Fire Road, along the crest of the ridge. Right leads to Panoramic Highway. To continue on Miwok, go left. In .1 mile, Miwok departs, dropping to the right. This section of Miwok is also part of the Bay Area Ridge Trail, for hikers and equestrians. (Cyclists still need to return right to Panoramic Highway; an off-road connection to Deer Park Fire Road has not yet been established.)

The descent is gradual, easy to walk down, not overly grueling to climb. In 100 yards is an old stone foundation from the days the area was part of a dairy ranch. The vegetation is lush. Buttercups, poppies, yarrow, irises, blue-eyed grass, and cucumber are some of the more colorful flowers. Blackberries, strawberries, gooseberries, and snowberries ripen in late summer. Spittle-bugs, ensconced in their protective foam, are found on many of the plants.

Two hundred yards down is the first tree, a young Douglas-fir. Just below is an oak, with hazel growing alongside. The Trail crosses over a few muddy seeps.

At .9 miles below Dias Ridge, Miwok Trail passes a horse hitching post and a bench. The Trail then descends into a remote, quiet, enchanted woodland of old oaks and laurels. Several species of ferns and numerous wildflowers, including many in the lily family, grow lushly. Unfortunately, so too does poison oak, demanding caution.

There is a brief return to grassland. Then, by a rock outcropping, Miwok literally passes over a magnificent oak. Its gnarled trunk writhes in several directions.

Miwok crosses a creek over a bridge. Begin looking, in late sping, for the lovely flower columbine, always a treat. A sign recognizes that the section of Miwok just passed was rebuilt by the Youth Conservation Corps in 1981. The Trail again hits grassland.

Miwok ends 50 yards later at its junction with Redwood Creek Trail in Franks Valley. Although a path (Redwood Creek Spur) on the opposite bank leads to Muir Woods Road by milepost sign 2.56, there is no dry crossing of Redwood Creek on foot here much of the year. The nearest bridge is .3 miles to the right, which is also the direction for continuing on the Bay Area Ridge Trail. Left leads to Muir Beach.

Coastal Miwok Indians resided for several thousand years on and around Tamalpais, particularly near the shorelines. Their primary foods in this abundant land were shellfish, acorns, berries, deer and elk, roots, and wild grains. The Miwoks were decimated, mostly by disease, very soon after Spanish settlement of Marin began with the establishment, in 1817, of Mission San Rafael Arcangel. One of the Miwok's last leaders was dubbed by the Spanish as "El Marinero" (The Mariner) or Chief Marin, and the name passed onto the County. Miwok middens, or shell mounds, can still be found on Tam by sharp-eyed visitors.

MORSE'S GULCH TRAIL
FROM: HIGHWAY 1 TO MORSE'S GULCH / .33 miles

Terrain: Grassland and woodland; riparian; unmaintained / GGNRA
Elevation: Around 50' / almost level
Intersecting Trails: None
Directions: Highway 1 north of Stinson Beach (milepost 14.86)

STEEP, DEEPLY WOODED, Morse's Gulch marks the northwest boundary of this book. This unmaintained Trail penetrates only the lowest reaches of the gulch.

The Trailhead is by a small parking area and gate at milepost 14.86 on Highway 1. A culvert brings the creek that carves Morse's Gulch under the highway to Bolinas Lagoon. There is only a generic "no pets, no bikes" GGNRA sign at the start. A path forks right.

The early yards are through grassland. Poison hemlock, tall in spring and summer, lines the way. Most of the trees lining the Trail's right edge are giant sequoias (*Sequoiadendron giganteum*). Native only to a few dozen Sierra groves, giants sequoias are the most massive of all trees. These cousins to our native redwoods were planted in Morse's Gulch in the 1950's, as part of a now-gone Christmas tree ranch.

In 300 yards, the Trail goes under a canopy of pines, Douglas-firs, and maples. The creekbed is just to the right. An old toilet stands surrealistically near it.

The Trail passes an old fence and narrows. Somewhat rough, but still clear, the route crosses another grassy patch. A steep trench can be avoided to the left. A short mound must be crested.

The Trail returns to the creek's edge and enters a second forest grove. While alders are the common riparian tree, a laurel on the left is the star here. Its huge base circumference, and height, make it one of the largest in the County.

The route basically ends here. Paths up the canyon are below this book's standard. There are no options out but to retrace your steps.

An 1873 H. H. Bancroft & Co. map shows an 800-acre Morse tract here. According to Louise Teather's *Place Names of Marin*, the Trail was originally the entrance to the "mansion" that Benjamin and Amelia Morse built in the 1880's. The house was destroyed by fire in 1930. Other ranch buildings were torn down when the GGNRA acquired the property. The Trail has no official name.

OWL TRAIL
FROM HIGHWAY 1 TO SLIDE RANCH / 1.05 miles

Terrain: Coastal scrub; unmaintained / GGNRA
Elevation: From 440' to 160' / gradual
Intersecting Trails: None
Directions: Highway 1 to Muir Beach Overlook, between mileposts 6.96 and 7.00

FOR DRAMATIC ocean-view scenery, few trails can match this one. Owl Trail is, however, not officially maintained (Slide Ranch residents clear it occasionally) so it is unsigned and can become narrow and overgrown.

Owl Trail sets off north from the parking lot of Muir Beach Overlook, a vista point high above sheer cliffs. In 200 yards the Trail meets a parking turnout and continues just to the left of four wooden posts.

In the next yards, the Trail skirts the edge of the cliff — the views down to the surf and rocks 400 feet below are spectacular. There is then more "breathing space," but no loss of views as the Pacific is always within sight and sound. Baccharis, lupine, blackberry and mustard may need to be brushed aside. Be particularly alert for the abundant poison oak; it becomes less of a problem ahead.

In .5 miles, a steep path crosses left and right. It connects a turnout on Highway 1 to the rocky shore below. Less than 100 yards later, a path forks left to a landmark, isolated Monterey cypress. Another path drops to a dome-shaped structure owned by Slide Ranch.

At .9 miles, Owl Trail bends right at a line of eucalyptus and cypress trees. Several great horned owls spend their days in these trees; look carefully.

The Trail bends left at the fence, then right. It goes under a massive cypress, then stays right of a line of planted trees. It meets a pen of noisy goats.

Owl Trail ends a few yards beyond at the Ranch's main dirt road. About 75 yards uphill to the right is the public parking area. The road also continues down to a former PG&E facility. Other paths descend from the ranch to the boulder-strewn shoreline.

Slide Ranch, a delightful blend of spectacular scenery, domesticated animals, and old buildings, covers 134 acres of the former Ranch U. The Nature Conservancy bought the property in 1970 when plans to develop it were emerging. In 1973, Slide Ranch became part of the Golden Gate National Recreation Area. Plans to tear down the buildings were overturned by a citizen advisory panel. The non-profit ranch (2025 Shoreline Highway) offers very popular tours for school groups; call the ranch manager at 415/381-6155 for details. Several of the buildings are used as private residences.

Great horned owls are the largest (nearly 24 inches) of several owl species found on the Mountain. They are very effective nocturnal predators, their muffled wings silent. Great horneds kill rodents, birds, and other prey as large as skunks.

RANCH M TRAIL
FROM DIAS RIDGE FIRE ROAD TO HIGHWAY 1 / .95 miles

Terrain: Grazing-disturbed coastal scrub and grassland; eroded / GGNRA
Elevation: From 700' to 50' / very steep
Intersecting Trails: None
Directions: Panoramic Highway — Dias Ridge F.R., 1.2 miles

RANCH M Trail connects Dias Ridge to near the ocean. The Trail sets off at the crest of Dias Ridge F. R., 1.25 miles west when coming from Panoramic Highway. Ranch M Trail forks left (southwest), through the old ranch fence which now marks the MTSP-GGNRA boundary. Please re-lock the gate; horses graze below.

The Trail follows an overgrown, rutted, ranch road. The entire descent route is in poor condition, due to grazing (cattle in the past, horses at present) and from other erosion. The views of the ocean and Muir Beach compete with the need to check footing over the rutted terrain.

Horses are often companions, although the status of grazing here is in flux at press-time (see below). The Green Gulch Zen Center, and its associated vegetable farm, become visible in the valley on the left (south).

The Trail meets a chert rock outcropping that blocks a direct descent to Muir Beach. The route bends sharply left in front of the rock.

Ranch M Trail presently ends rather unceremoniously, unsigned, at a barbed wire fence and old gate at Highway 1. A turnout and highway milepost 5.50 mark the spot. Exit by squeezing through to the right of the gate, where there is no barbed wire. Across the road is Green Gulch Farm, privately run amidst GGNRA lands. The vegetables grown there can be sampled at Greens Restaurant in San Francisco.

It is then a somewhat perilous walk along the road's edge down and right to

Muir Beach. The Pelican Inn, at Pacific Way, is a popular rest stop. Left on Pacific Way leads to Muir Beach, Pacific Coastal Trail and other Marin Headlands routes. Just up Highway 1 is Muir Woods Road and Redwood Creek Trail.

In 1835, the 19,000-acre Rancho Sausalito, comprising much of southern Marin, was granted to William Richardson by the Mexican government. In 1856, Richardson, deeply in debt and near death, ceded control of the grant to Samuel Throckmorton. Throckmorton carved much of his grant into some 26 tenant-run dairy ranches, identified by letters A through Z; this 194-acre parcel was Ranch M. In the 1890's, ownership of the grant lands passed to the Tamalpais Land & Water Company, which then sold the ranches, usually to their Portuguese tenants. Constantine Bello was the first purchaser.

For decades the ranch was the site of the Golden Gate Dairy. In 1962, the Pervier family (Richard and wife Tink, then daughter Caitlin) began leasing land for their Golden Gate Dairy Stables (locally called "The Dairy"). In 1968, William Caddell bought the parcel with plans to develop it as a resort. Ranch M, the cows gone, became part of the GGNRA in 1974, with Caddell maintaining private control under a leaseback arrangement through March 1999.

In 1997, faced with GGNRA-mandated improvements to stem erosion and runoff into Redwood Creek, the Perviers withdrew. At press-time, a non-profit group of horse owners, Ocean Riders, is seeking to take over what will likely be a smaller stable/grazing operation.

The name "Ranch M Trail" is unofficial; the newest State Park map labels the route as "Dias Ridge Spur."

RED ROCK TRAIL
FROM HIGHWAY 1 TO RED ROCK BEACH / .28 miles

Terrain: Coastal scrub / MTSP
Elevation: From 230' to 10' / very steep
Intersecting Trails: None
Directions: Highway 1 to milepost 11.43 (south of Stinson Beach)

THIS SHORT, deadend Trail is the principal, and usually only, access to Red Rock Beach. The trailhead is on Highway 1, two-thirds of a mile south of the Panoramic Highway junction. There is a sizable parking area atop the Trail but the former lot across Highway 1 is now closed due to slide danger.

Pick up the unsigned Trail at the lower edge of the parking area. Just in, a sign marks the State Park boundary. Red Rock Trail winds its way steeply down the red chert bluff. California blackberry lines the edge.

Suddenly, around a bend some 300 yards down, views of Red Rock itself and of the beach open. A first flight of steps leads to a path (unsafe and not for the fainthearted) onto this impressive, aptly named rock giant.

A final set of steps leads to the beach. One of these steps bears a carving— "In memory of Wendy Stoyka, the woman I love, lost at sea in seed"—that is now faded. A plaque notes the steps were built by a volunteer, Mike Silver, in 1986.

The beach is a favorite of "au naturel" sunbathers. It is possible to walk north to Stinson Beach during very low tides but be extremely cautious not to get trapped; the surf and currents here are unforgiving, and deadly.

ROCKY POINT ROAD
FROM HIGHWAY 1 TO ROCKY POINT / .94 miles

Terrain: Coastal scrub; upper part asphalt / MTSP
Elevation: From 380' to 50' / gradual
Intersecting Trails: Rocky Point Trail (.4m)
Directions: Highway 1 to mileage marker 11.04
Amenities: Fountains, outhouses, cabins, camping

THIS ROAD leads down from Highway 1 to the Steep Ravine (or Rocky Point) cabins and campground. A gate blocks cars — only overnight guests are given the lock's combination — so the route, though largely paved, is included in this book. With perfect footing and a gentle grade, Rocky Point Road is ideal for enjoying the fabulous ocean views.

The Trailhead is by Highway 1 mileage marker 11.04. There is parking for a few cars. (Do not mistake the turnout with the bigger one just to the north for Red Rock Beach.) Opposite, Steep Ravine Trail begins its long and lovely climb to Pantoll. In July and August, the top of the route and opening yards are covered with the purple-red flowers of *Clarkia amoena*, commonly known as "farewell-to-spring" or "summer's darling."

The descent to the cabins is glorious. The views of the Pacific are continuous, except in the common summer fogs, when the sound of the surf substitutes.

At .4 miles, signed Rocky Point Trail sets off left, by a fence line. It also connects to Highway 1. The bright reds of California fuchsia brighten the road edge from late August into fall. In another 200 yards, at a gate, a dirt fire road comes in on the left. It arcs around to again meet the paved road, making the lower half of Rocky Point Road a loop.

The pavement meets the Steep Ravine cabins. Perched just above the breaking surf, they are among Tam's man-made treasures. The cabins were on land owned by William Kent. In 1960, his estate donated 240 acres here to the State Park. The cabins themselves remained under private control (to the dismay of many) until the State renovated them and opened them to the public on a reservation basis. Be prepared for a rustic experience; none of the cabins have water, electricity, or bathrooms, and mice are regular visitors.

The ten cabins (there were once twelve) are numbered and carry names reflecting local history and features. They are: William Kent (#1, which is wheelchair-accessible); Dipsea (#2); Thaddeus Welch (#3); Rocky Point (#4); Willow Camp (#5); Webb Creek (#6); Hot Springs (#7); San Andreas (#8), Farallon (#9), and Whale Watchers (#10).

A path leads down to the mouth of Webb Creek, site of a once popular hot spring. The spring, inadvertently buried by falling boulders during reconstruction work on Highway 1 in 1960, is now accessible only in fall, at low minus tides. Then it is possible to dig in the sand to reach the spring's warm water. Another path, lined with poison oak, skirts the edge of the cliffs of Rocky Point cliffs. One of the offshore rocks is topped with an old concrete and metal foundation.

Continue on the dirt loop to the six campsites, with equally special settings. They are named Abalone (#1), Cormorant (#2), Starfish (#3), Pelican (#4), Kelp (#5) and Hot N Tot (#6, for the Hottentot Fig, a naturalized succulent abundant here). A pond is to the right, just before the uphill begins.

The climb back is reasonably gradual. Rocky Point Trail is a loop option but involves a half-mile walk along the edge of narrow Highway 1.

This Road was called Steep Ravine Road in early editions; the State Park prefers Rocky Point.

ROCKY POINT TRAIL
FROM HIGHWAY 1 TO STEEP RAVINE ROAD / .36 miles

Terrain: Coastal scrub / MTSP
Elevation: From 420' to 220' / steep
Intersecting Trails: None
Directions: Highway 1 to milepost 10.67

ROCKY POINT TRAIL offers a trail route down to the Steep Ravine cabins and campground; the other access is paved Rocky Point Road (which see).

The Trail descends from a turnout, with very limited parking, off Highway 1 just south of mileage marker 10.67. A signpost now marks the entry. Direclty across the highway here is the base of long, steep Lone Tree Fire Road.

In recent years, Rocky Point was narrow and lined with poison oak. The Trail has since been cleared and seemingly widened; the poison oak is still there but no longer unavoidable.

Veer right at the start to pick up the Trail. In 100 feet, the Trail crosses a gully over a bridge. In 400 feet, a path branches right. In another 100 yards, the Trail passes a large, resistant boulder of chert rock. Chert on Tam is often characterized by the evenly spaced layering that this boulder displays perfectly.

But it is the spectacular ocean view that is the Trail's main appeal. Below is a wild, stunning stretch of Pacific coastline.

Aromatic California sagebrush is one of the more common of the many shrubs. Amidst them, a few short, colonizing Douglas-firs have taken root. Coastal wildflowers abound in spring.

The Trail ends at paved Rocky Point Road, which continues down to the State Park's ten Steep Ravine cabins, six campsites, and to the rugged shore of Rocky Point. The paved road can be taken uphill for a loop but the half-mile walk on Highway 1's edge back to the Rocky Point trailhead is less than safe.

Roots in the Rainforest section of the Dipsea Trail.

Mill Valley Trailhead

Mill Valley Trailhead

Directions to downtown Mill Valley:

Highway 101 — East Blithedale Ave. (exit), Mill Valley — left on Throckmorton Ave. one block to Lytton Square

• Directions to base of Old Railroad Grade:
East Blithedale Ave. — West Blithedale Ave. to just past Lee Street

• Directions to Fern Canyon Road:
Throckmorton Ave. — right on Old Mill St. — left on Lovell Ave. — right on Summit Ave. to top

• Directions to Old Mill Park and Cascade Avenue:
Throckmorton Avenue, left on Cascade Avenue

• Directions to Glen Drive:
East Blithedale Ave., right on Carmelita Ave., right on Buena Vista Ave., left on Glen Drive

• Directions to Elinor Avenue:
East Blithedale Ave. to West Blithedale Ave., right on Oakdale Ave., left on Elinor Avenue

MILL VALLEY has been the principal entry onto Tam for San Franciscans and others ever since the town was founded in 1890. Day trippers and weekend and summer campers took a ferry to Sausalito, then rode the rail line to the depot in downtown Mill Valley. From there, many walked up Throckmorton Avenue to the Dipsea steps, or through Cascade Canyon (the old path is still evident) and up Ziz-Zag to Mountain Home, or took Temelpa Trail to East Peak. Others transfered at the depot onto the separate Mt. Tamalpais & Muir Woods Railway, which ran from 1896 through 1929, up the Mountain. There were also options for horse-drawn carriage (later motorized) excursions, camping, even burro rides. Passenger rail service into Mill Valley ended in 1940; driving over the new Golden Gate Bridge (opened in 1937) proved more popular.

The former depot area remains the heart of Mill Valley. It is bordered to the north by Lytton Square, for Lytton Plummer Barber, the first Mill Valley resident killed in World War I. The popular Depot Bookstore & Cafe now occupies the last station (built in 1929). There is a water fountain outside and a public restroom inside. Note that the two-hour parking time limit downtown is enforced even on Sundays.

Other Mill Valley trailheads involve negotiating very narrow, winding streets, with little parking and no amenities. One is the start of the surviving Old Railroad Grade, off West Blithedale above Lee Street. Another is the Cascade Falls area at the far end of Cascade Drive, from which Three Wells, Tenderfoot, Monte Vista, and Zig-Zag trails set off. Blithedale Ridge and Warner Canyon can be reached from the top of Elinor Avenue. Warner Canyon can also be accessed from the top of Glen Drive. Greenwood Way (West Blithedale Avenue, uphill on Eldridge Avenue to Woodbine Drive, right to Upland Avenue, then uphill on Greenwood past house numbers 24-60, 70, 74, and 78) offers access to Blithedale

Ridge. Mill Valley's highest trailhead is Fern Canyon Road, a paved section of Old Railroad Grade, reached via winding Summit Avenue.

Mill Valley also contains several potential new trailheads onto more recently acquired Marin County Open Space District properties. Paths set off from Fairway Drive, Val Vista Avenue, Tartan Road, Manor Drive, Del Casa Avenue and other locations on the east side of Mill Valley.

Suggested loops from Mill Valley:

• Glen Drive (elevation 280') — Glen F.R., .4m to Warner Canyon F.R. — left, .6m, to connector to Tartan Road-left, .3m, to Tartan Road — .1m, to Glen Drive — left, .4m, to start **1.8 miles.**

• Cascade Drive (elevation 270') — Tenderfoot Trail, .4m, to Cypress Trail — left, 1.1m, to connector to Rose Avenue — left, .5m, to Monte Vista Avenue and Monte Vista F.R., .5m, to Tenderfoot Trail by start **2.5 miles.**

• Old Railroad Grade trailhead (elevation 240') — Grade, .6m, to Horseshoe F.R. — right, .1m, to Corte Madera Trail — left, .6m, to Hoo-Koo-E-Koo Trail — right, .5m, to Blithedale Ridge F.R. — right, .5m, to H-Line F.R. — right, .6m, to Railroad Grade — left, .1m, to start **3.0 miles.**

• Old Mill Park (elevation 110') — Dipsea Trail, .5m, to Edgewood Ave. — right on Edgewood Ave. and Pipeline Trail, 2.0m, to Mountain Home — right on Tenderfoot Trail, 1.1m, to Cascade Drive — right, 1.1m, to start **4.7 miles.**

• Fern Canyon Road at Summit Ave. (elevation 820') — Temelpa Trail, .4m, to Hoo-Koo-E-Koo F.R. — right, 1.8m, to Blithedale Ridge F.R. — right, .8m, to Horseshoe F.R. — right, .3m, to Old Railroad Grade-right, 1.6m, to start **4.9 miles.**

BLITHEDALE RIDGE FIRE ROAD
FROM ELINOR AVENUE, MILL VALLEY, TO INDIAN F.R. / 2.33 miles

Terrain: Chaparral / MCOSD & MMWD
Elevation: From 520' to 900' to 650' to 1,040' / rolling, parts steep
Intersecting Trails: Maytag Trail (.1m, .5m), connector fire road to Greenwood Way (.1m), Corte Madera Ridge F.R. (.9m), H-Line F.R. (1.4m), Horseshoe F.R. (1.6m), Hoo-Koo-E-Koo Trail (1.9m), Hoo-Koo-E-Koo F.R. (2.3m)
Directions: Elinor Avenue to Via Van Dyke

BLITHEDALE RIDGE is a prominent feature on the east-southeast flank of Mt. Tamalpais, forming an imposing wall between Blithedale and Warner canyons. Homes cover the lowest reaches of Blithedale Ridge in Mill Valley, but this Fire Road tops its pristine upper 2.3 miles. Dramatic Mt. Tamalpais summit views are found most all the way.

Recent problems with public access to the lower end of the Fire Road seem to have been settled. In 1989, a gate had been placed at the foot of private Via Van Dyke at Elinor Avenue, cutting off entry. In 1998, a path around the gate, with a welcoming sign, was restored. At the first fork up Via Van Dyke, veer right to the water tank, then climb the adjacent access path to Blithedale Ridge.

Once on the Fire Road, a sign reminds that the way left is private property. Immediately to the right of the access path, Maytag Trail drops off the ridge. It parallels Blithedale Ridge F.R. for nearly half a mile, shaded and less steep.

Blithedale Ridge Fire Road is a roller-coaster, steeply rising and falling (mostly rising!). The first uphill leads to the initial Tam summit view. Just beyond, a fire road drops left. It leads to Mill Valley's Greenwood Way, an alternate access.

Broom lines both sides of the Fire Road, with oaks and madrones behind. Maytag Trail re-enters from the right at an easy-to-miss junction. Just beyond are a pair of MCOSD "boundary" signposts on a stiff rise to a fenced tank.

A level stretch then leads to a second fire road left. An orange gate, covered with warning messages, bars entry to the private residence below; keep out.

Another pair of uphills lead to a view north, to Bald Hill and Big Rock Ridge, the second highest peak in Marin after Tam. The canyon to the left is Blithedale, cut by Corte Madera Creek. The canyon right is Warner, carved by Warner Creek.

At .9 miles, at a very wide clearing, Corte Madera Ridge Fire Road, which tops the opposite wall of Warner Canyon, comes in from the right. The junction is known to some as "Judy's Corners."

A major descent begins. The views of Tam are particularly striking. The Fire Road then enters a redwood forest.

At the base of the descent, H-Line Fire Road drops left to Old Railroad Grade just in from West Blithedale. Twenty-five yards later, at another fork, Blithedale Ridge F.R. begins to climb again. Straight ahead, H-Line F.R. drops to Southern Marin Line (Crown) F.R.

The stiff uphill levels on the ridge line. Chinquapin, madrones, even a few redwoods, stand amidst the chaparral shrubs. A down part of the roller coaster leads to Horseshoe Fire Road, which drops left, also to Old Railroad Grade.

In another quarter-mile, Hoo-Koo-E-Koo Trail crosses Blithedale Ridge. Right leads to Kentfield's Crown Road; left, a shaded, level alternative for circling Blithedale Canyon, to Hoo-Koo-E-Koo F.R. There's a stiff uphill, rewarded by great views to the south from the head of Blithedale Canyon.

The Fire Road leaves MCOSD lands and enters the Marin Municipal Water District. Just above is the 1,091-foot summit of Knob Hill. To the left is the top of Hoo-Koo-E-Koo Fire Road. Climb the remaining yards to the end of Blithedale Ridge Fire Road at its junction with Indian Fire Road. Left leads up to Eldridge Grade, right down to Kent Woodlands.

In the 1870's, Dr. John Cushing, a pioneering homeopathic physician, opened a sanitarium "Blithedale" in what is now called Blithedale Canyon. The name stems from the novel "Blithedale Romance" written by Cushing's Bowdoin College classmate, Nathaniel Hawthorne. After Cushing's death in 1879, his son Sidney converted Blithedale into a resort, with cottages surrounding the main hotel building (at the present 205 West Blithedale Avenue). Sidney then became the chief mover behind the construction of the railway up Mt. Tamalpais, which boosted patronage for the track-side resort. The Mountain Theater is named for Sidney Cushing. Blithedale Ridge Fire Road was built in 1914 over an older trail.

CORTE MADERA TRAIL
FROM HORSESHOE F.R. TO HOO-KOO-E-KOO F.R. / .37 miles

Terrain: Deep redwood forest; riparian; several stream fordings / MCOSD & MMWD
Elevation: From 500' to 950' / extremely steep
Intersecting Trails: None
Directions: Old Railroad Grade trailhead — Grade, .6 miles

CORTE MADERA TRAIL follows the upper reaches of the creek properly called Corte Madera del Presidio, but frequently just Corte Madera Creek (not to be confused with the Corte Madera Creek that drains the Ross Valley a few miles to the north). The Trail is a lovely one, through a dense stand of redwoods. It is, however, extremely steep, narrow, and requires some potentially tricky stream crossings after winter rains.

To reach the lower end of Corte Madera Trail, follow Old Railroad Grade uphill from its start off West Blithedale Avenue. The first fire road on the right is H-Line. A half-mile later, at a bend and crossing over Corte Madera Creek, Horseshoe Fire Road also rises on the right. Follow it .1 mile to an MCOSD sign, on the left, that simply says "Trail" and marks the start of Corte Madera Trail. There is also a very steep path to the trailhead directly from Old Railroad Grade up the creek's right bank.

The Trail, rising beside the creek, immediately enters MMWD land. The first of the creek crossings, all without benefit of a bridge, is from the left to the right bank. After a heavy rain, this crossing requires a modest leap. If you make it, relax; the others are easier.

The Trail passes over a redwood downed in the storm of January 1982 and meets a confluence of two creek forks. The many rocks to the left here are not an accident. In 1988, a young artis gathered them here to build a rock wall. In 1997, a sizable redwood fell, taking down the wall. Cross and follow the left of the forks.

Continue climbing through the quiet woods. The redwoods and the water muffle outside noise. There is another, somewhat tricky fording. Actually, equal option routes ascend both banks up from here, and past the next fording.

A final push brings Corte Madera Creek Trail to its signed top at Hoo-Koo-E-Koo Trail, which goes right to Echo Rock. A few yards of scramble uphill is Hoo-Koo-E-Koo F.R., which goes right to Blithedale Ridge F.R. and left to Wheeler Trail.

"Corte Madera del Presidio" means "cut wood for the Presidio." Mill Valley redwoods, which grew closer to a since filled-in bay shore, were apparently used in erecting Spain's Presidio of San Francisco in 1776. (San Francisco was then virtually treeless.) The creek is also sometimes called "Widow Reed Creek," for Hilaria Sanchez Reed Garcia. Her first husband, who she outlived, was Irish-born John Reed, the original grantee of 8,000-acre Rancho Corte Madera del Presidio (which included the future Mill Valley) by Mexico in 1834. It was the first land grant to an individual in Marin County.

CYPRESS TRAIL
FROM TENDERFOOT TRAIL TO CYPRESS AVENUE, MILL VALLEY / 1.56 miles

Terrain: Woodland / City of Mill Valley
Elevation: 450' to 660' / early part gradual, then almost level
Intersecting Trails: Connector to Rose Avenue, 1.1m
Directions: Tenderfoot Trail, .4 miles

THIS IS A SURPRISING Trail — close to central Mill Valley yet quite long, near-pristine, and not part of any protected parkland. It typifies Mill Valley's charm, and its wisdom in preserving old byways. Cypress Trail does have drawbacks; it is narrow with poison oak bordering much of the route, several low trees menace the inattentive traveler, and the southern entry has a somewhat tricky stream crossing. The higher (southern) end of Cypress Trail is accessible by car but since most users join from the popular Tenderfoot Trail, that is how the route will be described.

Cypress Trail sets off left one-third mile up from the base of Tenderfoot Trail. Some rusty metal posts and siding mark the intersection, the third of fire road-width when climbing from Cascade Drive. There is a "No Bikes, No Horses" sign. (Cypress had earlier been open to bicycles; the change was made in 1996 after much debate.)

Most all of the Trail's elevation gain is in this opening section; the route is then nearly level. Redwoods dominate the early going, and are abundant all the rest of the way, particularly at the several streambed crossings. In some 100 yards is the first of numerous intersecting paths, most all leading to nearby homes.

At one-third mile, the upper reaches of Mt. Tam are visible through the tree canopy. At two-thirds of a mile, the Trail passes just above adjacent houses, skirting a backyard fence. But there are few other signs of civilization in the forest. The Trail crosses though a haunting double row of dead manzanita shrubs.

The only prominent intersection is just past one mile; Cypress is the upper, right route. Down left is a 125-yard connection (sometimes called Cypress Lane) to the unpaved 300 block of Rose Avenue. Rose offers a loop option back to Tenderfoot via Monte Vista Fire Road. At the intersection, amidst the deep forest, is an incongruous utility pole, anchored to a redwood.

In another 100 yards, Cypress Trail passes several massive eucalpytus trees and another house. The route is more open, but again returns to dense redwoods. There is a quiet grove of laurels. Just beyond, a downed redwood needs to be surmounted.

The Trail passes one more house, then drops steeply to a last stream crossing and its final yards. (The easier, lower exit route is now marked with a "No Trespassing" sign.) The Trail exits on a narrow easement beside the driveway of 100 Cypress Avenue, at the west end of the street. This entry is also signed, "No Bikes, No Horses."

Cypress Avenue, which offers striking Mt. Tam views on its way to Edgewood Road near the top of the Dipsea steps, is apparently named for its Monterey cypress trees, originally planted as windbreaks.

DIPSEA TRAIL
FROM OLD MILL PARK, MILL VALLEY, TO INTERSECTION OF HIGHWAY 1 AND
PANORAMIC HIGHWAY, STINSON BEACH / 6.9 miles

Terrain: Varied — deep and light woodland, grassland, riparian, and coastal scrub;
heavily used / City of Mill Valley, private (easement), MTSP, MWNM, GGNRA
Elevation: From 90' to 760' to 160' to 1,360' to 80' / mostly very steep, almost
no parts level
Intersecting Trails: Sun (1.3m), Deer Park F.R. (several times between miles
2.9m and 4.1m), Ben Johnson (3.9m), TCC (4.1m), Coastal F.R. (4.2m), Lone Tree
F.R. (4.4m, 4.6m, 4.8m), Steep Ravine (5.6m-5.7m), Hill 640 F.R. (5.8m)
Directions: Downtown Mill Valley — Throckmorton Ave. to Old Mill Park

THE DIPSEA is the most famous trail in the Bay Area, and, because of the footrace
held on it annually, even has a worldwide reputation. Few trails anywhere pack
such beauty, ruggedness, variety, and history into so short a distance. The Dipsea
Trail may well have been first blazed by the Coast Miwok Indians. It certainly
was popular, under the name Lone Tree Trail, with the County's first pleasure
hikers in the 1880's. In 1905 it became the route of the Dipsea Race, now the
oldest cross country race in the United States.

The origin of the name "Dipsea" remains unknown despite exhaustive research. A Dipsea Inn was built at Willow Camp (now Stinson Beach) in 1904 on
property owned by William Kent. That same year, a group of long distance hikers
from San Francisco's venerable Olympic Club conceived the idea of a race from
Mill Valley to the inn. They called themselves the Dipsea Indians and the race
"The Dipsea." But whether "Dipsea" itself refers to the practice of taking a plunge
in the Pacific after trekking the Trail, or to the Trail's apparent drop to the ocean
as viewed from Lone Tree, or to a name Kent picked up on his travels to British
seaside resorts, or a corruption of the words "deep sea," remains a mystery.

It must be pointed out that the course of the Dipsea Race (technically the
runners can take any itinerary to Stinson that is not specifically off-limits, but
most use a standard route) differs somewhat from the true Dipsea Trail. Since the
race is so closely tied to the Trail, I'll describe both ways (omitting, however,
environmentally dubious race day shortcuts). Two other cautions are in order.
The Dipsea Trail is arduous and may not be for everyone. And it's a one way
affair. Return options include Golden Gate Transit bus service back to Mill Valley (weekends only), a car shuttle, or a doubly tiring round trip. Another option
is to hike or run the Trail out and back in shorter sections, say from the start to
Muir Woods or to the top of Cardiac Hill, or from Muir Woods to Stinson Beach.

The Dipsea Race, now held the second Sunday of June, begins at Lytton
Square in downtown Mill Valley. The contestants run up Throckmorton Avenue
to Old Mill Park. The park has a bathroom and water fountain. It is the site of
John Reed's still-standing (partially restored) 1834 sawmill, which gave the town
its name. Also in the park is a re-built gravity car (#9) from the historic Mt.
Tamalpais & Muir Woods Railway.

Cut diagonally through the park and cross Old Mill Creek over the bridge. Continue straight across the street (Cascade Drive is to the right, Molino Avenue to the left) and up the pavement to encounter the Dipsea steps. (Don't take the first steps visible, to the left — they lead to the home of a very patient elderly lady.) The steps, technically Cascade Way, .3 miles into the Race, mark the start of the Dipsea Trail. White Dipsea arrows, sometimes faint, are painted on the pavement here and elsewhere. No part of the Dipsea Trail is better known than these both dreaded and beloved 676 steps. Originally of logs, they were all replaced in 1936 and subsequently as needed. They are in three flights. Private homes line the whole way. The first flight, to Millside Lane, is the longest, 313 steps. Its topmost 33 rock steps are the steepest.

At the pavement, go right, then immediately left on Marion Avenue. Just around the bend is the second flight, also the middle in length (222 steps). At the top, go left on Hazel Avenue a few yards to the third and shortest flight (141 steps). Think of the runners, who jam the steps to over-capacity, fatigued yet still short of the one mile mark. A famous quote by Jack Kirk, the legendary "Dipsea Demon" who has run every race since 1930, goes, "Old Dipsea runners never die. They just reach the 672nd step." (There were 671 steps until a rebuilding project in 1993; the number varies over the years.)

The steps top out at the intersection of Edgewood Avenue and Sequoia Valley Road at a junction once known as Inspiration Point for the views. Victorino's refreshment stand once accommodated hikers here. Across the road is Cowboy Rock Trail, part of the Homestead Valley Land Trust network. It descends a very steep .3 miles, past Cowboy Rock, to Tamalpais Drive and Stolte Grove in Homestead Valley. (The Homestead Valley trails are just outside this book's boundary.)

Go right up busy Sequoia Valley (not Edgewood, on the far right). This is a short but dangerous (due to cars) 100 yards. A safer, parallel hiker's path has recently been carved on the right.

The Dipsea then rises through the gates of the new Flying Y development on what is now called Walsh Drive, for the developer. This area is fondly remembered by generations of Dipsea runners and hikers as a dairy ranch, then the Flying Y Horse Ranch. Climb the paved street. There is a water fountain by 5 Walsh Drive.

A gate marks the first dirt section of the Trail. Look on the right for a Monterey cypress. In the early 1970's, the words "One Mile Tree" (the distance from the start) were carved where an overhanging branch was cut. The bark has now completely covered the words.

The Trail rejoins pavement as residential Bayview Drive. At its top, cross Panoramic Highway and veer right. This is the first of the route's two main summits, called Windy Gap. In under 50 yards, go left off the pavement at a Dipsea Trail signpost. The Trail is now in Mount Tamalpais State Park, and remains on public land the rest of the way.

This next section is known as "Hauke Hollow," for Jerry Hauke, who directed the Dipsea for more than 30 years. After the first big bend left on the downhill, a few yards past a small wooden bridge, are two junctions on the right.

The first is a path that parallels Panoramic Highway to Ridge Road. The second is the signed Sun Trail, which goes to the Tourist Club. The Dipsea takes the left fork and drops steeply to paved Muir Woods Road.

All the runners go right here, flying down the road. Hikers use a newer (built in 1981) Dipsea Trail section, marked by a post, directly across the road. This section is a little known part of the Dipsea. It follows a stream in the woods, and is quite attractive. The Trail and race route meet at a dirt road, Camino del Canyon, marked by a row of mailboxes. (Camino del Canyon is a winding, un-paved access road down to several dozen older homes on leased Federal lands.)

The Dipsea continues to the right off this dirt road at a sign. This next section of the Dipsea Trail was built in the late 1970's to replace a precipitous, 45-degree descent known as Suicide. Beware of poison oak, particularly in late winter and spring; good samaritans usually cut it back just before race day. A fence on the left near the top has a removable section which is opened on race day only.

The Trail meets a service road (mile 2 of the race), then crosses Muir Woods Road again. This was the site of a snack bar and dance pavilion called Joe's Place, popular in the 1920's and '30's. The main entrance to Muir Woods National Monument (with restrooms and water fountains) is to the right.

The Dipsea Trail passes through the Monument's overflow parking lot. It then drops a few steps to cross Redwood Creek on a footbridge. This crucial bridge is, however, only moved into place in spring, after the rainy season. The significantly longer alternative is to go left a half-mile on Muir Woods Road, then right, uphill, on Deer Park Fire Road to rejoin the Dipsea Trail. Across Redwood Creek, the Dipsea Trail begins an almost continuous climb to its high-est point. This first part, called Dynamite, is the steepest long section, around a half-mile. It is through a lush, fern-lined forest in the southwest corner of Muir Woods National Monument. It replaced an even steeper, more direct route, known as Butler's Pride, that is now off-limits. Here too, poison oak is abundant.

The climb eases a bit as the Trail leaves the deep forest and Muir Woods to again enter Mount Tamalpais State Park. A few feet to the left is Deer Park F.R. This is around mile 3 of the race.

The Trail first runs on the right of the fire road. The two then merge before the Trail departs left at a marked Dipsea sign post. Don't worry whether you should be on the fire road or the Trail; the two criss-cross for the next 1-1/2 miles.

The uphill eases a bit more through the open grassland called the Hogsback, for its appearance in profile. A prominent rock on the left, beside the telephone line, is known as "Halfway Rock"; Dipsea racers usually reach it in about half their total time. Splendid panoramas open, including the three summits of Tam. The Trail then again merges with and crosses Deer Park F.R.

After passing through a small grove, the Trail leaves the grassland, left of the fire road. This next heavily-wooded mile, back in Muir Woods National Monu-ment, is called the Rainforest. In summer, water drips off the fog-laden Douglas-firs and redwoods. It is another special stretch of the Dipsea. Here is one of the best places on Tam to see orchids.

Ben Johnson Trail, which also rose from Muir Woods, meets the Dipsea on the right and ends. Veer left. The Dipsea Trail joins Deer Park F.R. for the last time. Go left around 100 yards on the merged pair, then right as the Trail branches off.

This final stiff, 300 yard uphill is called Cardiac, not because it is that much steeper or longer than what has come before, but because the runners are already fatigued from the continuous climb out of Muir Woods. TCC Trail, from Pantoll, comes in on the right and the Dipsea re-enters Mt. Tamalpais State Park.

There is a last push to the summit, one of the loveliest places on the Mountain. The top of Cardiac Hill (formerly known as the Sugar Lump) is 1,360 feet and the highest point on the Dipsea Trail. The vistas of San Francisco and of the Pacific are dramatic. The knowledge that the Trail is now almost all downhill, plus the usual cooling ocean breezes, the views, and the water station here on race day, make this a place welcome to all Dipsea veterans.

The Dipsea crosses Coastal Fire Road. Just downhill to the left is the end of the now familiar Deer Park Fire Road and, well beyond, Muir Beach. Up to the right is Pantoll Ranger Station.

The narrow Dipsea Trail continues west, skirting the hillside. It then briefly merges with Lone Tree F.R. at a point only five inches lower in elevation than Cardiac. Early photos of this area show a single redwood, the "Lone Tree" that once gave its name to the Dipsea Trail. The redwood still stands, but the hillside above it is covered with Douglas-firs. Beneath the redwood, on a short path to the right, is a stone cairn. A pipe tapping into Lone Tree Spring here provides the only drinking water (untreated) on the Dipsea. The Tamalpais Conservation Club built the fountain in 1917.

The Dipsea Trail departs left from the fire road in a few yards. The two merge again for a down and up stretch. The Dipsea Trail leaves Lone Tree F.R. for the last time, to the right, at a post. Gone too, for a while, are the ocean views.

At a wooden fence, less than .1 mile from Lone Tree F.R., the runners leave the regular Dipsea Trail to plunge down the near vertical Swoop Hollow, so named by Jack Kirk.

Today's official Dipsea Trail, over a section built in 1977 by the Youth Conservation Corps, is to the right (north). Veteran racers dubbed it "The Gail Scott Trail" for the 1986 champion who accidentally took it while leading the '87 race and ended up second. It is one of the loveliest parts of the route, deeply wooded and quiet. The bent laurels and redwoods form separate, seemingly magical forests. A few Douglas-firs rise to enormous heights. The shortcut and Trail meet again 1/4-mile below.

A short passage through grassland brings the Dipsea Trail to the cool, wet forest of Steep Ravine. The Trail is extremely steep as it descends into the fern-lined canyon, with protruding rocks and roots. Stone and wooden steps, which Dipsea champions have been known to descend four at a time, help but caution is very much in order. Only racers have reason to rush through this lovely area.

The Dipsea crosses Webb Creek over a bridge. On the other bank, going right, is Steep Ravine Trail rising to Pantoll. The combined Dipsea and Steep Ravine trails go left. They pass a small reservoir, part of Stinson Beach's water supply.

The short stiff uphill now encountered is called Insult. It is the last uphill on the racer's route (but not on the regular Dipsea Trail); the course's final "insult" to those who thought it was all downhill to the finish line. Steep Ravine Trail branches left, to Highway 1.

Old timers refer to the area at the top of the hill as White Barn, part of the old White Gate Ranch. The old white barn was torn down around 1972, shortly after the Golden Gate National Recreation Area assumed stewardship of the land from here westward.

Knowledgeable Dipsea competitors depart the Trail to the right for the first of two stretches on Panoramic Highway. These well known shortcuts avoid the Trail's remaining uphills, but also cut off one of the Trail's most attractive sections.

The marked Dipsea Trail rises a few more yards left. It then descends through a rolling grassland known as the Moors, for its appearance during the frequent summer fogs. When the weather is clear there are striking views of Stinson Beach, tantalizingly close below. Hill 640 Fire Road is crossed; it goes right to Panoramic Highway and left to a deadend above a series of old military bunkers.

The Trail drops steadily. It then bends sharply right at a fence line and re-enters woodland. This is where the last of the race shortcuts re-joins. Veer left. The ocean's influence grows stronger. A bridge crosses a boggy area.

A short descent through grassland brings the Dipsea Trail to its end at Panoramic Highway, just above Highway 1. There is a large trail sign. (On race day, runners are routed left off the Trail a few yards earlier and have to make a perilous leap over a stile down to Highway 1. They go right, then left on Marine Way, then left again to finish at the southernmost Stinson Beach parking lot.)

The Dipsea Trail offers a special experience, among the best the Mountain has to offer, any time of year. It gets a trifle crowded with runners practicing on the several weekends before the race. Come race day to cheer the runners on. The race uses a handicap format, with women and older and younger entrants starting ahead, in one minute intervals, of the "scratch" runners. Three 52-year-old women, a man of 70, and a nine-year-old boy and girl have been champions. The race record is a hard-to-believe 44 minutes, 49 seconds, by Ron Elijah in 1974. The women's record is 55:47, by Peggy Smyth in 1988. The Double Dipsea, from Stinson Beach to Mill Valley and back, is held 13 days after the Dipsea. On the Saturday after Thanksgiving, the Quadruple Dipsea, four crossings starting in Old Mill Park, is contested.

(A more detailed description of the Dipsea Trail, and a removable, two-sided, large-scale, four-color map of the Trail, is found in my book, *Dipsea, The Greatest Race*. See the back page for order information.)

GARDEN PUMP TRAIL
FROM OLD RAILROAD GRADE TO HOO-KOO-E-KOO FIRE ROAD / .38 miles

Terrain: Redwood forest; riparian; unimproved and MARGINAL / MMWD
Elevation: From 560' to 1,040' / extremely steep
Intersecting Trails: None
Directions: Old Railroad Grade trailhead — Old Railroad Grade, 1.1 miles

THIS UNMAINTAINED Trail has not appeared on maps. It is extremely steep and wouldn't be included here were it not for the relatively good footing that redwood forest soils provide. There are also tricky forks; a mistake could lead to unpleasant scrambling through manzanita.

To find the unmarked lower end of the Trail, ascend Old Railroad Grade from West Blithedale Avenue. A half-mile past Horseshoe Curve (the MMWD-MCOSD boundary), and 200 yards beyond a private property fence, the grade crosses a redwood-lined creek. Garden Pump Trail heads right, up the creek's right bank.

The lower yards follow an old pipeline which can also be seen embedded in Old Railroad Grade just down from the Trail's base. The Trail meets a pump, which supplied water to the former Ralston White estate, known as the Garden of Allah, across Old Railroad Grade. The 43-acre estate is now a retreat run by the United Church of Christ, and is open only by reservation.

Continue up to the old stone dam and wood hatch cover. This is the start of the pipeline. Make sure to cross the stream bed here. The Trail continues up the left bank, where it remains the rest of the trip.

The Trail rises extremely steeply beside the creek, through deep forest. Almost halfway up, in a clearing, is a faint fork. Veer left or face manzanita. The Trail departs from the first creek and crosses over a divide to meet another. The remaining stiff uphill, up the left bank, is again through redwoods.

Garden Pump Trail ends at Hoo-Koo-E-Koo Fire Road, amidst a redwood grove. The unsigned junction (the MMWD has placed an "HK 6" post just across) may be hard to identify, as there are several similar groves along this section of Hoo-Koo-E-Koo. Wheeler Trail is 1/3 mile to the left and Corte Madera Trail is 1/2 mile to the right.

Long-time area hikers have never heard of a name for this Trail. The water pump for the Garden of Allah suggests one.

GLEN FIRE ROAD
FROM GLEN DRIVE, MILL VALLEY, TO CORTE MADERA RIDGE F.R. AT
HUCKLEBERRY TRAIL / .87 miles

Terrain: Broom-lined hillside / MCOSD
Elevation: From 280' to 800' / steep
Intersecting Trails: Warner Canyon (Elinor) F.R. (.4m)
Directions: Highway 101 — East Blithedale Ave. (exit), Mill Valley — right on
Carmelita Ave. — right on Buena Vista Ave. — Glen Drive to end

FIRE ROADS RISE on both the west side (from Elinor Avenue) and east side (from
Glen Drive) of Mill Valley's Warner Canyon. These two fire roads merge and
continue up the canyon to Corte Madera Ridge. Warner Canyon was dairy grazing land in the late 1800's and early 1900's, then a wild area open for Mill Valley
youth to explore. The golf course in the lower part of the Canyon opened in
1919.

Glen Fire Road starts from a gate at the upper end of Glen Drive. An
MCOSD sign reads "Northridge-Blithedale Summit." The early going is quite
steep; the grade soon eases. Broom, both French and Scotch, lines the Fire Road's
edge. Sage and monkeyflower are among the native shrubs holding out. Oaks
also border the route, but provide little shade.

Warner Canyon (Elinor) F.R., across Warner Canyon, is visible most of the
way. It joins Glen F.R. at .4 miles. Left leads, in 1.2 miles, to Elinor Avenue in Mill
Valley. The continuation straight, uphill, is considered Glen Fire Road here. Look
back for fine views of the San Francisco skyline as you climb the pristine canyon.

Glen Fire Road ends, presently unsigned here, at the top of Warner Canyon
at a four-way intersection. Corte Madera Ridge F.R. goes left to Blithedale Ridge
and right to Summit Avenue in Corte Madera. Huckleberry Trail, straight ahead,
drops to the Larkspur end of Southern Marin Line Fire Road. Be sure to go up a
few yards left for an outstanding view of Tam's East Peak.

"Glen" is a relatively recent name, applied to the main street of the Warner
Canyon residential area developed after World War II.

H-LINE FIRE ROAD
FROM OLD RAILROAD GRADE TO SOUTHERN MARIN LINE F.R. / .89 miles

Terrain: Chaparral / MCOSD
Elevation: From 320' to 660' to 510' / very steep
Intersecting Trails: Blithedale Ridge F.R. (.6m)
Directions: Old Railroad Grade trailhead — Grade, .1 mile

H-LINE IS A KEY connection in traveling between the Larkspur-Corte Madera
(east) and Mill Valley (south) sides of Tam.

H-Line is the first Fire Road to rise from Old Railroad Grade, 200 yards up from the West Blithedale start. The Fire Road quickly leaves the canyon's forest canopy and enters chaparral. In .1 mile, there is some asphalt at the first big bend. A path departs right from it up to Blithedale Ridge. A few yards above, H-Line passes the first of two water tanks, called "Lower Tank." Just beyond, dramatic views of the summit of Mt. Tamalpais open.

The Fire Road climbs relentlessly. Non-native acacias line the way. The utility poles appear incongruous. In .5 miles, the "Upper Tank" is passed. There is a last bend, and a leveling.

H-Line then crosses Blithedale Ridge F.R. at an important, but presently unsigned, intersection. Blithedale rises on both sides, to the left toward Indian Fire Road and to the right toward Corte Madera Ridge. Between these two branches, H-Line F.R. continues, downhill.

The remaining steep quarter-mile descent is lined with madrones and manzanita. H-Line Fire Road ends at its junction with Southern Marin Line F.R., by a pump station. It is 1.2 miles left to Crown Road in Kentfield, 1.6 miles right to Sunrise Lane in Larkspur.

H-Line was built just after World War II as part of the Southern Marin Line project, which brings water from the lakes on the north side of Tamalpais, through the Bon Tempe treatment plant, to users in southern Marin. From the pump station at the H-Line/Southern Marin junction, water is sent over Blithedale Ridge, where it then drops to the two storage tanks and on to Mill Valley.

The name H-Line, used by Water District personnel, arose when sections of the Southern Marin Line pipeline were marked by a grid; A-Line, B-Line, etc. This Fire Road straddled the H-Line. The newest MCOSD brochure labels the Mill Valley side of the route as "Two Tanks Road," a name used by many visitors.

HORSESHOE FIRE ROAD
FROM OLD RAILROAD GRADE TO BLITHEDALE RIDGE F.R. / .28 miles

Terrain: Chaparral / MCOSD
Elevation: From 440' to 700' / very steep
Intersecting Trails: Corte Madera Creek (.1m)
Directions: Start of Old Railroad Grade — Grade, .6 miles

HORSESHOE is the second of the two fire roads that connect the lower part of Old Railroad Grade to Blithedale Ridge. It sets off a half-mile above the first, H-Line (Two Tanks), and .6 miles from the Grade's dirt start at West Blithedale.

The Fire Road rises from a rare downhill (the result of storm damage) on Old Railroad Grade, where the Grade crosses over Corte Madera Creek. In railroad days, this bend was well-known as Horseshoe Curve. It was the sharpest turn on the entire 8.5 miles of track. Signs at the bend mark the demarcation between MCOSD and MMWD lands.

The uphill is a tough one. In .1 mile, at a green MCOSD "Trail" signpost,

Corte Madera Creek Trail departs left to begin its very steep climb to Hoo-Koo-E-Koo Fire Road. Horseshoe F.R. leaves the redwood forest into open chaparral. Splendid views of Mt. Tamalpais and the San Francisco skyline open.

Horseshoe ends when it hits Blithedale Ridge F.R., which goes left to Hoo-Koo-E-Koo Trail and right to Mill Valley.

MAYTAG TRAIL
BETWEEN BLITHEDALE RIDGE FIRE ROAD / .40 miles

Terrain: Redwood forest / MCOSD
Elevation: From 520' to 620' / gradual
Intersecting Trails: Connector path to Warner Canyon F.R., .1m
Directions: Start (southern end) of Blithedale Ridge F.R.

THIS TRAIL PROVIDES a shaded, less steep, alternative to lower Blithedale Ridge Fire Road. It sets off on the east side of the ridge, a few yards from the private property sign at the southern end of Blithedale Ridge Fire Road. Almost adjacent, closer to the private property boundary, is the access path from Elinor Avenue.

Maytag Trail immediately drops into woodland. In 100 yards, there is a fork. Left, up, leads back to the ridge. To the right is an extremely steep path down to Warner Canyon Fire Road (.4 miles in from its start off Elinor Avenue).

The Trail winds through the woods, Blithedale Ridge never far above. The shrub hazel is abundant. It has soft, serrated leaves and tasty nuts that are hard to find; squirrels and other forest residents harvest them first.

Sections may be overgrown, particularly with broom; the route is little used and only infrequently maintained. Redwoods line most of the rest of the way, and down the steep slope below.

At another fork, a quarter-mile in, a path bends left up to Blithedale Ridge Fire Road and another drops to Warner Canyon Fire Road.

The continuing route of Maytag straight ahead has only recently been beaten through. The Trail climbs a few steep yards to Blithedale Ridge F.R. and ends. A pair of "Boundary" signposts on the fire road are just to the right.

The Trail was originally cleared by a local boy scout troop. The name Maytag was then informally applied when an abandoned appliance was found. Hazel Trail might be a more fitting appellation.

MONTE VISTA FIRE ROAD
FROM TENDERFOOT TRAIL TO MONTE VISTA AVENUE, MILL VALLEY / .45 miles

Terrain: Redwood forest / City of Mill Valley
Elevation: From 240' to 360' / gradual
Intersecting Trails: None
Directions: Tenderfoot Trail, 100 yards

THIS DELIGHTFUL, redwood-lined Fire Road appears as a street on some road maps. Yet it is pristine, free of cars, and passage is open.

The lower trailhead is the same as for Tenderfoot Trail, beside #477 Cascade Drive. Enter quietly, respecting the adjacent homeowner's privacy. In just under 100 yards, there is a major fork. Tenderfoot, heading toward Mountain Home, branches off to the right. Monte Vista rises left (straight) up the creek canyon.

Redwoods dominate. In 100 yards, on the left, is a particularly striking one. Two trunks split about 20 feet up, then twist around one another. One trunk of an aged laurel leans against the tree.

Monte Vista bends left over and around the creek at .2 miles. Another huge, double-trunked redwood stands sentinel at the crossing. The uphill is gentle. A common shrub is California hazel, with its velvety soft leaves. Where the forest thins, look left for the views of Mt. Tamalpais that gave the Fire Road its name.

The Fire Road ends at a chain just before #420 Monte Vista Avenue. Monte Vista's intersection with Rose Avenue is about 100 yards ahead. There is a connection up from the unpaved part of Rose to Cypress Trail, which can then be taken right, to Tenderfoot, for a loop option.

OLD PLANE TRAIL
FROM JUNCTION OF OLD RAILROAD GRADE AND HOO-KOO-E-KOO F.R. TO JUNCTION OF TEMELPA AND TELEPHONE TRAILS / .51 miles

Terrain: Mostly chaparral, parts wooded / MMWD
Elevation: From 1,220' to 1,580' / steep
Intersecting Trails: None
Directions: Upper end of Fern Canyon Rd. — Old Railroad Grade — Murray Trail, OR Mountain Home trailhead — Gravity Car Grade — Old Railroad Grade uphill

OLD PLANE Trail is little used because it is unmarked, is very steep, and ends at even steeper trails. Yet it offers outstanding views, passes through some haunting woodland near an old plane crash site, and leads to one of the Mountain's jewels, the Sitting Bull plaque.

Old Plane is one of two unsigned trails (the other is Murray Trail, which descends) that leave from the Hoo-Koo-E-Koo Fire Road/Old Railroad Grade junction. It is on the northeast corner, rising from ten feet above the Old Railroad Grade signpost.

The entire route is narrow but the opening yards, through manzanita bushes, are the most overgrown. It does somewhat clear above.

Splendid vistas of San Francisco, Mt. Diablo, and the Golden Gate Bridge immediately open. In the first 100 yards is a curious intermingling of manzanitas, denizens of the dry chaparral, and slender redwoods, known for their high moisture requirements. A bit above, chinquapin trees border the Trail as well.

The stiff climb levels, then even drops, to a wonderful forest of laurels. A rivulet is crossed. Just beyond, .3 miles from the start, is a second laurel grove. Look here for a path to the right. (It is more noticeable when descending Old Plane, when it can be mistakenly followed.)

This path leads down the bed of Cascade Creek. Take it to find remnants of the Navy plane that went down here in 1944, killing its eight crew members. The plane was flying from Alameda to the Hawaiian island of Oahu when it slammed into the fog-shrouded Mountain. Remember, it is unlawful to remove historic artifacts from Tam.

The continuation of the Trail beyond the crash site was built a few years later. There is a cooling redwood forest; note that all the redwoods grow below the Trail, none higher. A rock offers a resting site with a choice southern panorama.

The evergreens ahead are mostly introduced Bishop and Monterey pines. This grove is quite prominent when viewing Tam from the south.

Old Plane ends when it hits Temelpa Trail. Bush poppies color the intersection bright yellow in late spring. A few yards uphill on Temelpa, to the left, is the lower end of extremely steep Telephone Trail, which rises to the East Peak parking lot. The equally steep Temelpa Trail climbs to Verna Dunshee Trail. Straight ahead is an overgrown path to Devil's Gulch. Go downhill 25 yards on Temelpa to visit the wonderful Sitting Bull plaque (see Temelpa Trail) embedded in a boulder. Temelpa continues down to Hoo-Koo-E-Koo F.R. for a loop option. (It is safer to do the loop in reverse, up Temelpa and down Old Plane.)

The Erickson map calls the Trail the Old Plane since its lower half was cut in 1944 specifically to reach the plane wreck site. The Olmsted map labels it as Vic Haun Trail; Victor Emmanuel Haun was one of the founders of the California Alpine Club. Some call it "Airplane Trail."

OLD RAILROAD GRADE
FROM WEST BLITHEDALE AVENUE, MILL VALLEY, TO RIDGECREST BOULEVARD /
6.72 miles

Terrain: Lower part wooded, upper part mostly chaparral; heavily used / MCOSD
& MMWD
Elevation: From 240' to 2,220' / gradual
Intersecting Trails: H-Line F.R. (.1m), Horseshoe F.R. (.6m), Garden Pump (1.1m),
Temelpa (1.8m, 2.2m), Connector to Hoo-Koo-E-Koo F.R. (2.6m), Murray (2.6m),
Gravity Car Grade (2.9m), Hoo-Koo-E-Koo (3.1m), Hoo-Koo-E-Koo F.R. (3.2m), Old
Plane (3.2m), Hogback F.R. (3.8m), Fern Creek (4.2m), Miller (4.3m, 6.0m), Nora
(5.3m), West Point (5.3m), Old Stage Road (5.3m), Rock Spring (5.3m), Tavern
Pump (6.2m)
Directions: Downtown Mill Valley — West Blithedale Ave. to just beyond Lee
Street
Amenities: Restrooms, fountains, picnic tables

A CASE CAN BE MADE that Old Railroad Grade is the most important route on
Mt. Tamalpais. It was graded in 1896, then covered, until 1930, by the track of
the Mt. Tamalpais & Muir Woods Railway, "The World's Crookedest Railroad."
The railway carried hundreds of thousands of riders to the summit and to Muir
Woods, and brought the Grade and the Mountain world-wide fame. The Grade
remains the most heavily used base-to-summit route on the Mountain, particularly for dirt bikers. Because it intersects so many trails, the Grade also plays a
part in most visits to the Mountain's south side.

The train departed from the downtown Mill Valley train station (now The
Depot Bookstore & Cafe) shared with the commuter line from Sausalito. The 8.5
miles of single track up the Mountain rounded a total of 281 curves, the equiva-
lent of 42 full circles. The longest straight section, ironically in the middle of the
celebrated series of turns known as Double Bow Knot, was only 413 feet. The
uphill never exceeded a modest 7 degree grade. There were originally 22 trestles;
all were late filled.

Most of the line's first 1.3 miles, beside Corte Madera Creek, is now blocked
by private homes. Some glimpses of the bygone era can be captured by walking
along Corte Madera Avenue. Around fifty yards beyond Lee Street is the start of
the surviving Old Railroad Grade. (From 1905 to 1927, a local commuter service
operated on the Mountain Railway track between Lee Street and the depot.)
The MCOSD sign on the gate does not mention the route's famous name, only
the designation "Northridge, Blithedale Summit."

This lower section skirts private property. Homes are visible across Corte
Madera Creek. The area is well wooded and the abundant big-leaf maple trees
bring New England-like colors in fall.

In 200 yards, the steep H-Line Fire Road (also called Two Tanks Road) rises
on the right to Blithedale Ridge. Farther along, a fence adjoins the Grade on the
left.

The Grade reaches a bend called Horseshoe Curve, the sharpest on the entire route, over Corte Madera Creek. On the near side of the creek, Horseshoe Fire Road, also going to Blithedale Ridge, sets off uphill to the right. Corte Madera Trail splits from Horseshoe F.R. some 100 yards higher. A path on the far (right) bank of the creek also connects to Corte Madera Trail. Storm damage has also brought a rare dip to the Grade at Horseshoe Curve. Here too Old Railroad Grade leaves Marin County Open Space District lands to enter the jurisdiction of the Marin Municipal Water District, where it remains the rest of the way.

There is a marked change in the vegetation as the Grade now climbs the hotter, drier, south-facing slope; chaparral largely replaces the redwoods, except at creek crossings. The site of an old wood post Mile 2 marker (as calibrated from the Mill Valley depot; deduct 1.3 miles to match our start) is passed.

A fence line on the left marks the upper boundary of the private, 43-acre Ralston L. White Memorial Retreat Center. Ralston White (1877-1943) built his dream home (completed in 1915) on the property, which he named Garden of Allah after a book popular at the time. Supplies to build the home came over the Mountain Railroad track and were dropped at the still-evident White Siding. The huge steel-framed, concrete-walled main house, now hidden by trees, was so sturdily built it survived the terrible 1929 Tam fire that started so nearby. (A newer house on the property now sits just left of the Grade.) The estate was deeded in 1957, for 100 years, to the United Church of Christ by Mrs. Ralston White. Several paths, all off-limits, cross the property.

From the water tank left, a pipeline is visible embedded in the Grade. Follow it some 150 yards to a bend that takes the Grade over a creek. This is the foot of unsigned, unmaintained Garden Pump Trail. It follows the water pipeline (which supplied the Garden of Allah) on the creek's right bank, then continues extremely steeply up the left bank to Hoo-Koo-E-Koo Fire Road.

Seventy-five yards before Milepost 3 (elevation, 700 feet), the Grade enters its largest road cut, the McKinley Cut. At its start, look for a boulder on the left with the words "McKinley Cut." President McKinley was scheduled to ride on the railroad in 1900 and the Mill Valley depot was properly festooned, but his wife became ill and the trip was cancelled.

Around .3 miles above, the Grade meets an MMWD gate and, immediately after, a private residence. Just higher, ten yards before the Grade meets the junction of Summit Avenue and Fern Canyon Road, unmarked Temelpa Trail sets off uphill toward the Mountain's summit.

The Grade is paved and open to auto traffic for .6 miles along Fern Canyon Road, but is included to avoid a discontinuity. Sweeping views, including of the San Francisco skyline, help compensate. The Grade can be reached by car here via Summit Avenue from downtown Mill Valley. Temelpa Trail again touches Fern Canyon Road, on the right. A restored sign in the old style marks the junction, by a yellow fire hydrant.

The Grade reenters woodland, and its surface is again dirt, beyond a gate at the upper end of Fern Canyon Road. A fence on the left marks the boundary of a private estate, with a new home at the edge. Just past milepost 4 is the East Fork of Cascade Creek. On the near bank, a path climbs 1/6-mile beside the creek to

Hoo-Koo-E-Koo Fire Road. Unsigned Murray Trail climbs the creek's other (right) bank to the Bow Knot, a one-third-mile shortcut to the Grade.

The Grade leaves the tree cover for the chaparral that characterizes much of the rest of the climb. (Early Tam photos show the whole upper part of the Grade as treeless). Views to the east, south, and west become ever more expansive. A path, marked by a "no bikes" sign, drops left between a line of Monterey pines to a homemade bench.

The Grade then enters the famous Double Bow Knot (also spelled as Bow-Knot and Bowknot, and without the "Double"). Here the tracks ran parallel to themselves five times, over a straight line distance of just 600 feet, to gain 168 feet of elevation. It used to be easy to go wrong in the maze here, losing the Grade by not bending right and ending up on Gravity Car Fire Road toward Mountain Home. New signposts should end the problem.

The Grade passes the stone platform remnant of Mesa Station, at Milepost 4.5, elevation 1,120 feet. Here, beginning in 1907, passengers could switch to gravity cars to descend to the Muir Woods Inn, above the new Muir Woods National Monument. A couple of small paths left and right offer Bow Knot shortcuts for impatient hikers.

The Grade bends left. There is a stand of introduced coulter pines, which carry the world's heaviest cones. A path drops to the right.

Just before the Bow Knot's final bend, Hoo-Koo-E-Koo Trail branches sharply left to Hogback (Throckmorton) F.R. A shortcut path to higher on the Grade rises from the same junction.

One hundred yards beyond on the Grade, Hoo-Koo-E-Koo departs right, as a fire road. The top of Murray Trail is fifteen yards away on it, unmarked and on the right. The Grade itself bends left here. In this bend unmarked Old Plane (Vic Haun) Trail sets off uphill to Temelpa Trail.

The Grade is now on a steady course west. A shortcut path back to the Bow Knot leaves left. Past Milepost 5 is the intersection with Hogback Fire Road, which drops directly to Mountain Home. To the right is the now-closed, precipitous, rocky Throckmorton Trail, a once popular route to East Peak.

The Grade re-enters woodland. Fern Creek Trail rises to the right from a marked signpost at the bend over Fern Creek itself. Just ahead, a reliable spring flows down a rock on the right.

At the next big bend, rebuilding after the major storm of January 1982 has introduced another short downhill to the Grade. Here, near where the now-gone Milepost 6 was, Miller Trail begins its very steep climb by ascending nearly 100 steps. Look for a redwood spouting young trees from its cut stump. Miller crosses the Grade again higher up, offering a steep, shaded, shortcut.

The Grade climbs another mile through the chaparral without a trail intersection. Finally, the cluster of buildings of West Point Inn appears. The inn sits at the westernmost edge of Old Railroad Grade. It was built by the railroad in 1904 to provide lodging for visitors, and still does provide rustic accommodations (call 388-9955 well in advance for reservations). West Point was also the transfer point for passengers taking the stagecoach on to Bolinas; a proposed rail line to Bolinas was never built. The inn is run by the West Point Inn Association, which also hosts a series of popular Sunday pancake breakfasts that are open to all. At the inn are public bathrooms, picnic tables with great views, a fountain, and interesting exhibits on the Mountain's geology, flora and fauna, and history.

Four trails meet the Grade at West Point: Nora and West Point, both dropping very steeply left to Matt Davis; broad Old Stage Road descending to Pantoll; and Rock Spring heading to the Mountain Theater. There was a siding at West Point for the extra railway cars used on Mountain Play weekends. Playgoers then walked to the theater.

The Grade rounds the inn and soon passes Milepost 7. The final stretch is largely treeless, and often hot in summer. Miller Trail again meets the Grade. It continues left uphill to Ridgecrest Boulevard and International Trail.

Soon after, Tavern Pump Trail joins from the right, having risen from Fern Creek Trail. Milepost 8 is passed.

The Grade ends at paved Ridgecrest Boulevard in the saddle between East and Middle peaks. Across the pavement is Middle Peak Fire Road and, to its right, the top of Eldridge Grade.

The track continued east up to the famous Tavern of Tamalpais, or Summit Tavern, at the far edge of today's East Peak parking lot. The tavern, offering gracious dining, dancing, and overnight accommodations, was built in 1896 (then expanded) as part of the railway project. Fires started by cinders from the train were a constant problem. The tavern burned to the ground in 1923, was rebuilt, then ironically survived the Mountain's 1929 conflagration. The tavern continued as a commercial enterprise until 1942, 13 years after the railroad's demise. It was then leased to the Army as a barracks. The structure fell into such disrepair after World War II that it was deliberately burned down in 1950. Its foundation now blends into the overlook picnic area.

The story of the Mt. Tamalpais & Muir Woods Railway is one of the Mountain's most colorful. It is well told in the book, *The Crookedest Railroad in the World*, by Ted Wurm and Al Graves. The Railway's flavor is also charmingly recaptured in Cris Chater's 1988 award-winning film *Steaming Up Tamalpais*.

Among the private railroad's principal financial backers were: Sidney Cushing, who owned the Blithedale Hotel near the start; William Kent, who went on to donate Muir Woods, Steep Ravine and other lands to the public; and the Tamalpais Land and Water Co., which was then developing its Mill Valley holdings.

The route was graded and the track laid with remarkable speed, under eight months. The groundbreaking was on February 5, 1896, the formal opening that August 27. During the Pan-American Exposition year of 1915, over 100,000 people took the ride to the top.

The line fell victim to the increased popularity of the automobile, and construction of Ridgecrest Boulevard and Panoramic Highway in the 1920's made it possible to drive to the top. The fire of 1929 was a final blow. The tracks were pulled up in 1930 but it is still possible, if you're sharp eyed and lucky, to find old spikes along the Grade.

TELEPHONE TRAIL
FROM TEMELPA TRAIL TO EAST PEAK PARKING AREA / .6 miles

Terrain: Chaparral; loose rocks; unmaintained and MARGINAL / MMWD
Elevation: 1,600' to 2,320' / extremely steep
Intersecting Trails: None
Directions: Fern Canyon Rd. at Summit Ave. — Temelpa Trail, .8 miles

TELEPHONE TRAIL is one of the steepest on Mt. Tamalpais. Loose rock on its upper half makes it extremely dangerous to descend; don't try it unless you're a mountaineer. Uphill is grueling, particularly on a warm day. The Trail is also overgrown (Olmsted now omits it save for the opening yards), so wear protective clothing to avoid being scratched by protruding chaparral shrubs. On the positive side, the Trail provides unique, spectacular vistas from high on the Mountain.

Two trails, both unsigned, branch left off Temelpa Trail about 25 yards above the Sitting Bull plaque boulder. First is Old Plane (Vic Haun), dropping to Old Railroad Grade. A few feet beyond is the foot of Telephone Trail.

From the start, the views are sweeping and extraordinary. You'll welcome every opportunity to rest and look. Manzanitas line the way, their sharp points often too close for comfort. Sticky monkeyflower adds orange color much of the year. A path branches left, downhill.

In less than .2 miles, the Trail meets the first of the telephone poles that give it its name. Stumps of the older poles are alongside. Higher, you can look left and see the entire phone line down to Mill Valley's Summit Avenue.

Halfway up, the Trail enters a grove of laurels, and laurels line much of the remainder of the ascent. A couple of paths set off right, back to Temelpa.

The Trail route becomes strewn with rocks. Soon after, the first in a series of boulders are encountered; they'll test your agility.

Sounds from the summit parking area carry down. The route levels. The Trail passes a prominent Monterey pine. Remnants of the long-gone Tavern on Tamalpais, the terminus of the railroad line, are visible above.

Telephone Trail ends at a path, the former Throckmorton Trail. The route downhill to the left is blocked for erosion control. Uphill leads to the stop sign by the edge of the East Peak parking lot. Just yards away are water fountains, a snack shack, the Visitors Center, bathrooms, and Verna Dunshee and Plankwalk trails.

Telephone Trail apparently dates from the early 1930's, perhaps tied to the rebuilding of the lookout tower atop East Peak then. There used to be another Telephone Trail, labeled #2 on older maps, running from the Mountain Theater to Old Stage Road.

TEMELPA TRAIL
FROM OLD RAILROAD GRADE AT FERN CANYON ROAD, MILL VALLEY, TO VERNA DUNSHEE TRAIL / 1.5 miles

Terrain: Overgrown chaparral; loose rocks; unmaintained and MARGINAL / MMWD
Elevation: From 820' to 2,380' / extremely steep
Intersecting Trails: Old Railroad Grade (.2m), Hoo-Koo-E-Koo F.R. (.5m), Old Plane (.8m), Telephone (.8m)
Directions: Summit Ave., Mill Valley, to top; limited or no parking

TEMELPA IS THE STEEPEST long Trail on Mt. Tamalpais. It rises more than 1,000 feet per mile directly atop what is called Middle Ridge. As a corollary, Temelpa is part of the fastest route from the Mountain's base to its summit. During a race in 1987, Tom Borschel ran from Lytton Square in downtown Mill Valley, elevation 64 feet, to the East Peak fire lookout, elevation 2,571 feet, via Summit Avenue, Temelpa Trail, and shortcuts in 30 minutes, 32 seconds.

Needless to say, Temelpa Trail is only for the very fittest hikers. Downhill is even more arduous because loose rock in the upper section makes footing treacherous. It is also somewhat difficult to follow, with many unsigned intersections. Those who do venture up Temelpa get fantastic views and a visit to a little-known treasure, the Sitting Bull plaque.

Temelpa Trail presently starts uphill, unmarked, off Old Railroad Grade a few feet below the junction of Summit Avenue and Fern Canyon Road. Not many years ago it started by the bridge on Summit Avenue, before upper Summit was paved. Earlier still, Temelpa started even lower, in Blithedale Canyon.

In .2 miles, Temelpa Trail meets an access path coming from Fern Canyon Road (by #39) to the left. After another hundred yards, Temelpa briefly touches Fern Canyon Road, which is a paved section of Old Railroad Grade. The junction is identified by a pair of restored signs, by a yellow fire hydrant. Keep climbing the Trail.

This next section, to Hoo-Koo-E-Koo F.R., was greatly improved in 1997. Most of an old two-inch pipeline that cut a gully through the Trail has been removed, dozens of wood steps added, and brush cleared. Much of the work was done by local Eagle Scouts, under the direction of the MMWD. The views are sweeping, and get ever better. Look up to see the distant goal; East Peak. At .3 miles, a short connector to Hoo-Koo-E-Koo F.R. branches right; some call it Easter Lily Trail. Stay left.

In just under a half-mile, Temelpa crosses Hoo-Koo-E-Koo Fire Road. A new MMWD 6x6 signpost marks the junction. Left on Hoo-Koo-E-Koo leads to the top of the Double Bowknot, right to Wheeler Trail. Cross the fire road and keep climbing. Shrubs, including sharp-pointed manzanita and chaparral pea, line the way; long sleeves are some protection.

In another tough 1/3 mile, be alert for a large boulder on the left. The boulder itself, a block of erosion-resistant quartz tourmaline that fell from East Peak during a slide in the distant past, is wonderful enough; the plaque affixed to it is one of the Mountain's jewels. It contains one of the most eloquent environmental statements ever made, expressed by the Sioux chief Sitting Bull in 1877. (The quote is also found in *The Portable North American Indian Reader*, edited by Frederick W. Turner III, Viking Press, 1974.) It reads:

BEHOLD MY BROTHERS, THE SPRING HAS COME; THE EARTH HAS RECEIVED THE EMBRACES OF THE SUN AND WE SHALL SOON SEE THE RESULT OF ALL THAT LOVE! EVERY SEED IS AWAKENED AND SO HAS ALL ANIMAL LIFE. IT IS THROUGH THIS MYSTERIOUS POWER THAT WE TOO HAVE OUR BEING AND WE THEREFORE YIELD TO OUR NEIGHBORS, EVEN OUR ANIMAL NEIGHBORS, THE SAME RIGHT AS OURSELVES, TO INHABIT THIS LAND. YET HEAR ME, PEOPLE, WE HAVE NOW TO DEAL WITH ANOTHER RACE; SMALL AND FEEBLE WHEN OUR FATHERS FIRST MET THEM BUT NOW GREAT AND OVERBEARING. STRANGELY ENOUGH THEY HAVE A MIND TO TILL THE SOIL AND THE LOVE OF POSSESSION IS A DISEASE TO THEM. THESE PEOPLE HAVE MADE MANY RULES THAT THE RICH MAY BREAK BUT THE POOR MAY NOT. THEY TAKE TITHES FROM THE POOR AND WEAK TO SUPPORT THE RICH WHO RULE. THEY CLAIM THIS MOTHER OF OURS, THE EARTH, FOR THEIR OWN AND FENCE THEIR NEIGHBORS AWAY; THEY DEFACE HER WITH THEIR BUILDINGS AND THEIR REFUSE. THAT NATION IS LIKE A SPRING FRESHET THAT OVERRUNS ITS BANKS AND DESTROYS ALL WHO ARE IN ITS PATH.
SITTING BULL 1877

The original plaque, placed in the 1980's, was defaced in 1990. A good samaritan attempted to replace it in 1993 (with permission from the MMWD) and inadvertently shattered it. Then his own replacement duplicate quickly fell off. Today's plaque, hopefully more enduring, was installed soon after.

Twenty-five yards uphill, two trails depart left. First is Old Plane (Vic Haun) going sharply left, downhill, to Double Bow Knot. A few feet above, Telephone Trail begins an extremely steep, rocky climb to the East Peak parking lot. To the right, a path winds to Devil's Slide and, a few feet above, Temelpa continues.

There is more steep scrambling. Temelpa crosses Devil's Slide, a massive rockfall that swept more than 1,000 vertical feet down the gully during the great rainstorm of early January 1982. Tam geologist Salem Rice ponders the thunderous roar the slide must have generated; apparently no one was nearby on the Mountain during the storm to hear it.

The uppermost part of Temelpa is tricky, laced with paths. You may end up on the old route straight up, or a more gradual, switchbacked one. In both cases you'll meet the Verna Dunshee Trail loop roughly halfway around from the East Peak parking area. Forty yards to the right of the Temelpa signpost is the top of a huge slide shored by an elaborate wood structure labeled "The Great Wall of Mt. Tamalpais."

Temelpa (variously spelled) is one name for the legendary lovelorn Indian

"Sleeping Maiden" who reposes on the Mountain to give the summit ridge its famous profile. While this legend, inspiration for countless poems and stories, may or (more likely) may not be of native American origin, it's a cherished one. The most famous recounting of the myth is Dan Totheroh's play, "Tamalpa," which has been presented a record eight seasons at the Mountain Theater. Its closing line, recited as the maiden Tamalpa is borne to her final resting place, is, "Throw over her the purple cloak that she will always wear — a shroud of amethyst from tip of toe to crown of hair."

Temelpa Trail was formerly part of Summit Trail, one of Tamalpais' oldest, dating from 1875. The name was changed in 1914. It has also been called Cushing's Trail, because it led up from the Cushing family's hotel in Blithedale Canyon.

TENDERFOOT TRAIL
FROM CASCADE DRIVE TO EDGEWOOD AVENUE, MILL VALLEY / 1.09 miles

Terrain: Deep woodland; open to bicycles / City of Mill Valley & private (easement)
Elevation: From 270′ to 840′ / steep
Intersecting Trails: Monte Vista F.R. (.1m)
Directions: Downtown Mill Valley — Throckmorton Ave. — Cascade Drive to near #477

A PAIR OF TRAILS, Zig-Zag and Tenderfoot, rise toward Mountain Home from the west end of Mill Valley's Cascade Drive. They can be combined (although Ziz-Zag is extremely steep) for a loop, with rest and refreshments available halfway through at Mountain Home Inn.

Cascade Drive is a quintessential Mill Valley street; alongside a creek and lined with redwoods and attractive homes. To reach Tenderfoot, follow Cascade Drive just over a mile from Old Mill Park and .2 miles past Cascade Falls. A sign beside the driveway of #477 Cascade reads "Tenderfoot Trails." The plural is no mistake; the hillside south of Cascade is laced with unmarked paths and intersections. Start the climb by passing quietly to the left of the private residence.

The first junction on Tenderfoot is in just 30 yards. Left (straight) is half-mile-long Monte Vista Fire Road. Veer right. In another 50 yards, the broad Tenderfoot passes through a gate. A sign here says that bicyclists — Tenderfoot is presently the only trail described in this book open to bikes — are to dismount when passing.

The second fork is at .2 miles. Spine-covered fruits fallen off chinquapin trees cover the ground here in early fall. The right path immediately enters private property; veer left. Fork #3, by an old corrugated iron switchback siding, is at .4 miles. Unmarked Cypress Trail goes left, winding more than a mile-and-a-half to Cypress Avenue. Veer right.

At a brief clearing in Tenderfoot's woodland canopy, a striking vista of East Peak opens. Around 75 yards beyond is fork #4. The upper, right option ends in 25 yards; veer left. The fifth and last fork, at .7 miles, is in deep woodland. The two left branches narrow are overgrown. Go right. Tenderfoot's sequence of turns is therefore easy to remember — right, left, right, left, right.

Tenderfoot's remaining climb is through a quiet redwood forest. A slide is bypassed. A few yards later, the Trail crosses a stream over a bridge of roughly lashed redwood logs.

The topmost yards of Tenderfoot Trail were rerouted in 1990 to skirt the carport of a new home. The Trail ends at Edgewood Avenue, beside a fire pump protected by fencing. Just to the left is Pipeline Trail, leading toward the top of the Dipsea Steps. A half-mile to the right on Edgewood is Mountain Home Inn, with Zig-Zag Trail just beyond.

There have been various proposals over the years to develop homesites along the historic Tenderfoot Trail. In 1980, concerned citizens mounted a major effort to keep it open. Evidence was cited that Tenderfoot had been used by local Coast Miwok Indians, then by the earliest loggers. Additional adjoining private acreage was acquired in 1997-98.

The name Tenderfoot may refer to the Trail being gentler graded than the Dipsea steps, Zig-Zag Trail (which is twice as steep), the former (now overgrown) adjacent Mill Creek Fire Trail, or other old routes up out of Mill Valley.

THREE WELLS TRAIL
FROM CASCADE DRIVE TO LOVELL AVENUE, MILL VALLEY / .27 miles

Terrain: Redwood forest; riparian / City of Mill Valley
Elevation: From 250' to 330' / lower part level, upper part steep
Intersecting Trails: None
Directions: Downtown Mill Valley — Throckmorton Avenue — left on Cascade Drive to near #320

WHEN SAMUEL THROCKMORTON controlled some 19,000 acres of southern Marin from the mid-1850's until his death in 1883, Mill Valley's Cascade Canyon was gated, with entry granted only to his favorite visitors. After the railroad came to Mill Valley and the town developed in 1890, the canyon and its jewels Three Wells and Cascade Falls immediately became popular tourist destinations for train-loads of visiting San Franciscans. They likely used this same Trail.

The Trail sets off opposite #320 Cascade Drive, from a "Three Wells" sign affixed to a redwood. (Traces of the original path all the way from Old Mill Park are still evident along Cascade Drive, but pass through private property.) Descend toward the creek, past a faded old "Keep Out" sign; the path is now open. The creek, which roars in winter, is called both Cascade and Old Mill.

In 80 yards, an alternate entry path forks right, meeting Cascade Drive by its junction with Throckmorton Ave. Beyond is a stone revetment shoring the bank.

The Trail enters a garden of boulders and the lower of three pools, or "wells," separated by small falls, that give the landmark its name. Cross the pedestrian bridge to the creek's right bank. A narrow section of Trail goes under a bridge serving adjacent homes. Another footbridge brings the Trail back to the left bank.

Three Wells Trail crosses Cascade Drive where two forks of the creek join. Enter the City of Mill Valley park (as it has been for more than 100 years) signed as "Cascade Falls." The small parking lot fills following winter storms as Mill Valleyites flock to see the falls.

There is a fork in 75 yards. Right leads down to the closest view of the falls. Veer left and up. It seems hard to believe in this lovely redwood forest that downtown Mill Valley, which many bemoan as too busy, is but a mile away.

A path left rises to another entry near 800 Lovell. Continue around the canyon. The Trail ends at Lovell Avenue, near #766. The trailheads for Zig-Zag, Tenderfoot, and Monte Vista trails are just to the left.

The Trail has no formal name, and Cascade Trail would be just as likely a candidate. But there is already a Cascade Falls in Fairfax. Three Wells is a historic name, and uniquely Mill Valley.

WARNER CANYON FIRE ROAD
FROM ELINOR AVENUE, MILL VALLEY, TO GLEN FIRE ROAD / 1.20 miles

Terrain: Lower part redwood forest; upper part chaparral / MCOSD
Elevation: From 360' to 580' / lower part steep, upper part almost level
Intersecting Trails: Warner Falls (.3m)
Directions: West Blithedale Avenue — right on Oakdale Ave. — right on Elinor Ave. to past #245; virtually no parking

MILL VALLEY's Warner Canyon, cut by Warner Creek, lies between Corte Madera and Blithedale Ridges. Its lower end is covered by the Mill Valley Municipal Golf Course. Both sides of the canyon are topped by fire roads, this one and Glen.

To reach Warner Canyon F.R., follow Mill Valley's winding and narrow Elinor Avenue uphill. Past #245, the road is unpaved. Veer right at the next intersection; left goes up to private residences. In thirty yards there is a gate marking the start of Warner Canyon Fire Road, also commonly called Elinor Fire Road. The opening yards of the Fire Road abut private property; the rest of the way is through MCOSD lands.

Within 30 yards, a path, sometimes shielded by broom, drops right to Bay Tree Lane. The Fire Road is fairly level at first. It is alternately lined with broom and, at creek crossings, with redwoods. In .2 miles, a path branches right through the broom and drops 300 yards to Tartan Road.

In another 100 yards, in the middle of a sharp, horseshoe bend left amidst redwoods, Warner Falls Trail (called Warner Canyon Trail on the MCOSD signpost) departs to the right. It runs a half-mile to a lovely, little known waterfall.

The uphill steepens. One hundred yards above Warner Falls Trail, at a bend right, an extremely steep path goes up to Blithedale Ridge. This path may one day be upgraded as an access to the ridge.

Warner Canyon F.R. passes in and out of redwood groves. The grade lessens, and there is even a short downhill. After the last quarter-mile stretch of redwoods, the Fire Road opens. There are views of the San Francisco skyline. At one such vista point, a delightful little "shrine" has been cut into a rock on the hillside left; anyone disturbing it should expect bad luck!

Two hundred fifty yards later, Warner Canyon F. R. ends at its junction with Glen F.R. Downhill leads, in .4 miles, to Mill Valley's Glen Drive. The remaining half-mile of uphill, to Corte Madera Ridge F.R., is called Glen Fire Road in this book, but can just as logically be considered part of Warner Canyon F.R.

Alexander Warner was a San Francisco physician who bought 170 acres of dairy grazing land in what was then called Juanita Canyon for $6,000 in 1885. For years, he brought his large family to summer there. The family sold the parcel (including 35 additional acres acquired in 1917) at the end of World War II.

Elinor Burt was a granddaughter of one of Mill Valley's first settlers, Jacob Gardner. Her father, John Burt, worked for the Tamalpais Land & Water Co., which opened Mill Valley for development in 1890. In 1916, he became the first superintendent of the Marin Municipal Water District. Gardner and Burt developed the tract through which Elinor Avenue runs. Elinor Burt was a widely respected teacher, a dietitian for the U.S. Air Corps during World War II, and the author of two cookbooks, *Olla Podrida* and *Far Eastern Cooking*. She died in 1973 at age 74. Her oral history is found in the Mill Valley Public Library.

The Marin County Open Space District began making acquisitions in Warner Canyon in the 1970's.

WARNER FALLS TRAIL
FROM WARNER CANYON FIRE ROAD TO WARNER FALLS / .48 miles

Terrain: Riparian; mostly redwood forest; parts sometimes overgrown by broom; deadend / MCOSD
Elevation: Around 380' / almost level
Intersecting Trails: None
Directions: Top of Elinor Ave. (virtually no parking) — Warner Canyon F.R., .3 miles

THERE IS A LOVELY WATERFALL on Warner Creek, little visited except by local residents. The falls are known both as Warner, for the canyon, and as Elinor, because most access it by Elinor Avenue. The Trail to the falls was only signed in 1994.

To reach the trailhead, follow Warner Canyon (Elinor) Fire Road .3 miles from its start off Elinor Avenue. Other connector paths to the right are passed along the way but Warner Falls Trail (called Warner Canyon Trail on the MCOSD signpost) is obvious in the middle of a redwood-shaded, horseshoe bend.

The early yards are wide. The Trail was originally a road but, like other old cuts in the area, became heavily overgrown with French broom and narrowed. Continued use by visitors to the falls, and recent broom pulls by MCOSD personnel and other passersby (a sign at the gate at Elinor says "Please pull broom"), now keep it reasonably open.

Redwood and hazel are abundant, with maples and madrones also common.

The Trail rises almost imperceptibly. At a prominent clearing, broom reigns, at times almost blocking through passage. Poison oak also intrudes, so be careful.

The Trail begins to rise noticeably as it meets Warner Creek. The falls, and end of the Trail, are just ahead. (The Trail's apparent continuation above the falls quickly deteriorates.) The flow in the falls is lively after a winter rain; nonexistent by late spring. This quiet place, bordered by huge redwoods and colored in spring by abundant trillium, makes for a special picnic spot.

Background on Alexander Warner and on Elinor Burt is found in the Warner Canyon Fire Road description.

WHEELER TRAIL
FROM HOO-KOO-E-KOO FIRE ROAD TO ELDRIDGE GRADE / .53 miles

Terrain: Light woods, chaparral / MMWD
Elevation: From 1,120' to 1,570' / very steep
Intersecting Trails: None
Directions: Fern Canyon Rd. at Summit Ave. — Temelpa Trail — right on Hoo-Koo-E-Koo F.R., .2 miles

Wheeler Trail often plays a role in circuit routes around Tamalpais as it offers a key link across the Mountain's east face. Otherwise it is little used, being far from any trailhead.

Wheeler sets off uphill from Hoo-Koo-E-Koo F.R. at Slide Gulch (also called Devil's Slide). The gulch, a named feature on Tam for more than 100 years, is a long, prominent slide that runs southeast from below East Peak. At Wheeler's base are a dam and pipeline, remnants of the old Slide Gulch water intake.

Begin uphill from the Wheeler signpost. Bear sharply right a few feet up the Trail, not crossing the creek. Wheeler rises very steeply, in parts extremely steeply, through a forest of thin redwoods. There are intersecting paths, including a prominent one right at .1m, but Wheeler is easy enough to follow.

After a quarter-mile, the Trail emerges into chaparral, with manzanita the dominant shrub. There are sweeping views, including the San Francisco skyline.

Keep climbing over the rocky terrain. There is, at last, a welcome downhill. Fifty yards later Wheeler ends at a signed, horseshoe curve in Eldridge Grade. Right leads down to the lakes, left up to Northside Trail and East Peak.

The Trail was largely built by Alfred Wheeler. He was an attorney who sailed to San Francisco from New York in 1849. In the 1850's, Wheeler accumulated large parcels of San Francisco real estate. He loved to hike on Tam, and, seeing the need for a connection between the north and south sides of the Mountain, decided to do the work himself.

The *San Francisco Chronicle* covered the dedication ceremony in September 1902 when bronze tablets honoring Wheeler were placed at both ends of the Trail. The account reads, in part, "For over two years, through summer's heat and winter's cold, this philanthropist, 80 years of age, toiled away with pick and shovel on the stubborn slopes of Tamalpais. He pursued his end with infinite patience, clearing a path over flinty rocks, hewing away the resisting chaparral, prying boulders out of the way, and all for a labor of love . . . He is now only able to move about with the help of crutches, and will probably never see his trail again . . . His thoughts dwell constantly on the heights of Tamalpais, and in his dreams he is still working away . . . on the winding path." Wheeler died 11 months later. His *Chronicle* obituary said, "the (trail) work cost him his life."

ZIG-ZAG TRAIL
FROM CASCADE DRIVE, MILL VALLEY, TO MOUNTAIN HOME / .50 miles

Terrain: Mostly redwood forest, some chaparral; unmaintained and MARGINAL / City of Mill Valley and private, with easement
Elevation: From 290' to 900' / extremely steep
Intersecting Trails: None
Directions: Cascade Drive to end at Lovell Avenue

ZIG-ZAG Trail is part of the quickest route from Mill Valley to Mountain Home. Indeed, in 1983, some enterprising runners in the Dipsea Race used it as part of a faster route to Stinson Beach than the Dipsea Trail itself. (The new route was then promptly banned.) Zig-Zag is in fact so steep that many might find descending it dangerous; it will be described uphill.

The trailhead is to the left of the driveway for the private residence of 550 Cascade Drive. Please be courteous. A separate road leads to the off-limits Cascade Dam, the drained Cascade Reservoir, and the former Cascade Fire Trail up to Old Railroad Grade. The reservoir was the site of much hippie-era carousing during the 1960's and '70's. It was closed to the public after a drowning death.

Zig-Zag starts by crossing a bridge. The Trail goes uphill, beside a fence surrounding a covered reservoir that served as Mill Valley's early water source. Nine-feet-deep, it holds 68,000 gallons.

Almost immediately, the extremely steep climbing begins. The switchbacks that gave the Trail its name help a little. Much of the route is through redwood forest, some of it mature, some with young, thin, crowded trees.

The Trail skirts several private parcels. Well up, Zig-Zag enters an open, rocky gully. There are fine views above the chaparral shrubs, to Mill Valley, "Little Tamalpais" (Corte Madera Ridge), and Tam's summit ridge. This is the most slippery part when descending. Huckleberry becomes abundant.

Zig Zag re-enters woodland. After passing a few paths, it ends, presently unmarked (there had been a sign here for decades) at a dirt driveway. Go right. In 50 yards is Gravity Car Grade. Mountain Home Inn and Panoramic Highway are then just uphill to the left.

Zig-Zag Trail is shown unnamed on the 1898 Sanborn map and named on the 1914 Tamalpais Fire Association map. The Trail was long part of a popular route over Throckmorton Ridge and down to Muir Woods.

Old Railroad Grade, above Mountain Home, as seen from West Peak.

Mountain Home Trailhead

Mountain Home Trailhead

Directions to Mountain Home:
Highway 101 — Highway 1 — Panoramic Highway near milepost 2.69

MOUNTAIN HOME has been a popular Tamalpais trailhead since early in the century. Six trails set off from it, with several more nearby, fanning out to cover the Mountain's south side. Many organized hikes start here and each Saturday morning for more than 25 years now a hardy group of runners gathers for long jaunts.

The parking lot usually fills early on weekends. There is some off-road parking to the south and a small overflow lot (which the MMWD has considered closing) just north across Panoramic Highway down the dirt road. The trailhead has a fountain built by the Tamalpa Runners in 1982, and outhouses. Golden Gate Transit bus #63 stops here on weekends.

The Mountain Home Inn, which gives the area its name, was built in 1912 by a Swiss couple, Claus and Martha Meyer. The inn had an Alpine flavor and fare and was a popular dining spot for decades. Later, guest rooms and a beer garden were added. After several ownership changes, and a few years of being closed altogether, the inn was completely remodeled in the early 1980's. Today it offers both light refreshments and elegant, full course dining, served indoors and outside on the splendid patio. Ten guest rooms, each with a spectacular view, are available for overnight stays.

South of Mountain Home off Panoramic Highway, Ridge Avenue offers access to the Sun and Redwood trails. The Dipsea Trail crosses Panoramic Highway opposite Bayview Drive.

Suggested loops from Mountain Home (elevation 920'):
• Gravity Car Grade, 1.0m, to Old Railroad Grade — left, .9m, to Hogback F.R. — left, .7m, to start **2.6 miles.**
• Hogback F.R., .3m, to Matt Davis Trail — left, .9m, to Nora Trail — right .5m, to West Point — right (downhill), 1.6m, on Old Railroad Grade to Hogback F.R. — right, .7m, to start **4.0 miles.**
• Hogback F.R., .3m, to Matt Davis Trail — left, 2.3m, to Bootjack Picnic Area — left on Bootjack Trail, .4m, to Troop 80 Trail — left, 1.5m, to Camp Eastwood Road — left, .5m, to start **5.0 miles.**
• Panoramic Trail, .5m, to Redwood Trail — right, .7m, to Tourist Club — Sun Trail, .7m, to Dipsea Trail — right, 1.1m, to Frank Valley Road — right, .9m, into Muir Woods to Camp Eastwood Road — right, 2.2m, to start **6.1 miles.**

Circuit of Mt. Tamalpais
Gravity Car Grade, .9m, to Old Railroad Grade — left (uphill), .2m, to Hoo-Koo-E-Koo F.R. — right, .7m, to Wheeler Trail — left, .5m, to Eldridge Grade — left (uphill), .5m, to Northside Trail — right, 2.7m, to Rifle Camp — left on Rock Spring-Lagunitas F.R., 1.2m, across Ridgecrest Boulevard to Mountain Theater — left on Rock Spring Trail, 1.7m, to West Point — Old Railroad Grade downhill, 1.5m, to Hogback F.R. — right, .7m, to start **10.6 miles.**

CAMP EASTWOOD ROAD
FROM PANORAMIC HIGHWAY TO MUIR WOODS ROAD / 2.25 miles

Terrain: Mostly redwood forest; upper half paved; bicycles not permitted below Camp Eastwood / MTSP & MWNM
Elevation: From 900' to 220' / gradual
Intersecting Trails: Trestle Trail (.1m), Troop 80 (.6m), Sierra (1.4m), Fern Canyon (1.4m), Plevin Cut (1.4, 1.9m), Bootjack Spur (2.1m)
Directions: Mountain Home
Amenities: Outhouses, fountains, picnic tables

THIS BROAD ROUTE, through a strikingly beautiful canyon, was originally graded to carry the tracks of the Mt. Tamalpais & Muir Roads Railway. Beginning in 1907, passengers could disembark at Mesa Station when traveling in either direction on the main rail line connecting East Peak and Mill Valley and take the side trip toward Muir Woods. (The line never ran all the way to the floor of Muir Woods, only to the two successive Muir Woods inns built above the valley.) The descent from Mesa Station was generally by gravity car; the ascent by steam-powered engine.

The upper part of the old Muir Woods line, in Water District land above Panoramic Highway, is called Gravity Car Grade in this book. Camp Eastwood Road (also called Alice Eastwood Road and Old Railroad Grade on signs and maps) is the section between Panoramic and the Muir Woods valley floor.

Camp Eastwood Road begins at a gate south of Panoramic Highway just before Mountain Home Inn when coming from Mill Valley. A sign by the gate indicates it is 1.4 miles to the Alice Eastwood Group Camp, and gives the Pantoll phone number (415/388-2070) to call for booking information.

The entire upper section of Eastwood is paved to accommodate the groups renting the Camp. The asphalt may turn off some hikers. They are missing one of the loveliest routes on the Mountain, and vehicular traffic is rare.

Shrubs, punctuated increasingly over the years by Douglas-firs, dominate the opening section. The impressive breadth and depth of heavily wooded Redwood Canyon, at whose base is Muir Woods, is clearly evident. Highway shoulder signs along the edge are recycled safety markers from other Marin roads.

In around 1/6 mile, the Road passes below the Mountain Home trailhead parking lot; the outhouses are visible. The short connection to the parking lot is called Trestle Trail. At a scant .03 miles in length, Trestle (a trestle carried a water pipeline over the rail tracks here before Panoramic Highway was built) is the shortest named trail on Tam. Layered sandstone rocks prominently line the road cut.

Camp Eastwood Road makes a broad bend left as it crosses over Fern Creek, which can be a torrent in winter. Just on the other side of the creek, to the right, Troop 80 Trail sets off to Bootjack Trail.

Now, towering redwoods dominate. Indeed, the whole deep canyon left is called Redwood Canyon (or Sequoia Canyon on some old maps). Many of the giants still bear scars from long-ago fires.

At a highway sign reading "C107, 1.96" look to the right to spot a long, metal rail. It may be a remnant from the old railroad line.

One hundred yards below, the Road crosses Laguna Creek. A water tank here serves Camp Eastwood. In another 100 yards, a huge Douglas-fir leans over the Road, then rises perfectly straight. Look near here for tree poppies, a shrub with striking yellow flowers in spring.

After 1.4 miles, the Road meets a broad paved clearing, Camp Alice Eastwood. There are fountains, tables, outhouses and an amphitheater for campfire presentations.

This was the site of the first Muir Woods Inn, built in 1908 and the original terminus of the gravity car line. The inn was destroyed by fire in 1913. During the 1930's, members of the depression-era Civilian Conservation Corps (CCC) built and occupied their Camp Mt. Tamalpais here. The camp contained some 14 structures; the foundations of many are still evident.

On May 1, 1949, the former CCC camp was renamed in honor of Alice Eastwood. It was her 90th birthday, and she was present. Alice Eastwood is one of the most legendary of all Mt. Tamalpais figures. Beginning in 1891, she hiked regularly on the Mountain, often as the only woman in her group. Her passion was plants; she was the Curator of Botany at the California Academy of Sciences from 1892 to 1949. Eastwood identified and named several Tam plants, including five species of manzanita. Eastwood died in 1953. A collection of her articles on Tam's flora was recently reissued by the Mount Tamalpais Interpretive Association.

Several trails meet at the Camp. Just past the outhouses, to the left, are the Plevin Cut and Fern Canyon (Creek) trails. The former (at .1 mile, too short to be separately described) slices around one-third mile off the descent of Camp Eastwood Road while the latter is an alternate route to Muir Woods. To the right of Camp Eastwood Road is Sierra Trail, which rises to Troop 80 Trail.

Camp Eastwood Road, continuing to the right beyond a gate, is now unpaved. Some old maps call this section Stage Road, for the balance of the trip to Muir Woods could be made by stagecoach.

The Road passes through the rail line's Plevin Cut. Then, a few yards later, it meets the bottom of the short Plevin Cut Trail. Plevin Cut Trail goes uphill sharply left. Look to its right for an overgrown old road. This is the lower section of the rail line that was extended down to the second Muir Woods Inn in 1914. Its continuation, overgrown but obvious and traceable, is across Camp Eastwood Road some ten yards down.

Around a half mile below the camp, the Road makes a bend right at a clearing. A Douglas-fir stands somewhat alone. This was the location of the second Muir Woods Inn, which stood from 1914 until it was torn down in 1932. The inn actually had a view down to Muir Woods; the surrounding trees have since grown much taller. Just below, at another bend and beside a redwood of enormous girth, is the signed top of Bootjack Spur. It drops .1 mile to Bootjack Trail.

Soon the asphalt-covered Muir Woods Trail becomes visible. Camp Eastwood Road, now bordered by a wooden fence, meets it and ends. Just to the left is the lower end of Fern Canyon (Creek) Trail, a lovely loop companion. Beyond is the Muir Woods visitor center. Bridge #4 over Redwood Creek and the Ben Johnson and Bootjack trails are to the right.

GRAVITY CAR GRADE
FROM MOUNTAIN HOME TO OLD RAILROAD GRADE AT DOUBLE BOW KNOT
/ .97 miles

Spur: Upper end, .1 mile
Terrain: Former railroad cut; chaparral and lightly wooded / MMWD
Elevation: From 900' to 1,100' / gradual
Intersecting Trails: Connector to Hogback F.R. (.1m)
Directions: Mountain Home

THE MOUNT TAMALPAIS RAILWAY, from downtown Mill Valley to near East Peak, was built and opened in 1896. Its route is today's Old Railroad Grade. In 1907, a branch line, between Mesa Station in the Grade's Double Bow Knot and the Muir Woods Inn, was added, and the Railway was renamed the Mt. Tamalpais & Muir Woods. The descent toward Muir Woods was usually by an engineless gravity car. The ride was both scenic and thrilling, with the posted top speed of 12 miles per hour often surpassed.

The railway's financial condition was weakened by the new auto roads to the summit, the Depression, and the huge fire of July 1929. After the runs of October 31, 1929, the railway closed for the winter, then never reopened. Gravity Car Grade, now a dirt fire road with the tracks long gone, remains as a remnant of those special days. (The section of the old gravity car line below Mountain Home is here called Camp Eastwood Road, which see.)

Gravity Car Grade sets off just past the Mountain Home Inn (when coming from Mill Valley), to the right off the base of the paved road up to the fire station. An old MMWD wood sign marks the start. The Grade surprisingly begins by dropping a few yards. But there was no climb for the gravity cars here when they ran. Instead, the tracks crossed through the Mine Ridge Cut, which was subsequently filled during construction of Panoramic Highway. All the rest of the way is gently, almost imperceptibly, uphill.

Within a few yards, a path branches right to the top of Zig-Zag Trail. The Grade passes an overflow dirt parking area. Note the yellow-topped post. Found along several Tam trails, it marks the Mountain's section of a planned (but never finished) trans-California equestrian route. Just beyond is a gate.

In .1 mile, a connector fire road rises to the left; it goes to the fire station on Throckmorton Ridge (Hogback Fire Road). Introduced acacias, natives of Australia, mingle with redwoods.

The Grade leaves the forest, and views of southern Marin and San Francisco open. Shrubs then line most of the way, though the Grade passes through some half-dozen redwood groves at stream crossings.

Gravity Car Grade splits just before its end. Both forks (one considered a

Spur) connect, in 100 yards, to Old Railroad Grade, which is making a horseshoe turn through Double Bow Knot. Take the left fork to continue up the Mountain, the right to descend to Mill Valley. A path drops at the start of the right fork.

HOGBACK FIRE ROAD
FROM MOUNTAIN HOME TO OLD RAILROAD GRADE / .61 miles

Terrain: Chaparral; ridgetop; bicycles not permitted downhill / MMWD
Elevation: 940' to 1,450' / very steep
Intersecting Trails: Matt Davis (.3m), Hoo-Koo-E-Koo (.5m)
Directions: Mountain Home
Amenities: Fountain

THIS VERY STEEP Fire Road is well used, as it is part of direct routes from the Mountain Home trailhead to popular destinations such as West Point, Bootjack, and Pantoll. It is one of the Mountain's oldest routes, and was once even more renown when it was the principal hikers' access to East Peak from Mill Valley. However, its upper end, above Old Railroad Grade, is now closed for erosion control.

A paved road up to the Throckmorton Ridge Fire Station departs from Panoramic Highway 50 yards above Mountain Home Inn. Immediately, both a private driveway, then Gravity Car Grade, fork right. Hogback F.R. climbs the ridge line but most users stay on the slightly lower paved road. The trace of a former routing is visible just left of the road, including an old bench.

The dirt and paved options meet at the firehouse, which was built in 1959. There is an information board and a water fountain at the barrier blocking uphill vehicular traffic.

Continue climbing. The views are outstanding. Just above the fire station on Hogback is the lowest point in elevation (around 1,060 feet) on Tamalpais from which the snowcapped peaks of the Sierra Nevada, 160 miles east, can be seen on clear winter days.

Another treat along the route are the abundant bush poppies. In late spring, their striking, lovely yellow flowers stand out amidst the manzanita.

A huge green water tank has replaced three former smaller ones, and the old water spigot is also gone. Just above the tank is the start of Matt Davis Trail, heading left (west) to Bootjack. An uphill path at the very start of Matt Davis later rejoins Hogback.

The tough uphill continues and the views become even more sweeping. Hoo-Koo-E-Koo Trail crosses left and right. Left connects to Matt Davis in .2 miles, right goes to Double Bow Knot.

Hogsback's climb ends at Old Railroad Grade, beside a prominent road cut. Left on the Grade leads to West Point, right to Bow Knot. The rocky, uphill continuation across the Grade, quite visible when looking at the Mountain from Mill Valley, is now closed.

Many people call this Fire Road the Throckmorton, a name for the prominent ridge it climbs. The MMWD signpost at the Railroad Grade junction labels the Fire Road as Hogback, due to the ridge's shape in profile. The ridge has also been called Mine Ridge; there was a quicksilver (mercury) claim near the present California Alpine Club headquarters just south of Mountain Home.

San Francisco financier Samuel Throckmorton took over the huge Rancho Sausalito land grant, which covered much of southern Marin, from debt-ridden William Richardson in 1856. He built a ranch home, called Homestead, near the present junction of Montford Avenue and Linden Lane (Mill Valley). Much of the estate was divided into smaller dairy ranches, rented to Portuguese settlers. Throckmorton died in 1883 at age 75. His daughter, Susanna, ceded 3,790 acres, including the Mill Valley slope of Mt. Tamalpais, to the San Francisco Savings Union to settle debts against the Throckmorton estate. In 1890, what became central Mill Valley was auctioned off in lots.

Though a fire road, the very steep Hogback is presently posted as closed to bicycles in the downhill direction. Old Railroad Grade, then Gravity Car Grade, is an alternate route.

MATT DAVIS TRAIL
FROM HOGBACK FIRE ROAD TO BELVEDERE AVENUE, STINSON BEACH / 6.70 miles

Terrain: Mostly woodland; parts chaparral, grassland / MMWD, MTSP, & GGNRA; segment part of Bay Area Ridge Trail
Elevation: 1,100' to 1,500' to 60' / gradual, western part very steep
Intersecting Trails: Hoo-Koo-E-Koo (.3m), Nora (1.0m), West Point (1.2m), Boot-jack (2.3m), Easy Grade (2.6m), Old Stage Road (2.6m), Coastal (2.7m-4.3m)
Directions: Mountain Home — Hogback F.R., .3m
Amenities: Fountains, bathrooms, picnic area
Spur: To Buena Vista Avenue, Stinson Beach, .1 mile

MATT DAVIS Trail offers a wonderful east-west passage across the Mountain. The Trail traverses redwood-lined creeks, chaparral, magnificent open grassland, forests of towering Douglas-fir, and coastal flora on its way to Stinson Beach. Because of the Trail's 6.7-mile length, and all return routes involve at least 1,500 feet of uphill, taking Matt Davis its full length requires some planning. One option is to place a car at Mountain Home, another at Stinson, and take the Trail one way downhill. Another option, available weekends only, is to ride a Golden Gate Transit bus back from Stinson Beach. Many loop possibilities cover sections of the Trail.

Though the west end of Matt Davis is accessible by car, most users join the Trail at its east end, so we will too. From Mountain Home, climb Hogback (Throckmorton) F.R. .3 miles, past the fire station. The Matt Davis trailhead is just above the huge green water tank, to the left. A path, connecting to higher on Hogback, immediately branches right.

The Trail begins up a few steps, then passes a water pipeline. Matt Davis is initially wide for a trail. This opening section was a later addition, built to provide the MMWD with vehicular access to the water intake at Fern Creek. Tall chaparral shrubs alternate with redwood groves. The going is level to gently uphill. Panoramic Highway is occasionally visible, and audible.

In .3 miles, beside a splendid (and increasingly leaning) redwood with spiraled bark, Hoo-Koo-E-Koo Trail joins on the right. This is the start of the original Matt Davis Trail. Look above to see a very old, out-of-commission outhouse.

The bridge ahead, through which a redwood grows, fords Fern Creek, on its into Muir Woods. Remnants of the old intake, a one-time water source, are visible.

Matt Davis narrows to standard trail width. Stands of densely packed young redwoods are passed. There are fine southern vistas in the clearings. A small meadow known as Azalea Flat lies a few yards to the left of Matt Davis just before the noticeable uphill. Some azaleas mark the overgrown entry.

In nearly a mile, at a bend just before a bridge over Laguna Creek, is the bottom end of Nora Trail. It goes uphill to West Point. Thirty yards before the junction is an old, non-working, stone water fountain. Matt Davis levels and opens.

Ten yards past a solitary Bishop pine tree (pines are not native to Tam, a line of them was planted up the Mountain here around 1930) is the easy-to-miss, unmarked crossing of West Point Trail. It goes left down to Panoramic Highway and right uphill to West Point.

Matt Davis Trail passes through chaparral. A sizable controlled burn here in 1984 is now revegetated. One shrub quick to follow fire is golden-fleece (*Ericameria arborescens*), standing out in bright green patches. Monkeyflowers add orange color.

The Trail crosses Spike Buck Creek. As the terrain is now drier, redwoods do not line the creek here (although they do lower). Instead, hazels flank the bridge. The next bridge, also bordered by hazels, is over a fork of Rattlesnake Creek. A rocky uphill leads to another bridge over a second Rattlesnake Creek fork. Azaleas are abundant here.

Matt Davis then leaves the Water District and enters Mt. Tamalpais State Park just outside delightful Bootjack Picnic Area. Bootjack was once a major campground. Now it hosts picnics of small and large groups. Matt Davis crosses Bootjack Trail, on its way from Muir Woods to the Mountain Theater.

Matt Davis continues on the asphalt — follow the signs. It passes a fountain, crosses a bridge, skirts above the bathrooms, and passes more picnic tables. It leaves the asphalt at a "trail" sign. The Trail cuts across a grassy slope between Panoramic Highway below and Old Stage Road above.

In .3 miles from Bootjack, Easy Grade Trail, going uphill to the Mountain Theater, departs right. Climb a few steps to join and cross paved Old Stage Road. It goes right to West Point, left down to Pantoll.

Pantoll Ranger Station is just to the left. The continuation of Matt Davis beyond Pantoll is a bit tricky. Follow the sign down the steps, then cross Southside Road (not Panoramic Highway) to another Matt Davis sign. There is a bench with a view.

Matt Davis' remaining 3.5 miles to Stinson Beach is sometimes called Matt Davis Extension, since it was built later. For the first 1.5 miles of the Extension, Matt Davis and Coastal trails run together as a pedestrian section of the Bay Area Ridge Trail.

In the opening yards of the Extension, the striking yellow flowers of mariposa lily stand out in late spring amidst the serpentine. Matt Davis quickly enters a cool, deep, Douglas-fir dominated forest, where it remains for 1.2 miles. This nearly level stretch is one of the best places to see orchids; calypso (invariably associated with Douglas-firs on Tam), spotted-coralroot, and others, but you'll have to look carefully in spring. Several ravines, carrying the uppermost forks of Webb Creek, need to be forded. Many trees lay fallen, some across the Trail.

Matt Davis then emerges onto the open grasslands of Tam's west shoulder, one of the Mountain's most dramatic changes of scenery. This is a spectacular area, with Tam's west wall towering behind and the Pacific below. A photo from here has graced the cover of Dorothy Whitnah's well-researched *An Outdoor Guide to the San Francisco Bay Area*. When the weather is mild, these gentle knolls make impossible-to-resist rest sites. At a Bay Area Ridge Trail signpost, a path branches left to a cluster of trees atop "the Knolls," or "Big Knoll." Another path here heads right, steeply up. This is Matt Davis' highest point, at some 1,500 feet in elevation.

Matt Davis Trail enters a grove of laurels. At the far end, Matt Davis splits from Coastal Trail. Coastal continues right over the Bob Cook Memorial Section, built in 1979. Matt Davis drops left. The distance to Stinson Beach is 2.2 miles, not the 1.7 miles of the signpost; the Trail has been rerouted, using more switchbacks to make the descent gentler.

Matt Davis descends through the grassland. In the canyon bends are streams surrounded by laurels. There are great views, to Bodega Head beyond Point Reyes on clear days.

Next is a magical 1.5-mile downhill through a Douglas-fir forest. In summer, when the creeks are not flowing strongly, the ocean surf at Stinson Beach becomes audible, sometimes even the sounds of people on the beach. Numerous paths, traces of the former, steeper trail, lace the hillside. There are several series of steps. Huckleberry is abundant. So, unfortunately, is poison oak.

Matt Davis passes under a huge Douglas-fir. Though battered by lightning, it has sent several massive candelabra-like limbs skyward. Just beyond is the start of the wood railings that accompany the Trail most of the rest of the way down.

The Trail gets ever closer to Table Rock Creek. A signpost points the way the few yards to Table Rock, a splendid, level, resting place with sensational views. (The rock can clearly be seen from the beach at Stinson.) Be cautious of poison oak on the approach. California buckeye is the common tree around the rock.

Matt Davis continues steeply down past the base of impressive Table Rock. A new sign there reads "Bischof Steps." Gary Bischof has been ably handling State Park trail projects for many, many years. The vegetation increasingly shows the ocean's influence. There are also many exotic plants, likely naturalized escapees from Stinson Beach gardens.

Duck under a buckeye and cross a bridge to Table Rock Creek's right bank. Soon after, the Trail briefly exits the woods onto a grassy hillside laced with morning-glory. The Trail returns to woodland, then back to coastal scrub, then again into the forest.

Matt Davis then crosses Easkoot Creek, also over a bridge. At the next bend left is a magnificent old laurel with several downed, but still alive, trunks. There is a rattlesnake warning sign.

Fifty yards below the sign, Matt Davis meets an unsigned fork by a prominent red fire plug. Right is a .1 mile Spur to the junction of Belvedere, Buena Vista, and Laurel avenues, an alternate trailhead. Continue left, crossing another bridge beneath an alder tree.

Matt Davis actually rises a few yards to another fork. Left is a short path through grassland onto private property; veer right. The route continues dropping.

Matt Davis crosses a final bridge and ends on Stinson Beach's Belvedere Avenue at a prominent sign. Across the street is the Casa del Mar Bed & Breakfast Inn. Lower on the street are the Stinson Beach Community Church, the Community Center, the fire station, public telephones, and another B&B, The Redwoods Haus. Central Stinson Beach is then just to the right. Panoramic Highway and the western end of the Dipsea Trail are one-quarter mile to the left.

Perhaps no one has influenced Mt. Tamalpais' trails more than Matt Davis. Lincoln Fairley's book, *Mount Tamalpais, A History*, has a picture of Matt Davis and calls him "champion trailbuilder." The TCC labeled him "the dean of trail workers," no small accolade from that club. Davis, a one time upholsterer, was for years the TCC's paid trails man. Davis built and lived in a couple of cabins in the Bootjack-Mountain Theater area from the 1920's to his death. Davis suffered a heart attack on the Mountain in 1938; he died on the Golden Gate Bridge while being transported to a hospital. He worked on the Trail that bears his name in 1929; the Extension was constructed in 1931. The long, magnificent, superbly designed Trail is a fitting monument to Davis.

NORA TRAIL
FROM MATT DAVIS TRAIL TO WEST POINT / .51 miles

Terrain: Mostly heavily wooded; lower part riparian / MMWD
Elevation: From 1,360' to 1,780' / very steep
Intersecting Trails: None
Directions: Mountain Home — Hogback Fire Road — Matt Davis Trail, .9 miles

NORA TRAIL is part of a well-traveled route between Mountain Home and West Point. Combined with Matt Davis Trail and Old Railroad Grade, it offers a popular loop option.

Nora rises, signed, from Matt Davis Trail. Look for it to the right (when coming from Mountain Home) just before the bridge over lively Laguna Creek.

Elk clover, a common Tam shrub with huge leaves that die back each year, and chain ferns line the creek bed.

Nora crosses Laguna Creek over a bridge some 50 yards above. It then rises up the creek's right bank.

The Trail veers west, away from Laguna Creek and out of the redwood forest. In clearings, San Francisco is visible. The Trail goes over a second bridge. It winds into and out of tree cover. The going is very steep.

Nora crosses a small bridge, then another more sizable one. The opening around West Point becomes visible above. Near its top, the Trail passes some wood posts, once part of a stile to keep horses from passing through.

Nora ends at a signpost beside the picnic tables at West Point. A few feet to the left is a bench with the loving dedication to hiker Robert Schneider, "Who touched our lives as he passed this way." To the left is the top of the steep, unmarked West Point Trail. Old Stage Road, Rock Spring Trail, and Old Railroad Grade also meet at West Point.

Nora and Bob Stanton helped build the Trail while they were caretakers of the West Point Inn during World War I. They later operated a restaurant in San Francisco at the corner of Pine and Montgomery Streets. A card in the Mount Tamalpais History Project file offers the conjecture that Nora was a sister of Mickey O'Brien, who also has a trail named for him.

PANORAMIC TRAIL
FROM JUNCTION OF PANORAMIC HIGHWAY AND RIDGE AVENUE, MILL VALLEY, TO CAMP EASTWOOD ROAD / .92 miles

Terrain: Hillside; disturbed vegetation / MTSP
Elevation: Around 900' / almost level
Intersecting Trails: Redwood (.5m), Ocean View (.8m)
Directions: Panoramic Highway to Ridge Avenue

PANORAMIC TRAIL is well-used because of the easy access from either end. It is even served by Golden Gate Transit buses on weekends. The Trail will be described from closer-in Ridge Avenue although just as many, or more, users pick it up from Camp Eastwood Road by the Mountain Home parking area. Starting at Ridge offers Tam views; from Camp Eastwood Road, ocean views.

The Panoramic trailhead is at the northwest corner of Ridge Avenue and Panoramic Highway, at a State Park signpost. Ridge Avenue leads to the Muir Woods Park Improvement Association clubhouse, and to a private (but open to hikers) paved road down to the Tourist Club.

The Trail sets off parallel to the highway through a dense growth of blackberry bushes. The tasty berries ripen around July, and are invariably picked quickly. After passing the last private residence on the west side of the highway, the Trail drops lower on the hillside, somewhat escaping the traffic sounds.

The vegetation has changed dramatically since controlled burns began here in 1994. Most of the overcrowding broom is gone (although broom seeds are remarkably hardy and long-lived) along with other potential fire fuel. Green grasses now wave in early spring winds and native wildflowers, particularly morning-glory, poppies, and blue-eyed grass, are returning.

The Tourist Club can be glimpsed to the left. There are paths right, to the road, and left. The Trail enters a redwood grove. A rusted automobile sits below, as it has for decades.

In a half-mile, beside introduced Monterey pines, is the upper end of Red-wood Trail. It goes sharply left, down to the Tourist Club.

The Trail passes a prominent rock. Just beyond, Panoramic meets the top of Ocean View Trail, which descends 1.5 miles to Muir Woods.

Directly across Panoramic Highway here is Alpine Lodge, headquarters of the California Alpine Club, which was founded in 1914 and welcomes new members. The Lodge's Henry Hertenstein Hall, added in 1953, can be rented for parties. Dormitory-style accommodations upstairs can also be booked; call 388-9940.

Panoramic Trail ends when it hits the top of paved Camp Eastwood Road at a gate. Mountain Home Inn is a few yards farther ahead across Panoramic Highway.

Panoramic Highway was built in the 1920's. This Trail, a way to avoid walking on the road, was completed in 1969, largely by Ben Schmidt, who was born nearby. It originally extended south to the Dipsea Trail at Windy Gap. Private residences now block that segment, although parts of it can still be traced.

PIPELINE TRAIL
BETWEEN TWO SECTIONS OF EDGEWOOD AVENUE, MILL VALLEY / .27 miles

Terrain: Redwood forest / City of Mill Valley
Elevation: Around 820' / almost level
Intersecting Trails: None
Directions: Mountain Home Inn — Edgewood Avenue, .5 miles

PIPELINE TRAIL was once "the most traveled and fondly remembered of all approaches to the Mountain" (Fred Sandrock, *Mill Valley Historical Review*, Spring 1985). Hikers would come from San Francisco via ferry to Sausalito, take the Northwestern Pacific Railroad to Mill Valley, climb the Dipsea steps, then head deep onto the Mountain on the Pipeline. The Trail went from the top of the Dipsea steps to Mountain Home, crossed over the Muir Wood railroad track on a bridge, then split into an Upper Pipeline to Bootjack Camp and a lower branch to Rattlesnake Camp. Pipeline was so popular that refreshment stands were set up beside it on weekends.

Today Pipeline Trail, covered and carved up by Panoramic Highway and Edgewood Avenue and replaced by the Matt Davis and Troop 80 trails, remains a public access, closed-to-cars trail for fewer than 500 yards. It now simply connects two segments of Edgewood Avenue.

To pick it up, follow unpaved Edgewood Road south of the Mountain Home Inn guest parking lot. The road is used by local residents. In about a half-mile, at a fenced-off yellow fire pump, Tenderfoot Trail drops left down to Cascade Drive in Mill Valley. Just beyond is the surviving section of Pipeline.

The lovely Trail winds along the hillside. Redwoods dominate in the deep, quiet canyon below. The old pipeline itself, badly battered, is still very evident. At a small bridge of lashed logs, look for the lovely, non-native plant foxglove (*Digitalis purpurea*).

The Trail ends when it widens and is again open to cars as Edgewood Avenue. Edgewood continues to Sequoia Valley Road at the top of the Dipsea steps, becoming paved and passing many homes, the Swiss Club Tell, the site of the old Belvedere Reservoir (now a meadow off Sunnycrest Avenue) and a native plant garden (at Cypress Avenue).

Pipeline Trail, and the adjacent eight-inch riveted steel pipeline, were built in 1904. The pipeline brought water from intakes at Rattlesnake, Spike Buck, Laguna, and Fern creeks to the Belvedere Reservoir, to serve the then developing communities of Tiburon and Belvedere. The three-acre, open reservoir, plagued with leakage and a diminishing supply from the intakes, was replaced by a five million gallon steel tank in 1967. The pipeline was completely abandoned soon after. Many other segments of the old pipeline remain, such as alongside Troop 80 Trail.

Helen Wild wrote a charming poem entitled "The Pipe Line Trail" that was published in the TCC's *California Out-Of-Doors* newsletter at the time the Trail was being carved up, in 1927. The poem concludes:

"Dear little brown trail among the green,
Your allurement your own destruction has been."

REDWOOD TRAIL
FROM PANORAMIC HIGHWAY TO THE TOURIST CLUB / .74 miles

Terrain: Largely open hillside, some woodland / MTSP
Elevation: From 900' to 700' / gradual
Intersecting Trails: None
Directions: Panoramic Trail (from either end)

REDWOOD TRAIL is the principal route to the famous Tourist Club. To reach it, take Panoramic Trail from either Ridge Avenue or Camp Eastwood Road; Redwood, signed, lies roughly halfway in between. (When coming from Camp Eastwood Road, Ocean View Trail is passed first.) An introduced Monterey pine stands at the trailhead.

At the start there are fine views out to the Pacific. The Trail passes under the first redwood, here isolated. The downhill briefly steepens. The Trail enters a grove of bay trees. Poison oak is abundant.

In .3 miles, the Trail bends left at an old fence line. There is still some demarcation with the area ahead that was control burned in 1994. A few yards in, a bench commands a splendid vista. The Tourist Club is plainly visible, and you may hear German music from here on weekends.

The Trail re-enters woodland. After a downhill through burn-rejuvenated grassland, the Trail crosses a bridge beneath a huge rock. Redwood Trail finally meets redwood forest. The next creek bed carries remains of an old water intake. Redwood Trail passes above the Tourist Club building lodge; steps on the right lead down to it. Refreshments are sold here on weekends, and there are restrooms on the other side of the veranda. Paths lead up left to private Tourist Club residences.

Redwood Trail continues a bit farther through club property. It ends at the base of a steep, paved road (closed to vehicles except on Tourist Club business), which rises to Ridge Avenue. There is a classic Tourist Club sign at the intersection. Fifty yards uphill on the road is one end of Sun Trail, going towards the Dipsea Trail. Downhill right is an extremely steep path to Ocean View Trail above Muir Woods.

Redwood Trail, in different routings, dates to 1900 or earlier. There once were plans to widen it and build homes along it. The Trail has also been called Tourist Club Trail. The Club, whose full name is "Touristen Verein-Die Naturfreunde" (Tourist Club-Nature Friends), established its Tamalpais chapter in 1912 (see Sun Trail). The world-wide organization itself had been founded in Vienna in 1882. Two of its most popular weekends on Tam are beer fests in summer and fall.

SIERRA TRAIL
FROM PANORAMIC HIGHWAY TO CAMP ALICE EASTWOOD / 1.05 miles

Terrain: Mixed woodland and chaparral / MTSP
Elevation: From 1,000' to 600' / steep
Intersecting Trails: Troop 80 (.1m)
Directions: Panoramic Highway to milepost 3.66 sign (between Mountain Home and Bootjack)
Amenities: Outhouses, fountains, picnic tables

SIERRA TRAIL was once part of a broad fire break called West Point Fire Trail. That old route was severed by Panoramic Highway. Today, Sierra Trail still plays a role in several loop options out of Mountain Home.

The top of today's Sierra Trail is on the south side of Panoramic Highway near milepost marker 3.66. Across the highway is the unmarked entry to the old route's upper section, the present West Point Trail. Sierra's trailhead sign says it is .7 miles to Camp Eastwood; subsequent reroutings of the Trail have actually increased the distance fifty percent.

Just 40 yards down, Sierra crosses Troop 80 Trail. Left leads to Mountain Home and right to Bootjack. Sierra goes straight ahead. This early section is fairly level, with even a short uphill. The rest of the route down the unnamed ridge is a steady descent.

Huckleberry is abundant. Native bunchgrasses remain green in summer and fall. Whenever the Trail emerges from woodland into chaparral, southern views open. There are deep canyons left and right.

A sign recognizes that the Youth Conservation Corps worked on Sierra Trail in 1980; there was an earlier rerouting in 1972. Five yards beyond the sign is the first of many chinquapin trees. Switchbacks wind the route downhill. The Trail passes though several stands of crowded, short, thin redwoods. Old-timers recall these groves as little-changed over the decades. It may be that the soil here is too hard for even redwood's shallow roots to penetrate.

Well down, Sierra passes a stone octagon-shaped water tank foundation. There is a bench here, pointing the way to the "Picnicing and Camping Area."

Sierra Trail is fire road-width for the remaining descent. It meets the upper, Camp B, section of Camp Alice Eastwood. Seventy yards below, Sierra ends at the main clearing of Camp Eastwood. There are outhouses to the left, an amphitheater, and several picnic tables. The first Muir Woods Inn, original terminus of the gravity car rail line from Double Bow Knot, stood here from 1908 to 1913. Also meeting at the camp are the Fern Canyon and Plevin Cut trails (both going downhill) and Camp Eastwood Fire Road (uphill and downhill).

The Sierra Club, the nation's foremost environmental organization, has been active in Tamalpais trail work and conservation since it was founded by John Muir in 1892. The Club rebuilt this Trail in 1946. The Sierra Club offers more than 100 hikes, all without charge, annually on Tamalpais, and has introduced many thousands to the Mountain.

SUN TRAIL
FROM DIPSEA TRAIL TO THE TOURIST CLUB / .69 miles

Terrain: Open, grassy hillside; some woodland / MTSP
Elevation: 680' to 700' / almost level
Intersecting Trails: None
Directions: Panoramic Highway to Bayview Drive, Mill Valley — Dipsea Trail toward Muir Woods, .1 mile

SUN TRAIL CAN BE a "poster trail" for those advocating control of broom on Mt. Tamalpais. In the early 1990's, Sun Trail was choked by broom, blocking views and almost blocking through passage. Now, recently cleared, the sweeping vistas are reopened and native wildflowers are returning. Broom, however, is hardy, and its seeds long-lived; it will likely return.

Just under .1 mile down the Dipsea Trail from Panoramic Highway, past a wood plank bridge, a path (which winds along the backyards of homes to Ridge Avenue) goes right. Then, in another 20 yards, the marked Sun Trail veers right off the Dipsea.

The views come immediately. They range from Tam's summit ridge on the north to the Marin Headlands on the south, with the Pacific in almost constant sight. Remarkably, the whole panorama is of pristine open space, with virtually no homes visible.

Spring brings a riot of color to the green grass. There are the orange of poppies; yellows of buttercup, broom, and wyethia; blues and purples of blue-eyed-grass, lupine, and blue-dicks; pinks and reds from mallow, vetch, and paintbrush; and whites from the abundant morning-glory and wild cucumber.

The Trail passes through a few laurel groves. The route remains fairly level, with some rolling terrain.

Sun Trail then descends into a grove of eucalyptus and Monterey pines. Just beyond, the Trail ends at a broad, dirt road (paved uphill). This road is known as Muir Woods Trail or Hazel Trail, and connects the Tourist Club with Ridge Avenue. The Tourist Club lodge and Redwood Trail are just to the left.

The local branch of the Tourist Club, or, reflecting its Germanic roots, "Touristen Verein-Die Naturfreunde," was established here in 1912. There are over 800 club branches in Germany, Austria, and Switzerland, plus several scattered elsewhere, devoted to the outdoors ("nature friends") and fellowship. The club and its buildings are private. The main lodge, however, is open to all passing through on weekends, when drinks and light refreshments can be ordered from a well-stocked bar.

Sun Trail was long known as Cow Trail for the dairies in the area.

TROOP 80 TRAIL
FROM CAMP EASTWOOD ROAD TO BOOTJACK TRAIL / 1.48 miles

Spur: Between Troop 80 Trail and Van Wyck Meadow, .1 mile
Terrain: Light woodland / MMWD & MTSP
Elevation: From 780' to 1,120' / gradual
Intersecting Trails: Sierra (.4m), Troop 80 Spur (1.3m)
Directions: Mountain Home — Camp Eastwood Road, .4 miles

TROOP 80 TRAIL, near the Mountain Home trailhead, shaded and fairly level, plays a part in many loop trips. It also offers some fine view sites. Troop 80's drawback is its proximity to Panoramic Highway, with the concomitant road noise.

To reach Troop 80, take the short path down from the north edge (by the telephone) of the Mountain Home trailhead parking lot to Camp Eastwood Road. This short path is called Trestle Trail, for the trestle that once spanned the railroad cut through the ridge here. Follow the paved road downhill to Fern Creek, which flows below in a culvert. On the far bank, Troop 80 departs to the right.

The short opening stretch, rerouted in 1971, is Troop 80's steepest. Switchbacks quickly bring the Trail to more level terrain.

Troop 80 is heavily forested in this eastern part. The Trail crosses Laguna

Creek over a bridge. An old steel water pipeline is embedded in the Trail. It once brought water from several south side creeks (Rattlesnake, Spike Buck, Laguna, and Fern) to the Belvedere Reservoir in Mill Valley, then on to Belvedere (see Pipeline Trail).

In under a half-mile, Troop 80 crosses Sierra Trail. Left leads down to Camp Eastwood, while Panoramic Highway is a few yards uphill. Shortly after is another stream crossing and redwood grove, a common Mountain combination. Just ahead is an old wooden bench and a water trough in which hikers used to dip their cups.

Continuing west, next up is a 60-foot-long, curved, bridge that was built by Matt Davis. East Bay views open. In the next deep redwood grove, an old horse trough sits beside the Trail.

Troop 80 crosses Spike Buck Creek at around 1.1 miles. Next is Rattlesnake Creek, the westernmost creek tapped and the start for the pipeline. Again the Trail is in dense redwoods. A steep, heavily wooded canyon drops to the left.

At 1.4 miles, there is a clearing and a fork. Look behind you at the junction to spot steps down to Memorial Tree. A plaque beside the huge Douglas-fir reads:

DEDICATED MAY 2, 1920 BY THE TAMALPAIS CONSERVATION CLUB
IN HONOR OF THE SERVICES RENDERED BY ITS MEMBERS
DURING WORLD WAR I.

Some 300 people attended the dedication service. The plaque is obviously not the original — the conflict of 1914-1918 was called the Great War and "World War I" did not come into usage until the second World War (1939).

A sign post (which, in 1994, replaced a classic old wood bench sign) points the way left to Van Wyck Meadow or straight. The left option is the short Troop 80 Spur. The delightful Van Wyck Meadow, a favorite resting spot, was the site of historic Lower Rattlesnake Camp.

Troop 80 continues to the right, passing above Van Wyck Meadow. It ends at a poorly-marked intersection with Bootjack Trail. Bootjack Trail goes left downhill to Muir Woods, and right, uphill to Alpine Trail, Panoramic Highway, and Bootjack Camp.

The Trail was built in 1931, largely by the Troop 80 Boy Scouts from the Ingleside district of San Francisco. It basically replaced the once very popular Lower Pipeline Trail, which was disrupted when Panoramic Highway was constructed in the late 1920's.

Peeling madrone bark, Northside Trail.

Redwoods and understory, lower Bootjack Trail.

Muir Woods National Monument

Muir Woods National Monument

Directions to Muir Woods National Monument:
Highway 101 — Highway 1 — Panoramic Highway to "Four Corners" intersection — left down Muir Woods Road to parking areas.

MOST ALL of Mt. Tamalpais' virgin redwood and Douglas-fir forests were logged in the years just after the 1849 California Gold Rush. The stand in Redwood Canyon — today's Muir Woods — escaped early cutting because of its relative inaccessibility. After the opening of a rail line into Mill Valley in 1890, and the grading of a crude wagon road into the canyon in 1893, the area became a tourist attraction.

But soon after, plans were advanced to dam Redwood Creek to create a reservoir. The huge trees would have been logged, then the canyon flooded. To save Redwood Canyon, wealthy Mt. Tam landowners William and Elizabeth Kent purchased 611 acres in 1905. William asked Elizabeth, "If we lost all the money we have and saved the trees it would be worthwhile, wouldn't it?" In 1908, the Kents donated 295 acres, the heart of the canyon, to the American people. The Kents insisted the monument be named for John Muir, dean of the nation's environmental movement. Muir said, "This is the best tree lover's monument that could be found in all the forests of the world."

Automobiles first entered Muir Woods in 1908; cars were banned from the grove proper in 1924. Kent's private access road was widened in 1926 and tolls were then collected at the two entry points, Four Corners and Frank Valley Road. In 1939, the road passed to the County. A stone portal at Four Corners remains.

The Monument now attracts some 1.5 million visitors annually. The grandeur of the redwoods, some more than 1,000 years old and over 200 feet tall, makes this a unique place on this special Mountain, and a national treasure.

The Monument is open daily from 8 a.m. to sunset. After decades of free entry, a $2 daily admission fee ($15 for an annual pass) was instituted on a trial basis in 1997. There is no charge for children 12 and under, those entering during the first or last of the Monument's open hours, or by other than the main entrance.

A visitor center, completed in 1989, is at the main entrance. Books, maps and advice are cheerfully dispensed. Just inside the entrance are a gift shop and cafeteria, both run by a concessionaire, and the Monument's administrative offices. There are restrooms and telephones in the parking lot and by the cafeteria, and several water fountains along the Muir Woods Main Trail. Note that there is no picnicking inside the Monument.

Parking near the main entrance is almost always difficult; try the overflow lot first. If it is full, plan on a walk on Muir Woods (also called Franks Valley) Road.

On Muir Woods Road between the monument and Muir Beach are access points to Deer Park Fire Road (at milepost 2.09), Redwood Creek Trail (several) and to Kent Canyon Trail (past milepost 2.56).

Suggested loops from Muir Woods main entrance (elevation 160'):
• Muir Woods Trail, .9m, to bridge #4 and Hillside Trail — left, .7m, to bridge #2 — right .3m, on Muir Woods Trail to start **1.9 miles.**
• Muir Woods Trail, .2m, to Ocean View Trail — right, 1.3m, to Lost Trail — left, .6m, to Fern Canyon (Creek) Trail — left, .4m, to Muir Woods Trail — left, .6m, to start **3.1 miles.**
• Dipsea Trail west from overflow parking lot (or Deer Park Fire Road when the Redwood Creek bridge is out), 1.6m, to Ben Johnson Trail — right, 1.3m, to Muir Woods Trail — right, 1.0m to start (1.5m to Deer Park F.R.) **3.9 miles.**
• Muir Woods Trail, .9m, to Bootjack Trail — right (straight), 1.5m, to Van Wyck Meadow — right, .9m, on Troop 80 Spur and Trail to Sierra Trail — right, 1.0m, to Camp Eastwood — right, .9m, on Camp Eastwood Road (downhill) to Muir Woods Trail — left, .7m, to start **5.9 miles.**
• Muir Woods Trail, .9m, to bridge #4 and Ben Johnson Trail — left, 1.3m, to Dipsea Trail — right, .3m, to TCC Trail — right, 1.8m, to Van Wyck Meadow — right on Bootjack Trail, 1.5m, to Muir Woods Trail — left (straight), .9m, to start **6.7 miles.**

BEN JOHNSON TRAIL
FROM MUIR WOODS TRAIL TO DIPSEA TRAIL / 1.27 miles

Terrain: Redwood forest / MWNM
Elevation: From 230' to 860' / very steep
Intersecting Trails: Hillside (.1m), Stapelveldt (1.0m), Deer Park F.R. (1.2m)
Directions: Muir Woods Trail, .9 miles to bridge #4

BEN JOHNSON TRAIL passes through one of the quietest, deepest, wettest forests on Mt. Tamalpais. It plays a role in several wonderful loop walks out of Muir Woods.

To reach the Ben Johnson trailhead, take the asphalt-covered Muir Woods Trail to its end at bridge #4 (the fourth bridge over Redwood Creek from the main entrance). Bootjack Trail continues straight ahead while Ben Johnson rises, across the bridge, to the left. A signpost points the way toward the Dipsea Trail, Pantoll, and Stinson Beach.

Just on the other side of the bridge, to the left, is Hillside Trail, which connects to bridge #2. Ben Johnson veers right, uphill.

The climb is a long one, but the route is well graded and the certain coolness of the woods brings relief. Steps carry the Trail up over the steepest early part. Runners would find Ben Johnson one of the most glorious downhill trails; over soft redwood duff and relatively free of roots and rocks.

Ben Johnson crosses several streambeds, two of them over bridges fashioned from a single redwood. The redwoods and Douglas-firs are enormous; several of the former, opened by fire, can be entered. Huckleberry is abundant.

A welcome seat is embedded in the hillside. Just beyond, a small clearing in the tree canopy permits glimpses of Throckmorton Ridge. Higher, a downed redwood took out another bench and forces a slight detour.

After a mile of climbing, Ben Johnson Trail meets a signed, three-way junction. A pause at the sign bench here in the deep woods is obligatory. Straight ahead is the start of Stapelveldt Trail, rising to Pantoll. Ben Johnson continues left, following the sign to the Dipsea Trail. Newer switchbacks, bordered by fences, carry it uphill another well-wooded quarter-mile.

Ben Johnson crests a ridge. It crosses Deer Park Fire Road in the magical area known as Deer Park. To the left is a magnificent stand of virgin redwoods. Just to the right is the fire road's junction with the Dipsea Trail. Ben Johnson Trail goes another 20 yards straight ahead to end at the Dipsea.

Ben Johnson was once a superintendent of Samuel Throckmorton's southern Marin dairy ranches. He apparently also worked at the San Francisco Mint. He then moved to a cabin just downstream from the present bridge #4. There is an 1892 reference to Redwood Creek called "Johnson's Creek." Johnson built the Trail that carries his name around 1900, when he became the gamekeeper for the Tamalpais Sportsman's Club. The Trail provided hunters with access to the club's extensive lands higher on Tam. (After the Mountain's bears, elk and mountain lions had been hunted out by the 1880's, deer and quail remained as quarry.) Johnson died of tuberculosis in 1904, at age 51. The Trail has been known as Dead Horse Trail and as Sequoia Trail.

BOOTJACK TRAIL
FROM MUIR WOODS TRAIL TO THE MOUNTAIN THEATER / 2.77 miles

Terrain: Lower part riparian redwood and Douglas-fir forest; upper part tanbark oak woodland with some grassland / MTSP & MMWD
Elevation: From 230' to 1,980' / steep
Intersecting Trails: Troop 80 Spur (1.5m), TCC (1.5m), Troop 80 (1.6m), Alpine (1.9m), Matt Davis (2.0m), Old Stage Road (2.2m)
Directions: Muir Woods Trail to end
Amenities: Bathrooms, fountains, picnic tables
Spur: To Camp Eastwood Fire Road, .1 mile

No MT. TAM TRAIL (and only three fire roads — Willow Camp, and the Eldridge and Old Railroad grades) has a greater differential between its start and end elevations than Bootjack does. So ascending, or even descending, its full length is no easy task. But the journey is worthwhile for Bootjack Trail passes through some of the Mountain's loveliest and most diverse areas and connects treasures such as Muir Woods, Van Wyck Meadow, Bootjack itself, and the Mountain Theater.

Bootjack Trail starts at the far end of the asphalt-covered Muir Woods Main Trail, at bridge #4. Here, too, left across the bridge, Ben Johnson Trail begins its climb. Bootjack immediately leaves Muir Woods National Monument into Mount Tamalpais State Park.

The early going, along the left bank of Redwood Creek, is fairly level. Giant redwoods, rivaling those passed on the approach walk, tower above. Beside one is a plaque, dating from the late 1920's, to "the memory of Andrew Jay Cross, Pioneer in Optometry, 1855-1925." The broad area here was once a picnic site maintained by Muir Woods; a later, more precise survey moved the boundary southeast.

In .1 mile, Bootjack Spur departs to the right. It climbs .1 mile to meet Camp Eastwood Fire Road beside a particularly huge redwood. That upper junction was the site of the second Muir Woods Inn (1914-1932). The Spur was used by visitors walking between the inn and Muir Woods.

There is not another trail intersection for 1.4 miles, one of the longest such stretches on the Mountain. Bootjack passes through wondrous terrain; deep in forest, beside vigorous, waterfall-laden Redwood Creek. The crowds of Muir Woods seem miles away. Here Bootjack rivals the Cataract and Steep Ravine trails as Tam's best waterfall walks after a heavy rain.

The Trail crosses several bridges over feeder streams. Azaleas are abundant. Around 1/3 mile in, the Trail has been rerouted; keep off the blocked path. There is another split soon after. The climbing begins is earnest.

In fall and winter, begin looking for hibernating ladybugs (*Hippodomia convergens*, also called ladybird beetles). Swarms of them miraculously find their way to the exact same site year after year, carried by the wind. At peak times, they cover rocks, bridges, live and dead branches and trunks, and ferns. An early and reliable haunt is the 30-foot wood fence opposite a bench.

Just above, Bootjack Trail crosses Redwood Creek to its right bank. The relatively long bridge, built in 1983, had a "Surf Unsafe" sign embedded in the railing. A respite is all but mandatory. Azalea, elk clover (with enormous leaves), goldcup oak, redwood, hazel and poison oak border the bridge. Maples add color.

The going gets steeper as the Trail ascends several series of steps. Bootjack Trail enters a lovely grassy ridge. Douglas-firs now dominate. Choice picnic sites present themselves. Look in summer for Indian pink. Its bright red petals, deeply cleft, would stand out any time; they are particularly striking as among the year's last woodland wildflowers.

Some of the steps are recycled from old trail signs, such as "No Dogs, 8 p.m.-7 a.m." and "Groups Only." The Trail recrosses upper Redwood Creek. A fallen Douglas-fir, dated when cut for passage (2/1/94), will be a landmark for years.

A tough haul of some 100 wood and stone steps lead to the delightful, grassy clearing of Van Wyck Meadow. On one side is the charming sign "Population, 3 Stellar Jays" (Stellar is misspelled; it should be Steller). In the middle of the meadow is a large sandstone boulder, Council Rock. A plaque dedicated to the Tamalpais Conservation Club, "Guardian of the Mountain," was placed on the old stone fireplace left, now shaded by a goldcup oak, in February 1989. The meadow was the site of Lower Rattlesnake Camp, later called Van Wyck Camp, one of the most popular of the Mountain's old gathering spots.

Sidney M. Van Wyck, Jr. (1869-1931) was a lawyer who helped the TCC during the crisis that led to the creation of Mt. Tamalpais State Park. Donating his services, he headed condemnation proceedings in 1927-28 against James Newlands and William Magee of the North Coast Water Company. They refused to sell their 500-plus acre parcel between Mountain Home and Bootjack to the State, hoping instead to develop it. The land, when finally purchased for $52,000, became the State Park's initial acreage. Van Wyck, a graduate of the University of California, had been president of the TCC and an unsuccessful candidate for governor of California.

A signed trail through the grass to the right is Troop 80 Spur (also called Van Wyck Trail) leading to Troop 80 Trail at Memorial Tree. At the meadow's left, TCC Trail begins a 1.4-mile trip to Stapelveldt Trail.

Bootjack continues left through a patch of false lupine. It immediately resumes climbing, passing a huge, smooth-faced boulder. The Trail is back in woods, largely tanbark oak and redwood. The next intersection is with the west end of Troop 80 Trail; it goes right, to Mountain Home.

Just beyond is a bench made from an old trail sign, and the remains of an old fountain. This was the site of Upper Rattlesnake Camp, another one-time popular hikers haunt.

Alpine Trail comes in from the left; it rises to Pantoll. A bench at this junction is made from a classic old Rattlesnake Camp sign.

The sound of cars on Panoramic Highway becomes evident. After crossing a couple of bridges, Bootjack Trail meets the highway at a Golden Gate Transit bus stop. Cross the road into the parking lot and go right, up steps past a fountain, into the Bootjack Picnic Area, formerly Bootjack Camp, and generally known simply as Bootjack. There are picnic tables and restrooms at this historic site. There were 29 State Park campsites here until the early 1970's; now the nearest camping is at Pantoll.

Wind your way through Bootjack, passing a huge stone grill, to pick up the Trail at its intersection with Matt Davis Trail. Matt Davis goes left to Pantoll and right toward Mountain Home while Bootjack continues straight up.

The Trail passes below an MTSP residence. It was originally built by the Tamalpais Conservation Club as their "Trailsman" Matt Davis' cabin, then was enlarged by the State Park in 1955.

Bootjack meets an asphalt road. To the far right is the entry to the residence. Above is Old Stage Road, to the right heading to West Point and left to Pantoll. A few yards to the left, opposite a fountain and chlorinator building, is the foot of Riding & Hiking Trail.

Bootjack continues steeply uphill. Above a rocky stretch, the Trail hits a grassy hillside. This clearing is prominent from many vantage points south of the Mountain. In the 1880's, it struck someone as having the shape of a bootjack, a device used to help remove boots, particularly riding boots, and the name has stuck. In late spring, the clearing is ablaze with yellow from poppies and mariposa lilies. There are splendid southeast vistas. The view from a bench, carved "RANGER," is being blocked by a spreading Douglas-fir.

This is a good area to see, in late spring, the Tamalpais jewelflower, a plant that grows only on the Mountain. Its 4-petaled purple flowers decrease in size higher on the stalk. The upper leaves are perfoliate; that is, they surround the stalk.

Switchbacks, one with a small sign dubbing it "the Gucci," carry the Trail ever upward, although not so steeply as the earlier, still evident route. A sign credits the former Youth Conservation Corps with doing the rerouting in 1980. The next bench was made out of the "STATION" part of the same sign as the bench lower.

Bootjack Trail ends at a junction with Easy Grade Trail just below the "stage" of the Mountain Theater. Easy Grade descends to Old Stage Road near Pantoll. To the left are the theater's dressing rooms. Sit in the theater, conjure an image of a Mountain Play (or prepare for a real one if coming during Play weekends) and enjoy!

Bootjack Trail appeared on the 1898 Sanborn map.

DEER PARK FIRE ROAD (#2)
FROM MUIR WOODS ROAD TO COASTAL FIRE ROAD / 2.39 miles

Terrain: Upper part redwood forest, middle part grassland, lower part lightly wooded / MTSP & MWNM; Bay Area Ridge Trail
Elevation: From 1,300' to 140' / steep, parts very steep
Intersecting Trails: Dipsea (several times between .9m and 2.1m), Ben Johnson (1.9m)
Directions: Muir Woods Road to milepost 2.09

THIS FIRE ROAD is a close companion of the Dipsea Trail; they run together for four stretches and intersect several other times. But the Fire Road's haunting topmost section, one of the loveliest on Tam, is not part of the race route and remains relatively little visited.

Deer Park Fire Road (also known as Dipsea Fire Road, and, on State Park signs, as Deer Park Fire Trail) sets off from Muir Woods Road at a gate between road mileage signs 2.09 and 2.10. The trailhead is a half-mile west of the Muir Woods overflow parking lot. In winter, when the bridge over Redwood Creek there is out — it is removed during high water — those traversing the Dipsea Trail are directed to Deer Park F.R. as a detour.

The uphill is immediately very steep. Shrubs, including abundant native blackberries (not nearly as tasty as the introduced species), line the left. To the right is woodland. A path down through Rocky Canyon branches right in .1m; it is laden with poison oak.

After .5 miles of stiff climbing, the Fire Road meets the Dipsea Trail (technically, they remain a yard or two apart), entering from the right. A sign marks the junction. This is the end of the winter detour (or the start of it when descending the Dipsea Trail).

The uphill eases somewhat. This next mile-long section, in which the Deer Park F.R. and Dipsea Trail intertwine, is known as the Hogsback, for its appearance in profile. Pictures from 75 years ago, when the land here was fenced and grazed, show only grassland. Now baccharis (coyote brush) is a common shrub and Douglas-firs have gained more than a foothold.

The Dipsea Trail combines with the Fire Road. They rise together, until the trail continues straight and the Fire Road veers right. (Many Dipsea racers remain on the Fire Road, which is marginally longer but has more room to pass.) There are sweeping views toward the Pacific and of the Tam summit ridge.

Again the Dipsea Trail briefly joins the Fire Road, this time to depart to the right. (Each intersection is signed.) The two meet again, with the Trail now exiting to the left.

Deer Park Fire Road then enters Muir Woods National Monument; the State Park boundary sign beside a huge fallen tanbark oak. This is one of the special parts of Tam: an unexpected stand of giant, virgin redwoods and Douglas-firs high on the Mountain. Their relative inaccessibility, then William Kent's protection, spared these giants from the logging that decimated virtually all of the Mountain's other first growth redwoods. This cool, haunting, magical area is little known even to Mountain veterans, as most visitors follow the Dipsea Trail. It was once known as Kent's Deer Park, hence the Fire Road name. George Lucas filmed part of his fantasy movie "Willow" here. There is evidence of a 1997 fire.

At a signpost, Ben Johnson Trail crosses. Right leads to Stapelveldt Trail, then on down to Muir Woods for a loop option. Left connects, in a few yards, to the Dipsea Trail. The Dipsea Trail itself then joins. The two then run uphill together for 100 yards until the Trail departs for the last time, to the right.

The Fire Road continues rising through deep woodland, to the westernmost tip of Muir Woods National Monument. Huge redwoods and Douglas-firs tower above. One of the latter, on the left, is particularly enormous, with a huge girth supporting three tall trunks.

Deer Park Fire Road ends when it meets Coastal F.R. Just uphill to the right, the Dipsea Trail, at its highest point (Cardiac Hill), crosses Coastal F.R. It too makes a good loop choice. Further to the right is Pantoll. Coastal F.R. drops left to Highway 1.

The route has also been known as Old Mine Truck Road, because it went on to the old mine below Pantoll. It appeared as a trail on the 1898 Sanborn map, then was widened in the 1930's. There is another Deer Park F.R. out of the Deer Park trailhead in Fairfax.

FERN CANYON TRAIL
FROM MUIR WOODS TRAIL TO CAMP ALICE EASTWOOD / 1.03 miles

Terrain: Redwood forest; riparian / MWNM & MTSP
Elevation: 210' to 580' / lower part almost level, upper part steep
Intersecting Trails: Lost (.4m), Plevin Cut (1.0m)
Directions: Muir Woods Trail, .5 miles
Amenities: Outhouses, fountains, benches, picnic tables

THIS IS A LOVELY Trail, as enchanting as the more famous one through the heart

of Muir Woods, but without crowds. Visitors to the Monument should well consider traversing it, or at least the almost level section to the third bridge over
Fern Creek.

The trailhead (where it is called Fern *Creek* Trail) is a quarter-mile past
Cathedral Grove and bridge #3 when coming from the main Muir Woods en-
trance. It is here that Fern Creek itself, one of the longest and liveliest streams on
Tamalpais, ends at its junction with Redwood Creek.

At the start, a plaque informs visitors, "Ferns Return to Fern Creek." The
fencing and plantings are part of a MWNM effort to restore the creek's habitat

One hundred yards in, just past a bench, is a massive Douglas-fir, the Kent
Tree. It was a favorite of William Kent, who donated the land that became Muir
Woods. The Kent Tree was once 273 feet in height and the tallest tree not only
in Muir Woods but in all Marin County. During a storm in 1982, its top 50 feet
fell. (Marin's tallest tree is now a redwood in Roys Redwoods, off Nicasio Road.
The Monument's tallest is a redwood in Bohemian Grove.) Still, with its circumference of 26 feet, 8 inches, the Kent Tree remains most impressive.

Beside the Kent Tree is a plaque affixed to a boulder. It reads:

WILLIAM KENT, WHO GAVE THESE WOODS
AND OTHER NATURAL BEAUTY SITES TO PERPETUATE THEM
FOR PEOPLE WHO LOVE THE OUT-OF-DOORS, 1864-1928 . . . TCC.

The three-ton boulder was brought to the second Muir Woods Inn by railroad car, then further down the canyon by wagon. Just before its placement, the
boulder slipped into Fern Creek and had to be rolled back by hikers. The dedication ceremony was in May, 1929, a year after Kent's death (March 13, 1928).

The Trail heads into the canyon of Fern Creek, seemingly a world apart
from the sometimes bustle of the main Muir Woods Trail. The Trail actually does
leave MWNM in .1 mile, to enter Mt. Tamalpais State Park. Bridges cross first to
the creek's right bank, then back to the left. A more noticeable uphill begins.

The Trail crosses a feeder stream. It then meets Lost Trail, which rises very
steeply right to Ocean View Trail. Fern Canyon Trail then crosses Fern Creek for
the third and last time over a wonderful, downsloping bridge. At 103 feet, it is is
perhaps the longest trail bridge on Tam. A small plaque dates the span, but-
tressed by a fallen redwood, to 12/24/77. On the other side, a re-placed old sign
directs hikers right, away from the closed shortcut steps.

The Trail now climbs steeply out of Fern Creek Canyon. Still, there remain
many giant redwoods to enjoy, including several fire-scarred monarchs joined at
the base to form double or triple trees. Traces of the asphalt that once covered
the Trail are still visible.

Near its top, Fern Canyon Trail meets the signed Plevin Cut Trail, a shortcut if returning to Muir Woods via Camp Eastwood Road. Look to the right here
to see the concrete foundations from the first Muir Woods Inn, built in 1908 and
destroyed by fire in 1913.

Fern Canyon Trail ends at the paved, open clearing of Camp Alice Eastwood,
near the outhouses. The area was once the terminus of the gravity car line from

Double Bow Knot, then a Civilian Conservation Corps camp during the 1930's. Now it is a popular group camp (by advance reservation only). The other trails meeting here are, clockwise: Camp Eastwood Road downhill (a loop option), Sierra, and Camp Eastwood Road uphill.

The Trail appears on the 1898 Sanborn map. It was considered as the western half of Zig-Zag Trail until construction of Panoramic Highway in the 1920's severed the two. Muir Woods maps refer to it as Fern Creek Trail. But that name is more widely reserved for another trail (between the East Peak parking area to Old Railroad Grade) which follows the creek along its uppermost reaches, some 2,000 vertical feet above.

HEATHER CUTOFF TRAIL
FROM REDWOOD CREEK TRAIL TO COASTAL FIRE ROAD / 1.46 miles

Terrain: Coastal brush and grassland; horses permitted / MTSP
Elevation: From 60' to 440' / gradual
Intersecting Trails: None
Directions: Muir Woods Road at milepost 3.21

THIS UNUSUAL Trail was built with 21 gently graded switchbacks to make ascents and descents easier for horses. Heather Cutoff also plays a role for those on foot as part of loops on the southwest flank of Mt. Tamalpais.

The Trail technically begins from Redwood Creek Trail, at an MTSP signpost, south of Muir Woods Road from the new horse camp (milepost 3.21). Since the lush, riparian opening 200 yards to the road involves crossing Redwood Creek without a bridge, most hikers pick it up from the entrance gate to the Franks Valley Horse Camp. The camp, directly ahead, opened in 1991 to accommodate equestrian groups. Heather Cutoff goes left from the trail sign, through the meadow.

There is no true trail here; follow the overgrown vehicle track toward the horse corral. Just before it, veer right to the Heather signpost. The route is then unmistakable.

The climbing now begins. The switchbacks provide extra time to enjoy the expanding views. The first vista is of the western end of Franks Valley. Banducci's Gardens, the flower farm in the valley, can still readily be distinguished, but, its water supply cut off, it is returning to a natural state. The shrub baccharis is the most abundant plant along the Trail but blackberry, thimbleberry, monkey flower, sage, strawberry, Indian warrior and, alas, poison oak, are also common. After 1/3-mile of climbing, a stand of chain ferns mark the crossing of a muddy seep.

The Trail ever rises. You can easily see how far you've climbed, and what remains. Near the top, views open over Dias Ridge to San Francisco and beyond.

Heather Cutoff ends at its junction with Coastal F. R., which goes left to Highway 1 and right up to Pantoll. There are lovely ocean vistas.

Also just to the left is the MTSP-GGNRA boundary, and the old Heather Farm. Founded by Amadeo Banducci, Sr. in the 1920's, it was an important Bay

Area wholesale flower supplier for decades. Heather, in many varieties, was a key crop. The farm remained in the Banducci family until 1980, when, after a court battle, the GGNRA condemned and took over the land. The Banduccis continued their operation through a lease. In 1994, the GGNRA cut off the Banducci's main water source, wells near Redwood Creek, as a danger to the salmon run. Banducci family members still live on the property.

In late winter, heather, a non-native shrub, covers the hills here with its pink-purple flowers, hence the Trail name. Plaques affixed to railroad ties in some of the switchbacks credit re-building of the Trail — called by its earlier name of Perkins Trail — to the Marin Conservation Corps in 1983. The former routing was closed due to erosion problems.

HILLSIDE TRAIL
BETWEEN MUIR WOODS TRAIL, FROM BRIDGE #2 TO BRIDGE #4 / .70 miles

Terrain: Redwood forest; heavily used / MWNM
Elevation: From 180′ to 360′ to 240′ / gradual
Intersecting Trails: None
Directions: Muir Woods Trail, .3 miles

SINCE Hillside Trail is part of the easiest loop option in Muir Woods off the asphalt-covered main trail, it is heavily used. Indeed, more people cover its full length each year than any other dirt trail on Tam.

The signed entrance to Hillside Trail is at bridge #2 over Redwood Creek, a quarter-mile from the Muir Woods National Monument entrance archway. The Trail immediately climbs a few steps, frightening off some Monument visitors, but the route is then quite easy. The trailhead sign says it is 1/2-mile to Ben Johnson Trail; it is actually .7 miles.

Hillside Trail gently rises above the creek floor. The "hillside" of the name is the western wall of Redwood Canyon. Redwoods, of course, dominate. While you will not likely be alone, Hillside is always a quieter alternative to the main Muir Woods trail, visible, and its visitors sometimes audible, below.

About halfway through, two pairs of steps carry the Trail up and over a fallen redwood. Douglas-firs begin to appear, rivals of the redwoods in height and girth. A particularly large and prominent one is in the middle of the sharp bend to the right, which has a bench and footbridge. Also at this bend, I've seen trillium growing directly out of one of the redwoods, several feet above the soil.

Beyond the bend the route begins dropping. Hillside ends at its junction with Ben Johnson Trail, which is starting its climb left to the Dipsea Trail. A few steps lead down to bridge #4 over Redwood Creek. Cross and go right to return to the start. Left is the start of Bootjack Trail, which rises to the Mountain Theater.

Hillside Trail, which appears on maps from the 1920's, was restored in the mid-'30's and renamed Hillside Nature Trail. There were signs for a self-guided nature tour along it until 1964.

KENT CANYON TRAIL
FROM MUIR WOODS ROAD TO KENT CANYON FALLS / .5 miles

Terrain: Riparian; woodland; unimproved / MTSP
Elevation: Around 140' / almost level
Intersecting Trails: None
Directions: Muir Woods Road to "Kerri Lane," between mileposts 2.56 and 2.67

IN 1914, this Trail was opened from Franks Valley up what was then known as Rocky Canyon. It was to serve as a new, shaded route for walking to the then-new Mountain Play. The Trail was originally named for its builders, Fred Robbins and William Higgins. Robbins was a newspaperman who wrote books and articles about the outdoors. Logging in the 1950's contributed to the Trail's disrepair and abandonment. Today only the lower section survives, and just barely, as Kent Canyon Trail.

To reach the Trail, which bears no signs whatsoever, walk down the driveway (unofficially, "Kerri Lane") of 2700 Muir Woods Road. There are State Park residences on both sides. Kerri is the daughter of the late Randy Hogue, a much beloved and respected Mt. Tamalpais State Park ranger. The Hogues lived many years in the house on the left. The buildings were once part of the sizable Brazil Ranch, which extended from here up to near Pantoll. In the early 1970's, a proposal was advanced to open a hostel here.

Veer right in front of the barn. The Trail begins at fire road-width. Kent Creek is to the left. Oaks, buckeyes, madrones, and especially laurels line the way.

In .2 miles is a clearing used as a target practice range by rangers; it is closed much of the year so as not to disturb spotted owls resident in the upper canyon. A few yards beyond it, Kent Canyon Trail narrows as it enters deeper woodland. It crosses the creek, which may require some rock-hopping in winter. A pipeline is embedded alongside. Posts, now knocked down, carry the sign, "Kent Canyon Blow Off" water valves.

The Trail meanders streamside. An overgrown ranch road branches uphill left. It actually can be followed a bit deeper into the canyon, above the falls, than the lower route, then deteriorates.

Kent Canyon Trail meets Kent Creek again and ends. To the left, a waterfall cascades down a rocky gorge. Across the creek is an old quarry site, likely the source of the rocks shoring the creek bank. This is one of the loveliest, most peaceful, and little visited parts of Mt. Tamalpais. It gives a hint of how delightful the trail-less upper Kent Canyon (also called Kent Ravine) is. But resist trying the several visible paths; all are extremely steep, poor, and lined with poison oak

The canyon was renamed to honor William Kent, who once had a hunting cabin on its upper slopes. It is is one of three trails on Tam named for him (see Kent Trail). There is some sentiment to rename the Trail in the memory of Ranger Hogue, who so often explored it.

LOST TRAIL
FROM FERN CANYON TRAIL TO OCEAN VIEW TRAIL / .52 miles

Terrain: Deeply wooded, lower half redwoods, upper half Douglas-firs / MTSP
Elevation: From 310' to 750' / very steep
Intersecting Trails: None
Directions: Muir Woods Trail — Fern Canyon Trail, .4 miles

LOST TRAIL, when combined with Ocean View and Fern Canyon trails, offers a lovely loop walk out of Muir Woods. Lost Trail leaves Fern Canyon (also called Fern Creek) Trail to the right at a marked intersection, .4 miles above Muir Woods Trail. The junction is a few feet before the long bridge over Fern Creek.

Lost Trail opens with steps — there are nearly 250 in total — and remains very steep, with few respites, throughout. The Trail, in deep woods, is quiet and peaceful, drawing only heartier Muir Woods visitors. A bridge is crossed at .2 miles.

At .3 miles, a giant Douglas-fir towers above a flight of steps and Douglas-firs replaces redwoods as the dominant tree. As the stiff climb continues, the forest canopy opens slightly. A pair of steep stream canyons are crossed.

Lost Trail actually drops a few feet and then ends at its junction with Ocean View Trail, amidst a redwood grove. Ocean View goes left uphill to Panoramic Trail and Panoramic Highway, and right downhill back to Muir Woods.

The Trail dates to around 1914. It was partly buried by a landslide in the 1930's and "lost" for some 30 years — it didn't even appear on post-World War II Freese maps. The Trail was finally recleared and given the name "Lost." Then, for years, the upper Trail sign was lost. Now all that is "lost" is the "i" in "Muir Woods" in the sign at Ocean View.

MUIR WOODS (MAIN) TRAIL
FROM MUIR WOODS ENTRANCE TO JUNCTION OF BEN JOHNSON AND BOOTJACK TRAILS / .88 miles

Terrain: Redwood forest; riparian; asphalt surface; heavily used / MWNM
Elevation: 150' to 230' / almost level
Intersecting Trails: Ocean View (.2m), Hillside (.3m), Fern Canyon (.6m), Camp Eastwood Road (.7m)
Directions: Muir Woods trailhead
Amenities: Wheelchair accessible, cafeteria, gift shop, fountains, bathrooms, interpretive signs, guided nature trail
Spur: Between bridges #1 and #3 / .4 miles

THIS IS MUCH the most heavily used Trail on Mt. Tamalpais. Perhaps 1.5 million visitors a year, from scores of countries and speaking dozens of languages, follow it at least part way along Redwood Creek north from the main Muir Woods National Monument entrance. Along the Trail tower some of the County's tallest and oldest trees. Salmon still swim up the pristine stream to their spawning grounds. Come to the Monument early (it opens at 8 a.m. daily) or in winter to enjoy the area in relative solitude, or take pleasure in sharing this very special place with others. Adjoining trails, which head high on the Mountain, are uncrowded any time of the year. The Trail is presently the only one on Mt. Tamalpais completely accessible to those in wheelchairs.

Oddly, this busiest of trails does not have a widely accepted name. Erickson labels it part of Bootjack Trail. Olmsted leaves it nameless. Muir Woods staffers refer to it as Main Trail. The newer Spur part of the Trail, on Redwood Creek's right bank (between bridges #1 and #3), has also been called Nature Trail.

The asphalt-covered Muir Woods Trail begins under the newly restored entrance arch. An admission fee is now collected. On the right is the new (1989) visitor center, constructed in the style of 1930's Works Progress Administration buildings. A ranger or volunteer will answer questions and dispense the free park brochure and the guide ($1) to the 10-stop nature trail which begins at bridge #2. Inside, books, videos, maps and cards are sold; proceeds go to the Monument. There are maps and attractive interpretive signs along the way as well.

The prominent first redwood on the right stands 190 feet tall and is estimated at 500-800 years in age. Just beyond, a path on the right leads to a gift shop and cafeteria run by a concessionaire, restrooms and park offices. In a few more yards is bridge #1, rebuilt in late 1993, across Redwood Creek. (We won't cross yet.) Traces of no fewer than 16 now-gone bridges across Redwood Creek in Muir Woods have been uncovered.

Redwoods are, of course, the stars of this Trail. These long-lived monarchs have thick bark, up to 12 inches, which keeps out enemies such as insects and fungi. The bark also helps make redwoods exceptionally fire-resistant; many healthy redwoods still show evidence of the last great fire to sweep through the area, in 1845. In winter, the tree's male cones release their clouds of pollen, imparting a golden cast to the area.

There is a water fountain beside a cross-cut section of a redwood. Just beyond, Ocean View Trail departs uphill to the right. Opposite is a plaque dedicating a redwood to Gifford Pinchot, first head of the National Forest Service. Ironically, Pinchot, called "Friend of the Forest, Preserver of the Common-Wealth" on the plaque placed by the Sierra Club in 1910, was becoming the club's, and John Muir's, bitter enemy as he supported the damming of Hetch Hetchy in Yosemite, a project Muir fervently opposed.

Just behind the Pinchot Tree is a double-trunked giant, the Emerson Tree. A plaque, still affixed to the far side (visible to sharp-eyed observers from the Spur trail on the opposite bank), was placed in 1903 to mark the 100th anniversary of the birth of Ralph Waldo Emerson. Jack London was among those attending the ceremony. It reads, "1803 EMERSON 1903" and may be the oldest surviving plaque on Mt. Tamalpais.

Across bridge #2, gently rolling Hillside Trail begins. It connects to bridge #4, and offers a popular loop option. Here too is the start of the new nature trail. Brochures, interpreting the 10 numbered stops, are available here; leave $1.

The bridges are good spots to look, in December and January, for two species of salmon (coho and steelhead) heading upstream to spawn, although their numbers are down drastically from years past. The adult coho salmon never make it back. Only the small percentage of surviving young return, after the first heavy fall rains open the sandbar downstream at Muir Beach, back to the ocean. After a few years in the Pacific, they too return to Redwood Creek and complete their own life cycle. Steelhead, however, can spawn more than once.

Note the rock revetment along the creek bank. It was built by the Civilian Conservation Corps in the 1930's to control erosion.

By Bridge #3 (.4m) is Cathedral Grove. Here in 1971, at nature trail stop #6, a 225-foot redwood fell, taking a second redwood down as well. The soil around its shallow roots had become overly compacted from visitor's feet and could no longer hold sufficient moisture. The incident led to the construction of the wood barriers that now line the whole Trail.

The Trail forks around Cathedral Grove, which contains some of the Monument's largest trees. Azaleas grow beside the creek. On the right fork, a plaque and sign mark where delegates from around the world, meeting in San Francisco to frame the United Nations charter, came on May 19, 1945. They were honoring President Franklin D. Roosevelt, who had died a month earlier. Fifteen feet beyond, another sign stands by a 200-foot, 800-year-old redwood that toppled May 19, 1995.

There is a bench just after the forks reunite. A plaque behind dedicates it to William Montanary (1915-1985), whose children donated it. MWNM policy now restricts such trailside plaques.

At .7 miles, Fern Canyon (also called Fern Creek) Trail goes uphill to the right. One hundred yards up Fern Canyon is the famous Kent Tree, well worth a visit. Fern Canyon Trail also offers excellent loop options, with Lost and Ocean View trails or with Camp Eastwood F. R. About 50 yards past the junction, on the right, is an albino redwood tree. Note the pale foliage. Unable to photosynthesize, the albino relies on nourishment from the roots of an adjacent redwood.

In 50 more yards, on the left, a turnout marks the site of a cabin that stood from around 1885 to 1928. Ben Johnson lived there in the 1890's when he was gamekeeper for the Tamalpais Sportsmen's Club, whose members hunted deer in the area. Just beyond, Camp Eastwood F.R. begins its climb to Mountain Home.

Muir Woods Trail ends at bridge #4 by the Monument's boundary. The unpaved trail straight ahead is Bootjack, which climbs all the way to the Mountain Theater. Ben Johnson Trail sets off left on its way to the Dipsea Trail. A few yards up on Ben Johnson, just over the bridge, is the far end of Hillside Trail.

On the return, cross Redwood Creek at bridge #3 to make a loop back on the right bank Spur. Some 15 yards before bridge #2, look on the right for a redwood with a particularly large burl, about 20 feet up. Burls, which can weigh up to 50 tons each, are swollen masses of undeveloped buds, an alternative, non-sexual method of reproduction to seeds.

At bridge #2 is Hillside Trail and the Bohemian Grove. The Bohemian Club had its annual summer camp here in 1892. The members quickly decided that Muir Woods was too cold, so they purchased a permanent camp (which draws some of the nation's most prominent leaders each summer) in Sonoma County. In the Bohemian Grove is Muir Woods' tallest tree, a 252' redwood.

A plaque marks the Bicentennial Tree, estimated to have sprouted in 1776. The redwood is now a full-fledged giant. Just before bridge #1, the route passes through a downed redwood. It fell across the Trail in April 1993 and blocked passage for a year. The Trail was slightly rerouted. The loop ends back at bridge #1.

President Theodore Roosevelt wanted to name the park Kent Monument in honor of William Kent, who donated its initial acreage to the nation in 1908. Kent declined, saying, "I have five good husky boys . . . if (they) cannot keep the name of Kent alive, I am willing it should be forgotten." He also said, "I deserve no more credit than if I had protected my children from a kidnapper." Kent suggested honoring John Muir, then 70 and the dean of American conservationists.

OCEAN VIEW TRAIL
FROM MUIR WOODS TO PANORAMIC HIGHWAY / 1.52 miles

Terrain: Deeply wooded; heavily used / MWNM & MTSP
Elevation: 180' to 900' / steep
Intersecting Trails: Lost (1.3m)
Directions: Muir Woods Trail, .1 mile

As THE FIRST Trail out of Redwood Canyon when entering Muir Woods from the main entrance, Ocean View is well trod. While many turn back, others complete lovely loops with Lost and Fern Canyon trails, or with Camp Eastwood Road. Be forewarned that there are no ocean views until near the Trail's top.

The trailhead is .1 mile in from the Visitor Center, opposite the Pinchot Tree. Gifford Pinchot, founder of the National Forest Service, later proved an arch enemy of John Muir when he supported damming Yosemite's Hetch Hetchy Valley, a project Muir passionately fought.

Ocean View begins its long uphill on steps. Towering redwoods line the Trail along with associated forest plants such as trillium, fairy-bells, and sword ferns. Unfortunately, poison oak is also abundant, so be cautious. In .1 mile, a huge Douglas-fir straddles the Trail's left margin. Above, Douglas-firs replace redwoods as the common tree.

At .4 miles, the Trail levels somewhat as it leaves Muir Woods National Monument and enters Mt. Tamalpais State Park. Thirty yards past the sign, an extremely steep path rises to the Tourist Club. (Its use is discouraged because of erosion problems.) Soon after crossing a creek, Ocean View steepens.

At .8 miles, in a clearing known as "Fir Tree Point," the Trail opens. Look here for aromatic pitcher sages (*Lepechinia calycina*). They are woody shrubs, one to four feet tall, with two-lipped white flowers in spring. Rub the opposite leaves to capture the strong mint fragrance. There is another stand of redwoods. Just beyond, at a signpost, Lost Trail departs to the left.

Broom begins to make incursions, but less so since regular pulls and burns began in the 1990's. The Trail leaves deep woodland at an old barbed wire fence post. Ahead is open grassland, and, finally, views. First there is a vista of Tam's summit ridge. A few yards later look back to see the Pacific, and how the Trail got its name. The Trail passes beneath a huge rock, a favored picnic site.

Ocean View ends when it meets Panoramic Trail. To the left is Camp Eastwood Road, which drops gently to Muir Woods. Further left is the Mountain Home Inn. To the right, toward Ridge Avenue, is another loop option back, via Redwood Trail to the Tourist Club, then the Sun and Dipsea trails. A few yards up is Panoramic Highway. Alpine Lodge, headquarters of the California Alpine Club, is directly across the road.

REDWOOD CREEK TRAIL
FROM MUIR WOODS ROAD TO SHORELINE HIGHWAY / 2.04 miles

Terrain: Riparian; coastal grassland; muddy / MTSP
Elevation: From 100' to 20' / almost level
Intersecting Trails: Miwok (.3m), Heather Cutoff (1.2m), Dias (1.3m)
Directions: Muir Woods Road, mile marker 2.09
Spur: To Muir Woods Road, .1 mile

THIS TRAIL, along Redwood Creek, plays a role in many long-distance Marin County hikes as it links Mt. Tam's trail system with the Marin Headlands trail network. Heavy equestrian use, however, keeps it muddy in winter. Another drawback is that much of the Trail is within a few yards of Muir Woods Road.

While the western end of the Trail is only 50 yards off Highway One, it will be described from the more commonly joined Muir Woods side. This inland end is directly across Muir Woods Road from Deer Park Fire Road, between road mile markers 2.09 and 2.10, a half-mile west of the Muir Woods overflow parking lot and just west of the Muir Woods-Mt. Tamalpais State Park boundary. At the trailhead, on the south side of the road, is an MTSP sign and one for the Bay Area Ridge Trail, of which Redwood Creek Trail is a part for .3 miles.

The abundant lacy-leaved plant on the left in the opening yards (and much of the rest of the way) is poison hemlock. Its scientific name is *conium maculatum* ("maculatum" means "spotted," referring to the blotched stems). The poison which killed Socrates was prepared from the root of this hemlock, an Old World native introduced to California.

In .1 mile, the Trail meets and crosses Redwood Creek. The long-time bridge here was destroyed by a falling red alder in the winter of 1993-94, then replaced several months later.

The Trail now winds along Redwood Creek's left bank, through what is known as Franks Valley, but just who "Frank" was remains an unsolved mystery. Redwood Creek, which cuts through the heart of Muir Woods, is one of the strongest flowing, undammed creeks in Marin. It still supports a salmon run, albeit at a fraction of former levels. A new book about Redwood Creek, *Web of*

Water, by Maya Khosla, came out in 1997.

At .3 miles is the junction with the north end of Miwok Trail. Miwok, one of the longest trails in Marin, rises left to Dias Ridge Fire Road, then continues its roller-coaster route through Tennessee Valley and on to Rodeo Valley. It is a hiking and equestrian section of the Bay Area Ridge Trail.

The next section, through a grassy meadow, is most likely to be muddy in winter. At .6 miles, a signpost marks an entry, "Redwood Creek Spur," from Muir Woods Road (at milepost sign 2.56), but there is no bridge over the creek. Kent Canyon is across Muir Woods Road here, behind a pair of State Park residences.

In 100 yards, the Trail meets an incongruous stone building foundation. It is one of many remnants here of the old Ponte Ranch, from the area's dairy days.

In another 100 yards, the Trail crosses Redwood Creek over a hikers bridge (horses ford on the right). There are vestiges of a dam in the creek here. Just beyond, the Trail skirts to within 25 yards of Muir Woods Road (at road milepost 2.81) and a signpost marks the connecting path.

At 1.1 miles, another marked path connects right with Muir Woods Road. A few yards past, the Trail crosses Redwood Creek for the last time on a long (and a bit shaky) pedestrian-only bridge.

At 1.2 miles, a signpost marks Heather Trail. Heather crosses Redwood Creek (without a bridge), then Muir Woods Road by the new group horse camp, before rising to Coastal Trail.

The Trail enters a wooded area. In late winter, you may spot giant wake-robin (*trillium chloropetalum*) in bloom here. It has three deep maroon petals clustered above three stalkless large leaves. This is the rarer of the two trillium wildflower species found in Marin County. Not rare here, however, is poison oak.

The Trail emerges from the woodland. Fifty yards later (25 yards past a utility pole), unmarked Dias Trail begins an extremely steep climb left to Dias Ridge. This very poor trail may one day be replaced with a longer, more gradual, multi-use route.

Redwood Creek itself crosses to the opposite (north) side of Muir Woods Road, where it remains. Just beyond is a fork. A sign points to the upper, left fork as the continuation of Redwood Creek Trail to Muir Beach. The lower, right option connects to Muir Woods Road (at milepost sign 3.43).

The road remains in view. Look across it to the Heather, or Banducci, Farm, on leased GGNRA land. The extensive flower farm here, dating from the 1920's, is now largely gone. In the mid-1990's, the GGNRA cut off the farm's supply of Redwood Creek water, saying withdrawals were detrimental to the severely depleted and endangered salmon run.

There is a small bridge over a rivulet. The Trail passes a grove of eucalyptus trees, and skirts where several giants were felled. There is a final bridge crossing.

The purple flowers of periwinkle, a non-native garden plant, alongside the Trail indicates homes are nearby. Sure enough, a few switchbacks bring Redwood Creek Trail down to the town of Muir Beach at the signed western trailhead. Fifty yards ahead is Shoreline Highway (Highway 1). To the right, the Highway crosses Big Lagoon Bridge. To the left, less than a quarter-mile, is the Pelican Inn, a great place to pause. At the Inn is the entry (Pacific Way) to the ocean at Muir Beach proper. From there, signs point the way to Marin Headlands trails.

Southeast flank of Tam, and East Peak, from Corte Madera Ridge F.R. at Blithedale Ridge intersection.

Old Highway 101 Trailhead

Old Highway 101 Trailhead

Directions to Crown Road area trailheads, Kentfield:
Highway 101 — west on Sir Francis Drake Blvd. (exit), Greenbrae — left on College Ave., Kentfield — right on Woodland Road — left on Evergreen Drive — left on Ridgecrest Rd. to end; OR left on Crown Road to end OR right on Crown Road to Phoenix Road; OR straight on Evergreen Drive to end.

Directions to Baltimore Canyon, Larkspur:
Highway 101 — west on Tamalpais Drive (exit), Corte Madera to Redwood Ave. — right on Corte Madera Ave. (which becomes Magnolia Ave.) — left on Madrone Ave. to Valley Way.

Directions to Escalon Drive, Mill Valley:
Highway 101 — East Blithedale Ave. (exit), Mill Valley — right on Camino Alto — left on Overhill Road — right on Escalon Drive.

THE COUNTY ROAD that was forerunner to today's Highway 101 now has four different names in the four communities it crosses below Mt. Tamalpais; College Avenue in Kentfield, Magnolia Avenue in Larkspur, Corte Madera Avenue in Corte Madera, and Camino Alto in Mill Valley. It was Marin's main north-south road for some 75 years. (Today's Highway 101, which dates from the late 1920's, hugs the flatter, land-filled bay margin.) This old road has been the traditional eastern boundary of Mt. Tamalpais maps, and is here.

There are many trailheads leading westward from the corridor, generally onto Marin County Open Space District lands. None have any facilites; most have very limited parking. These access points are described in order, north to south.

A few trailheads (with the best parking possibilities) are in Kent Woodlands, an elegant residential area that the Kent family began subdividing in 1936. The most popular, for Southern Marin Line Fire Road, is at the southern end of Crown Road. There are other public access points nearby off northern Crown Road, at the upper end of Ridgecrest Road (for the newly opened King Mountain trails) and at the top of Evergreen Drive.

King Mountain can also be accessed in Larkspur, from the top of Skylark Drive (off Magnolia) and from Cedar Avenue, near downtown. Just south of downtown Larkspur is shaded, creek-side Baltimore Canyon (also called Larkspur or Madrone canyon), another favorite starting point.

In Corte Madera, there are three fire road access points off steep Summit Drive. Continuing south, there are three public open space entries directly adjacent to the road near the Corte Madera-Mill Valley border. Two are just before the road's crest (where Corte Madera Avenue changes names to Camino Alto), and one just after. In Mill Valley, there is a popular access at the end of Escalon Drive.

Suggested loops from Old Highway 101:

• Ridgecrest Road (Kent Woodlands) trailhead (elevation 600') — King Mountain Loop Trail (either direction) **1.4 miles**

• Baltimore Canyon trailhead (elevation 160') — Dawn Falls Trail, .1m to Barbara Spring Trail — uphill, .3m, to Southern Marin Line F.R. — right, 1.3m, to Dawn Falls Trail — right, 1.2m, to start **2.9 miles.**

• Southern Marin Line F.R. trailhead (elevation 510')-Southern Marin Line F.R., 2.8m, to Huckleberry Trail — right, .6m, to Corte Madera Ridge F.R. — right, .5m, to Blithedale Ridge F.R. — right, .8m, to Hoo-Koo-E-Koo Trail — right, .9m, to Southern Marin Line F.R. — left, .1m, to start **5.7 miles.**

BARBARA SPRING TRAIL
FROM DAWN FALLS TRAIL TO SOUTHERN MARIN LINE F.R. / .34 miles

Terrain: Riparian; deep woodland / MCOSD
Elevation: From 170' to 490' / very steep
Intersecting Trails: None
Directions: Dawn Falls Trail from Valley Way — right, 50 yards

ALTHOUGH NEAR A TRAILHEAD, Barbara Spring Trail's steepness keeps it relatively little-used. But, combined with Dawn Falls Trail and Southern Marin Line Fire Road, it offers a nice wilderness loop within a mile of downtown Larkspur. Be cautioned that the Trail has very steep sections which can be slippery when taken downhill.

Barbara Spring Trail rises from an MCOSD signpost 50 yards upstream (right) from the bridge over Larkspur Creek at Valley Way. The Trail's steep, slide-prone early yards are among the worst on the route, but not atypical. The Trail climbs beside a deep creek canyon. In .1 mile, two rivulets merge at a small waterfall. The Trail follows the left-hand feeder.

The forest muffles any urban noise. There are usually downed madrones blocking sections of the Trail. This is common in maturing, fire-free forests on Tam; redwoods and Douglas-firs rise above the older madrones, outcompete them for sunlight, and the madrones die and fall.

The Trail ends when it meets level Southern Marin Line Fire Road. An MCOSD signpost marks the intersection. It is 1.2 miles left to the fire road's Larkspur end, .3 miles right to H-Line Fire Road and 1.3 miles right to Dawn Falls Trail.

One account says the Trail was built by Larkspur firemen for fitness training runs. It is also commonly called "S" Trail, for its shape. The "Barbara" of the Trail's name is unknown.

CAMINO ALTO FIRE ROAD
FROM CAMINO ALTO TO MARLIN AVENUE, MILL VALLEY / 1.19 miles

Terrain: Broom-dominated grassland / MCOSD
Elevation: From 350' to 490' to 200' / parts very steep
Intersecting Trails: Escalon-Lower Summit F.R. (.6m)
Directions: Highway 101 — East Blithedale Avenue (exit), Mill Valley — right on Camino Alto to summit (Mill Valley town limits sign)

FEW TRAVEL SPECIFICALLY to Camino Alto Fire Road; its users are almost entirely nearby residents. The Fire Road is exposed, dusty, lined with broom, near homes, and you can even hear Highway 101 as a dull roar. But it does offer very easy access and some splendid views.

The Fire Road begins at an MCOSD gate signed "Camino Alto" just below the summit of the auto road Camino Alto, to the left (west) when coming from Mill Valley. There is limited parking across from the gate.

The route opens with a very steep climb to a water tank. Immediately there are vistas of the San Francisco skyline. A path to the right heads down into the forest; forks lead to the base of Corte Madera Ridge F.R. and to the Octopus Junction. Farther, another path branches right to Escalon-Lower Summit F.R. Broom, both French and Scotch, completely lines both sides of the Fire Road, somewhat obscuring both the native oaks behind and the views.

The Fire Road drops. At .6 miles it crosses a four-way junction dubbed "the Escalon Octopus" by MCOSD rangers. Escalon-Lower Summit F.R. goes left to Escalon Drive in Mill Valley and right, past a bigger junction known as "The Octopus," to Summit Drive in Corte Madera.

Camino Alto F.R. rises again. A few yards up, a path goes right, down into deeply wooded MCOSD lands above the Mill Valley Municipal Golf Course. The Fire Road crests again beside a row of private homes. The far house, where the Fire Road bends right and down, burned in 1993 when an MCOSD worker accidentally set off a grass fire while welding a gate. It was owned and occupied at the time by singer Grace Slick of Jefferson Airplane fame; she received a sizable settlement.

There are more fine views of Mt. Tamalpais, towering over the nearer ridge called Little Tamalpais. The Fire Road then drops very steeply. Lupine, clover, and yarrow are among the few native wildflowers holding out against the otherwise all-pervasive broom.

The Fire Road meets a gate, marked with an MCOSD "Camino Alto" sign, at the crest of Mill Valley's Del Casa Drive (opposite #270). Del Casa is an alternate access to the Fire Road. Camino Alto F.R. continues beyond another MCOSD-signed gate immediately to the left; duck under the oak guarding the entry. This lower section was only added to the Open Space District in 1989.

The downhill is steeper still. Camino Alto Fire Road ends at a gate beside the private residence of #150 Marlin Drive. Downtown Mill Valley is a half-mile due east.

The Fire Road has no accepted name. I called it Camino Alto-Marlin F.R. in earlier editions; Camino Alto Fire Road, matching the new MCOSD signs, is simpler. Camino Alto means "high road" in Spanish.

CEDAR FIRE ROAD
FROM CEDAR AVENUE, LARKSPUR, TO KING MOUNTAIN LOOP TRAIL/ .72 miles

Terrain: Grassland, some woodland / MCOSD
Elevation: From 200' to 575' / steep
Intersecting Trails: King Mountain, .7 miles
Directions: Same as to Baltimore Canyon except continue north on Magnolia Avenue — left on Ward Street — right on Hawthorne Avenue — left on Ajax Street — left on Cedar Avenue to end

THIS FIRE ROAD was only formally opened to the public in 1993, when it was added to the Marin County Open Space District.

There are two accesses, both unpaved, to Cedar Fire Road's lower trailhead from downtown Larkspur. One is at the southern end of Larkspur's Cedar Road. The other is up a 150-yard lane, signed "Fire Road, Do Not Block," above Willow Avenue. There is no provision for parking by the trailhead gate and virtually no legal spots (marked by white lines) on Cedar Avenue. The gate carries an MCOSD "King Mountain" sign.

The first prominent tree on the left edge is an old oak. One can easily get the feeling that here, so close to downtown Larkspur, is land that appears as it did for hundreds of years. But a closer look reveals that, except for that oak, virtually all the prominent vegetation is non-native, introduced following European settlement of the County. That includes the abundant broom, the acacia and eucalyptus trees, and basically all the grasses. A few poppies and blue-eyed grass wildflowers hold out; more may return after an extensive clearing in 1997.

The Fire Road rises both gently and moderately steeply. The hillside, grassy as recently as the early 1970's, is now covered with broom. In spring, white patches of morning-glory stand out amidst the sea of yellow broom flowers. Views continue to expand.

In a half-mile, a broad path veers right; it quickly ends at private property. One hundred yards later, a short descent leads to a fence line. Beyond, left and down on the asphalt, is a water tank. Right and down is an alternate entrance to the Fire Road from the Skylark Apartments, atop Larkspur's Skylark Drive. (That entrance, at the southwest corner of the complex, has been marked by forbidding "Do Not Enter" lettering on the pavement, but there is a public easement. Veer right twice when descending, left twice when coming up from Skylark.)

Cedar F.R. continues left and up. There is a fine vista of Tam's East Peak. Two-hundred-fifty yards from the fence line, the new (1994) King Mountain Loop Trail loop sets off left and right at MCOSD signposts.

The public portion of the Fire Road ends just above King Mountain Trail at another fence line, signed as off-limits by the MCOSD. Beyond is the privately-owned upper slope of King Mountain.

Although numerous Marin streets are named "Cedar," and many cedar trees have been planted as ornamentals, true cedars (genus *Cedrus*) are not native to North America.

CORTE MADERA RIDGE FIRE ROAD
FROM CORTE MADERA AVENUE, CORTE MADERA, TO BLITHEDALE RIDGE FIRE ROAD / 1.69 miles

Terrain: Chaparral and light woodland / MCOSD
Elevation: From 300' to 850' / rolling, parts very steep
Intersecting Trails: Harvey Warne (.1m), Escalon-Lower Summit F.R. (.1m), Huckleberry (1.6m), Glen F.R. (1.6m)
Directions: Highway 101 — west on Tamalpais Drive (exit), Corte Madera — left on Corte Madera Avenue to opposite Chapman Avenue

CORTE MADERA RIDGE Fire Road is one of the more easily reached routes on Tam, departing directly from a main road. It also offers splendid views — of Mt. Tam when ascending, of San Francisco when dropping. It is, however, quite steep, bordered largely by the weed French broom, and has a .2-mile discontinuity that is paved and open to automobiles.

The Fire Road begins from an MCOSD-signed gate to the right, when going up Corte Madera Avenue from Corte Madera, a few yards before the Mill Valley town limits sign. There is very limited nearby off-road parking.

The initial uphill is through dense woods. A path left rises to Camino Alto Fire Road.

In .1 mile, the Fire Road meets a major, currently unsigned junction dubbed "The Octopus" by MCOSD rangers. An MMWD pumphouse is the main landmark. The eight options (hence the name) are noted clockwise. Far left, two paths head into the wooded ridge. The fire road left is Escalon-Lower Summit, to Escalon Drive in Mill Valley. A paved driveway, added in 1990, goes down to Sarah Drive in Mill Valley and up (private) to the new home higher on the ridge. Straight across, Corte Madera F.R. continues climbing. Escalon-Lower Summit F.R. right leads to Summit Drive in Corte Madera. On the far right, signed, is Harvey Warne Trail (not separately described, shorter than a quarter-mile). It leads back to Corte Madera Avenue just to the north of this Fire Road's base, with forks that wind through the forest.

Continue the very steep climb. Until a major fire management clearing effort here during the winter of 1996-97, both sides of the Fire Road were completely lined with broom. Now, the ridge's lovely native oak woodland is revealed.

The Fire Road passes within yards of the home accessed by the long driveway. In 1997, a deal was finalized in which five more homesites off Sarah Drive would be developed (the lots were listed at $1.8 million each!) but 42 acres of the remaining adjacent private lands south and west of the Fire Road protected and added to the MCOSD. Neighborhood residents, the City of Mill Valley, the MCOSD, and the Tamalpais Conservation Club were among major contributors to the purchase fund.

The route dips. Paths branch left and right from the saddle. The uphill resumes. Splendid views open behind, particularly now that much of the encroaching brush has been cleared.

In .7 miles, the Fire Road meets a gate at Corte Madera's narrow Summit Drive. There are two options up — .2 miles on the asphalt or an overgrown path to the left, behind a separate gate. (Each December, the houses on this section of Summit Drive form the very top of the Christmas Tree Hill night lights.) The path and road meet atop Summit Drive near the gate and MCOSD sign that mark the continuation of Corte Madera Ridge F.R. There are only a couple of parking places here. The road to the left of the gate leads to a private residence.

The Fire Road circles high above Warner Canyon. The actual ridge top of what is called Little Tamalpais is a few yards up on the right; a path traverses it. A fire road that old maps showed branching left is now overgrown by broom in its early yards, and completely impassable later.

There are several outstanding Mt. Tam vista points. Look back to get equally dramatic City skyline views. In .6 miles from the Summit Drive gate, the Fire Road meets a four-way intersection. Huckleberry Trail drops right to Southern Marin Line Fire Road. To the left, Glen Fire Road descends Warner Canyon to Mill Valley.

Corte Madera Ridge F.R. rises to command a glorious view to the north and south. It drops, then rises again. The Fire Road ends at its junction, called Judy's Corner by some equestrians, with Blithedale Ridge F.R. The top of 937-foot Blithedale Knoll is just above. This is another stunning view site. Blithedale Ridge F.R. goes left to Mill Valley and right to Indian Fire Road.

Corte Madera del Presidio ("cut wood for the Presidio" in Spanish) was the name of the 8,000 acre rancho, covering much of the southeast of the Mountain, granted to John Reed by the Mexican government in 1834. The land, in which redwoods once ran down to the bay margin, was logged early in the European settlement of the Bay Area (San Francisco's Presidio dates from 1776) and more heavily in Gold Rush days. There is a separate Corte Madera Trail running between Hoo-Koo-E-Koo F.R. and Old Railroad Grade.

DAWN FALLS TRAIL
FROM WEST BALTIMORE AVENUE, LARKSPUR, TO HOO-KOO-E-KOO TRAIL /
1.84 miles

Terrain: Deep woodland; riparian / MCOSD
Elevation: 160' to 640' / eastern half almost level, western half very steep
Intersecting Trails: Barbara Spring (.6m), Ladybug (1.1m), Southern Marin Line
F.R. (1.6m)
Directions: Baltimore Canyon (Valley Way) trailhead — cross bridge

DAWN FALLS is one of the more accessible of the Mountain's larger waterfalls, just 1.5 miles west of central Larkspur. The redwood-lined Trail to it is well-used all year; in winter, for viewing the falls, in summer as a cool escape.

As there is presently no public passage through from West Baltimore Avenue, Dawn Falls Trail is usually joined midway. From Magnolia Avenue, follow Madrone Avenue to its end at Valley Way, park in a designated white zone, then cross the bridge over Larkspur Creek. Dawn Falls Trail goes both left and right.

First, I'll describe the route to the right, upstream, which leads to the falls and other trail options. In 50 yards, marked by an MCOSD sign, is the lower end of Barbara Spring Trail. It rises very steeply to Southern Marin Line F.R.

In another .1 mile is an old fence. When it was erected, in 1971, a public outcry ensued and passage was reopened. (A colorful story is told in the fine book, *Larkspur, Past and Present*, of how longtime landowner Adolph Tiscornia and a hired hand once patrolled the area with shotguns.) The lands south-southwest of the creek, known as Northridge and extending into Mill Valley, were purchased as open space in the late 1970's (for the now hard-to-believe price of $650 per acre) and the full Trail is now open to the public.

Just beyond, the Trail goes over a short hill. In the creek here are remnants of a dam that once stored drinking water for Larkspur. After a drowning here in the 1920's, the dam, no longer in use, was dynamited. The route narrows to trail width; the broader road was maintained as a vehicular access to the dam from the east.

The Trail skirts the edge of lively Larkspur Creek. After a sizable rain, the creek overruns sections of the Trail, requiring some scrambling along the bank. Redwoods line the way. There are several old quarry sites, where blue basalt was taken from rock faces. Some of the basalt went into downtown Larkspur's historic Blue Rock Inn.

A path rises left, immediately passing two wood "forts." It leads to Southern Marin Line Fire Road near H-Line F.R.

In a small meadow on the right is a wintering ground for ladybugs; I've seen them completely cover the vegetation. The ladybugs apparently ride thermal winds here from the Sacramento Valley in fall, then back in spring. Across the creek here, which is not fordable in winter, is the recently re-cleared Ladybug Trail. It rises steeply to King Mountain Loop Trail. (The MCOSD has talked of relocating the base of Ladybug Trail some 300 yards upstream and building another bridge over Larkspur Creek there.)

The Trail begins rising, soon steeply. Switchbacks, cut in the mid-1980's, help. Then Dawn Falls themselves are reached. Two forks of Larkspur Creek converge and promptly plummet 25 feet. Come after a mid-winter rain and you'll be rewarded with a torrent; in the summer the falls are barely a trickle. There are rocks on which to sit and enjoy this special place.

More switchbacks and steps lead up to Southern Marin Line F.R. at a signed junction. It is .3 miles right to Kentfield's Crown Road, actually a closer trailhead to Dawn Falls.

Cross the fire road to continue. This upper part of Dawn Falls Trail, though old, was improved and signed only in 1988. It rises very steeply up the redwood-lined creek canyon.

Dawn Falls Trail ends at its junction with Hoo-Koo-E-Koo Trail. To the right is a downhill back to Southern Marin Line F.R., to the left a climb to Blithedale Ridge.

Now let's "jump" back to the bridge over Larkspur Creek to visit the broader, eastern section of Dawn Falls Trail (separately called Baltimore Canyon Fire Road on some old trail maps). Homes line the left bank of the creek. There are no other bridges. Second-growth redwoods tower above.

Soon after a prominent clearing on the right, the Trail deadends abruptly at a fence. Beyond is the private property of the last house on West Baltimore Avenue, in which the late singer Janis Joplin once lived.

Until 1990, passage was informally permitted through the property or on a path along the creek's edge. Both options have since been closed, to the dismay of the MCOSD and many users. The only way out, other than retracing your steps, is over a path on the right, at the fence line. This path, which improves beyond the first creek crossing, winds a half-mile, past a couple of homes, to the paved upper end of Piedmont Road. Piedmont is the first street south of West Baltimore off Magnolia Avenue.

The name Baltimore Canyon comes from a Maryland concern, the Baltimore & Frederick Mining and Trading Co. The firm brought a sawmill around Cape Horn to the head of the heavily wooded canyon in 1849. Company employees took the shorter route across the Isthmus of Panama, which proved miserable, and several died. They began logging the canyon's giant redwoods, some said to be nearly 300 feet high and one reputed to be the tallest tree ever found. The lumber was carted by oxen to an estuary of Corte Madera Creek, floated to the docks at Ross Landing (by today's College Avenue-Sir Francis Drake intersection), then shipped to San Francisco. The firm, its workers afflicted by gold fever, sold the mill after just five months. All the remainder of Baltimore Canyon's old growth redwoods (with apparently a few exceptions above the canyon floor) were cut in the next few years. Today's route along the creek follows the original logging road.

Since Dawn Falls faces southeast, the "Dawn" perhaps refers to the wooded area's early morning light. Larkspur Creek was also earlier known as Arroyo Holon.

ESCALON-LOWER SUMMIT FIRE ROAD
FROM ESCALON DRIVE, MILL VALLEY, TO SUMMIT DRIVE, CORTE MADERA /
1.26 miles

Terrain: Southern half grassland, northern half woodland / MCOSD
Elevation: Around 400' / almost level
Intersecting Trails: Camino Alto F.R. (.1m), Corte Madera Ridge F.R. (.7m), Harvey Warne (.7m)
Directions: Escalon Drive trailhead

A LEVEL FIRE ROAD runs from one end of Mill Valley's Escalon Drive to Summit Drive in Corte Madera. It is the southernmost section of the long Southern Marin Line, under which water from the Bon Tempe Treatment (Filter) Plant is piped. Because the Southern Marin Line has several discontinuities as a fire road, only the 2.8-mile section between Kent Woodlands and Larkspur is given that name in this book. Here, this Fire Road is unofficially called Escalon-Lower Summit, for its two ends and because MCOSD rangers use the name. There is adequate street parking only on the Mill Valley end, in the Northridge subdivision, so that is our starting point.

Pass the gate and almost immediately, behind, are lovely views of the San Francisco skyline. Broom, which thrives along disturbed Tam road cuts such as here, lines the way.

In .1 mile, the Fire Road crosses Camino Alto F.R. This four-way junction is called "Escalon Octopus" by the rangers. Left leads to Del Casa Drive in Mill Valley. Right connects to Camino Alto. Note the first of many signs of the pipeline.

The next virtually flat stretch is lightly wooded. Redwoods mix with madrones and oaks. There are striking Mt. Tamalpais vistas.

The Fire Road then meets the unsigned "Octopus" junction. Corte Madera Ridge F.R. crosses left (up to higher on Corte Madera's Summit Drive and on to Blithedale Ridge) and right (down to Camino Alto). A paved driveway drops to Sarah Drive and up (private) to a residence. Harvey Warne Trail (to Camino Alto) and other paths also meet here. Escalon-Lower Summit F.R. continues directly across, past the water pump building.

The last half-mile, in which the slight uphill is noticeable, is well-wooded. Madrone, laurel, redwood and the shrub hazel are most common. Several paths veer off right to cross the woodland between the Fire Road and Camino Alto. There is also a path up left to Corte Madera Ridge Fire Road.

The Fire Road ends at a gate with an MCOSD "Northridge, Blithedale Summit" sign between the private residences of #151 and #155 Summit Drive in Corte Madera. Parking is extremely limited on this northern end; use only designated spaces outlined in white. This access point is called Lower Summit by the rangers because there are two MCOSD entry gates higher (Middle Summit and Upper Summit).

From the gate you can go uphill a few yards on Summit to steps labeled

Spring Trail, and follow them (in total, called Hill Path), down to the junction of Tamalpais Avenue and Camino Alto in central Corte Madera. Higher on Summit are loop options with Corte Madera Ridge F.R. The hill itself is known as "Christmas Tree Hill"; in December, residents collectively display lights in the shape of a tree.

The Fire Road was built in 1950 as part of the Southern Marin Line project, bringing water from the Bon Tempe treatment plant to southern Marin users. Escalon is a city in Mexico where a key battle in that country's war for independence was fought. The name has come to signify "stepping stone."

HOO-KOO-E-KOO TRAIL & FIRE ROAD
FROM SOUTHERN MARIN LINE FIRE ROAD TO MATT DAVIS TRAIL / 4.04 miles

Terrain: Part woodland, part chaparral / MCOSD & MMWD
Elevation: From 510' to 1,200' / gradual, short parts steep
Intersecting Trails: Dawn Falls (.5m), Blithedale Ridge F.R. (.9m), Corte Madera (1.5m), Garden Pump (2.0m), Wheeler (2.3m), connector to Temelpa (2.5m), Temelpa (2.7m), Murray (3.1m), Old Railroad Grade (3.1-3.2m), Old Plane (3.1m), Hogback F.R. (3.9m)
Directions: Southern Marin Line Fire Road trailhead, Kentfield — Southern Marin Line F.R., .1 mile
Spur: To Blithedale Ridge F.R., .2 miles

Hoo-Koo-E-Koo (most people emphasize the second syllable, some the third) is among the more colorful of the Mountain's trail names. One version of the origin says it was purely an invention of Dan Totheroh in his oft-performed Mountain Play, "Tamalpa." Others say a band of Coast Miwok Indians of that name once lived around the base of the Mountain. Harry Allen, president of the TCC when the Trail was started in 1915, applied the name after Indian middens, or waste sites, were found near the route. It has also been known as Kentfield-Ocean Trail since, combined with Matt Davis Trail, it could be taken to the Pacific. In the 1950's, Hoo-Koo-E-Koo's lower, easternmost section was covered during the development of Kent Woodlands, and the middle segment, half its length, was widened to a fire road. Still, Hoo-Koo-E-Koo remains a well-used Mountain route. The trail and fire road designations are used as appropriate.

Hoo-Koo-E-Koo Trail presently begins 100 yards in (from the Kentfield end) of Southern Marin Line Fire Road. It rises to the right, at an MCOSD sign, at the Fire Road's first bend. Hoo-Koo-E-Koo Trail immediately enters woodland, and climbs. The opening yards are the steepest (and least distinct) of the entire four mile distance. In .1 mile a path, actually an old segment of the Trail, enters on the right; veer left.

The Trail runs parallel to, and above, Southern Marin Line F.R., which is occasionally visible. A rich variety of native plant life is quickly evident. A steep path drops left. Fifty yards beyond, signed Dawn Falls Trail descends to the fire road and on to Dawn Falls and Madrone Canyon.

The Trail rises into open chaparral, and offers striking views over Madrone (Baltimore) Canyon. It then meets and crosses Blithedale Ridge Fire Road. The fragrance of ceanothus pervades this intersection in spring.

Directly across the ridge top, the Trail begins circling above Blithedale Canyon. (The newest MMWD map labels this section of Hoo-Koo-E-Koo as Echo Rock Trail.) Around a quarter-mile past the Blithedale intersection, the Trail encounters, on the right, a massive outcropping of greenstone basalt, Echo Rock. Basalt is formed in ocean floor fissures; the greenish tinges are from the mineral chlorite. Echo Rock is well named; give it a try. Sound carries remarkably well here. In certain conditions, you can hear every word of conversations nearly a mile away in the canyon.

Hoo-Koo-E-Koo then enters a dense stand of young redwoods; mature groves have larger, more spaced trees. Just ahead, at Corte Madera Creek, there is a signed intersection. Corte Madera Trail drops steeply left toward Old Railroad Grade. An old pre-slide Hoo-Koo-E-Koo Trail routing continues straight, quickly to end. Clamber right up a few root-covered yards to Hoo-Koo-E-Koo Fire Road. The route right (called a Spur here) runs 400 steep uphill yards to a junction with Blithedale Ridge F.R., just below Knob Hill and Indian Fire Road. It offers a loop option back to Crown Road.

Continuing left, Hoo-Koo-E-Koo Fire Road crosses over the creek, which flows even in mid-summer. A horse trough is a fairly new addition.

The climb is noticeable, but gradual. Open areas with fine views alternate with, at stream crossings, groves of redwoods. A half-mile beyond Corte Madera Trail, in the second dense redwood grove, an unsigned trail drops left. It is the top of very steep Garden Pump Trail, which drops to Old Railroad Grade. A pipe (marked HK6) brings a creek under Hoo-Koo-E-Koo F.R. here.

In another 1/3 mile is the signed, lower end of Wheeler Trail. A concrete platform, part of the old Slide Gulch water intake, is in the creek bed to the right. Wheeler rises very steeply to Eldridge Grade.

In .2 more miles, just after an exceptional view spot, a connector to Temelpa Trail descends left. A small tanbark oak guards its entrance, which now has a generic MMWD sign. In 1/8 mile, Hoo-Koo-E-Koo F.R. crosses the infamously steep Temelpa itself at a newly signed junction. Left leads down to Fern Canyon Road (the paved section of Old Railroad Grade) and right up to Verna Dunshee Trail below the East Peak summit.

Hoo-Koo-E-Koo has turned from the eastern to the southern flank of the Mountain. Excellent vistas continue. At a creek crossing, lined with redwoods, two generically signed paths drop left on opposite banks. The first is unnamed, the second is Murray Trail. Both descend .2 miles to Old Railroad Grade a few yards in from Fern Canyon Road.

Fifteen yards later, Hoo-Koo-E-Koo meets the Grade itself near the top of the Double Bowknot. The Grade goes uphill to the right, on its steady climb up Tamalpais. Unmarked Old Plane Trail also rises from this junction. Hoo-Koo-E-Koo continues left, combined with the Grade.

Within less than .1 mile of downhill, Hoo-Koo-E-Koo branches to the right as a Trail again. At this same junction, a connector path rises to higher on Railroad Grade.

Next is another lovely stretch of Hoo-Koo-E-Koo. It runs in and out of redwood groves, and has sweeping southern panoramas. After .6 miles as a Trail, Hoo-Koo-E-Koo crosses Hogback Fire Road. To the left is Mountain Home Inn (which had been visible for a while) and up to the right is Old Railroad Grade.

Hoo-Koo-E-Koo has less than .2 miles remaining. Near its end, it crosses a stream over a bridge and passes a magnificent redwood with spiraled bark. Scientists remain uncertain about what causes this spiraling, which is also found in sequoias, cousins of the redwoods. Above to the right are two old outhouses.

Hoo-Koo-E-Koo ends at its junction with Matt Davis Trail, by Fern Creek. Matt Davis fulfills the promise of a trip to the ocean. Left on Matt Davis is a return to Hogback F.R. above Mountain Home.

HUCKLEBERRY TRAIL
FROM SOUTHERN MARIN LINE F.R. TO CORTE MADERA RIDGE F.R. / .61 miles

Terrain: Mixed, redwoods and chaparral / MCOSD
Elevation: From 480' to 800' / very steep
Intersecting Trails: None
Directions: Magnolia Ave., Larkspur — Wiltshire Ave. — Marina Vista Ave. — Sunrise Lane; very limited nearby parking

HUCKLEBERRY TRAIL rises from the Larkspur end of Southern Marin Line Fire Road. The Trail's start, marked by an MCOSD signpost, is ten yards before the second gate when approaching from Sunrise Lane in Larkspur, ten yards past the fire road gate when coming from Kentfield's Crown Road.

Most of the stiff uphill is in the early going. Huckleberry bushes line the Trail. Chinquapin is the common short tree.

About a quarter-mile up, at a forest edge by a stand of tanbark oaks, are a handful of western rhododendron (*Rhododendron macrophyllum*) bushes on both sides of the Trail. They are in the same genus as the more locally abundant western azalea but, unlike the azalea, keep their leathery leaves all year. Rhododendrons are more associated with coastal woodlands to the north; this is one of only some five places that they grow naturally in Marin. Ben Schmidt, who helped build the Trail in the 1950's, prefers his original name of Rhododendron Trail.

The Trail passes several redwood groves and occasionally narrows to squeeze through. A promising-looking path left quickly deadends.

In its upper reaches, Huckleberry Trail is more open, through chaparral, with broad views. Manzanita joins huckleberry as the common shrubs.

One last redwood grove and Huckleberry meets Corte Madera Ridge Fire Road at a four-way intersection. Left on Corte Madera Ridge goes to Summit Drive in Corte Madera and right to Blithedale Ridge F.R. Be sure to climb a few yards to the right for an exceptional Tam view. Glen Fire Road goes straight ahead; it branches into two forks that descend both sides of Warner Canyon.

Huckleberry is abundant along many of Tam's trails. The three-to-eight foot shrub has toothed leaves and white-to-pink bell-shaped flowers in clusters. In late summer and fall, the small berries make delicious eating; they're sweetest when black.

INDIAN FIRE ROAD
FROM PHOENIX ROAD, KENTFIELD, TO ELDRIDGE GRADE / 1.33 miles

Terrain: Open ridge top; chaparral bordered by madrones / MMWD
Elevation: From 560' to 1,400' / lower half rolling and very steep, upper half gradual
Intersecting Trails: Kent F.R. (.4m), Blithedale Ridge F.R. (.8m)
Directions: Woodland Road, Kentfield — right on Goodhill Road — left on Crown Road to Phoenix Road

INDIAN FIRE ROAD starts almost 500 feet higher than nearby Phoenix Lake trailhead, offering quicker access to high on the Mountain. It traverses an exposed ridge above the deep canyon of Bill Williams Gulch. There are wonderful views almost the whole way. Sections are as steep as any fire road on the Mountain. To make the going even more tiring, some of the elevation gains are lost in four separate dips, requiring additional climbing.

Indian Fire Road once rose directly from atop Kent Woodlands' Windy Ridge. Its lower part is now paved over as Phoenix Road. The start is now at an MMWD-signed gate, on the right when going uphill on Phoenix Road. A few yards past, at the end of Phoenix Road, is another gate behind which the continuing Harry Allen Trail drops and Kent Fire Road rises. The latter, shaded and more gradual, rejoins Indian F.R. for a short loop option.

Indian Fire Road is immediately steep; there's more of the same ahead. The stiff uphills are followed by short level or downhill stretches, earning this stretch the designation of "the roller coaster." (Another "roller coaster" on Tam is lower Blithedale Ridge F.R.) At the first crest, in 200 yards, is a great Mt. Tamalpais summit scene. A 250,000 gallon water tank is on the left. Ceanothus shrubs provide blue color and a pleasing fragrance in early spring.

The Fire Road is criss-crossed with overgrown paths, remnants of a more extensive trail network here before the development of Kent Woodlands after World War II. In .2 miles, a path connects down and left to Kent Fire Road.

In .4 miles, there is a four-way junction, presently unsigned. Kent (Evergreen) Fire Road crests here, dropping left back to Phoenix Road and right to Evergreen Drive.

A stiff up, down, then up again leads to another fire road on the left. This is the northern end of Blithedale Ridge F.R., 100 yards above its junction with Hoo-Koo-E-Koo F.R. Continue uphill. An old sign points the way to Larkspur's Baltimore Park, once the nearest railroad station (train service ended in 1941).

About 150 yards higher, just before a bend right, now-closed Indian Fire Trail sets off straight uphill. One of the oldest trails on the Mountain (referred to in an 1876 article), it offered a precipitous trip to the summit. It was widened to a 100-foot fire break in the 1930's. Indian Fire Trail is now off-limits, blocked at its several crossings of Eldridge Grade above, to limit erosion and to allow vegetation to cover its still highly visible slash.

Indian Fire Road enters some shade, and the uphill finally eases. Look right, over Bill Williams Gulch, to see the part of Indian F.R. you've already climbed. There's even a brief downhill.

The Fire Road continues climbing, into redwoods. An old water tank stands at a crossing of a fork of Bill Williams Creek. Another 100 yards of uphill brings Indian Fire Road to its end at Eldridge Grade. It is 2.4 miles left up to the East Peak parking area; right leads down to the lakes.

"Indians" began settling Marin's shores some 5,000 years ago, possibly earlier. The local Coast Miwoks lived largely on acorns, shellfish, fish, and berries and other vegetation. They had year-round settlements along Tam's bay margins and seasonal camps higher on the Mountain.

Within just a few years of permanent European settlement in Marin, which began with the establishment of Mission San Rafael Arcangel in 1817, the Coast Miwoks lost all their land and were virtually extirpated by disease. A Marin population of some 3,000 in 1800 was reduced by 90 percent by 1840. Sharp-eyed Tam hikers still find mounds of crushed white shells from Miwok middens (waste piles).

The native Indians revered Mount Tamalpais, possibly never venturing to its top. Experts debate whether the famous story about a "sleeping maiden" forming the profile of the Mountain's summit ridge is an Indian legend or, more likely, a later creation.

KENT FIRE ROAD
FROM PHOENIX ROAD TO EVERGREEN DRIVE, KENTFIELD / .67 miles

Terrain: Woodland and chaparral / MCOSD
Elevation: From 580' to 800' to 620' / steep, parts very steep
Intersecting Trails: Indian F.R. (.4m)
Directions: Woodland Road, Kentfield — right on Goodhill Road — left on Crown Road to Phoenix Road

SEVERAL ROADS AND TRAILS branch off from near the junction of Crown and Phoenix roads high in Kent Woodlands. Proceeding up Crown from Goodhill Road, the first is Harry Allen Trail, which drops to Phoenix Lake. Just ahead, at the Phoenix-Crown junction, Crown Road branches left, unpaved, for one-quarter mile, and Tucker Cutoff Trail starts precipitously right behind the steel barrier. Next, Indian Fire Road sets off uphill to the right. At the upper end of Phoenix Road, behind a wood barrier with an MCOSD "Northridge/Baltimore Canyon" sign, Harry Allen Trail continues to the left, dropping to reconnect with the southern half of Crown Road. And, directly ahead, Kent Fire Road begins its climb.

Kent is presently its true fire road-width. In the past, broom narrowed the route to trail-width and threatened to block it altogether.

The climb is through a forest of mostly young redwoods, with tanbark oaks and madrones common as well. At .3 miles, a short connector to Indian Fire Road rises to the right.

Kent Fire Road crests at a presently unsigned four-way junction with fine Tam views. To the right, Indian Fire Road returns to Phoenix Road. (Kent is used as a shaded, less steep alternative to Indian F.R.) Immediately left, Kent Fire Road continues. In the middle, Indian F.R. continues up to Eldridge Grade.

The descent route is separately designated as Evergreen Fire Road by the MMWD. It is heavily eroded and, in recent wet winters, has been posted as closed. The loose rocks demand caution. There are fine northern views. A water tank, now topped with communication equipment, is a landmark.

Kent Fire Road ends at a gate atop Evergreen Drive in Kent Woodlands. (There are presently no parking restriction signs lower on Evergreen, but the emergency vehicle minimum mid-road clearance requirement must be observed.) Kent F.R. originally connected to the Ross Valley and the Northwestern Pacific Railroad line. Its entire course was through property of the Kent family, although through passage by hikers was generally permitted. The family developed Kent Woodlands after World War II. The original Kent family home (now owned by others) still stands at the base of Evergreen, across Woodland Avenue.

KING MOUNTAIN LOOP TRAIL
AROUND KING MOUNTAIN / 1.95 miles

Terrain: Mostly oak-madrone woodland / MCOSD & private (easement)
Elevation: Around 600' / mostly level
Intersecting Trails: Cedar F.R.(.6m), Ladybug (1.5m)
Directions: End of Ridgecrest Road, Kent Woodlands
Spur: To Wilson Way, .1 mile

In 1994, a delightful new loop trail on the hitherto private upper reaches of King Mountain was opened to the public. Marin County Open Space District workers, led by Senior Ranger John Aranson, who hiked the area as a boy, cleared old routes, cut new paths, opened fences and added trail signs. The County had acquired 131 acres outright and 129 acres of easement in a deal with the Tiscornia Estate, long-time owners of King Mountain. In exchange, the County approved plans for estate-sized homes to be built on the mountain's still pristine 161 acre summit.

King Mountain Loop Trail can be accessed from four trailheads: Wilson Way, Cedar Avenue, and Skylark Drive, all in Larkspur, and Ridgecrest Road in Kent Woodlands. Wilson Way (from Madrone Avenue via Redwood Avenue and Oak Road) is long, narrow and circuitous, with limited parking. Cedar Avenue requires a .7 mile uphill trek. The Skylark Drive entry, beside a huge apartment complex, has virtually no public parking. Ridgecrest Road may become the main public access, so is used here.

The entry from Ridgecrest Road will probably change when the home sites atop King Mountain are developed. Presently, a dirt road sets off behind a gate by the last house on Ridgecrest. There is a fork in 100 yards. Straight ahead (presently a dirt fire road) will likely be the paved extension of Ridgecrest. To the right is an MCOSD "Public Trail" sign, one "end" of the King Mountain Loop Trail. To the left, just uphill, is another "Public Trail" sign, which will mark our start. Many visitors note that the loop somehow feels net downhill when followed in this clockwise direction.

Certainly the start is sharply downhill, with steps and wood fences aiding. This is an entirely new (1995-96) Trail section, replacing an old route called Pipeline. In 200 yards, a path branches off at a bend right. Immediately after, the Trail enters a redwood forest. There is a quiet, timeless quality to this woodland, although it is less than a mile, as the crow flies, from busy Magnolia Avenue.

A bridge crosses a creek. Look up the bed to see stands of pampas grass (*Cortaderia*), a hardy South American invader that some regard as almost as menacing to native flora as broom is.

In a half-mile from the start, look left for a handful of what appear to be first growth redwoods. Why these giants escaped the loggers who cut here in the 1850's is unknown. Beyond, laurels dominate.

At .6 miles, the Loop Trail crosses Cedar Fire Road. Left goes to the Skylark Apartments and on to Larkspur's Cedar Avenue. Right is a deadend at the private property line. The Trail continues directly across, immediately passing a massive old oak.

Fifty yards in, the Trail meets an open area with splendid views extending to Mount Diablo and the San Francisco skyline. This pattern of light woodland and open areas is repeated the rest of the way. A few feet beyond, a path drops left and another rises right, both to Cedar F.R.

The Trail runs almost level through a typical Tam broad-leaved forest of coast live oaks, madrones, tanbark oaks and buckeyes. Broom, however, has crowded out many of the native wildflowers.

There are views across Baltimore Canyon of the heavily wooded, seemingly untouched north wall of Corte Madera Ridge, also known as "Little Tamalpais." There are also breathtaking shots of Tam's East Peak.

At 1.4m, after a short downhill, the Trail meets a signed junction. Left is a 100-yard Spur to the top of Wilson Way. To the right is a now overgrown path signed as closed. Continue straight across and bend right.

This next section was built by the MCOSD in 1994. In 200 yards there is another fork, also marked by an MCOSD signpost. Left and down is Ladybug Trail to Baltimore Canyon (and to Dawn Falls Trail if Larkspur Creek is fordable). Take it at least a few yards to a clearing offering one of the finest of all Mt. Tamalpais vistas.

The Trail continues winding around King Mountain. Homes high in Kent Woodlands come into view. There is a fork; the option left is less steep. The loop ends within 100 yards.

Patrick King and his partner William Murray bought 1,234 acres of the southern Ross Valley from the Ross family in the late 1860's. The two then divided the parcel. Murray got the northern part, which included today's Kent Woodlands. King took the southern half, including today's downtown Larkspur and the hill that came to be known as King Mountain. (There is also an adjacent smaller hill called Little King.) Much of King's land was then used for dairying and grazing. The name King Mountain Loop Trail is my own; the MCOSD has not yet formally selected one.

LADYBUG TRAIL
FROM KING MOUNTAIN LOOP TRAIL TO BALTIMORE CANYON / .47 miles

Terrain: Broad-leaved woodland / MCOSD
Elevation: From 575' to 180' / steep, parts very steep
Intersecting Trails: None
Directions: King Mountain Loop Trail north from Spur to Wilson Way, .1m

LADYBUG TRAIL was an informal path upgraded by John Aranson of the MCOSD (but not yet fully to standards regarding steepness) as part of opening King Mountain to the public. The Trail sets off left and downhill from the King Mountain Loop Trail, .1m from the Wilson Way (Larkspur) access Spur. An MCOSD sign marks the junction.

A few yards down, the wood canopy clears to open splendid view. A tree-framed vista of Tam's entire east face is among the more dramatic Mountain shots anywhere.

A quarter-mile down, a haunting, level madrone grove is reached. There are still signs of the "hippie" commune that camped here, drawing water from the creek below, in the 1960's. Below are the Trail's steepest and most slippery sections, demanding extra caution.

The Trail ends when it meets Larkspur Creek. There is no sign, and the last yards are indistinct. (The MCOSD has considered making the lower part of the Trail more gradual by bringing it out some 300 yards west, where a new bridge over Larkspur Creek may be built.) In winter, there is no dry fording; a return uphill is the only option. In summer and early fall the creek bed can be easily crossed and the connection to Dawn Falls Trail, at a grassy clearing on the other bank, completed.

This clearing has been a wintering home to tens of thousands of ladybugs (also known as ladybird beetles). The ladybugs ride wind currents here from the Central Valley in fall, then ride them back again in spring. *Hippodomia convergens* is the most common, and familiar, of some 125 California ladybug species. The clearing was disturbed in 1996; hopefully the ladybugs will return.

The Trail was carved as an access to the Tiscornia Estate atop King Mountain. The route originally went higher, traces of which are still evident. MCOSD field personnel called it Contractors Trail for want of a better designation. I use the more attractive appellation Ladybug Trail; an official name will be designated by the MCOSD after discussion with community groups.

SOUTHERN MARIN LINE FIRE ROAD
FROM CROWN ROAD, KENT WOODLANDS, TO SUNRISE LANE, LARKSPUR / 2.78 miles

Terrain: Moderately wooded hillside; heavily used / MCOSD
Elevation: Around 500' / level
Intersecting Trails: Hoo-Koo-E-Koo (.1m), Dawn Falls (.3), H-Line F.R. (1.2m), Barbara Spring (1.6m)
Directions: Southern Marin Line trailhead, Kent Woodlands

BECAUSE SOUTHERN MARIN is the longest level fire road on Tam, and is easily accessible, it is popular among many user groups; walkers, dog-owners, runners, and bikers. It is very commonly called Crown Road because it appears to be a continuation of that Kent Woodlands street. Crown Road is also the principal access point because parking is better than at the Larkspur end. (Be mindful of nearby residents, and of the several "no parking" signs added in 1989.) But Southern Marin Line Road is a better designation as the route was completed in 1951 as part of the MMWD's Southern Marin Line project to bring a 24-inch water pipeline from the new Bon Tempe treatment plant to southern Marin.

The Fire Road begins beyond the gate. There is an inspiring view of Mt. Tam's summit right at the start. To the east is King Mountain, Corte Madera Ridge and, on clear days, Mount Diablo.

French broom has become the dominant road-side vegetation. There are periodic broom cuts, but the hearty shrub invariably returns quickly.

In 100 yards, Hoo-Koo-E-Koo Trail rises on the right. It climbs to Blithedale Ridge Fire Road, then continues to Matt Davis Trail. Loops can be made by taking Hoo-Koo-E-Koo and returning to Southern Marin Line by either Dawn Falls Trail, H-Line Fire Road, or Huckleberry Trail.

In .3 miles, Dawn Falls Trail crosses. To the left is a short descent to the falls. A loop can be made by continuing down Dawn Falls Trail and returning to Southern Marin Line on the very steep Barbara Spring Trail. To the right, Dawn Falls Trail rises to Hoo-Koo-E-Koo. A few yards beyond the Dawn Falls junction is a small suspension bridge nicknamed "the Little Golden Gate." It carries the Southern Marin water pipeline over a bend, then back under the Fire Road.

A few vista spots open but the route is now mostly wooded. The deep canyon below is Baltimore Canyon. The MMWD recently marked all culverts, here and on other fire roads, with coded green stakes.

At 1-1/4 miles, at a pump station, H-Line Fire Road sets off uphill to the right. Branches of the pipeline diverge here, from within the fenced enclosure, to various southern Marin water tanks. Just beyond, on the left, is a rough path down the canyon.

In another one-third mile, an MCOSD signpost on the left marks the top of Barbara Spring Trail, which descends very steeply down to Baltimore Canyon. Beyond, a pair of fences block off a slide area.

Continue winding around the many bends. The terrain again opens. Look back for more splendid Tam shots.

At a bend right at 2.5 miles, its entrance only faintly visible between a madrone and a manzanita bush, is the top of unmaintained Big Dog Trail. It drops steeply for just under a quarter-mile (so not separately described) to the unpaved west end of Larkspur's Piedmont Road. (Big Dog is an unofficial name. In 1996, an area couple, bereaved over the death of their dalmation, placed a professional-quality signpost carved "Big Dog Tr." 50 yards above the trail's lower end.)

Southern Marin Line Fire Road ends at a gate. A few yards beyond, on the right, is Huckleberry Trail, which goes uphill to Corte Madera Ridge F.R. The street ahead is Sunrise Lane, off Marina Vista Avenue, in Larkspur. A sign at this end, "#10 Fire Road," points to a private residence; it has led many users to mistakenly call Southern Marin Line, "Fire Road 10." The Southern Marin pipeline itself continues to the Alto water tanks in Mill Valley.

TUCKER CUTOFF TRAIL
FROM CROWN ROAD TO TUCKER TRAIL / .26 miles

Terrain: Light woodland
Elevation: From 510' to 420' / gradual, top extremely steep
Intersecting Trails: None
Directions: Woodland Road, Kentfield — right on Goodhill Road — left on Crown Road to Phoenix Road

TUCKER CUTOFF offers the shortest route to Tucker Trail, and that accounts for virtually all its use.

The Cutoff descends, presently unsigned or unmarked, from directly opposite the Crown Road/Phoenix Road street sign. Go over the railing and carefully negotiate the precipitously steep opening downhill. In 25 yards, the plunge abates at a pair of MMWD trail signs and the rest of the descent is gradual.

In another 25 yards, a short bypass skirts a small slide. There is a glorious Mt. Tam view here. Rub the California sagebrush (*Artemesia californica*) leaves for a delightful fragrance.

By .1 mile, the Trail enters a light tree canopy. You can glimpse Bald Hill to the right. The woods deepen, with redwoods, laurels, madrones, and tanbark oaks.

The Cutoff ends at an unmarked crest of Tucker Trail. The Bill Williams Trail junction is 50 yards to the left. Harry Allen Trail, which offers a loop option back to Crown Road, is .7 miles to the right.

The Cutoff has long appeared on maps. It was more heavily used in the days of the Northwestern Pacific Railroad (local passenger service ended in 1941), which brought hikers to Tam's east slope.

San Francisco skyline above the fog. (Randall Hogue)

Pantoll Trailhead

Pantoll Trailhead

Directions to Pantoll (and Bootjack):
Highway 101 — Highway 1 — Panoramic Highway

PANTOLL (or Pan Toll) is a junction on *Panoramic* Highway where a *toll* house once stood, hence the name. Earlier the area was known as Summit Meadow. Two fire roads — Coastal and Old Stage — and six trails — Alpine, Easy Grade, Matt Davis, Old Mine, Stapelveldt, and Steep Ravine — converge here.

At Pantoll, the Southside (or Pantoll) Road branches uphill from Panoramic Highway to Rock Spring, Ridgecrest Boulevard, and the summit. A gate bars access before sunrise and after sunset, during high fire danger days, and in rare snowfalls. The main parking turnout on Southside Road is a mile uphill, where paths have been worn in through the grassland to stunning view knolls.

Pantoll serves as the headquarters of Mount Tamalpais State Park. Tam maps, books, and the like are sold at the ranger station, which is not always staffed due to budget cutbacks. Nearby are fountains, a large map, a telephone, and bathrooms. Down the asphalt road are ranger residences and a maintenance facility.

Pantoll is also the principal campground on the Mountain. The 16 walk-in campsites are assigned at the ranger station on a first come, first served basis. In 1998, the overnight campsite fee is $15 ($16 on Friday and Saturday nights, $2 less for seniors). Campsite #3 is reserved for hikers/bikers arriving without a car; the fee is $3. If any of the Steep Ravine cabins or campsites are available, they also can be booked at Pantoll.

Golden Gate Transit bus #63, which runs between the Golden Gate Bridge and Stinson Beach on weekends (runs may be cancelled in inclement winter winter), stops at Pantoll.

Around 1/4 mile east of Pantoll on Panoramic Highway is the Bootjack Picnic Area, another popular trailhead. Bootjack has a large parking lot, bathrooms, water fountains, picnic tables and outdoor grills. Call 456-5218 for group reservations. Matt Davis Trail connects Pantoll and Bootjack.

In 1991, a $5 vehicle parking fee was instituted at the Bootjack and Pantoll lots. At press-time, there were four or five free spaces directly across the road from Pantoll and a few road-shoulder spots just across from, and above, Bootjack.

Suggested loops from Pantoll Ranger Station (elevation 1,500'):
• Alpine Trail, .4m, to Bootjack Trail — left, .8m, across Panoramic Highway, through Bootjack Camp, to Mountain Theater — Easy Grade Trail, .7m, to Old Stage Road — right, .1m, to start **2.0 miles.**
• Stapelveldt Trail, 1.0m, to Ben Johnson Trail — right, .2m, to Deer Park F.R. — right, .4m, to Coastal F.R. — right, .6m, to start **2.2 miles.**
• Steep Ravine Trail, 1.6m, to Dipsea Trail — left, 1.4m, to Coastal F.R. — left, .2m, to Old Mine Trail — right, .3m, to start **3.5 miles.**
• Old Stage Road, .1m, to Old Mine Trail — left, 1.0m, to Mountain Theater Trail — right, .2m, through Mountain Theater to Rock Spring Trail — right, 1.4m, to

West Point — right, 1.8m, on Old Stage Road to start **4.5 miles.**
• Matt Davis Trail west, 1.6m, to Coastal Trail — right, 1.4m, to Willow Camp F.R.
— right, .1m, across Ridgecrest Blvd. to Laurel Dell F.R. — straight, .5m, to Laurel
Dell — right on Cataract Trail, 1.2m, to Rock Spring and across Ridgecrest Blvd.
— left, .1m, on Mountain Theater Trail to Old Mine Trail — right, 1.0m, to Old
Stage Road — right, .1m, to start **6.0 miles.**

ALPINE TRAIL
FROM PANTOLL TO BOOTJACK TRAIL / .35 miles

Terrain: Redwood forest / MTSP
Elevation: From 1,500' to 1,280' / steep
Intersecting Trails: None
Directions: Pantoll

ALPINE TRAIL is short and catches traffic noise of Panoramic Highway. Still, it is
well-used in journeys between Pantoll and both Muir Woods and Mountain Home.

The signed Trail begins at the Golden Gate Transit bus stop by Pantoll
Ranger Station. Also beginning here, on the right, is Stapelveldt Trail.

Alpine immediately enters a redwood forest, and begins its steep, steady
descent. Panoramic Highway is nearby, 25-100 yards across the gully. Several
trees downed in a 1989 wind storm remain where they fell.

Alpine Trail crosses a small bridge. Huge redwoods tower above. The highway noise is muted.

Alpine ends when it meets Bootjack Trail by an old bench. Left on Boot-
jack leads up to Panoramic Highway and Bootjack Camp. Right goes downhill to
Troop 80 Trail and Van Wyck Meadow, with options on to Muir Woods and
Mountain Home.

The Trail was one of the first projects of the California Alpine Club, and
has been called Alpine Club Trail. The club, formed in 1914 and active on Tam
and in the Sierra, has its headquarters at Alpine Lodge, 730 Panoramic Highway,
just below Mountain Home. The name "Alpine," synonymous with mountains,
appears elsewhere on Tamalpais. Alpine Dam, creating Alpine Lake, was built at
the old Alpine Bridge over Lagunitas Creek.

EASY GRADE TRAIL
FROM MATT DAVIS TRAIL TO THE MOUNTAIN THEATER / .60 miles

Terrain: Tanbark oak woodland / MTSP
Elevation: From 1,540' to 1,980' / steep
Intersecting Trails: Old Stage Road (.1m), Easy Grade Spur (.1m), Riding & Hiking (.2m)
Directions: Pantoll — Matt Davis Trail east, .1 mile
Amenities: Restrooms, fountains
Spur: .1 mile, to Old Stage Road

EASY GRADE TRAIL offers the most direct route from Pantoll to the Mountain Theater. The Trail starts from Matt Davis Trail, though it is more commonly joined 20 yards higher, at a pair of entrances on Old Stage Road.

Easy Grade sets off uphill into a mostly tanbark oak forest. In a bit over .1 mile of climbing, a brief opening on the right offers a view of Mountain Home and, well beyond, of Mt. Diablo.

Twenty-five yards after Easy Grade crosses a rivulet, there is a fence line and T-intersection. Easy Grade Spur comes in on the right from Old Stage Road; the single, united Easy Grade Trail rises to the left.

Just beyond in the grassy clearing is another three-way intersection. Veer right along the fence; left is a short connector to Riding & Hiking Trail. Look here for one of the Mountain's classic old signs, with both color and shape codes to show direction and route. The green and yellow shapes are still visible, but not the writing.

At the end of the fence, Riding & Hiking Trail crosses at a four-way intersection. To the left it goes to Old Mine Trail, to the right down to Old Stage Road. Both old and new signposts mark the junction. Continue straight and uphill.

Easy Grade reenters a deep woodland. There is a particularly impressive old oak on the right. A pipeline is embedded in the Trail's left margin. There is another opening, with a great shot of Tam's summit peaks.

Easy Grade ends when it meets the top of Bootjack Trail at the Mountain Theater. To the left are the stage players' dressing rooms. Follow the asphalt path to the Mountain Theater stage. Look there for the plaque — MY FEET WILL MARK THE TRAIL OF STARS — dedicated to the memory of longtime play director Dan Totheroh.

The Civilian Conservation Corps built Easy Grade in the late 1930's as a new route to the the Mountain Theater. It was less steep, an "easier grade," than older traditional Bootjack Trail up. Since Bootjack itself was rerouted in 1980, with more switchbacks, the two routes now differ little in grade.

HILL 640 FIRE ROAD
FROM PANORAMIC HIGHWAY TO HILL 640 / .30 miles

Terrain: Grassland / GGNRA
Elevation: Around 640' / rolling
Intersecting Trails: Dipsea (.1m)
Directions: Pantoll — west on Panoramic Highway to mileage marker 7.86

THIS FIRE ROAD WAS CARVED to construct and access a World War II military installation on the coastal bluff. Enter through the "Fire Lane" gate opposite milepost 7.86 on Panoramic Highway. (Another gate, behind which a short fire road drops to the Dipsea Trail, is 75 yards uphill.)

Hill 640 F.R. sets off southwest. There are immediately glorious views, of the sweep of Stinson Beach, of Bolinas, and of the Pacific. In 100 yards, the Fire Road crosses the Dipsea Trail. Stinson Beach is a mile to the right, Mill Valley six miles left. Clinging to a rock on the left are an isolated Douglas-fir and many poppies.

The Fire Road gently rises, then descends. A broad path forks uphill to the right. It leads past a few planted Monterey pines to the top of the knoll and some bunker remnants.

Hill 640 F.R. meets a lone eucalyptus. A path right across the grass connects with the Dipsea Trail.

Beyond the eucalyptus, the route simply peters out at the edge of the steep drop to Highway 1. The ten Steep Ravine cabins are visible well below.

A path to the right leads to a descending row of abandoned concrete bunkers that once served as "base end stations." Triangulation measurements were taken from here and from other similar coastal stations, such as those by Muir Beach Overlook, to calculate the distance of enemy ships. The data was then relayed to Marin Headlands gun batteries overlooking the Golden Gate.

Since the hill at the Fire Road's end is 640 feet in elevation, the U.S. Geological Survey map calls it Hill 640. The GGNRA *Park Guide* labels it White Gate Ranch Trail, for the historic ranch of that name once here.

LONE TREE HILL FIRE ROAD
FROM JUNCTION OF COASTAL F.R. AND OLD MINE TRAIL TO TOP OF LONE TREE
HILL / .27 miles

Terrain: Douglas-fir forest / MTSP
Elevation: From 1,460′ to 1,600′ / steep
Intersecting Trails: None
Directions: Pantoll — Old Mine Trail south to end

THIS BROAD ROUTE was originally a road carved in preparation for a housing development that, fortunately, was never built.

It rises directly across Coastal Fire Road from the lower end of Old Mine Trail. The signpost at the junction does not point to it, but the route does appear on the newest State Park map.

Douglas-firs dominate, and provide a haunting backdrop in the area's frequent fogs. Resident owls add to the mood.

Many of the Douglas-firs are impressive, older "wolf trees," so-called because they have massive lower limbs that "devour" (block sunlight to) vegetation below. Such trees are found where Douglas-firs advanced without competition for sunlight, certainly the case here on this formerly grazed, grassy knoll. Several remain downed from the February 1989 wind storm that closed the route for some time.

Lone Tree Hill F.R. reaches the hill's summit ridge. It continues a bit more then forks just before its end. A few yards away is grassland, and some of the best view and picnic sites on Tam. A path runs down to the Lone Tree/Coastal fire roads junction.

This hill was once known as Bald Hill; its summit was treeless through much of the first part of the 20th century. Another common name was Lone Tree Hill, for the famous, isolated "Lone Tree," a redwood, on the south face. Lone Tree Hill forms the "feet" of Tam's Sleeping Maiden summit ridge profile as seen from many vantage points, such as in the East Bay.

The route dates to the 1950's, when the hill was sold by the Brazil Ranch to developers. The road was to provide access from Panoramic Highway to the homesites. After a public outcry, the land was returned to the Brazil Ranch, whose entire 2,150 acres were then acquired by the State Park in 1968.

A separate Lone Tree Fire Road starts from the hill's southeast base and runs down to Highway 1.

OLD STAGE ROAD
FROM PANTOLL TO WEST POINT / 1.83 miles

Terrain: Lower part paved, woodland; upper part chaparral / MTSP & MMWD
Elevation: From 1,500' to 1,785' / gradual
Intersecting Trails: Matt Davis (.1m), Old Mine (.1m), Easy Grade (.1m), Easy Grade Spur (.3m), Riding & Hiking (.4m), Bootjack (.4m)
Directions: Pantoll
Amenities: Fountains, bathrooms, picnic tables

OLD STAGE ROAD was originally graded in 1902 as a wagon road to connect the Mt. Tamalpais Railway at West Point with the coastal towns of Stinson Beach (then called Willow Camp), Bolinas and Olema. There was a daily morning stage-coach departure from the West Point Inn and a return trip, with six horses pull-ing uphill, in the afternoon. A plan to extend the railway itself to Stinson — William Kent owned the entire right-of-way — never came to fruition; the auto-mobile was already making its mark.

Much of the original stage road below Pantoll has been covered by Pan-oramic Highway. The surviving Old Stage Road is now itself paved between Pantoll and Bootjack Trail. Its upper 1.4 miles, however, remain a dirt road from which the old stage days can still be imagined.

Across Panoramic Highway from Pantoll Ranger Station, two paved roads rise. The one on the left is Pantoll, or Southside, Road, open to cars heading higher on the Mountain. On the right, behind a gate, is Old Stage Road. A sign marks it as part of the Bay Area Ridge Trail.

Old Stage is very gently graded throughout. There are several trail intersec-tions in the opening .1 mile. The first, in 50 yards, is with Matt Davis going west to Stinson Beach. Ten yards later, Matt Davis departs on the right, going east toward Bootjack. In another 60 yards, Old Mine Trail heads up left to Rock Spring. Twenty yards farther, also to the left, are two entrances to Easy Grade Trail; they join and rise to the Mountain Theater. Between the two entrances, to the right, Easy Grade descends its last few yards to Matt Davis.

Trees line the Road, but breaks permit outstanding views. Incongruous high-way reflector signs, recycled from other county roads, dot Old Stage's margin.

In a half-mile is a water chlorination building, beside which is a drinking fountain. Across the Road here, behind a horse trough, Riding & Hiking Trail rises toward Rock Spring.

A few yards beyond, an asphalt road veers right; it leads to a State Park residence. Ten yards down that paved road, Bootjack Trail comes in from Boot-jack Camp. Follow Old Stage Road straight ahead. In a few yards, Bootjack Trail continues up to the left, on to the Mountain Theater. Soon, Old Stage Road becomes dirt-surfaced.

Open chaparral replaces the forest canopy, and the views are superb the rest of the trip. A gate marks the boundary between Mt. Tamalpais State Park, which you are leaving, and MMWD lands. The uphill is gentle, noticeable only when you look back or ahead. There are no intersecting trails for 1.3 miles.

Old Stage Road crosses the upper reaches of several important Tam creeks; they are, in order, Bootjack (near Bootjack Trail), two forks of Rattlesnake, and Spike Buck. Old stonework, chain ferns, and azaleas mark each crossing. Sticky monkeyflower, manzanita, chamise, toyon, and chaparral pea are common shrubs growing amidst the serpentine. Prominent is a stand of Sargent cypress trees.

West Point Inn becomes visible well before it is reached. Here stage passengers could connect with the Mt. Tamalpais & Muir Woods Railway, dine, or spend the night. The inn still offers overnight lodging (by advance reservation only) and light refreshments. There are restrooms, a fountain, and lovely view sites, some shaded, to rest and picnic. Many trails meet here. In order, clockwise, they are: Rock Spring to the Mountain Theater, Old Railroad Grade uphill, the Grade downhill, Nora to Matt Davis, and the extremely steep West Point Trail to Panoramic Highway.

RIDING & HIKING TRAIL
FROM OLD STAGE ROAD TO OLD MINE TRAIL / .40 miles

Terrain: Mostly woodland, parts grassland; horses permitted / MTSP; equestrian section of Bay Area Ridge Trail
Elevation: From 1,580' to 1,700' / gradual
Intersecting Trails: Easy Grade (.2m)
Directions: Bootjack Picnic Area — Bootjack Trail uphill, .2 miles
Amenities: Fountain

In 1945, the California State legislature authorized establishment of an equestrian route to wind through 36 counties between the Mexico and Oregon borders. It was to pass through Mt. Tamalpais. After some debate, a decision was made to use existing Tam trails and fire roads, rather than to build new ones. This Trail was an exception, built specifically to accommodate horse riders (though hikers, of course, can also take it). Redwood signposts, painted yellow on top, mark the never fully completed cross-California project. In 1989, Riding & Hiking Trail became an equestrian section of the new Bay Area Ridge Trail.

Riding & Hiking Trail sets off from the upper end of the paved section of Old Stage Road, a few yards west of the Bootjack Trail crossing. The trailhead is opposite a chlorinator building, where there is a water fountain. The Marin Horse Council donated the horse trough at the start.

Riding & Hiking Trail begins in a peaceful woodland of laurel, tanbark oak, and Douglas-fir. The uphill is gradual.

In around 1/6 mile, just past a huge oak, the Trail enters a grass clearing. There is a four-way junction where Easy Grade Trail crosses left down to Old Stage Road and right up to the Mountain Theater. Riding & Hiking Trail continues straight. In 50 yards, over a slight rise, is another junction. The path to the left is a short connector back to Easy Grade.

Riding & Hiking continues gently up. At the edge of the next grassland is one of the historic yellow-topped signposts. There are splendid views, back to Tam's three summits and Mt. Diablo and ahead to the Pacific.

The Trail returns to tanbark oak woodland. There are level sections, even dips. Riding & Hiking Trail ends when it meets Old Mine Trail. Horse riders can then continue on Old Mine (uphill only) to Rock Spring.

STAPELVELDT TRAIL
FROM PANTOLL TO BEN JOHNSON TRAIL / 1.02 miles

Terrain: Deep woods; lower half riparian / MTSP
Elevation: From 1,500' to 920' / steep
Intersecting Trails: TCC (twice at .4m)
Directions: Pantoll

VISITORS TO PANTOLL seeking the joys of a redwood-lined, creekside trail usually opt for justly famous Steep Ravine. But Stapelveldt Trail, part (with Ben Johnson Trail) of a direct route between Muir Woods and Pantoll, serves just as well.

The Trail sets off behind the Golden Gate Transit bus stop at Pantoll Ranger Station. Alpine Trail also begins here; it veers left while Stapelveldt goes right.

The early yards through the Pantoll campground may be a bit confusing; campers have worn in many paths. There is a trail sign at a crest above campsite #15, after which the route is clear.

Stapelveldt leaves the camp's ridge line and begins its steady, all-downhill journey. A huge, downed Douglas-fir may remain a feature for years. Beside it, another Douglas-fir shows the effect of a lightning strike.

In .3 miles, three small bridges are crossed in quick succession. Honeysuckle and huckleberry border the first; the delicate shrub wood rose the next two.

Just beyond, Stapelveldt meets TCC Trail at a bridge. A bench has been fashioned from an old trail sign. Old maps indicated a Camp Stapelveldt here. Left, TCC goes 1.4 miles to Bootjack Trail at Van Wyck Meadow. TCC and Stapelveldt descend together for 20 yards to a second three-way junction, where TCC departs right to the Dipsea Trail.

Stapelveldt descends the ever-deepening canyon. Switchbacks, shored by railroad ties, were built by the Youth Conservation Corps in 1978. (The added turns also make the route from the TCC junction to Ben Johnson a bit longer than the signs indicate.) The unnamed creek left is heading to Redwood Creek, then on to Muir Woods. Three feeder rivulets are crossed on bridges.

Ever more massive redwoods, some branchless for 100 feet, line the way. A fire-scarred giant can be entered. The Trail squeezes between another towering pair. Low growing oxalis, or redwood clover, borders the Trail from late winter.

Stapelveldt drops steeply to its end. The terminus is at its junction with Ben Johnson Trail, which goes straight ahead down to Muir Woods, and right up to Deer Park F.R. and the Dipsea Trail. There is a bench to rest at this peaceful spot.

In 1989, Fred Sandrock of the Mt. Tamalpais History Project published evidence that the Trail was named for Wilhelm (William) Stapelfeldt. Stapelfeldt was born in Germany in 1839. He came to San Francisco, where he worked as a grocer. He was apparently a hiking partner of legendary Tamalpais figures such as Emil Barth, Edward Ziesche, and Alice Eastwood, and did much trail work. He died in 1912. The Trail has known some half-dozen different spellings.

STEEP RAVINE TRAIL
FROM PANTOLL TO HIGHWAY 1 / 2.12 miles

Terrain: Riparian; redwood forest / MTSP
Elevation: From 1,500' to 430' / very steep
Intersecting Trails: Dipsea (1.6m, 1.7m)
Directions: Pantoll

STEEP RAVINE is widely considered among the most beautiful trails on Mt. Tamalpais, if not in all of California. Few who traverse it come away unmoved by its beauty. There are so many treasures to be found along its way that I am loath to single out just a few.

The Trail begins a few yards below Pantoll Ranger Station, to the right off the road leading to the maintenance area. The upper part has been rerouted, with switchbacks added to lessen the steepness and to help prevent erosion.

The route starts, and remains, fairly near to Panoramic Highway. But a bit lower, Webb Creek, adjacent the rest of the way, muffles any road noise and drowns it completely in winter.

Early on are downed trees that must be ducked under, a feature of the Trail throughout. In .3 miles, at the base of the switchbacks, is a bench, particularly welcome to those ascending. At this bend are the uppermost redwoods in the canyon. One in particular is enormous, among the most impressive on Tam outside of Muir Woods. Redwoods remain companions the rest of the route down.

The Trail crosses a few rivulets, feeders to Webb Creek. Then, in .5 miles, the Trail meets Webb Creek, which began above Panoramic Highway. The Trail makes the first of its eight bridged crossings of Webb Creek, here to the right bank. Just beyond, the Trail squeezes between two towering redwoods, joined at their shallow roots.

If your attention can be diverted from the creek, from the redwoods, and from the carpets of sword ferns covering the hillsides, you'll find many other floral treasures. An abundant and showy favorite is trillium, or wake-robin. Look for its characteristic three broad leaves and, atop a slender stalk, the three-petaled flower. The color varies, with white later fading to pink.

An abundant shrub along the creek is red elderberry (*Sambucus racemosa*). It rises to ten feet, with a characteristic five-parted compound leaf. Its clusters of creamy white flowers, in spring, form pyramids. In fall, they bear red berries.

At the second Webb Creek bridge (rivulets are forded by smaller bridges), look for Clintonia, in the lily family. It has large glossy leaves, deep rose flowers, and, in early summer, blue berries.

Just beyond this bridge is the famous Steep Ravine ladder. It takes the Trail down a precipitous rock face, beside a waterfall. Proceed down cautiously. (Legendary Tam trail runner Byron Lowry, on his first trip down Steep Ravine Trail, came upon this unexpected sheer drop at breakneck speed. He went down the ladder forward, still running.)

The Trail continues ever down, with the grade usually gradual enough to permit gazing at the sylvan wonders. Just before bridge #3, a "doorway" has been cut in a downed redwood. It will continue to remain a feature of the Trail for many years. Past the bridge is another waterfall. The bright red berries of baneberry (*Actaea rubra*) brighten the green foliage here in summer.

Just after bridge #4 there is a slight rise in the Trail, then a steep drop over steps to bridge #5. It, and the next two bridges, are close together. Beyond the last, a downed redwood serves many as a well-sculpted bench. An old pipeline lies in the creekbed.

Steep Ravine Trail then meets the Dipsea Trail, which descended the other side of the same canyon (this section of the Dipsea Trail is known to racers as "Steep Ravine"). The Dipsea is here crossing Webb Creek (but do not go over the bridge now unless you are taking the Dipsea back to Pantoll, a classic loop).

The Dipsea and Steep Ravine trails run together beside the reservoir, part of the Stinson Beach water supply. At the base of the uphill (known as Insult in the Dipsea Race), a path branches left to Webb Creek. Continue uphill a few yards. Beside a power pole (which buzzes when water is being pumped to the storage tank above), Steep Ravine Trail veers left at a marked intersection.

This lower stretch of Steep Ravine (sometimes called Webb Creek Trail) is less visited. Many find it as appealing as the more renown upper section. It is lush, and may well have a greater variety of native plant species than any comparably sized stretch of trail in the Bay Area.

After a slight rise, the Trail meets a clearing. A broad path branches right, soon to reconnect with the Dipsea. Steep Ravine continues, also broad. Incredible as it may now seem, this was the original routing of Highway 1, before this section was rebuilt closer to the coast.

A sharp left leads the Trail away from the former roadbed and under an impressive, old, spreading buckeye. Also passed here is a massive redwood, the last on the Trail. Delicate blue forget-me-nots, originally garden escapees but now established in Tam's redwood forests, dot its base. A bridge provides the last crossing of Webb Creek.

Thaddeus Welch, whose landscapes of Tamalpais are considered among the finest ever painted, lived in this tranquil area from 1900 to 1905. He and his artist wife Ludmilla built a cabin in a level clearing on the creek's right bank. Only the sharpest-eyed observers will find any traces of the Welches' stay, such as some introduced German ivy. It was Welch who coined the name Steep Ravine.

Soon after the bridge is a bench, recycled from an old trail sign. There aren't many lovelier settings on the Mountain. The flora here is verdant all year. In late summer and fall, berries abound. They include (with botanic name when not otherwise cited): elderberry, baneberry, oso berry (*Osmaronia cerasiformis*), twinberry (*Lonicera involucrata*), strawberry, California blackberry (*Rubus ursinus*), thimbleberry (*R. parviflorus*) and salmonberry (*R. spectabilis*).

The last .1m of the Trail was rerouted in 1992, both to keep it beside Webb Creek and to bring it out directly across from Rocky Point Road (eliminating the previous short but dangerous walk on Highway 1). The final yards now face a glaring, large yellow sign warning drivers on Highway 1 to slow to "20 MPH." The spell is broken.

Steep Ravine Trail exits beside a parking area at mile sign 11.04. Down the gated road are the Steep Ravine cabins, an environmental campground, and the mouth of Webb Creek at the ocean.

William Kent purchased the Steep Ravine area in 1904 with the intention of extending the Mt. Tamalpais Railway to Stinson Beach, where he also owned land. In 1928, on the day before his death on March 13, he deeded Steep Ravine to the State of California. One of the Steep Ravine cabins is named for him, another for Welch. The present Steep Ravine Trail was built over an earlier route in 1935-36 by the Civilian Conservation Corps.

TCC TRAIL
FROM BOOTJACK TRAIL AT VAN WYCK MEADOW TO DIPSEA TRAIL / 1.80 miles

Terrain: Douglas-fir forest / MTSP & MWNM
Elevation: 1,040' to 1,280' / gradual
Intersecting Trails: Stapelveldt (1.4m)
Directions: Bootjack parking lot — Bootjack Trail toward Muir Woods, .5 miles

THIS IS ONE OF THE BETTER designed of the Mountain's trails. It crosses some eleven deeply wooded canyons, yet runs fairly level its whole 1.8-mile length.

TCC Trail sets off from Van Wyck Meadow to the right (when descending Bootjack Trail from the Bootjack parking lot) of an old stone fireplace. The rock structure, in which pipes are still evident, was part of Lower Rattlesnake Camp, a favorite haunt of Tam hikers in its 1920's heyday. On the fireplace beneath a goldcup oak is a plaque, placed in February 1989, dedicated to the Tamalpais Conservation Club, for which the Trail is named.

The Trail immediately enters deep woodland, where it remains the whole length. In 20 yards, the first creek is crossed on a bridge. Affixed to a laurel 25 yards beyond is one of the old trail signs the TCC once placed throughout the Mountain; it is now illegible. Douglas-firs, many of them huge "wolf-trees" (having sizable branches circling the base), are dominant. Redwoods line all the creek canyons. Somehat similar in foliage to both are a few California nutmegs. At the second creek is a restored old sign bench, pointing the way to the Ben Johnson, Stapelveldt, and Dipsea trails.

The Trail winds around canyon after canyon, some with bridges over the creeks, some with only rivulets to step over. Huckleberries line the route in a profusion perhaps unmatched on any other trail. The fairly steady elevation gain is barely noticeable (unless you're tired!).

In 1.4 miles, TCC Trail crosses a bridge and meets Stapelveldt Trail. A signpost and sign bench mark the junction. Straight ahead, Stapelveldt rises to Pantoll. To the left, TCC and Stapelveldt run together for 20 yards to a second junction. Stapelveldt departs downhill left, to Ben Johnson Trail; veer right.

Another bridge is crossed. The building crew left a sign — similar ones are found on many of the more recent State Park bridges and switchbacks — naming the workers and date of construction (1/12/83).

TCC Trail enters Muir Woods National Monument, then soon after ends when it hits the Dipsea Trail. Just uphill to the right is the crest of Cardiac Hill, a stunning view site. Downhill leads to Deer Park F.R. and Ben Johnson Trail.

The Tamalpais Conservation Club (TCC) was formed by a band of hikers in 1912 for "Preservation of the scenic beauties and fauna of Mt. Tamalpais and its spurs and slopes." The club's first major activity was a trail cleanup day and they have done more trail building and maintenance than any other volunteer group since. The TCC was a leader in the fight to create Mt. Tamalpais State Park and remains vigilant in living up to its motto, "Guardian of the Mountain." Information on membership can be obtained by writing the TCC at Room 562, 870 Market Street, San Francisco 94102.

This Trail was built during the first World War by TCC trail crews. It was originally named Houghton Trail for Samuel Monroe Houghton, a founder of the TCC and its president from 1913 to 1914, the year he died. The Trail is also spelled as "T.C.C."

WEST POINT TRAIL
FROM PANORAMIC HIGHWAY TO WEST POINT / .65 miles

Terrain: Chaparral with planted pines; loose rock; unmaintained and MARGINAL / MMWD
Elevation: From 1,000' to 1,780' / extremely steep
Intersecting Trails: Matt Davis (.3m)
Directions: Panoramic Highway to milepost 3.66
Amenities: Fountains, bathrooms, picnic tables

WEST POINT TRAIL rises from the north side of Panoramic Highway at milepost marker 3.66, across the highway from a parking turnout and the signed top of Sierra Trail. The Trail is unsigned; the MMWD considers it dangerous and does not maintain it. The steepness, loose rock and deep ruts certainly do make it hard to climb and hazardous to descend. It has also become overgrown with shrubs.

Begin up the stone steps into the trees. The Trail, more a gully, quickly enters chaparral, dominated by manzanitas. There are views of the three Tamalpais summits and, left of them, of the pine grove that tops West Point Trail. Look back for sweeping, and ever-expanding, panoramas to the east, south and west.

Extremely steep sections are mixed in with somewhat easier stretches.

Three hundred yards up are the first of the Monterey and Bishop pines that accompany the Trail the rest of the way up. They were part of a planting in the area around 1930. Bishops are the only pine native to Marin, but are normally found only west of the San Andreas Fault. They have egg-like cones clinging to the branches and the needles are in bunches of two. Monterey pines, native only to a strip of central coastal California, have been widely planted throughout the world for both ornamental and, particularly, commercial purposes. Its cones are larger than those of the Bishop, and the needles are in bunches of three.

Halfway up, West Point Trail crosses Matt Davis Trail at an unmarked inter- section. Left, Matt Davis goes to Pantoll, right to Hogback F.R. above Mountain Home. Above, there are again extremely steep segments. This upper half is more wooded, directly through the row of pines, and thus more shaded and sheltered.

Near its top, West Point Trail forks several times and becomes indistinct, particularly since many downed pines now lie across the route. Just go directly uphill and you'll surely hit West Point Inn. The main outlet is below the picnic table area, by the Nora Trail signpost. The bench there carries the plaque "IN LOVING MEMORY OF ROBERT SCHNEIDER, WHO TOUCHED OUR LIVES, 10-20-1928, 12-11-1982." The other trails converging at West Point are, clockwise: Old Stage Road, Rock Spring, Old Railroad Grade going up, the Grade going down, and Nora.

West Point Inn was built in 1904 at the westernmost point of the rail line up the Mountain. The first of its cabins was added in 1918, the wonderful lounge in the early 1920's. It was a popular resting, dining, and lodging site for decades. When the railway went bankrupt in 1930, the MMWD assumed ownership and leased the inn as a private tavern. By 1942, with the top of the Mountain closed to the public by the military, patronage had declined so significantly that the MMWD was planning to raze the inn as a fire hazard. The West Point Club was formed to save the inn after some Tamalpais Conservation Club members learned, reportedly through overhearing a remark by MMWD patrolman Joe Zapella, that its destruction was imminent.

The club, now the West Point Inn Association and separate from the TCC, still manages the inn. The association sells light refreshments (coffee, tea, lem- onade, energy bars) to visitors. On selected Sundays in spring and summer they serve justly popular, bounteous pancake breakfasts.

Rustic rooms and cabins can be rented for overnight stays. Call 388-9955, Tuesday through Friday between 11 a.m. and 6 p.m., to make the necessary reser- vation. In 1998, the rates were $25 per person ($12 for those under 18, free to children under 5). There is no electricity. Guests provide their own food and linen or sleeping bags. Be prepared to walk or bike in.

West Point Trail, which dates from World War I, originally connected Muir Woods Inn, at the present Camp Eastwood, with West Point Inn. Its lower half, today's Sierra Trail, was cut off by the construction of Panoramic Highway. In the 1930's, the Trail was widened as part of a fire break that stretched from Camp Eastwood to West Peak. The 1898 Sanborn map calls today's Rock Spring Trail the West Point Trail.

Old fence line, and Bald Hill cliffs, from Worn Spring Fire Road.

Phoenix Lake Trailhead

Phoenix Lake Trailhead

Directions to Phoenix Lake:
Highway 101 — Sir Francis Drake Boulevard (exit) west, Greenbrae — three miles, left on Lagunitas Road in Ross to end

PHOENIX LAKE has long been the most popular trailhead on the north side of Mt. Tamalpais. Indeed, it has become so heavily used that the Town of Ross has recently felt it necessary to discourage visitors.

Entry to the lake is through Ross' Natalie Coffin Greene Park. Follow Lagunitas Road, which is unpaved past the park's stone entry portal. (The entry gate is closed to cars every night, on high fire danger days, and after heavy winter rains.) Lagunitas Road was part of the 19th century San Rafael-Bolinas County Road and stage route. At the road's is a parking area (often filled) and a charming creekside picnic area.

A quarter-mile, connector fire road rises to the right, behind a gate, onto Water District land. At the top is Phoenix Dam, constructed in 1905 to form Phoenix Lake. Ross Trail, which sets off south of Lagunitas Road before the entry pillars, also leads to the parking lot and dam. There is a separate path to the dam from the picnic area. Phoenix Junction, where four fire roads and a trail meet, is at the far, western tip of Phoenix Lake, .6 miles from the dam counterclockwise.

Greene Park was a gift to the public by the Greene family, with ownership later transfered from the Water District to Ross (and the name changed from Phoenix Lake Park). Natalie Coffin Greene (1885-1966) was a descendant of one of Ross' pioneer families and active in civic affairs.

In 1994, the Town of Ross banned weekend and holiday parking on sections of Lagunitas Road, Glenwood Avenue, and other streets near Greene Park. The closest long-term (although still limited; observe the signs) weekend parking is near Ross Common at the east end of Lagunitas Road.

There are outhouses by the parking area and at Phoenix Dam. Also at the dam is an MMWD information board and a telephone. (The phone in the parking area was all but buried by a slide in 1986; its top is still visible). There are water fountains at the start of Ross Trail beside the private Lagunitas Country Club, in the picnic area, and 50 yards north from the dam.

It is 3.6 miles around Phoenix Lake from the junction of Glenwood Avenue and Lagunitas Road and 2.33 miles, eschewing shortcuts, around the lake itself.

Suggested loops from Phoenix Dam (elevation 180'):
• Around Phoenix Lake ***2.3 miles.***
• Phoenix Lake F.R. counterclockwise, .6m, to Phoenix Junction — right on Shaver Grade, .3m, to Hidden Meadow Trail — right, .7m, to Six Points Junction — right, 1.3m on Yolanda Trail to Phoenix Lake F.R. — left .4m, to start ***3.3 miles.***
• Phoenix Lake F.R. clockwise, .5m, to Bill Williams Trail — left, .6m, to Tucker Trail — right, 1.1m, to Eldridge Grade — right, 1.6m, to Phoenix Junction — left, .6m, on Phoenix F.R. to start ***4.4 miles.***
• Phoenix Lake F.R. counterclockwise, .4m, to Yolanda Trail — right, 2.2m, to

Worn Spring F.R. — right, 2.2m, to Phoenix Lake — left, .1m, to start **4.9 miles.**
• Phoenix Lake F.R. counterclockwise, .1m, to Worn Spring F.R. — right, 2.5m, to
Deer Park Trail — left, .8m, to Deer Park F.R. — left, 1.1m to Shaver Grade — left,
1.2m, to Phoenix Junction — Phoenix Lake F.R. left, .6m (OR right, 1.7m), to start
6.3 (or 7.4) miles.

BILL WILLIAMS TRAIL
FROM SOUTHERN TIP OF PHOENIX LAKE TO TUCKER TRAIL / .64 miles

Terrain: Redwood forest; riparian / MMWD
Elevation: From 200' to 380' / gradual
Intersecting Trails: None
Directions: Phoenix Dam — Phoenix Lake F.R., clockwise, .5 miles

BILL WILLIAMS TRAIL starts from the southern tip of Phoenix Lake, where the
fire road and trail sections of the loop route around the lake meet.

Bill Williams, signed, leaves the lake shore at fire-road width. It climbs
gently into the deep woodland of Bill Williams Gulch. Maples and redwoods
predominate. In around 200 yards is a wide area, used as an MMWD vehicular
turnaround. A sign points the way toward Tucker Trail.

The Trail, now narrow, dips and crosses a pipeline which brings water from
the Bon Tempe Treatment Plant. A pump above, off Eldridge Grade, drives the
water up out of the gulch to Kent Woodlands.

Bill Williams follows Bill Williams Creek, one of the sources of Phoenix Lake.
This lovely, fern-covered area remains cool on the hottest of summer days, and the
creek roars in winter. In .5 miles, the Trail crosses the creek on a bridge. You can
see remains of the old stone Bill Williams Gulch Dam. A wood plaque affixed to
the base of a redwood beside the bridge dates the dam to 1886. The dam played a
role in supplying Marin's water until Phoenix Lake was filled after 1905.

The Trail crosses back over the creek, now without a bridge. The fording,
just above where a fork of Bill Williams enters, can be a wet one in winter. A
short, steep uphill leads to an unsigned fork. To the right and up is a path —
almost unpassable 20 years ago but now becoming so used and worn in that it
may soon meet trail standards — that snakes up to Eldridge Grade. Veer left
downhill to another bridge, which again takes the Trail over the creek.

Bill Williams Trail rises steeply a few more yards to end at a signed junction
with Tucker Trail. Left leads to Harry Allen Trail, right is a climb to Eldridge Grade.

Bill Williams lived in a cabin in the first gulch upstream from the dam in
the 1860's. His background is little known; some thought he was a Confederate
Army deserter. Alice Eastwood referred to him as "an old wood-chopper." The
legend persists that his hidden treasure remains buried somewhere in the gulch.
A story relates that laborers building Phoenix Dam in the early years of this
century spent more time looking for Bill Williams' gold than working. There was
another fruitless treasure hunt when Phoenix Lake was drained in the mid-1980's.

ELDRIDGE GRADE
FROM PHOENIX JUNCTION TO RIDGECREST BOULEVARD / 5.46 miles

Terrain: Lower part forested, upper part mostly chaparral / MMWD
Elevation: From 200' to 2,250' / gradual
Intersecting Trails: Filter Plant Road (.8m), Tucker (1.6m), Lakeview F.R. (2.0m), Indian F.R. (3.1m), Wheeler (3.7m), Northside (4.3m), East Peak Fire (5.0m), Redwood Spring (5.3m)
Directions: Phoenix Junction
Amenities: Fountain

ELDRIDGE GRADE, opened December 13, 1884, is the oldest road to the summit of Mt. Tamalpais. Construction took five months and cost $8,000, with most of the work done by Chinese laborers. Long-time Tam explorer Brad Rippe has located one of their camps high off Eldridge. The Grade was built for horse-drawn wagons, with wide turnouts and a slope rarely exceeding one foot in 14 (7 per cent). Six-horse, ten-passenger Tally-Ho wagons then made regular excursions on it from the Rafael Hotel in San Rafael.

The road project was headed by John Oscar Eldridge. He had come to California from New York by ship in 1849 at the age of 21. Instead of rushing to the gold fields, he stayed in San Francisco and became a successful auctioneer. Later, he brought street lighting to San Rafael as founder of the San Rafael Gas Company. His daughter married Sidney Cushing, for whom the Mountain Theater is now named. Eldridge died just two months after his road opened.

In the early 1900's, when horse-drawn carriages became obsolete, Eldridge Grade fell into disrepair and plans were advanced to pave the route for auto use. Today, Eldridge Grade remains the principal summit route on the Mountain's north side, a position held on the south side by Old Railroad Grade (financed largely by Eldridge's son-in-law Cushing).

Eldridge is one of three fire roads that rise from Phoenix Junction at the northwest tip of Phoenix Lake. With your back to the lake, Eldridge is to the left; Fish Grade is in the middle, then Shaver Grade right. Be prepared for a long journey as there are basically no direct, non-precipitous options back to Phoenix Lake.

Eldridge begins under a dense canopy of trees; mostly bay but with redwoods plentiful. In recent years, there have been serious slide problems in the first half-mile, permanently narrowing the Grade in places. Skunks are regular daytime denizens of culverts in the canyon crossings.

In .8 miles, Filter Plant Road, which connects to Fish Grade, comes in right. A fountain was added here in 1992. The next fork is just a re-grading; veer right.

As Eldridge rises, the terrain becomes ever drier. Madrones and tanbark oaks are more prevalent, with redwoods only at stream crossings. Tucker Trail, which offers a lovely but steep route back toward Phoenix Lake, joins at a righthand bend in the Grade. Just ahead a sign on a trough identifies Bear Wallow Spring; there were once both black and grizzly bears on Tam. Views continue to open, particularly to the east.

Lakeview F.R., from Lake Lagunitas, joins the Grade on the right. An old trail sign marks the intersection. Just above, chinquapin, a small tree in the oak family, is common. In season, its spiny bur-like fruit capsules line the edge of the Grade here. Eldridge's surface becomes increasingly rocky.

A quarter-mile above the Lakeview junction, just around a bend and past a grove of redwoods, a short path on the right connects to East Peak Fire Trail. The next fire road to enter is Indian, on the left. It goes to Kent Woodlands.

Continue right. Extremely steep Indian Fire Trail crosses several times, the intersections deliberately blocked by branches. Indian Fire Trail was an old route up the Mountain broadened in the 1930's as a fire break. It is now closed for erosion control.

Views to the south, of San Francisco and the San Mateo coastline, expand. To the east it is possible, on the clearest of winter days, to see the snow-capped Sierra, 160 miles away, through a gap (the Sacramento River delta) in the interior Coast Range north of Mt. Diablo.

At a wide horseshoe curve, Wheeler Trail enters on the left. Descending to Hoo-Koo-E-Koo F.R., it offers a key north-south Tam link.

Indian Fire Trail is crossed again. The next big bend to the left is known as Sawtooth Point. Soon after, at a horseshoe curve left, an old sign points the way up a short fire road to Northside Trail, which runs all the way to Rifle Camp. Also just up this connector is East Peak Fire Trail and scenic Inspiration Point.

The next big bend, to the right, is below the rock formation known as North Knee. East Peak Fire Trail joins on the right.

Eldridge passes atop the deep canyon formed by the East Fork of Lagunitas Creek, which is beginning its long cross-Marin journey to Tomales Bay. Unmarked Redwood Spring Trail crosses Eldridge. To the left, it climbs steeply up to the East Peak parking lot, a significant shortcut if that is your destination. To the right, it descends to Redwood Spring and Northside Trail.

Two-hundred-fifty yards above Redwood Spring Trail, Eldridge Grade ends at paved Ridgecrest Road. Eldridge originally terminated at West Peak but construction of Ridgecrest in the 1920's covered the old route, shortening its total length two miles. East Peak is to the left. Middle Peak Fire Road and Old Railroad Grade are a few yards downhill.

FISH GRADE
FROM PHOENIX JUNCTION TO SKY OAKS ROAD / .76 miles

Terrain: Redwood forest; riparian; upper part paved / MMWD
Elevation: 200' to 720' / very steep
Intersecting Trails: Fish Gulch (.6m)
Directions: Phoenix Junction

THE STEEPNESS of Fish Grade is legendary, intimidating some visitors. Yet many hike, run and bike up it regularly as the most direct route between Phoenix Lake and the "upper lakes" of Lagunitas, Bon Tempe and Alpine. Lined by redwoods, it is also quite pretty.

Fish Grade is the middle of the three fire roads — Eldridge and Shaver grades are the others — that rise from Phoenix Junction. Narrower Fish Gulch Trail, on the opposite bank from Fish Grade, also sets off uphill here.

There is no getting lost on Fish Grade; just keep climbing up, up, up through the cool, quiet forest. The canyon below is Fish Gulch. The creek through it is not officially named but Fish Creek seems obvious.

Fish Gulch Trail rejoins Fish Grade. Combined, they directly meet paved Filter Plant Road, which goes left to the MMWD filter plant and Eldridge Grade.

There is another 225 yards of stiff uphill on asphalt. The array of water valves to the right, the Bon Tempe Headworks, brings water from Bon Tempe Lake to the treatment plant and on to southern Marin.

The Grade ends at a gate beside Sky Oaks Road. Pumpkin Ridge Trail rises here on the right. Bon Tempe Lake is across the road. Left (straight) on the road leads to the Lake Lagunitas parking area.

The "Fish" in the name refers to a Mr. Fish who had a camp in the present Lake Lagunitas area in the 1860's. The original grade was built around 1873, when Lagunitas Dam, creating the lake, was completed. That first grade is now the Fish Gulch Trail. The current Fish Grade was carved in 1903 to carry water pipelines down from the planned Tamalpais Dam, which was never completed.

FISH GULCH TRAIL
FROM PHOENIX JUNCTION TO FISH GRADE / .57 miles

Terrain: Heavily wooded; riparian / MMWD
Elevation: From 200' to 600' / very steep
Intersecting Trails: Concrete Pipeline F.R. (.4m)
Directions: Phoenix Junction

Fish Gulch Trail is the only trail out of Phoenix Junction; the other four spokes are all fire-road width. It sets off uphill between Fish and Shaver grades.

The climb, through oak-madrone woodland, is very steep. A water pipeline is visible beside the Trail. The Trail — originally broader — was cleared in the early 1870's to bring a water line down from then newly filled Lake Lagunitas. The Trail is actually the original Fish Grade (the present Fish Grade was built in 1903), and is sometimes called Old Fish Grade.

Fish Gulch Trail meets the southern end of Concrete Pipeline F.R., which connects to Five Corners (left) and Fairfax-Bolinas Road (right). The remaining ascent is the steepest yet. The fire road (Fish Grade) across redwood-lined Fish Gulch gets steadily closer. In winter, water rushes through the creek below. There's a last incline past a Water District building known as a baffle chamber.

Fish Gulch Trail veers left to rejoin Fish Grade. A path goes straight ahead to the Bon Tempe Headworks. A few yards uphill on Fish Grade is paved Filter

Plant Road, which goes left to the filter plant and Eldridge Grade. Fish Grade continues steeply up 225 yards to Sky Oaks Road.

HARRY ALLEN TRAIL
FROM PHOENIX LAKE TO CROWN ROAD, KENT WOODLANDS / 1.15 miles*

Terrain: Heavily wooded; quarter-mile paved / MMWD & MCOSD
Elevation: From 200' to 580' to 480' / steep
Intersecting Trails: Tucker (.3m), Tucker Cutoff (.6m), Indian F.R. (.7m), Kent F.R. (.7m)
Directions: Phoenix Dam — Phoenix Lake F.R., clockwise, .4 miles
*Includes .24 miles of paved Phoenix Road, which separates the two sections of Harry Allen Trail.

HARRIS (HARRY) STEARNS ALLEN built this Trail on Sundays over a three-year period in the early 1920's. It connected his home at 55 Olive Avenue in Larkspur's Baltimore Canyon to Phoenix Lake. The development of Kent Woodlands following World War II covered much of the old route, and diminished its importance. Today the Trail is in two parts, severed by paved Phoenix Road atop Windy Ridge. The less known eastern half, on MCOSD land, was re-cleared and signed only in 1987. Although both ends of that segment are accessible by car and offer adequate parking, most users join Harry Allen at Phoenix Lake, so we will too.

The Trail rises from Phoenix Lake Fire Road at a marked intersection. The steep initial grade lessens when the Trail enters the forest. Look in winter and spring for delicate maidenhair fern, with its green, fan-shaped fronds (leaves) branching off slender black stalks. The spores are found under the reflexed outer margins of the fronds. "Adiantum", the fern's genus name, comes from the Greek word "unwettable," because the fronds shed water.

Just beyond a creek crossing, the Trail meets the start of Tucker Trail. Most visitors leave Harry Allen here, taking Tucker either up to Eldridge Grade or, with Bill Williams Trail, back to Phoenix. Harry Allen continues up left.

Several paths cross. They are remnants a more extensive trail system here from the days when hikers approached the Mountain from Northwestern Pacific Railroad stops to the east. Passenger train service was discontinued in 1941.

The Trail climbs out of its forest canopy and passes the introduced garden shrub called Pride of Madeira, a sure sign that homes are near, which indeed they are. The Trail unceremoniously runs into a gap in a rusted guard rail opposite 123 Crown Road. A pair of MMWD signs mark the junction.

To pick up the second half of Harry Allen (called Windy Ridge Trail on the latest MCOSD brochure), go right on the pavement along the spine of Windy Ridge. In .1 mile, a fire road goes left. It is an unpaved segment of Crown Road. Tucker Cutoff Trail, to Tucker Trail, drops right. Continue up Phoenix Road. In another .1 mile, an MMWD gate to the right marks the start of Indian F.R. A few yards beyond, at the end of the pavement, is a wood barrier with an MCOSD sign.

Behind it is Kent F.R. Left, signed "Trail to Crown Road," Harry Allen continues.

Squeeze through two redwoods. Narrow and, unfortunately, rapidly eroding, Harry Allen (Windy Ridge) Trail descends through a redwood forest. Huckleberry is abundant. In 1/4-mile, there is an MCOSD sign at a fork; take the left option. The upper path loops back to near Harry Allen. In another .1 mile, a sign, for the opposite direction, notes "Trail to Windy Ridge."

Harry Allen ends 75 yards below this sign, just east of #320 Crown Road. The entry is marked with an MCOSD sign. Crown Road goes right, past Idlewood Road and Evergreen Drive, to the Southern Marin Line (Crown) Fire Road trailhead, and left back to Phoenix Road.

Harry Stearns Allen was president of the Tamalpais Conservation Club in 1916-17. He died in 1947.

HIDDEN MEADOW TRAIL
FROM SHAVER GRADE TO SIX POINTS / .77 miles

Terrain: Grassy hillside; lower part riparian; horses permitted / MMWD
Elevation: 270' to 550' / gradual, upper half very steep
Intersecting Trails: Logging (.2m)
Directions: Phoenix Junction — Shaver Grade, .3 miles

HIDDEN MEADOW Trail is barely a mile from the popular Phoenix Lake and Deer Park trailheads, yet it offers peace and an unspoiled quality reminiscent of early California. It also has several inviting picnic sites to savor that tranquility.

From Phoenix Junction, follow Shaver Grade one-third mile up Phoenix Creek. Hidden Meadow Trail sets off to the right, signed, just before Shaver begins rising steeply. The Trail follows Phoenix Creek, then fords it at the entrance to lovely Hidden Meadow itself.

The meadow's grassy knolls are indeed hidden from the rest of the world. Oaks dot the slopes, laurels line the creek. On the left, unsigned Logging Trail rises toward higher on Shaver Grade. The site was formerly known as Marshall Gulch. The Marshall family operated a dairy here around the turn of the century. Cattle grazed the area until 1916. A Mt. Tamalpais History Project walk in 1988 turned up an old milk bottle from the ranch. (Note that it is unlawful to remove historic artifacts from the Mountain without a permit.)

Linger in the meadow, or continue if you prefer to a picnic site with views. The Trail begins climbing up the southwest face of Bald Hill. Across a rivulet, railroad-tie switchbacks built by the Marin Conservation Corps in 1997 ease the steepness and an erosion problem.

A path forks left to an inviting level knoll with a stunning Mt. Tam view. Some 75 yards up the Trail, a "Keep Off" sign marks a former spur to Bald Hill Trail now closed for erosion control. The Trail leaves the oaks onto the grassy hillside and snakes its way higher. The pastoral setting calls for a leisurely pace.

Hidden Meadow Trail ends at Six Points Junction. The continuing options, from left to right, are: Bald Hill Trail to Five Corners, Six Points Trail to Deer Park, Yolanda Trail to Worn Spring F.R., and Yolanda back to Phoenix.

Hidden Meadow Trail was apparently built, or improved, in the 1930's.

PHOENIX LAKE F.R. & ORD TRAIL
LOOP AROUND PHOENIX LAKE / 2.33 miles

Terrain: Riparian; oak-buckeye woodland; half trail, half fire road; horses permitted on fire road only; heavily used / MMWD
Elevation: Around 175' / level to slightly rolling
Intersecting Trails: Clockwise from dam; Ross (at dam), Harry Allen (.4m), Bill Williams (.5m), Eldridge Grade (1.7m), Fish Grade (1.7m), Fish Gulch (1.7m), Shaver Grade (1.7m), Yolanda (1.9m), Worn Spring F.R. (2.2m)
Directions: Phoenix Dam
Amenities: Fountain, outhouses, telephone

THE WALK AROUND Phoenix Lake is one of the most beloved routes on Mt. Tamalpais. The loop's popularity arises from its easy accessibility, level terrain, and beauty. The full circuit comprises two distinct parts of almost identical distance; a fire road (open to horses and bicycles) that goes left and right from the dam, and a pedestrian-only trail along the Lake's south shore.

Phoenix Lake was formed when the Marin County Water Company, a predecessor to the MMWD, constructed today's dam in Phoenix Gulch in 1905. Phoenix, with a capacity of 178 million gallons, is now the second smallest of the MMWD reservoirs. It is also the lowest in elevation, in fact so low (some 300 vertical feet below the Bon Tempe Filter Plant, through which its water must pass) that it is not regularly used as part of the regular County supply. Its water, however, can be used in an emergency; a pump was installed in the center of the lake when a drought threatened in 1989. Phoenix Lake was most recently drained in 1984, when the current concrete spillway replaced an old wooden one.

Most visitors to Phoenix come from Ross, reaching the dam by climbing either Ross Trail or the quarter-mile-long fire road from the parking area. We'll follow the circle route clockwise from where this fire road meets the dam. This offers views of Tam's summit; going the other way affords better vistas of Bald Hill.

Start by crossing the dam. Many visitors go no further than the benches here. Ross Trail enters on the dam's far side, the junction marked with a signpost pointing the way to Ross. Continuing on the Fire Road, you'll notice several paths to the lake's shore. Fishermen often line the bank.

In a bit under a half-mile, Harry Allen Trail rises on the left. It connects to Tucker Trail, then continues up to Kent Woodlands. The Fire Road then drops to the lake's southern tip, which is sometimes dry here before the first winter rains. Straight ahead, into the redwoods, is Bill Williams Trail, which starts at fire road width. It too leads to Tucker Trail.

To continue the loop around the lake, go right, up the steps. This next

1.2-mile trail section has been officially designated by the MMWD as the Ord Trail (although few visitors call it that). Gertrude Ord was a popular equestrienne and her husband Eric was a president of the Tamalpais Trail Riders. Somewhat ironically, horses are no longer allowed on the Trail portion.

The Trail rolls gently along the lake's quieter southwest shore. It would be rare not to meet at least a few other walkers or runners.

There are two short steep sections over unnamed streams. The first is by a bridge, built in the mid-1980's. After a second bridge, installed in 1987 when the Trail was rerouted, forks branch left and right. Both lead back to the Fire Road, with the right fork a 100-yard shortcut. When back on the Fire Road, go right to complete the loop. To the left, at the northwest tip of the lake, is Phoenix Junction, from which the Eldridge, Fish, Old Fish, and Shaver grades rise.

The circuit continues on the historic County Road, which once connected San Rafael to Bolinas. It passes several buildings (some used as MMWD residences and all off-limits) of the former Porteous Ranch. Prominent is the handsome Phoenix Log Cabin. It was built in 1896 by Porteous Ranch coachman and foreman Martin Grant and restored by the MMWD in 1989. In the next bend, lovely Yolanda Trail sets off uphill onto the slope of Bald Hill.

The loop's last junction is with broad Worn Spring F.R., which climbs to the top of Bald Hill. A few yards beyond are a water fountain and trough for horses. Just ahead is a private MMWD ranger's residence. A plaque across from it honors Clayton Stocking, an MMWD employee who lived there for 42 years (see Stocking Trail). Back at the dam, there are outhouses and a telephone.

The distance around Phoenix Lake, avoiding the few shortcuts, has been accurately measured at 2.33 miles. Tam historian Fred Sandrock says the name "Phoenix" is corrupted from the William Phenix family, emigrants from Great Britain who settled in what is now the lake bed sometime around 1850.

ROSS TRAIL
FROM LAGUNITAS ROAD, ROSS, TO PHOENIX DAM / .66 miles

Terrain: Wooded hillside; heavily used / Town of Ross & MMWD
Elevation: From 80' to 200' / gradual, parts steep
Intersecting Trails: None
Directions: Same as Phoenix Lake, to intersection of Lagunitas Road and Glenwood Avenue
Amenities: Fountain

Ross Trail is an alternate to the open-to-autos road to Phoenix Lake, so is well-used. It may be considered to start at the intersection of Lagunitas Road and Glenwood Avenue in Ross. It winds on the southern side of the street, among redwoods beside the Lagunitas Country Club. Within the first yards is a water fountain, installed by the Club for "thirsty joggers." The path then leaves the road's edge, heading left and uphill. It joins Greene Park above the stone entrance pillars.

The woods here are rich in vegetation. Spring wildflowers usually begin bloming here in early January. Leading the way, and abundant along the Trail, are milk-maids and fetid-adder's-tongue. The latter, in the lily family, can be recognized by its pair of broad leaves spotted with brown. It displays its three-petaled, purple-striped flowers ever so briefly. The slender flower stalks then droop downward, implanting their own seeds. Later in the year, the fragrant mint yerba buena blossoms abundantly along the Trail. Downed madrones, losers here in the battle for light in the maturing forest, may necessitate scrambling.

Ross Trail drops to near the Phoenix Lake parking lot, but remains above it. Ross, or Windy, Hill, 763 feet high, looms above to the left. A still visible major slide here in 1986 cut Ross Trail. A wood bridge crosses the heart of the slide.

The Trail runs above the park's picnic area and Ross Creek. A few steep paths drop to the right. As you approach Phoenix Lake you might, in winter, hear the sound of water roaring down the dam's spillway. Just before the Trail's end, steps bring a path up from Ross Creek.

The Trail ends at Phoenix Lake Fire Road on the southeast edge of Phoenix Dam. An MMWD sign, carved "Ross," is at the intersection.

Scotsman James Ross was a pioneer settler who bought much of the Ross Valley in 1857. He died, at age 50, in 1862. Later, his wife Anne had to sell most of the holdings to provide the substantial dowries called for in James' will upon the marriages of the couple's two daughters. The North Pacific Coast Railroad stop of Sunnyside (at today's post office) was renamed Ross in 1882. The Town of Ross was incorporated in 1908.

SHAVER GRADE
FROM PHOENIX JUNCTION TO SKY OAKS ROAD / 1.69 miles

Terrain: Wooded, parts deeply; lower part riparian; heavily used / MMWD
Elevation: From 180' to 775' / steep
Intersecting Trails: Hidden Meadow (.3m), Logging (.6m, 1.5m), Concrete Pipe-line F.R. (1.0m-1.1m), Elliott (1.1m, 1.4m, 1.5m), Deer Park F.R. (1.1m), connector fire road to Bald Hill Trail (1.1m), Sky Oaks-Lagunitas (at top)
Directions: Phoenix Junction

SHAVER GRADE IS QUITE POPULAR with travelers on the north side of Mt. Tamalpais. It is less steep than Fish Grade in going between Phoenix Lake and the upper lakes and is the direct connection between Phoenix and the important Five Corners junction. Though Shaver's upper end is accessible by car, most users join the Grade from Phoenix Lake.

Shaver Grade has a long history. Isaac Shaver (or Shafer or Schaffer) came overland to California from New York in 1852. In 1864 he built a sawmill near the present Alpine Dam and graded a road to haul the lumber and cordwood to Corte Madera Creek at Ross Landing (by the junction of today's College Avenue and Sir Francis Drake). Shallow-draft schooners completed the trip to San Francisco. The Tam section of that route was the original Shaver Grade, part of which is today's Logging Trail. The mill closed in 1873. The present Shaver Grade was a section of the old County road from San Rafael to Bolinas.

Shaver was credited with constructing many of San Rafael's earliest homes. Ever enterprising, he bought the redwood timbers, for $50, when the original San Rafael Mission was torn down. He was president of San Rafael's first library and a street near today's library site bears his name. Shaver reportedly drowned himself after being accused of wrongdoing in a land transaction.

Shaver Grade is the fire road on the right at Phoenix Junction when your back is to Phoenix Lake. Shaver begins only slightly uphill. It has a timeless, pastoral feel in the woodland beside Phoenix Creek. Hidden Meadow Trail, to Hidden Meadow, branches right at a signpost. Then the uphill begins in earnest.

In the middle of a redwood-lined horseshoe bend to the right (MMWD "SG9"), easy-to-miss Logging Trail crosses the Grade. To the left, Logging Trail (the old Shaver Grade) goes uphill between a laurel and a madrone. Thirty-five yards farther up the Grade, Logging Trail drops right, down to Hidden Meadow.

Through the trees are views of Bald Hill. The Grade then meets Concrete Pipeline F.R. Left leads to Madrone Trail and Lake Lagunitas. Shaver and Concrete Pipeline run together uphill, above a tunnel for the water pipeline, for 200 yards to the key junction of Five Corners. Clockwise, the five other spokes (yes, there are six), are: Elliott Trail, Shaver Grade continuing uphill, Concrete Pipeline F.R., Deer Park F.R., and a connector fire road up to Bald Hill Trail.

Madrones line the way above Five Corners. Shaver again meets Elliott Trail, crossing left and right. There's actually a brief downhill. At a saddle, Elliott Trail meets Shaver a last time and, opposite, Logging Trail sets off downhill.

A final climb leads to Sky Oaks-Lagunitas Trail and, a few yards above, paved Sky Oaks Road. Across Sky Oaks is a path and the auto access (also part of the old County road) to the Bon Tempe Dam parking area and Alpine Lake.

TUCKER TRAIL
FROM HARRY ALLEN TRAIL TO ELDRIDGE GRADE / 1.65 miles

Terrain: Deep forest; riparian / MMWD
Elevation: From 300' to 800' / middle section very steep, rest gradual
Intersecting Trails: Tucker Cutoff (.7m), Bill Williams (.7m)
Directions: Phoenix Dam — Phoenix Lake F.R. clockwise — Harry Allen Trail, .2 miles

THE HEAVILY WOODED Tucker (or Camp Tucker) Trail is one of the loveliest on the mountain. In summer, it offers a cool respite from summer heat. In winter, rushing creeks and a waterfall are added attractions. The Trail's proximity to Phoenix Lake adds to its popularity. It is, however, steep, and requires, after winter rains, some agility in crossing streams.

Tucker Trail branches to the right off Harry Allen Trail at a signed intersection .2 miles up from Phoenix Lake. California buckeyes line Tucker's early yards, then the Trail heads into deeper woods. Bill Williams Creek can be heard, and glimpsed, rushing below.

After a winding .7 miles, Tucker meets Tucker Cutoff Trail on the left. The Cutoff rises a quarter-mile to Windy Ridge, and is actually much the quickest access to Tucker from any trailhead. Tucker Trail then drops 50 yards to meet Bill Williams Trail at a signed junction. Bill Williams descends to the bridge below and returns to Phoenix Lake.

Veer left to the head of the canyon for the first of the Trail's three crossings of Bill Williams Creek, here of the east fork. A short leap may be required immediately after a rainstorm. The Trail becomes steeper, rising to a ridge above the canyon of the Creek's middle fork. At 1.1 miles is the second stream crossing. Continue climbing through this peaceful, isolated forest. The third and last crossing is of the Creek's west fork. There's another stiff uphill to a trail sign at 1.5 miles.

This level spot is the site of old Camp Tucker. Here one Mr. Tucker, who logged the area in the late 1800's, apparently built and lived in a cabin. Later, the clearing housed picnic tables. There is a waterfall just above the Trail here, with a very steep path leading to it and then on to Eldridge Grade.

The last .2 miles of Tucker are fairly level. The Trail finally leaves the forest canopy for its first broad views.

Tucker ends at a bend in Eldridge Grade just below Bear Wallow Spring. Phoenix Lake is 1.6 miles downhill on the Grade and Lakeview Fire Road is .4 miles uphill.

Tucker Trail appeared on the 1898 Sanborn map.

WORN SPRING FIRE ROAD
FROM PHOENIX LAKE TO TOP OF DEER PARK TRAIL / 2.51 miles

Terrain: Grassland; some light woodland / MMWD & private (easement)
Elevation: From 200' to 1100' to 510' / very steep
Intersecting Trails: Spur of Yolanda (.1m), Yolanda (2.1m), connectors to Redwood Road and Oak Avenue (2.1m), Buckeye (2.2m, 2.5m), Deer Park (2.5m)
Directions: Phoenix Dam — Phoenix Lake F.R., counterclockwise, .1 mile

BALD HILL OCCUPIES A SPECIAL PLACE for residents of the Ross Valley. Baldy, as it is affectionately called, is visible from just about everywhere in the valley and its pristine upper slopes have become an integral part of the quality of life for the area. Up close, Baldy is even lovelier, a quintessential California hill, green in winter and spring, golden in summer and fall. Worn Spring Fire Road traverses the entire west side of Baldy. It offers a splendid trip any time of the year.

Worn Spring is the first fire road rising above Phoenix Lake when going counterclockwise from the dam. The climb is unrelentingly steep all the way to the top of Baldy. At the first bend to the right, in less than 100 yards, a steep spur of Yolanda Trail branches left. Views open; the whole journey is a visual treat.

In less than .4 miles, the Fire Road passes a wood structure covering the Ross Reservoir. The reservoir dates from 1921. It has a capacity of one million gallons. You can often smell chlorine, added to sterilize the water. Just beyond is a fork. The road right goes the few yards to the reservoir. Worn Spring's continuation, widened to a fire road after World War II, is to the left. Just above is a gate.

The Fire Road climbs even more steeply. A grove of trees is watered by Worn Spring. Right begin vistas of the treeless, upper, grassy slopes of Baldy.

In .5 miles the Fire Road drops slightly, the only downhill, and crosses over Worn Spring for the second time. Worn Spring, emerging from Bald Hill here in this grove of madrones, oaks and laurels, was tapped as an important water source for Marin from 1881 until the completion of Alpine Dam in 1919. It was pressed into service again during the drought of 1976-77. A trough to the left is carved "Worn Springs." This grove offers the last shade of the climb.

A path goes left; it is the steep, overgrown Burnt Trail (below minimum standards, so not described), connecting to Yolanda Trail. The scenery is superb. Mt. Tamalpais rises behind you, Baldy's gentle contours in front. You could be in the Marin of 200 years ago.

Above, there are signs of a more recent (1993) fire. Broad views, first of the East Bay, then of the San Francisco skyline, then of the greenbelt to the northwest, open to ease the uphill burden.

Near the summit, the Fire Road passes an MMWD boundary sign. Few visitors realize that much of Baldy, including its summit, is privately held. Though access has long been permitted, it cannot be guaranteed. A 1992 attempt to form a tax assessment district in San Anselmo and Ross and acquire this uppermost 60-acre parcel narrowly missed the necessary two-thirds majority.

The summit, 1.7 miles from the start, is reached via a 50 yard connector to the right. A U.S. Geological Survey post is buried near the peak. As splendid as the views have been, those from the very top are even more spectacular, as the north opens up as well. It might be windy but, in any case, enjoy the 360 degree panorama. You've earned it!

If you are not returning directly to Phoenix Lake (and the views on the way back, facing Tam, are among Marin's best) continue on Warm Spring F.R. Across is a second summit of Baldy. In .1 mile, there is a fork. The unnamed fire road to the right, over private property but long open, runs .8 miles down to Upper Road West in Ross.

Veer left to stay on Worn Spring. You are descending the north side of Bald Hill, and this stretch was once known as Bald Hill Fire Trail and as Corral Trail. A half-mile down from the summit is a fence line of a residence, the highest home on Baldy. The house was rebuilt in 1994.

Just beyond, the Fire Road drops to a saddle. To the left is one end of Yolanda Trail. To the right, behind a gate, is a short, broad connector, on private property, to Oak Avenue in San Anselmo. After a bitter legal fight in 1993-94 (more than 100 hikers, including the author, were sued by the adjacent property owners), the public's right to an easement across this connector was secured.

A few feet beyond, also to the right, an extremely steep and slippery path descends a quarter-mile through newly acquired Marin County Open Space District lands. It exits near the summit of San Anselmo's Redwood Road, where it is marked by an MCOSD sign. Hopefully, this below-standards connector will someday be upgraded to a trail.

The boundary between Water District and private lands runs down the center of the Fire Road. There is a short uphill, then a short downhill through oak woodland. At the bottom of this saddle, Buckeye Trail goes left to bypass the next climb. The path right, and its several offshoots, all enter private property.

Worn Spring crests its final hill, then descends. There are fine vistas.

The Fire Road forks. Right leads to a gate of the privately owned Sky Ranch, from which equestrians set off. Veer left. The steep downhill drops past the other end of Buckeye Trail, then the signed top of Deer Park Trail, which connects to Deer Park. A path on the right crosses private land, then descends to Fairfax.

A few yards beyond, Worn Spring Fire Road comes to an abrupt end. The precipitous path straight ahead plummets directly down to the Deer Park trailhead.

James and Anne Ross bought, in 1857, most of today's Ross Valley. A daughter, also named Anne, married San Franciscan George Worn. James' will called for a large cash dowry for Anne; most of the land holdings had to be sold to pay it. Worn later recovered much of the acreage. The couple operated a dairy ranch on the Ross slope of Bald Hill. The Worn residence, called Sunnyside, is the present site of Ross' Marin Art & Garden Center.

YOLANDA TRAIL
FROM PHOENIX LAKE TO WORN SPRING FIRE ROAD / 2.23 miles

Terrain: Woodland, middle part grassy hillside with steep dropoff; horses permitted (except on Spur) / MMWD
Elevation: 180' to 650' / gradual, southern part steep
Intersecting Trails: Hidden Meadow (1.3m), Bald Hill (1.3m), Six Points (1.3m)
Directions: Phoenix Dam — Phoenix Lake F.R., counterclockwise, .4 miles
Spur: Between Yolanda and Worn Spring F.R., .2m

YOLANDA is one of the most beautiful, and best loved, trails on Tam. Most of the year it captures the early morning sun; in summer, the last light as well. The Trail makes a semicircle around the western side of Bald Hill, with Mt. Tamalpais' summit almost constantly in view. The Trail is also among Marin's richest in wildflowers. After a riot of color in spring, pink willow-herbs bloom after mid-summer and California fuchsias add red into November. Yolanda's proximity to the Phoenix Lake and Deer Park trailheads further contributes to its popularity.

The Trail rises from Phoenix Lake at a marked signpost just before the restored log home when going counterclockwise around the lake. An alternate entry Spur, closer to the dam but steeper, is just up Worn Spring F.R. from Phoenix.

Yolanda starts uphill through oak-madrone woodland. There is an MMWD residence and a corral in the fenced-in, off-limits enclosure just below, part of the old Hippolyte Dairy Ranch. The Porteous family bought 1,100 acres here in 1883, and renamed the property Porteous Ranch.

The Spur from Worn Spring enters right, on the ridge line, by a "no horses" sign. In spring, this part of the Trail is lined with irises. After a good climb, the bulk of the Trail's total rise, you leave the trees for another special part of Yolanda.

The Trail, carved onto the steep southwest slope of Bald Hill by the Civilian Conservation Corps in the 1930's, offers stunning Mt. Tam vistas, and an equally stunning drop down the hillside if you're inattentive!

Though but a mile as the crow flies from the heavily populated Ross Valley, Yolanda appears tranquil and timeless. Fifty yards into the open area, the Trail passes entrances on the right to Burnt Trail, a steep and overgrown (so not described) connection to Worn Spring F.R. Yolanda winds its way, gently rising and dropping, around Bald Hill. There is more woodland nearing Six Points.

At Six Points Junction (which see), Yolanda bends to the right. This last section of Yolanda (called Yolanda North on Erickson, as opposed to the Yolanda South just covered) is along Baldy's north face. Except for one open stretch, it is well wooded; it is only Baldy's sun-dried south face that doesn't support trees.

The Trail, which rises gently, is every bit as peaceful as before. At a lovely Mt. Tam view knoll, a path veers left. It passes some old growth redwoods, then, overgrown and steep, connects to Deer Park F.R. near Oak Tree Junction. Soon another path goes up, right, to Worn Spring F.R. Occasionally visible below on the left is the old Deer Park School. There are some muddy patches in winter as the Trail is used by horseback riders from the nearby Sky Ranch and Marin Stables.

Yolanda re-emerges into the open at its terminus at Worn Spring Fire Road. Both left on the fire road, toward Deer Park, and right, to the top of Baldy, border private property on the far (northeast) side. The fire road straight ahead, to Oak Avenue in San Anselmo, has been the subject of litigation; in 1993, adjacent landowners sued more than 100 hikers who had been using it for years.

Also at the Yolanda/Worn Spring junction, a very steep path, which may someday be upgraded to trail standards, drops through deep woodland to the crest of San Anselmo's Redwood Avenue. It passes over land acquired in the mid-1990's by the Town of San Anselmo and the Marin County Open Space District, which manages the parcel.

The name Yolanda comes from an area, now part of San Anselmo, that was the first stop west of the Hub on the old Northwestern Pacific commuter rail line. The Trail originally connected to the station. An attractive San Anselmo street still carries the name.

Snow on upper Old Mine Trail.

Rock Spring Trailhead

Rock Spring Trailhead

Directions to Rock Spring:
Highway 101 — Highway 1 — Panoramic Highway — Southside (Pantoll) Road to junction with Ridgecrest Boulevard

ROCK SPRING has been a named feature of Mt. Tamalpais for more than 100 years. Around the turn of the century, it was a popular deer hunting area. A shoot here in 1912 helped galvanize hikers into forming the Tamalpais Conservation Club, which in turn spearheaded the long battle to establish Mt. Tamalpais State Park. (Hunting is now banned everywhere on Tam.) Rock Spring remains popular for the stunning views and for the access it offers to trails high on the north and west slopes of the Mountain. But another plus — free parking — just came to an end. The parking lot, which is in the State Park on the edge of Water District lands, was paved in 1998; a $5 parking fee may be imposed.

The trailhead is at the junction of Ridgecrest Boulevard and Southside (Pantoll) Road. Gates at Pantoll and on Ridgecrest near Fairfax-Bolinas Road bar automobile access to Rock Spring from around an hour after sunset until morning. During exceptionally hot and dry weather, or during rare snowfalls, vehicular access to the summit may be blocked at Rock Spring; call 499-7191 for a recorded message. On Sundays from mid-May through June, Rock Spring is jammed with Mountain Play patrons. By the parking area are outhouses and an interpretive display. There is no water fountain — the nearest are at the Mountain Theater to the east. Some use the untreated water from Rock Spring itself, which flows into a stone enclosure just down Cataract Trail.

Across Ridgecrest Boulevard from the parking lot, paths climb both view knolls flanking Southside Road. The one right (southwest) is separately described as O'Rourke's Bench Trail. The other tops at Forbes Bench, honoring John Franklin Forbes. He and other hikers of the Cross Country Boys Club used to gather on the knoll; Alice Eastwood read Sherlock Holmes installments from Collier's Magazine. The bench was placed by Forbes' son, John Douglas Forbes, in 1981.

Many call the area Rock Springs, but purists correctly point out that there is only one spring.

Suggested loops from Rock Spring (elevation 1,940'):
• Cataract Trail, 1.1m, to Mickey O'Brien Trail — right, .7m, to Barth's Retreat — connector fire road, .2m, to Laurel Dell F.R. — right, .2m, to Benstein Trail — right, 1.2m, to Cataract Trail — left, .1m, to start **3.5 miles.**
• Rock Spring Trail, .1m, to Ridgecrest Blvd. — left, .1m, to Rock Spring-Lagunitas F.R. — left, .8m, to Potrero Meadow — left, 1.6m, on Laurel Dell F.R. to Cataract Trail-left, 1.2m, to start **3.8 miles.**
• Cataract Trail, .1m, to Simmons Trail — right, 1.0m to Barth's Retreat-connector fire road, .2m, to Music Stand Trail — straight, .5m, to High Marsh Trail — left, 1.5m, to Cataract Trail — left, 1.5m, to start **4.8 miles.**

BENSTEIN TRAIL
FROM SIMMONS TRAIL TO LAUREL DELL F.R. / 1.16 miles

Terrain: Deep woodland / MMWD
Elevation: 1,920′ to 2,250′ to 1,980′ / steep
Intersecting Trails: Connector (Ziesche Trail) to Simmons Trail (.4m), Rock Spring-Lagunitas F.R. (.6m-.7m), Lincoln Fairley Trail to Barth's Retreat (.9m)
Directions: Rock Spring trailhead — Cataract Trail — Simmons Trail, .1 mile
Spur: Benstein Extension, to Ridgecrest Boulevard, .1 mile

THE LOVELY Benstein Trail is the most direct route from Rock Spring to Potrero Meadow and on to other north side treasures.

The start of Benstein Trail was rerouted north in the mid-1980's to stem erosion damage to the meadow. To reach the trailhead, follow Cataract Trail 100 yards downhill from Rock Spring and veer right at the MMWD signpost, "To Benstein." In .1 mile, Benstein splits off to the right from Simmons Trail at another signpost.

Benstein climbs, with occasional help from stone and wood steps, at the edge of a Douglas-fir forest. Steve Petterle, former lands manager of the Marin Municipal Water District and now with the Marin County Open Space District, dubbed the area right as "Serpentine Swale." Beyond, the main entrance to the Mountain Theater is visible. In .3 miles, a signed spur (sometimes called Benstein Extension) to Ridgecrest Boulevard and the theater branches right. In early summer, the dried grassland here is dotted bright yellow with showy flowers of yellow mariposa-lily and blue with brodiaea.

At .4 miles, Benstein crosses Ziesche Creek. A .2-mile connector, known as Ziesche Trail, for Edward Ziesche, who had a cabin in the area, drops left to Simmons Trail.

A bit more uphill brings Benstein across a Ziesche feeder. Just above, an MMWD "Erosive Area" sign warns to stay off the hillside. Ten yards past, a path drops left; it winds through the serpentine chaparral triangle between Benstein, Simmons, and Laurel Dell Fire Road. Veer right and go up through the serpentine rock outcrop, where the Trail is briefly indistinct. At .6 miles, Benstein meets and joins Rock Spring-Lagunitas Fire Road along Tam's summit ridge. Go left, toward Rifle Camp. In 100 yards, Benstein departs from the Fire Road to the left at a signpost.

The Trail heads into deep woodland. This was once one of the few places on Tam to spot the celebrated calypso orchid, *Calypso bulbosa*. They are still there, beneath Douglas-firs in early spring for the sharp-eyed to spot, but happily are not as rare on Tam as just 20 years ago. Never pick, or even risk trampling, any wildflower on the Mountain. In 150 yards, a path forks left behind a Douglas-fir, into the same triangle as the earlier path.

Benstein descends, at times steeply. A giant Douglas-fir, with low branches, stands isolated in a forest clearing. One hundred yards below, a seven-trunked tanbark oak borders the Trail's left edge.

Benstein enters an open serpentine outcrop. There are splendid views north. Mt. St. Helena, and higher peaks in Mendocino County, can be seen on clear days. The nearby trees, many dead or almost so, are Sargent cypress. A path, which the Mt. Tamalpais History Project has named for the group's founder, Lincoln Fairley, goes left just under a quarter-mile to Barth's Retreat. Benstein becomes rock-strewn, and slippery when wet.

Benstein drops to its end at Laurel Dell F.R. A path has been worn in across to Potrero Camp, a favored picnic site. Nearby to the right is the main Potrero Meadow, and to the left is Barth's Retreat.

Henry Benstein was an inveterate Mountain hiker and a "regular" at Potrero Camp. In 1921 he recruited his youngest son Albert to build this Trail as a shortcut between Rock Spring and Potrero. Originally called Potrero Camp Trail, it was renamed in Benstein's honor after he died in 1938. (A mis-carved trail sign, reading "Bernstein," helped trigger a lively debate over just whom the Trail was named for. In 1992, I received a letter from Henry's daughter Diane, which seems to settle the issue in favor of "Benstein.")

CATARACT TRAIL
FROM ROCK SPRING TO ALPINE LAKE / 2.89 miles

Terrain: Heavily wooded; riparian; parts rocky / MMWD
Elevation: From 1,970' to 650' / very steep, parts extremely steep
Intersecting Trails: Simmons (.1m), connector to Laurel Dell F.R. (1.0m), Mickey O'Brien (1.2m), Laurel Dell F.R. (1.2m-1.3m), High Marsh (1.5m), Helen Markt (2.3m)
Directions: Rock Spring Trailhead

CATARACT TRAIL is always listed near the top of favorite Tamalpais trails. It is lovely at any time of year but really comes into its own in winter, particularly after a storm. Cataract Creek, which the Trail parallels, is then a torrent, cascading down waterfall after waterfall amidst deep woods. Since Cataract Trail is accessible on both ends by road, and because it is so steep and has only very strenuous loop possibilities, a car shuttle is ideal for those wishing to cover its full length. Leave one car at the turnout where the Fairfax-Bolinas Road bends sharply uphill past Alpine Dam (eight miles from downtown Fairfax), and drive to Rock Spring. You'll then have an all-downhill, three mile walk back. (However, because the Trail has many very steep and often wet and slippery rock steps, many users find it safer and more enjoyable to walk it uphill.)

Note: At press-time (early 1998), the Water District was getting ready to begin an $80,000 reconstruction effort on Cataract Trail, to protect it from erosion and to make it safer. There will be more stairs, more railings, and more overlooks, but no changes to the route described, except possibly a slight rerouting through wet Laurel Dell Meadow.

The Trail begins from the gate at the Rock Spring parking lot. There are outhouses to the left. To the right, in a rocky, shaded grove, are picnic tables. Below the rocks is the source of Rock Spring. Cataract Creek begins its flow to Alpine Lake from the area farther to the right, called Serpentine Swale. In about 100 yards, the combined Simmons and rerouted Benstein trails branch right. Just beyond, Rock Spring is fed, untreated, into a stone pool (right) from the storage tank (left). This historic pool is now choked with watercress and tall rushes.

A fence and sign mark the first of two Cataract Trail reroutings built by the MMWD and Marin Conservation Corps in 1991. The Trail enters riparian forest, where it remains the rest of the way. At the first bridge, two Cataract feeders merge. Stay on the right bank. There is another bridge, crossing Ziesche Creek at its merger with Cataract Creek.

The Trail used to remain on the creek's right bank, passing through a meadow. To protect this meadow, a new bridge, at .4m, takes the Trail over Cataract Creek at the start of the second rerouting. A huge, ancient laurel stands next to the bridge. This new section, through a forest of Douglas-firs, is a delightful addition to the Mountain's trail network. Azaleas dot the creek bank and maples add color in fall.

At .8m, another new bridge brings Cataract Trail over Cataract Creek, back to the right bank and its old routing. About a quarter-mile beyond, where a faint path goes left, look carefully in the creek bed to spot an old airplane engine. It is a remnant from a two-plane collision over Mt. Tam in 1945 (see Mickey O'Brien Trail). Less than 50 yards below, a bridge, unofficially called Ray Murphy Bridge for the ranger who built it, goes left over Cataract Creek to connect with Laurel Dell Fire Road. (The engine was visible upstream from the bridge, until a massive Douglas-fir toppled in 1997 and blocked the view.) There is no other bridge over Cataract Creek for 1.3 miles.

The Trail emerges briefly from the forest in the wonderful meadow known as Laurel Dell. At the start of the clearing, to the right, is Mickey O'Brien Trail, heading to Barth's Retreat. After winter rains, the crossing of Barth's Creek here will likely be a wet one; a small bridge helps. A few yards through the grass and Cataract Trail joins Laurel Dell F.R. The two run together, past a water trough, down to the Laurel Dell sign. To continue on Cataract, veer left into the picnic area; Laurel Dell F.R. continues straight toward Potrero Meadow.

Laurel Dell — with its quiet, shaded, creekside picnic tables — has been a beloved resting spot for decades. A long-time water fountain was recently removed. Across the fire road are outhouses. A few yards downstream of the picnic area a path, known as Old Stove Extension, once rose on the opposite bank; it is now overgrown.

Just below Laurel Dell, Cataract Trail encounters the first of the several impressive waterfalls that accompany it the rest of the way down. Cataract meets the west end of High Marsh Trail, which winds to Kent Trail. The junction is signed, and has a bench. Other paths to High Marsh branch off Cataract near here.

The Trail and adjacent creek begin plunging more steeply; caution is in order, particularly on the slippery rock steps. Continue down through the lush woodland. A steel railing offers some protection when passing beside another of the falls. Look near the railing in May for the lovely blue and white flowers known as Chinese houses. The redwoods and Douglas-firs beside the creek are tall, among the most impressive on the Mountain. Far from any road, this is a magical stretch.

At 2.3 miles, by another waterfall and a pool reminiscent of Hawaii, Cataract meets the signed west end of Helen Markt Trail. It rolls nearly two miles, without an intersection, to Kent Trail.

Cataract Trail now descends very steeply left (avoid the even steeper short-cut). In about 100 yards it crosses the creek. The angled bridge is an old one; countless photos have been taken from it. Few cover the Trail without lingering here above the torrent. The pool above was once a water source.

The Trail continues down, often extremely steeply. (A hiker fell into the creek here during the winter of 1991-92.) Some new steps and a bridge over a wet fording were added in 1989. There are turnouts to get special views of falls. The Trail and Cataract Creek meet the shore of Alpine Lake. Anglers often line the bank. The creek's journey is over but the Trail, now level, continues another one-third mile. Trillium (in late winter) and Clintonia (in early summer), both in the lily family, are two of the showiest among many wildflowers. This broader stretch was once part of the old San Rafael-Bolinas stagecoach road.

Cataract Trail ends at Fairfax-Bolinas Road at a big bend near milepost 8.09. Alpine Dam is a couple of hundred yards to the right. Cataract Trail appeared on the 1898 Sanborn map. The Civilian Conservation Corps rebuilt it in the 1930's.

MOUNTAIN THEATER TRAIL
FROM ROCK SPRING TO MOUNTAIN THEATER / .25 miles

Terrain: Grassland; horses permitted to Old Mine Trail / MTSP; part of Bay Area Ridge Trail
Elevation: From 1,980' to 2,020' / gradual
Intersecting Trails: Old Mine (.1m)
Directions: Rock Spring

MOUNTAIN THEATER TRAIL rises behind a gate, across Ridgecrest Boulevard from the eastern side of the Rock Spring parking area. There are both State Park and Bay Area Ridge Trail signs. A second path here climbs the knoll to Forbes Bench.

The broad Trail rises up the grassy hillside. In 150 yards, at a spectacular view site, Old Mine Trail branches off right. Mountain Theater Trail skirts a hill, with more excellent vistas. A path branches left to Old Mine.

The Trail enters Madrone Grove (also called Sherwood Forest), a picnic area just below the amphitheater itself. "Tanbark Grove" would also be apt, as there are magnificent old tanbark oaks here as well. Beyond is the Mountain Theater.

The first Mountain Play, "Abraham and Isaac," drew 1,200 spectators in 1913. William Kent donated the theater site to the Mountain Play Association in 1915 as a memorial to his friend and business partner Sidney Cushing. Cushing, for whom the theater is now named, was the prime mover behind the Mt. Tamalpais Railway. He committed suicide in 1909.

The present stone-seat amphitheater was constructed by the Civilian Conservation Corps in the 1930's based on a design by Emerson Knight. As condition for the CCC's involvement, the 7-acre site was dedicated to the State Park. The stone blocks, weighing up to two tons, were quarried elsewhere on Tam, brought by truck, then placed in position using a cable and winch system. There are 40 rows of seats, each 1,000 feet long. They are invariably filled to capacity during Mountain Play weekends in May and June.

MUSIC STAND TRAIL
FROM LAUREL DELL FIRE ROAD TO HIGH MARSH TRAIL / .49 miles

Terrain: Wooded; riparian / MMWD
Elevation: From 2,000' to 1,760' / steep, lower half very steep and rocky
Intersecting Trails: None
Directions: Rock Spring — Cataract Trail — Simmons Trail to Barth's Retreat — broad connector to Laurel Dell Fire Road

IN THE 1950's, Mountain veteran Ben Schmidt placed a music stand and some seats for his musician friends in one of the remotest parts of Tam. In the decades that followed, only hard core Tam hikers knew the exact location of the "Music Camp," and finding it was a badge of accomplishment. In 1997, the MMWD, bowing to the many requests, finally signed the main entry although the route is well below their usual standards. There will now undoubtedly be many more visitors to this treasure of Mt. Tamalpais.

The upper end of Music Stand Trail is north off Laurel Dell Fire Road, directly opposite the sign and broad connector to Barth's Retreat. Descend 30 or 40 yards, over the serpentine rocks and through the chamise. A creek bed, which doubles as the upper end of the Trail, comes into view. The Trail branches left of the creek bed in a few more yards, and is then clearer to follow.

The downhill, through forest, is gradual to steep. The adjacent creek, dry much of the year, is the uppermost reaches of the West Fork of Swede George Creek. The Trail crosses to the right bank of the creek, then back to the left bank. Thirty yards from this re-crossing, and a quarter-mile from the start, by a double-trunked Douglas-fir tree and a spring, a path departs left. By now more well-worn than the continuing Trail itself, the path leads a level 50 yards to the Music Camp itself.

There, in a sylvan setting, is an old rusted music stand. Visitors leave coins where the sheet music would rest and messages in the waterproof bags. Battered chairs, tables, and benches complete the camp's "permanent" furnishings. Other decorations, such as the chimes, vary over the months and years. Sing as loud as you want here for it is, after all, the Music Camp. A path continues from the other side of the camp back to Laurel Dell F.R.

Return to the Trail and go left to continue downhill. The Trail becomes more open, and very rocky and steep. Descend with care. A path branches right to High Marsh Trail. A common shrub is the very fragrant pitcher sage.

The Trail crosses the creek, spends 10 yards in the creek bed itself, then recrosses. All this can be quite wet and slippery in winter. The final 100 yards are on the left bank; be careful over a very narrow section.

Music Stand Trail ends when it hits High Marsh Trail, which goes left 1.6 miles to Cataract Trail and right .6 miles to Kent Trail. The creekbed, a massive Douglas-fir whose trunk straightens 10 feet up, and a sizable boulder are landmarks of the unsigned junction. A continuing path straight ahead in the creek canyon is being worn in.

Ben Schmidt, who opened the camp, may know more about the Mountain's hidden trails than any other Tam veteran and is also one of the most important trail builders. Schmidt, now well past 80, was raised on Tam in a cabin near the Tourist Club. He is a music lover, among many other interests. The Trail has also been called the Frank Meraglia, for another Mountain veteran who died in the mid-1970's. Music Camp is another alternate name.

OLD MINE TRAIL
FROM MOUNTAIN THEATER TRAIL TO COASTAL FIRE ROAD / 1.49 miles*

Terrain: Upper part grassland, lower part tanbark oak woodland; horses permitted above Riding & Hiking Trail / MTSP; part of Bay Area Ridge Trail
Elevation: From 2,000' to 1,460' / upper half steep
Intersecting Trails: Riding & Hiking (.6m), Old Stage Road (1.0m)
Directions: Rock Spring — Mountain Theater Trail, .1m
Amenities: Bathrooms, fountains, telephone
*Includes .2m discontinuity below Old Stage Road

OLD MINE TRAIL is a lovely Trail, with spectacular vistas. From the Rock Spring parking area, cross Ridgecrest Boulevard, veer left, and follow Mountain Theater Trail uphill. In around 100 yards there is a signed junction. Mountain Theater Trail continues left to the theater and Old Mine Trail branches right. To the right of the intersection, atop the tree covered hill, is Forbes Bench.

This upper section of Old Mine, to Riding & Hiking Trail, is a hiker-equestrian segment of the Bay Area Ridge Trail. The views out over the grassland are among the finest anywhere on Tam. A path departs left toward the theater. Old Mine crosses a serpentine outcropping. The first path to the top of the hill is presently closed for erosion control; users have worn in another just beyond. Make the short ascent for even more stunning views. On clear days, the snow-capped Sierra may be visible, along with Mt. Diablo, the San Francisco skyline, both towers of the Golden Gate Bridge, and the Pacific. The hill is popular as a wedding site and as a place to fly kites.

Old Mine begins dropping steeply. It passes beside, and then through, a woodland. Tanbark oaks become the most common tree. Found in all Tam forests, tanbarks are dominant on Old Mine. At .4 miles, a massive Douglas-fir, with huge lower limbs, sits aside the Trail's left margin. Pantoll, the Trail's destination, briefly comes into view.

After some switchbacks, Old Mine meets Riding & Hiking Trail, which goes left to Easy Grade Trail and Old Stage Road. Veer right, back into forest. A former shortcut to Pantoll, closed due to erosion problems, branches right. Old Mine swings left and meets asphalt-covered Old Stage Road at a signed junction.

The original Old Mine Trail is now severed and paved over by Old Stage Road and Panoramic Highway. To pick up the remainder of the Trail, go right to Pantoll and cross Panoramic. Follow the paved road (Coastal Fire Road, but originally called Old Mine Fire Road) downhill from the ranger station. Forty yards past the Steep Ravine Trail turnoff, Old Mine Trail resumes, well marked, on the left. This fairly level lower section is a pedestrian segment of the Bay Area Ridge Trail.

A quarter-mile into the Douglas-fir forest, at a 6x6 post, is the site of the old mine, just above on the right, that gave the Trail its name. The mine site was only rediscovered in 1952, by State Park ranger Jim Whitehead. A re-done sign fixed to the post, copying the original filing, dates this "Denos Claim" to May 1863. Louis Denos was a pioneer Marin settler. (The sign is now missing.) There was a modest gold rush on Tam then with over a dozen claims, none profitable, filed. There are traces of gold in some Tam quartz outcroppings.

The Trail ends shortly after, when it again meets Coastal Fire Road at a four-way intersection. Coastal goes left to the Dipsea Trail and to Deer Park Fire Road, which is the southern continuation of the Bay Area Ridge Trail. Right is a return to Pantoll through the State Park's maintenance yard. Straight across is the bottom of unsigned Lone Tree Hill Fire Road.

O'ROURKE'S BENCH TRAIL
FROM ROCK SPRING TO O'ROURKE'S BENCH / .41 miles

Terrain: Grassland / MTSP
Elevation: From 1,980' to 2,070' / gradual
Intersecting Trails: None
Directions: Rock Spring

THIS TRAIL LEADS to the stunning view knoll on which O'Rourke's Bench sits. It sets off directly across from the Rock Spring parking area, up the grassy slope to the southwest. The start is marked only by a "no dogs" sign.

O'Rourke's Bench Trail climbs 100 yards to the top of the knoll. A fenced-in wind gauge is passed on the right. This splendid, open area that O'Rourke's Bench Trail enters, formerly the Scott property, was only added to Mt. Tamalpais State Park in 1953. The 265-acre addition was financed largely by William Kent, Jr. and John Miller, for whom Miller Trail is named.

The views are sweeping the rest of the way. The Trail meets a serpentine outcropping, barren of plants save for an occasional poppy. Go directly over the rocks; the route is momentarily indistinct. Keep ever uphill.

The Trail passes a laurel shielded from the west winds by a huge boulder. Just beyond, the Trail passes through a small grove dominated by three trees; a tanbark oak, a goldcup oak, and a Douglas-fir riddled with woodpecker holes.

The Trail veers left up into an isolated stand of laurels. (A path continues through the grassland, toward the "hang glider" knolls.) Enter to savor one of the Mountain's treasures, O'Rourke's Bench. Carved from the rocks, it commands a spectacular, panoramic view (even of the Sierra on clear winter days, when standing on the bench). The plaque on the bench reads:

'GIVE ME THESE HILLS AND THE FRIENDS I LOVE,
I ASK NO OTHER HEAVEN.'
TO OUR DAD O'ROURKE, IN JOYOUS CELEBRATION OF HIS
76TH. BIRTHDAY, FEB. 25TH. 1927. FROM THE FRIENDS
TO WHOM HE SHOWED THIS HEAVEN.

You'll surely want to stay a while, even if the area's notorious winds and fog are swirling. Many visitors leave flowers. Richard Festus "Dad" O'Rourke was an impeccably dressed Mountain veteran who led his wife and four daughters, and legions of others, on hikes over Tamalpais. He is credited with being a catalyst for both the founding of the Tamalpais Conservation Club and the building of the Mountain Theater. Much beloved, he was honored by this bench at his favorite resting place, which he called "Edge of the World." There is a splendid picture of O'Rourke and his wife, sitting on the bench on the day of its dedication, in Lincoln Fairley's book *Mount Tamalpais, A History*.

POTRERO TRAIL
FROM POTRERO CAMP TO RIFLE CAMP / .33 miles

Terrain: Meadow and riparian woodland / MMWD
Elevation: Around 2,000' / almost level
Intersecting Trails: None
Directions: Rock Spring — Cataract Trail, .1m — Simmons Trail, .1m — Benstein Trail to end — Connector to Potrero Camp
Amenities: Outhouse, picnic tables

THIS TRAIL, with no official name, connects the two Potrero meadows. It sets off from Potrero Camp, a favorite picnic area. Also beginning here is unsigned Swede George Trail, which descends north into the woods. Potrero Trail enters Lower Potrero Meadow. It immediately crosses a short bridge. To the left, Kent Trail begins its long descent to Alpine Lake. A horse hitch is a reminder that this is a long-time equestrian gathering site.

The Trail enters a delightful woodland. It ascends gently along the edge of a stream. Beyond is Upper Potrero Meadow, one of Tam's crown jewels. It is lovely any time of day, any time of year. Savor the short walk across its northern edge. The early yards may be somewhat boggy; other routes across the even wetter parts of the meadow are now closed. Near the end, on the left, is the site of a once well-tended garden.

The Trail ends, marked by an MMWD signpost, at its intersection with Rock Spring-Lagunitas Fire Road. Rifle Camp, another favored picnic site, is a few yards ahead. (From Rifle Camp, Arturo Trail rises to East Ridgecrest Boulevard; it offers a slightly shorter entry to Potrero Trail.)

ROCK SPRING TRAIL
FROM ROCK SPRING TO OLD RAILROAD GRADE AT WEST POINT / 1.70 miles

Terrain: Mostly wooded, parts open; short section asphalt / MTSP & MMWD
Elevation: 1,970' to 1,780' / gradual
Intersecting Trails: Eastwood (1.3m)
Directions: Rock Spring

THIS IS A LOVELY TRAIL — well-graded, well-wooded, and with many breathtaking view sites. It is also popular because it connects three of the Mountain's special places; Rock Spring, Mountain Theater, and West Point.

Rock Spring Trail sets off from the Rock Spring parking lot, to the right (east) at the Cataract Trail sign. The Trail passes below the shaded tables. In early spring, look carefully in the grass under the trees for the purple-pink calypso orchids, always a challenge and treat to find. Beneath the rocks here is the source of Rock Spring itself. Work was done on the spring in 1933 to keep it flowing all year. In 1972, the spring's outlet was relocated to its present site, just down Cataract Trail.

In .1 mile, the Trail hits Ridgecrest Boulevard directly across from the main entrance to the Sidney B. Cushing Memorial (Mountain) Theater. Cross the pavement and enter the theater; it is open year round. The next section is on an asphalt path. In 40 yards, at a fork, is a plaque. Placed in 1986, it honors the Civilian Conservation Corps for constructing the amphitheater 50 years earlier. Hauling, shaping, and placing the thousands of serpentine rocks (some weighing over two tons) to make the seats was an extraordinary undertaking. Veer left. This approach to the upper seats of the theater, taken by thousands on Sunday play dates in May and June, seems oddly quiet any other time.

A second plaque, dating from 1983, is passed. It honors three men: Marin Congressman and land baron William Kent, who donated the theater's land; Sidney Cushing, the driving force behind the Mt. Tamalpais Railway; and Alfred Pinther, a past president of the Mountain Play Association, the California Alpine Club, and the Tamalpais Conservation Club.

A few yards beyond, a trail sign points the way, right, to the upper ends of the Bootjack and Easy Grade trails. Rock Spring Trail goes straight ahead, across the top row of the amphitheater. This is a special place, during the plays, when it is rented for weddings, or when it is deserted the rest of the year. Sit and enjoy the views over to the East Bay.

The Trail continues on the other side of the theater, past a pair of drinking fountains. It immediately encounters, on the left, massive Pohli Rock, which commands a stunning view site. Salem Rice, the leading authority of Mt. Tamalpais' geology, dates the Rock's greenstone to a sea floor lava flow some 400 million years ago.

Pohli Rock has long been intimately connected to the Mountain Play. It has been used as a prop in several productions, people still watch the play from atop it, and there are two haunting plaques affixed to it. The one on the far left, somewhat hidden, says:

I LINGERED ON THE HILL WHERE WE HAD PLAYED,
GARNETT HOLME, 1873-1929.

Holme, a drama instructor at the University of California, was one of the prime movers behind the creation of the Mountain Play, and served as its first director. He died in 1929, after a fall on the Mountain. His ashes are embedded in the rock.

The second plaque reads:

TO AUSTIN RAMON POHLI, A LOVER OF THIS MOUNTAIN,
WHO DIED MAY 20, 1913, AGED 20 YEARS,
THIS ROCK IS DEDICATED.

Pohli was the son of Emil and Kate Pohli. Mrs. Pohli was one of the founders of the Mill Valley Outdoor Art Club and chairwoman, in 1904, of a committee that was fighting to save Muir Woods (then called Sequoia Canyon). Ramon Pohli was a student at Cal when he met Holme, who then appointed him the Mountain Play's first business manager. Pohli fell to his death while climbing near Snow Creek Falls in Yosemite just 20 days after the triumphal opening of the very first Mountain Play, the success for which he was given large credit. Pohli's ashes were scattered on the Mountain. The rock was formally dedicated to him on May 17, 1914.

Just beyond, at a boundary post, the Trail leaves Mt. Tamalpais State Park into the Water District. (The Water District donated the acreage of Pohli Rock to the State Park.) A few yards past, a path, once known as Telephone Trail #2, heads off left up to a Mountain Theater parking lot. One hundred yards later, by a classic old MMWD sign, another path rises left to Ridgecrest Boulevard. Continue through the light woodland. The down grade is barely noticeable. A double bridge fords a rivulet, then another bridge crosses the headwaters of Rattlesnake Creek.

At .9 miles, the Trail passes through a treeless serpentine rock band. On the far side, look on the right for Colier Rock, a serpentine boulder commanding a great vista. It bears a patina-covered bronze plaque:

TO JOHN M. COLIER, A LOVER OF NATURE.

This is the same Colier of Colier Spring and Colier Trail (which see), and here was his favorite view spot.

A second, even more prominent open serpentine stretch is crossed. In the middle, the Trail is barely visible. This gray-green area is visible from many areas to the south of Tam. Serpentine rock steps continue the descent.

At 1.3 miles, a signpost marks the lower end of Eastwood Trail, which rises extremely steeply to Ridgecrest Boulevard. (The Eastwood Trail side of the post was covered in 1993; the Water District has abandoned the route.) Continue straight. You can begin to see glimpses of West Point Inn. Evidence of a burn remains on the left. The Trail crosses Spike Buck Creek.

By a Douglas-fir, Rock Spring Trail passes the remnant of an old stile that once kept horses off the route. In another 100 yards, the Trail ends at Old Railroad Grade, here circling around West Point Inn. Nora and West Point trails also meet the inn.

Rock Spring has been a named feature on Mt. Tamalpais for more than 100 years. Rock Spring Trail was shown on the 1898 Sanborn map as the West Point Trail. Since West Point was a name added to Tamalpais in 1896 during construction of the rail line, the Trail probably dates to 1896-98.

SIMMONS TRAIL
FROM CATARACT TRAIL TO BARTH'S RETREAT / .95 miles

Terrain: Mixed forest and open serpentine; parts rocky / MMWD
Elevation: 1,960' to 2,210' to 1,960' / very steep
Intersecting Trails: Benstein (.1m), connector (Ziesche Trail) to Benstein Trail (.2m)
Directions: Rock Spring — Cataract Trail, .1 mile

SIMMONS TRAIL plays a part in many loop trips from Rock Spring. It is also the direct route to two of the Mountain's treasures, Barth's Retreat and the Music Camp. The Trail offers splendid vistas as it passes over the haunting western edge of Tam's summit ridge.

To reach Simmons, follow Cataract Trail 100 yards down from the Rock Spring parking area to a signpost. Simmons, combined with the rerouted Benstein Trail, branches to the right.

Simmons crosses Cataract Creek, here only a trickle. In 100 yards, Benstein departs to the right, on its way to Potrero Camp. Since that is quite near Simmons' end (Barth's Retreat), Benstein makes a good loop partner.

Simmons veers left to follow the left bank of Ziesche Creek. Pioneer Tam hiker Edward Ziesche built a cabin here in the 1880's. It was razed around 1935. The exact site was only rediscovered in 1988 by Sausalitan Phil Frank, creator of the cartoon "Farley" and an avid Tam explorer. The area is criss-crossed with faint, old paths, including an earlier routing of Simmons.

The Trail crosses the creek over a bridge. There is a stand of introduced redwoods. This was the site of old Camp Norway. Two forks present themselves; they soon unite. Just up the main one, left, affixed to a dead Douglas-fir, is a replica of an old sign pointing the way to Barth's Retreat. (The original is in the Lucretia Little History Room of the Mill Valley Public Library.)

The Trail begins to climb. The ascent is first through a forest. Simmons then enters an open serpentine rock area. The Trail is lined with chaparral shrubs. The uphill is steep and rocky but the views ahead more than compensate.

Fifty yards before the crest, and some 15 yards before the first Sargent cypress tree, paths set off left and right. The one right, known to some as Perkins Pass Trail, goes to Rock Spring-Lagunitas F.R. between the two forks of Benstein. The one left leads to the "Throne," a man-made rock seat that is one of Tam's treasured hidden gems. If you can find it, sit in the "Throne" and enjoy the magnificent vista.

Simmons Trail levels at its crest of just over 2,200 feet. This starkly lovely area is the western edge of the Mt. Tamalpais summit ridge. The trees found amidst the serpentine rock are virtually all Sargent cypress. John Thomas Howell's description of Sargent cypress in his *Marin Flora* may well have been inspired here: "These gray-green trees blend with the gray-green rock of the serpentine barrens to form a picturesque and memorable part of the Mount Tamalpais scene." Look carefully at the trees and, on many, you'll see mistletoe (*Phoradendron densum*) growing off the branch tips. Mistletoe is a parasitic plant, robbing the trees of nutrients; "phoradendron" means tree-thief in Greek. This mistletoe species is also poisonous to humans.

The Trail passes briefly through another forest, then opens in an area known as Buck Meadows. There is a welcome bench from which a view of Point Reyes is framed.

Simmons continues its descent through a predominantly Douglas-fir forest. A path forks right at the Trail's final bend.

Simmons ends at Barth's Retreat. Mickey O'Brien Trail sets off from here to Laurel Dell. A bridge, dedicated to the memory of Harold Allen Atkinson (1903-1983), crosses Barth's Creek. Atkinson was an active member of the Tamalpais Conservation Club for decades; his name appears on an April 21, 1912, trail cleanup assignment list.

Barth's Retreat has been a popular picnic site for more than 100 years. There are picnic tables and a water spigot (untreated and signed as non-potable). Emil Barth was a versatile musician and music teacher. He was associated with the Mountain from 1886, when he arrived from Germany. He built a cabin here, named Casa Escondida, that he lived in, part-time, until his death in 1926. The obituary for him in the TCC newsletter, *California Out Of Doors*, of January 1927 said: "No one knew the trails and unfrequented paths as he did, no one loved them more, and few have done as much as he to find beauty spots and build trails to reach them." His extensive music collection was donated to the San Francisco Public Library by his wife in 1937.

A broad connector to Laurel Dell F.R. rises from Barths Retreat. Half-way up it, on the left, is a plaque to long-time MMWD patrolman Joseph Zapella, "Friend of the Hikers." Across Laurel Dell F.R. from the connector's junction is the unmarked upper end of Music Camp Trail.

Simmons Trail dates from around World War I. Fred Sandrock of the Mt. Tamalpais History Project speculates it may be named for Spanish-American War Colonel Charles A. Simmons, who made a film promoting the virtues of California and who was an early donor to the Tamalpais Conservation Club. Simmons also organized a series of "Hospitality Hikes," some of which were on Tam. He died in 1931, at age 57.

SWEDE GEORGE TRAIL
FROM POTRERO CAMP TO WILLOW MEADOW TRAIL / .86 miles

Terrain: Deep woodland; riparian; unmaintained and MARGINAL / MMWD
Elevation: From 1,985' to 1,460' / steep to very steep
Intersecting Trails: High Marsh (.5m)
Directions: Rock Spring — Cataract Trail — Simmons Trail — Benstein Trail to end — broad connector to Potrero Camp

THREE TRAILS — Kent, Potrero and Swede George — converge at lower Potrero Meadow (Potrero Camp). Kent sets off downhill from the east side of the foot bridge. Potrero Trail crosses the meadow and connects with Rifle Camp. Swede George Trail, unsigned, easy to miss, and absent on most maps, sets off from just behind (north of) the Potrero Camp sign. It passes through some of the Mountain's quietest and loveliest woodland.

From the old Potrero Camp sign, head directly into the forest, keeping the creek to the right. There is a fork in 25 yards; bend right and down toward the creek. A connector to Laurel Dell Fire Road departs on the left. Swede George Trail descends alongside the left bank of the Middle Fork of Swede George Creek.

Within 200 feet, by a prominent boulder outcropping, are azalea bushes. Many of the trees are Douglas-firs but those with longer, sharper needles are California nutmegs. In late fall, look on the ground for their green fruits, a favorite of forest denizens. The single seed is encased in a hard shell, in turn surrounded by a sticky, fragrant, outer envelope (aril).

The unmaintained Trail is at times rough, steep, and narrow, but reasonably clear to follow. If you lose it, stay near the creek's left bank.

At .3 miles, the Trail enters a delightful clearing, carpeted with native, perennial bunch grasses. These grasses, largely replaced throughout California by faster growing, Eurasian annual grasses after cattle grazing was introduced in the late 1700's, remain hardy and green here into fall. Dead Douglas-firs contain woodpecker-carved nesting holes.

The Trail continues dropping, in sections somewhat steep and indistinct. Just below a crossing of a Swede George Creek feeder, Swede George Trail meets

High Marsh Trail. The two trails run together to the right for 50 yards, when Swede George branches off left and downhill.

This lower section, also not signed or officially maintained, is in better condition, particularly the early section through a Douglas-fir forest. The canyon of the Middle Fork is near, then the Trail veers away from it. The Trail is narrower when it passes through sections of chaparral.

Soon, the East Fork of Swede George Creek becomes audible, a roar in winter. The Trail drops to it. The fording can be a tricky one after winter rains. Try it just upstream, and do your best to stay dry. A retreat to High Marsh Trail is another option.

Swede George Trail ends just 15 yards above the creek at Willow Meadow Trail. Kent Trail is .1 mile uphill, Stocking Trail .4 miles down.

Although likely a long-time route, Swede George Trail has no official name. "Swede George Trail" is my own suggestion, as it runs between two forks of that important northside creek. (Swede George Trail was, however, a former name of both Kent Trail and Stocking Trail.) Swede George was a woodsman who lived in a cabin in the area in the 1860's. Even his obituary in a Marin newspaper failed to reveal his last name.

Oaks, Casey Cutoff Trail.

Sky Oaks Trailhead

Sky Oaks Trailhead

Directions to Sky Oaks Road:
Highway 101 — Sir Francis Drake Blvd. (exit) west, Greenbrae, to San Anselmo — left on Center Blvd., which becomes Broadway in Fairfax — left on Bolinas Road, 1.4 miles, to Lake Lagunitas sign opposite #700 Bolinas Road

SKY OAKS ROAD provides access to Lakes Lagunitas, Bon Tempe, and Alpine. These "upper lakes," as they are sometimes called, are immensely appealing to a wide range of users. A vehicle use fee, currently $4 ($3 November through March), is collected at the toll booth opposite the MMWD Sky Oaks Ranger Station. Annual passes costing $30 ($15 for senior citizens) are sold at the station or at MMWD headquarters, 220 Nellen Avenue, Corte Madera.

Several trail junctions are encountered along Sky Oaks Road. With mileage from the ranger station, they are: Taylor (at the station), Scott Tank F.R. (at the station), Bullfrog F.R. (.1m), Sky Oaks-Lagunitas (.1m and 1.3m), Shaver Grade (.4m), Pumpkin Ridge (.7m and 1.5m), Bon Tempe (1.0m), Madrone (1.0m), and Fish Grade (1.5m).

Parking for Bon Tempe Dam and Alpine Lake is reached by the only right turn off Sky Oaks Road, .6 miles from the ranger station. This unpaved road was once part of the San Rafael-Bolinas County Road, dating to the stagecoach era of the 1870's. There are portable outhouses on both sides of Bon Tempe dam, but no other facilities. There is a ramp for wheelchair-bound fishermen at Bon Tempe's Redwood Cove, one mile from the toll booth.

The Lake Lagunitas parking lot, at what was known as Lagunitas Junction, is at the end of Sky Oaks Road, 1.6 miles from the Ranger Station. Adjacent are outhouses (new ones opened in 1997), fountains, a telephone, and an attractive picnic area with tables and grills. The dam, lake and loop road are just above.

Sky Oaks, by the present ranger station, was the site, from 1924, of Camp California, a University of California summer training camp for engineering students. During the 1930's, the Civilian Conservation Corps had one of its two Mt. Tamalpais camps here (the other was at today's Camp Eastwood). On December 9, 1941, two days after the bombing of Pearl Harbor, National Guard troops moved in and Sky Oaks was used for military training during World War II. After the war the university did not renew its lease and the area became Sky Oaks Girl Scout Camp. Today, the area houses the newly renovated headquarters for rangers of the Marin Municipal Water District.

Suggested loops from Lake Lagunitas parking area-elevation 730':
• To Lake Lagunitas F.R., .1m — left or right, 1.6m, around Lake Lagunitas — to start, .1m **1.8 miles.**
• Left or right on Bon Tempe Trail around Bon Tempe Lake **4.0 miles.**
• Sky Oaks Road, .2m, to Fish Gulch — .2m to Filter Plant Road — 1.0m to Eldridge Grade — right, 1.2m, to Lakeview F.R. — right, .8m, to Lake Lagunitas F.R. — right, .6m, to start (or left, 1.2m, to start) **4.0 miles (or 4.6 miles).**

• Bon Tempe (Shadyside) Trail, .3m, to Lower Berry Trail — left, .4m, to No Name Trail — right, .5m, to Rocky Ridge F.R. — right, .1m, to Stocking Trail-left, .6m, to Kent Trail — right, 2.3m, to Alpine — Bon Tempe Pump F.R. — straight, .5m, to Bon Tempe (Shadyside) Trail — right, 1.3m, to start **6.0 miles.**
• To Lake Lagunitas F.R., .1m — right (counterclockwise), .6m, to Colier Trail — right, 1.1m, to Northside Trail — left, 1.6m, to Eldridge Grade — left, 2.3m, to Lakeview F.R. — left, .3m, to Pilot Knob Trail — .8m to Bridle Path F.R. — .2m down to start **7.0 miles**

Circuit of Mt. Tamalpais:
• To Lake Lagunitas F.R., .1m — left (clockwise), .5m, to Lakeview F.R. — left (straight), .8m, to Eldridge Grade — right (straight), 3.5m, across Ridgecrest Blvd. to Old Railroad Grade — left, 1.5m, to West Point — right on Rock Spring Trail, .4m, to Eastwood Trail — right, .6m, across Ridgecrest Blvd. to Arturo Trail — left, .5m, to Rifle Camp — right, 2.4m, on Rock Spring-Lagunitas F.R. to start **10.3 miles.**

Suggested loops from Bon Tempe Dam — elevation 720'
• Cross dam, .3m — Alpine-Bon Tempe F.R., .4m, to Kent Trail — 2.3m to Stocking Trail — left, .6m, to Rocky Ridge F.R. — left, 1.4m, to Bon Tempe Dam — cross dam, .3m, to start **5.3 miles.**
• Cross dam, .3m — Casey Cutoff Trail, .5m, to Rocky Ridge F.R. — left .6m, to Stocking Trail — right, 1.1m, to Willow Meadow Trail — left, .5m, to Kent Trail — right, .1m, to Azalea Meadow Trail — left, .6m, to Cross Country Boys Trail — left, .3m, to Upper Berry Trail — left, .1m, to Rock Spring-Lagunitas F.R. — left, 1.0m, to Lower Berry Trail — left, .4m, to Bon Tempe Trail — left, 1.2m, to dam — cross dam, .3m, to start **7.0 miles.**

ALPINE PUMP FIRE ROAD
FROM BON TEMPE DAM TO KENT TRAIL / .50 miles

Terrain: Riparian; lightly wooded / MMWD
Elevation: From 720' to 650' / gradual
Intersecting Trails: Rocky Ridge F.R. (.1m)
Directions: Across Bon Tempe Dam from parking lot
Amenities: Outhouse

This Fire Road is the main access to Kent Trail, and therefore to many other northside trails. It sets off from Bon Tempe Dam on the opposite (west) side from the spillway and parking area. Here also, by an outhouse, are the starts of Bon Tempe (Shadyside) and Casey Cutoff trails.

In 20 yards, Rocky Ridge F.R. departs to the left, beginning a long, stiff uphill. Alpine Pump Fire Road descends toward Alpine Lake. This was the area where Tamalpais Dam was to have been erected. Work was started in 1903 but never completed. Instead, Phoenix Dam (1905), then Alpine Dam (1917-19), then nearby Bon Tempe Dam (1949) were built. The foundations of Tamalpais Dam are still visible across Alpine Lake here when the water level is low.

The Fire Road continues to drop. It meets Alpine Lake by a pump house, which dates to 1956. From here, water is delivered up to Bon Tempe Lake, then on through the treatment plant to southern Marin consumers. To the left is the signed start of Kent Trail, which winds its way to Potrero Camp. A line of orange-red markers stretches across Alpine's surface to a mid-lake pump. The Fire Road was built to provide access to the pump. It is also called Pumphouse F.R.

AZALEA HILL TRAIL
FROM FAIRFAX-BOLINAS ROAD TO (TRADITIONALLY) BON TEMPE CREEK / .85 miles

Terrain: Part grassland, part woodland / MMWD
Elevation: From 1,080' to 1,180' to 650' / steep; parts very steep
Intersecting Trails: None
Directions: Same as Sky Oaks but continue on Fairfax-Bolinas Road to parking area by milepost 3.76
Amenities: Outhouse

THE WEST END of this unusually stunning Trail is at a gate on the left (coming from Fairfax) side of Fairfax-Bolinas Road, at a parking area about a mile beyond the Meadow Club golf course. Across the pavement is Pine Mountain Fire Road, principal entry into the drainages of the Little and Big Carson creeks, a huge area of Water District land outside this book's coverage.

Azalea Hill Trail begins climbing at fire road-width, with only this broad section to the crest open to cyclists. A new sign warns that MMWD lands are open only sunrise to sunset; Azalea Hill had long been a popular site for stargazing.

Just about every step upward brings new landmarks into view. In rapid order, Pine Mountain, White's Hill, Loma Alta, and Big Rock (four of the tallest peaks in Marin County), become visible. There is then a view down to the Meadow Club golf course and, well beyond, San Pablo Bay. At a path left, is the first glimpse of Tam's East Peak summit. Next, Bald Hill, the ridges above China Camp, the Richmond-San Rafael Bridge, and Mt. Diablo, 40 miles east, are added. Hundreds of planted daffodils bring even more color in late winter to the rich native wildflower display.

At .2 miles the fire road crests with a view of Tam's full summit ridge. A path right leads to the 1,217-foot top of Azalea Hill (noted by a survey marker), a side trip definitely worth taking. Wade through the shrubby leather oak (*Quercus durata*) and the manzanita, over the serpentine rocks, to check out the even broader views.

Continuing on the Trail, Bon Tempe, 500' below, suddenly becomes visible at one of Tam's classic scenic vistas. The meadow here is among the loveliest on Tam, special to many. (I was best man at a wedding here.) A path sets off right.

Since there are currently no through options beyond the far side of the meadow, the Trail can be said to end there, but I'll describe the traditional route. The now narrow Trail begins a short but extremely steep descent over serpentine rock. Descend with care. There are intersecting paths, some now posted as closed for erosion control; aim toward the Bon Tempe Dam spillway. An unusual fern at the base of many of the rocks here is serpentine fern. Look carefully for the azalea bushes that gave the hill and Trail their names.

The Trail then resumes in reasonable condition, though it is still slippery, into a grove of black oaks and stately madrones. Isolated rest and picnic sites, with views of Mt. Tamalpais across Bon Tempe Lake, beckon in this idyllic area. There is some poison oak as well, however.

The Trail descends a steep, bracken-covered hillside. The traditional route, now blocked by an "erosion control" sign, went straight down to a path just above Bon Tempe Creek. Now, go left, to the driest creek crossing to Bullfrog Road.

There have been calls, particularly by mountain bicyclists, for improving the route over this eastern section slope of Azalea Hill to provide a direct connection between the lakes and Pine Mountain.

BON TEMPE TRAIL
AROUND BON TEMPE LAKE / 3.96 miles

Terrain: Half woodland, half grassland; riparian; .1 mile paved; horses permitted except at Pine Point / MMWD
Elevation: Around 730' / almost level
Intersecting Trails: Clockwise from Bon Tempe Dam; Hidden Cove (.6m), Madrone (1.0m), Sky Oaks-Lagunitas (1.0m, 2.2m), Rock Spring-Lagunitas F.R. (2.5m), Lower Berry (2.8m), Stocking (2.8m), Casey Cutoff (3.8m), Alpine Pump F.R. (3.8m)
Directions: Bon Tempe Dam parking lot
Amenities: Outhouses, fountain

IT IS POSSIBLE TO CIRCLE the shore of Bon Tempe Lake by trail, save for a short paved section at Redwood Cove. The loop is traditionally viewed as two segments; the southwestern, wooded "Shadyside," and the northeastern, largely open "Sunnyside." The circuit is described clockwise from Bon Tempe Dam, though the Trail is just as commonly joined from the Lake Lagunitas parking lot. The total distance of four miles is based on hugging the shore on the Sunnyside part, avoiding the several shortcuts.

Follow the steep dirt road up from the Bon Tempe Dam parking area (the nearer parking area uphill was closed in 1991), then veer left onto a fire road to begin the circuit of the lake. (There is also a trail, which quickly meets this route.) The broad road climbs through oak woodland then meets open grassland. This is clearly the "Sunnyside" half of the circuit. It was most recently widened and improved in 1997.

Opposite the spillway, the trail and broader options meet. The route rises to a level crest, then descends. At a building containing a pump, the broad section ends and becomes trail-width. A shortcut path goes left, the first of several that lace the Lake's northern and eastern shores.

The next inlet is Hamburger Cove, a popular fishing spot. Stick to the gently rolling lakeshore. The area has a pastoral quality, particularly appealing in the soft light of early morning and dusk. But it can also be quite hot here in summer, and muddy in winter.

The Trail circles a secluded inlet aptly called Hidden Cove. Unsigned Hidden Cove Trail rises from the bend of the cove to the unpaved auto access road to Bon Tempe.

About a mile in, at Redwood Cove, Bon Tempe Trail is routed onto Sky Oaks Road at a marked crosswalk. Go right. Across the pavement here is an entry to the Madrone and Sky Oaks-Lagunitas trails. Rounding the bend on the pavement, the route passes the splendid redwood tree that gives the cove its name. The outhouse and fishing ramp are wheelchair-accessible. About 75 yards beyond is the first of a few short connectors, all steep, back to the Trail by the lake shore.

Paths that parallel Sky Oaks Road offer shortcuts. Veer right, along the shore, to circle lovely, wooded Pine Point. (This section of the route is sometimes called Pine Point Trail.) Introduced pines have long provided shade for the picnickers and fishermen who frequent the peninsula's shore. A plan under discussion to restore native vegetation calls for removal of the pines.

The Trail runs into a junction of dirt roads at the lake's southeast tip. Continue right, around the lake. At the junction with the southern end of Sky Oaks-Lagunitas Trail (marked with a "Horse" route sign) is an array of valves. They regulate the flow of water from Bon Tempe to the nearby treatment plant. In summer, cooler water from the bottom of the lake is drawn. In winter, when the bottom of the lake is clouded by sediment raised from the overflow of Lake Lagunitas, the clearer water from the top of the lake is released.

The now broad Trail winds to the edge of the Lake Lagunitas parking lot. Nearby are water fountains, a lovely picnic area, outhouses and a phone. Cross the bridge over Lagunitas Creek. The "Shadyside" of Bon Tempe Trail continues around the lake to the right, up a short rise.

After hugging the shore at the lake's southeast corner, Shadyside emerges into an open area. Beyond a small stream is the unmarked bottom of Lower Berry Trail. It rises to Rock Spring-Lagunitas F.R.

Bon Tempe Trail re-enters the forest, where it remains until the dam. On the far side of the first of Shadyside's three bridges, unmarked Stocking Trail climbs steeply toward Rocky Ridge F.R. (This lower section of Stocking is so hard to find that it has been removed from the Olmsted map entirely; look carefully up the creek's left bank.)

The next mile is very gently rolling, and peaceful. Huge Douglas-firs tower above the Trail. There are lovely views out over the lake through the trees.

Around one-half mile past the third bridge, the Trail descends a few steps onto Bon Tempe Dam. Casey Cutoff Trail, to Rocky Ridge, rises uphill to the left before the last step. Alpine Pump F.R., on the left past the outhouse, leads to the starts of both Rocky Ridge F.R. and Kent Trail.

Cross the dam to complete the loop. To the left is the eastern tip of long, thin, Alpine Lake. To the right is one of the loveliest sights in the Bay Area; Mt. Tamalpais reflected in the waters of Bon Tempe Lake.

Bon Tempe is an Americanized version of the Swiss-Italian surname Bautunpi. Two brothers, Guiseppi and Pasquale Bautunpi, leased 1,180 acres here in 1868 to run a dairy ranch. By 1874, they had 88 cows on the ranch and produced 115 pounds of butter a day. The main ranch buildings, below Bon Tempe Dam, were removed in 1918 just before Alpine Lake was filled.

Bon Tempe Lake was formed in 1949 upon completion of the dam on Lagunitas Creek. It has a capacity of 1.3 billion gallons, ten times larger than Lake Lagunitas upstream but significantly smaller than Alpine and Kent lakes downstream. The loop Trail was built, largely by the Tamalpais Trail Riders, just after the lake was filled.

BRIDLE PATH FIRE ROAD
FROM LAKE LAGUNITAS PARKING AREA TO LAKE LAGUNITAS / .27 miles

Terrain: Woodland / MMWD
Elevation: 730' to 840' to 790' / very steep
Intersecting Trails: Pilot Knob (.2m)
Directions: Lake Lagunitas parking area

Two FIRE ROADS RISE from the old and now closed outhouses at the Lake Lagunitas parking lot. The unnamed one to the right (south) connects to Lagunitas Dam. The one to the left is signed as Lakeview Road, to Eldridge Grade. But the Lakeview designation, while technically correct, is nowadays more associated with the section of the road above Lake Lagunitas. The unofficial name Bridle Path Fire Road, from a long-time sign "Bridle Path," is still used here. The Fire Road has been an equestrian access to Lake Lagunitas, and more recently also a bikers bypass.

Bridle Path F.R. sets off steeply uphill, lined with pines. Immediately another fire road branches to the right. Closed to the public, it leads to the MMWD lake keeper's private residence.

At the summit of the Fire Road, Pilot Knob Trail sets off to the left, on its way to the famous large madrone tree and Lakeview Fire Road. Bridle Path F.R. drops right, to the loop road around the shore of Lake Lagunitas, and ends.

The Fire Road was built over the lower part of Pilot Knob Trail so that MMWD vehicles would not have to go directly past the lake keeper's house.

BULLFROG FIRE ROAD
FROM SKY OAKS ROAD TO EASTERN TIP OF ALPINE LAKE / .83 miles

Terrain: Meadow with boggy sections; half riparian / MMWD
Elevation: Around 680' / almost level
Intersecting Trails: None
Directions: Sky Oaks Road, 100 yards past toll booth

BULLFROG Fire Road is a level, dirt alternative to Sky Oaks Road in traveling between the ranger station and Alpine and Bon Tempe lakes. Bullfrog, however, is often a muddy bog in its first half in winter; messy and barely passable.

Bullfrog begins at the parking turnout, on the right, 100 yards past the Sky Oaks toll booth. A path from the toll booth also leads to it. Just inside the entrance gate, on the right, is a native rose bush (*Rosa californica*), usually in fragrant bloom in May. Just beyond is a fork. The option right (not described here because it enters private property) goes through to the Meadow Club clubhouse and Fairfax-Bolinas Road. Bullfrog goes left.

Paths branch left off Bullfrog to the top of the tree-lined ridge south. At one-third mile, a path to the right joins the Meadow Club route. In 1976-77, the 162 acres on which the golf course sits were traded by the MMWD to the Meadow Club (which had been leasing the land) in exchange for some 2,200 acres of a former hunting preserve above the Kent Lake area.

The Fire Road leaves the meadow near a service road, which veers right onto the golf course. Bullfrog swings south. A short rise brings the Fire Road to an old quarry site. From here were taken the rocks used to build Bon Tempe Dam. Across from the quarry is the best, but still not necessarily dry, crossing of Bon Tempe Creek. On the other side, a path leads to the Azalea Hill and Liberty Gulch trails. A bobcat family has been resident near here in recent years.

Bullfrog ends at a gate. The eastern tip of Alpine Lake is to the right. The dirt road beyond, which is open to autos, is part of the historic San Rafael-Bolinas County Road, dating from the 1870's. Bon Tempe Dam is just above.

The name Bullfrog is an old one, applied perhaps mistakenly as bullfrogs, though now widespread, were not introduced into California until the early 1900's. They are the largest of western frogs, up to eight inches. Their booming calls are unmistakeable. Other common, native Tam frog/toad species are western toad, redlegged frog and the smaller (two inches or less) Pacific treefrog. (See Amphibians chapter.)

CASEY CUTOFF TRAIL
FROM BON TEMPE DAM TO ROCKY RIDGE FIRE ROAD / .51 miles

Terrain: Oak woodland; unmaintained / MMWD
Elevation: From 730' to 1,200' / extremely steep
Intersecting Trails: None
Directions: Bon Tempe Dam parking lot-cross dam
Amenities: Outhouse

CASEY CUTOFF Trail "cuts off" around .3 miles of Rocky Ridge Fire Road in climbing from, or descending to, Bon Tempe Dam. The drawback is steepness, with at
least one section that some may find unacceptably precipitous.

At the far end of Bon Tempe Dam from the parking area, Alpine Pump F.R.
branches right and Bon Tempe (Shadyside) Trail goes left. At the top of the
Shadyside entry steps, unsigned Casey Cutoff Trail veers right. The first yards
may be a bit confusing but the Trail quickly becomes evident.

The Trail passes into a short clearing, going over serpentine rock. Back in
the woods, it hits an extremely steep 100-yard uphill through a grove of laurels.
More than a few visitors have slipped here on the return journey. There is a
second tough haul soon after, amidst a quiet woodland of mostly tanbark oaks.

Nearing the top of the Trail, views open behind. There is an MMWD sign,
the only one marking Casey Cutoff, 15 yards before the junction with Rocky
Ridge F.R. It is of some help locating the otherwise easy-to-miss Cutoff when
descending Rocky Ridge. At the junction, it is .8 miles downhill back to the dam
and .6 miles uphill left to Stocking Trail.

Casey May was chief ranger, now a superintendent, for the Marin Municipal Water District for many years. The Trail was named for him when MMWD
workers grew tired of talking about "that trail with no name from Bon Tempe
Dam."

COLIER TRAIL
FROM LAKE LAGUNITAS TO INTERNATIONAL TRAIL / 1.5 miles

Terrain: Riparian; deep woodland; parts rocky / MMWD
Elevation: 790' to 2,280' / extremely steep
Intersecting Trails: Northside (1.1m), Lower Northside (1.1m)
Directions: Lagunitas Dam — Lake Lagunitas F.R. to second bridge

COLIER (or Colier Spring) Trail follows the Middle Fork of Lagunitas Creek up
from Lake Lagunitas to Colier Spring, and continues toward the saddle between
West and Middle peaks. For riparian, woodland beauty, it rivals the more famous
Cataract Trail, but is even steeper. Indeed, its middle part is as steep as any trail
on the Mountain. Those prepared to tackle it will be challenged, and rewarded.

The Trail begins at a signpost beside the middle of the three bridges when circling Lake Lagunitas from the dam. Colier starts rather level beside the right bank of the Middle Fork of Lagunitas Creek, which is flowing unfettered for the last time in its long journey to Tomales Bay. Below, the creek is dammed to form Lake Lagunitas, and then, in order, Bon Tempe, Alpine, and Kent lakes.

Colier crosses the creek twice in the first quarter-mile; expect to rock hop after winter rains. Veer left at a fork and cross a feeder stream.

Above where two branches of the middle fork merge, Colier becomes extremely steep. It climbs the divide between two branches of the Middle Fork, and then follows the western branch. Because the Trail is infrequently cleared and used, it is often lined with fallen limbs. There is also some scrambling over rocks. The steepness forces rest stops. Enjoy the serenity of one of the most peaceful parts of the Bay Area. Ramrod straight redwoods mix with madrones and tanbark oaks. There is some slight relief in the uphill after a final creek crossing.

At 1.1 miles, the Trail meets Colier Spring at a five-way intersection. Huge redwoods, in one of the highest groves on Tam, tower above the site. The spring, once known as Butterfly Spring, has long been a favorite resting spot among veteran Mt. Tam visitors. Cool spring water poured from a pipe until 1982, when the great winter storm apparently shifted the flow. A redwood bench, placed by Boy Scout Troop 48 in 1997, offers a place to sit. Northside Trail comes in from the left. It leaves to the right, split as Northside (or Upper Northside) and Lower Northside. Colier Trail continues uphill to the left, past the second of the new footbridges.

The Trail is now above the headwaters of the Middle Fork. A shortcut path branches right; continue uphill to the left. An old TCC marker pointing the way to West Point is fastened to a California nutmeg tree.

Colier ends at International Trail. Go left 100 yards to the top of International on Ridgecrest Boulevard to enjoy one of the best views on Mt. Tamalpais. Or, if you don't want the solitude broken, take International right and downhill back to Upper Northside.

The late Louise Teather, in her book *Place Names of Marin* describes the man behind the Trail's and spring's name: "John Munro Colier (or Collier) was a Scot, described as a lovable and wealthy eccentric who sometimes pretended to be a tramp and went about asking for handouts. He hiked Mt. Tamalpais and worked on the trails for many years, and when he died in 1916 a marker was placed [at his favorite view site on Rock Spring Trail] in his memory." Colier was a vice-president of the Cross Country Club, and a charter member of the TCC. Harold Atkinson, in his unpublished *History of the Tamalpais Conservation Club*, said, "(Colier) was the original conservationist . . . He knew every shady nook and spot, every water course, every pool on Tamalpais." Besides this Trail, Colier is credited with building Alice Eastwood Trail. Colier, a bachelor, left a sizable bequest to Children's Hospital in San Francisco.

The Trail was rerouted in the mid-1960's, which accounts for several of the faint alternate routes. The section above Colier Spring was a later addition.

CONCRETE PIPELINE FIRE ROAD
FROM JUNCTION OF FAIRFAX-BOLINAS AND SKY OAKS ROADS TO FISH GULCH
TRAIL / 2.78 miles

Terrain: Light woodland; heavily used / MMWD
Elevation: Around 500' / almost level
Intersecting Trails: Taylor (.6m), Canyon (.7m), Deer Park F.R. (1.3m), connector fire road to Bald Hill Trail (1.3m), Shaver Grade (1.3m-1.4m), Elliott (1.3m), Logging (1.7m), Madrone (2.5)
Directions: Same as Sky Oaks to junction of Sky Oaks and Fairfax-Bolinas roads; limited road edge parking

CONCRETE PIPELINE is the second longest, basically level fire road on Mt. Tamalpais, behind only Southern Marin Line F.R. It would be the longest if its 1.3-mile continuation north of Fairfax-Bolinas Road (so just outside this book's boundary), to Happersberger Point, is added. The Pipeline is also popular because there is free parking at its trailhead (although the number of spaces was reduced after Fairfax-Bolinas Road was repaved and widened in 1994). And Concrete Pipeline has an excellent variety of wildflowers due to its varying habitats and the vigilance of passersby who pull out the invasive brooms.

The Fire Road sets off from a gate opposite #700 Bolinas Road, a few yards below Sky Oaks Road and the "Lake Lagunitas" sign. The trailhead signpost is in error; it is 1.3, not 1.9, miles to Five Corners.

The opening few yards are downhill. The Water District buildings, which regulate flow at this key intersection in Marin's water supply, are part of the Jory Gatehouse, for the Jory Ranch once here. Quickly, road noise fades and the redwood-lined route becomes lovely and peaceful.

Concrete Pipeline does indeed follow a pair of water pipelines, only one still active. The big pipes are just under the Fire Road's surface, and visible at bends in the road. The pipelines are graded downhill at a uniform one foot per thousand feet, though the Fire Road itself has undulations.

The first intersection, on the right, is with Taylor Trail, which goes up to the ranger headquarters on Sky Oaks Road. Just beyond, Canyon Trail, unsigned, drops to the left. The Drake High School cross country course, which is entirely on Concrete Pipeline, starts here.

There's a dip and then a rise around a sweeping bend. This area is particularly rich in wildflowers during spring. A pair of pipes on the left, one dark, marks the precisely measured one-mile mark.

The Fire Road rises as it approaches the key junction of Five Corners (which see). The pipeline itself goes under Five Corners through what is called Porteous Tunnel; this area was once part of the Porteous Ranch. At Five Corners, Shaver Grade and Concrete Pipeline briefly combine as they descend to the right. At the next junction, .1 mile below, Shaver Grade splits off downhill to the left.

It is just under one level mile on Concrete Pipeline from this split to the Madrone Trail intersection, which has made the route popular with runners doing timed workouts. A sign here informs bicyclists that there is no outlet at the far end of the Fire Road.

In winter, there may be some muddy patches just ahead. At the next broad bend, unsigned Logging Trail crosses. The first junction is to the left and down; the second, 20 yards later, is right and up. Both options meet Shaver Grade. Deer frequent this lovely woodland. Hound's tongue, common on the left margin, heralds spring with blossoms in January and February, and in some years as early as December.

The Fire Road passes two MMWD buildings, the Phoenix gate house and pump station. Between them, Madrone Trail rises uphill on the right, heading to Sky Oaks Road and Bon Tempe Lake. Bikes are not permitted beyond.

Concrete Pipeline then drops and narrows. It ends at its junction with Fish Gulch Trail, which comes in from the left. The uphill continuation, part of the original Fish Grade, is considered here as Fish Gulch Trail.

Concrete Pipeline Fire Road was built in 1918 as part of the Alpine Dam project. The adjacent pipeline, which originally was concrete, took water from Alpine Lake through the Pine Mountain Tunnel (which emerges at Happersberger Point) then on to the main distribution network. A second, parallel steel pipeline was added in 1926.

CROSS COUNTRY BOYS TRAIL
FROM UPPER BERRY TRAIL TO HIGH MARSH TRAIL AT HIGH MARSH / 1.00 MILES

Terrain: Heavily wooded, part chaparral; unmaintained, parts overgrown / MMWD
Elevation: From 1,760' to 1,520' / upper part gradual, lower half very steep
Intersecting Trails: Lagoon F.R. (.1m), connector to Upper Berry (.2m), Azalea Meadow (twice at .3m), Kent (.6m)
Directions: Lake Lagunitas — Rock Spring-Lagunitas F.R., 1.7 miles — right at first junction with Upper Berry Trail

IN RECENT DECADES, Cross Country Boys was one of the trickiest Trails on the Mountain to follow — there were no signs at either of its remote ends or at any of its some half-dozen tricky intersections. But just-placed MMWD signposts, trail clearing, and a new bridge should make this historic route more traveled.

Well up (1.7 miles) Rock Spring-Lagunitas F.R., opposite Rocky Ridge Fire Trail, Upper Berry Trail heads off into woodland. Follow it .1 mile, a few yards above a rivulet, to a fork. The branch to the right is the start of Cross Country Boys Trail. In less than 100 yards, Cross Country meets and crosses Lagoon Fire Road, marked by one of the new signposts.

Cross Country Boys heads into deep forest. In another .1 mile, it hits a three-way intersection, tricky and presently unsigned. Left is a 50-yard connector back to Upper Berry Trail. Veer right.

Cross Country drops to wondrous Azalea Meadow. In May and June, fragrance from the blossoming azaleas pervades this quiet area, which almost begs for a rest stop.

Continue around the meadow to another three-way intersection. Right is Azalea Meadow Trail, to Kent Trail. Left, Cross Country Boys and Azalea Meadow trails run combined for 15 yards, up a few steps, to yet another three-pronged intersection. Here Azalea Meadow Trail splits uphill left to Rifle Camp while Cross Country Boys continues to the right.

Continue through the peaceful forest. At .6 miles, Cross Country meets Kent Trail at a four-way junction by the edge of chaparral. This is the site of the old Cross Country Boys Club Camp; the Trail was built to it. Kent goes left up to Potrero Camp and right down to High Marsh Trail.

The steeper, more rugged continuation of Cross Country Boys Trail to High Marsh is a later addition. It plunges down into the manzanita-dominated chaparral, with outstanding northern vistas above and between the shrubs. Rattlesnakes have been known to nest just below the Kent junction. Also be careful not to brush the sharp-pointed chaparral pea.

A splendid isolated, multi-trunked oak tree is passed. Chinquapin trees, then madrones, become more common.

Cross Country Boys Trail ends at High Marsh Trail directly across from High Marsh. The marsh is gradually receding; old-timers note how much smaller it is now than just a few decades ago, and is dry in summer. Still, it remains a Mountain treasure. High Marsh Trail goes left to Cataract Trail, and right 200 yards to Kent Trail.

The Cross Country Boys Club was formed in 1891 as an offshoot for "fast hiking men" of the Sightseers Club, itself founded three years earlier. Only a handful of women, one being Alice Eastwood, were admitted as associate members. Lincoln Fairley reprints (*Mount Tamalpais, A History*, page 68) a delightful account of a splinter group of the club, called the "Hill Tribe," that was written in 1905: "(They) prowled these hills year after year . . . over the endless trails, light of pack and light of heart . . . Their sole object seemed to be the hills, and for wide views from them, and the silent places."

EAST PEAK FIRE TRAIL
FROM LAKEVIEW FIRE ROAD TO ELDRIDGE GRADE / 1.2 miles

Terrain: Chaparral, overgrown with shrubs; dangerous loose rock; unmaintained and MARGINAL / MMWD
Elevation: From 830' to 2,080' / extremely steep
Intersecting Trails: Northside (1.1m)
Directions: Lagunitas Dam — clockwise on Lake Lagunitas F.R. — Lakeview F.R., .2 miles

EAST PEAK FIRE TRAIL barely meets this book's minimum standards for inclusion. It is unmarked and hard to find, particularly at its lower end. The MMWD has abandoned it. Its extreme steepness and loose rocks make it difficult to climb and downright dangerous to descend; don't attempt it unless you're a "mountain goat" type. Overgrown shrubs on the lower portion are a hazard as well. The latest Olmsted map shows only a segment of it. You've been forewarned. But if you do take it, you'll enjoy extraordinary views and the quickest passage between the lakes and East Peak.

Finding the lower end of East Peak Fire Trail is the first obstacle. Look for it around 300 yards up Lakeview Fire Road from Lake Lagunitas. There is a prominent grassy clearing on the right, then a closely paired 20-foot oak and 15-foot laurel. A couple of yards beyond them, a faint path, East Peak Fire Trail, sets off.

Veer right of the huge Monterey pine. In around 35 yards, the Trail crosses a rivulet, then immediately veers left. The route is indistinct; follow the gully uphill to the left. A few remaining Coulter pines — the MMWD has been removing them as non-native — still stand along the lowest part of the Trail. Their huge cones are unmistakeable. If you don't like the rough climbing, head back, as the Trail only gets steeper.

Once clearly on the ridge line, the Trail becomes obvious and, except for one short section, remains so all the way up. There are stunning and ever-expanding views. The Trail climbs the west side of an unnamed hill, with several forking paths. There is a brief downhill, the only one on the route. At the bottom, a short connector goes left to Eldridge Grade. Deep canyons drop precipitously to the left (Bill Williams Creek) and right (East Fork of Lagunitas Creek). Across the canyon right, the almost equally steep Lagunitas Fire Trail tops the next ridge.

The Trail gains 600 feet in elevation over the next steep and slippery half-mile. Don't forget to look back during what will certainly be many pauses. Chinquapin is the common short tree, manzanita the most abundant shrub.

The Fire Trail meets Northside Trail at the splendid view site called Inspiration Point, 2,000 feet in elevation. A sign (which does not note East Peak Fire Trail) points the way left to Eldridge Grade and right to Northside Trail. East Peak Fire Trail is less overgrown in its remaining climb, but barely less steep. Near its upper end is a huge rock whose flat top offers a perfect place to rest and enjoy one of the Mountain's best vista points. Virtually all of Marin north of Tamalpais is visible.

The Fire Trail ends a few more yards up when it meets Eldridge Grade. The Grade, here making a bend, goes a half-mile uphill to Ridgecrest Boulevard and three miles downhill back to Lakeview F.R. for a loop option.

The Trail was originally a 200 foot-wide fire break, one of four (along with Indian, Lagunitas, and Rocky Ridge), carved on Tam's north face by the Civilian Conservation Corps in the 1930's.

FILTER PLANT ROAD
FROM FISH GRADE TO ELDRIDGE GRADE / 1.00 miles

Terrain: Wooded, mostly with redwoods; western half paved / MMWD
Elevation: From 620' to 520' / western part almost level, eastern part gradual
Intersecting Trails: None
Directions: Sky Oaks Road to top of Fish Grade, .1 mile
Amenities: Fountain

THOUGH PAVED most of its exactly one-mile length, Filter Plant Road is still popular as it opens several loop options in the lakes area. To reach the Road's western end, follow Sky Oaks Road 1.5 miles from the toll booth, to the final bend right leading to the Lake Lagunitas parking lot. On the left side of the bend, behind a gate erected in 1997, is the paved upper portion of Fish Grade. There are parking spaces on the right. Follow Fish Grade down one-sixth mile, passing the pipeline bringing water from Bon Tempe lake under Sky Oaks Road to the filter plant. Asphalt-topped Filter Plant Road splits off to the right while Fish Grade continues downhill.

The paved portion of Filter Plant Road is level. Redwoods line the way. Water District employees drive on the Road, so be alert.

In .6 miles the route meets the filter plant, properly called the Bon Tempe Water Treatment Plant. The structures, built in 1959, are painted green to minimize their visual impact. Much of southern Marin's drinking water, some 20 million gallons a day from Bon Tempe Lake, flows through the plant. Chemicals, particularly aluminum sulfate, are introduced here to gather foreign matter into "floc" particles. The water is slowly mixed, building up the size of the "floc" particles until they settle out. The water is then passed through filter beds of graduated gravel, sand, and anthracite coal to remove further impurities. Lime, to reduce corrosion, and chlorine, to kill bacteria, are also added. The District's one other treatment plant, built in 1962 and somewhat larger, is in the San Geronimo Valley.

Veer left around the huge tank to continue. A wastewater recovery pond is to the left. There is a unique perspective down to Phoenix Lake. A steep service road heads uphill as the pavement gives way to dirt.

A pleasant, gradual, tree-lined descent brings the Road to its end at Eldridge Grade. To the right, the Grade rises to the top of Tam, to the left it drops to Phoenix Junction. In 1992, a water fountain, one of the very few on Tam away from a trailhead, was installed at this intersection.

Olmsted, MMWD maps and Water District personnel call this Road the Southern Marin Line, which indeed it is a part. But since there is a sizable gap in the Southern Marin Line across Bill Williams Gulch to the east, I reserve the designation Southern Marin Line F.R. only for the section between Kentfield's Crown Road and Larkspur's Sunrise Lane. Filter Plant Road is a common name among many long-time users.

HIDDEN COVE TRAIL
FROM OLD SAN RAFAEL-BOLINAS ROAD TO BON TEMPE TRAIL / .33 miles

Terrain: Grassland; rolling; horses permitted / MMWD
Elevation: From 780' to 750' to 840' to 720' / steep
Intersecting Trails: None
Directions: Sky Oaks Road — dirt road to Bon Tempe Dam, 50 yards

ABOUT A HALF-MILE IN on Sky Oaks Road from the toll booth, an unpaved road, the auto access to Bon Tempe Dam, branches right. It is a surviving part of the old San Rafael-Bolinas stage road. Follow it a few yards and, just past a gate, look left to spot a "generic" MMWD trail sign. Two trails depart here. To the right, the .2-mile Dam Trail (not separately described) drops parallel to the road. Hidden Cove Trail sets off left (or straight), into some short oaks.

Within a few yards, a path forks left. Then an MMWD sign explains the area is being cleared of Coulter pines to restore native vegetation. In 100 yards, the Trail bottoms. Coffeeberry and coyote brush are the common shrubs. Continue uphill. Bracken fern is taking hold on the grassland. Poppies and lupine contribute to spring color.

Just before the Trail crests, the East Peak of Tam becomes visible. At the summit saddle, paths lead left and right to a pair of pastoral, oak-covered hills. The one left is called Cross Bar Knoll. On the descent, there are splendid views of the Mountain across Bon Tempe Lake. Once there were many Coulter pines here. They were introduced in the lakes area during a planting project in the 1930's. Coulters bear the heaviest cones of any pine in the world, weighing up to five pounds. You may still find a survivor and some of the massive cones.

Hidden Cove Trail ends when it hits Bon Tempe Trail at the head of a remote, quiet inlet aptly called Hidden Cove. A rivulet enters the lake a few feet to the left.

KENT TRAIL
FROM ALPINE LAKE TO POTRERO CAMP / 3.85 miles

Terrain: Deep woods, some chaparral; lower part riparian / MMWD
Elevation: From 650' to 1,980' / steep, parts very steep
Intersecting Trails: Van Wyck Creek (1.1m), Helen Markt (1.5m), Willow Meadow (2.3m, 2.8m), Stocking (2.3m), connector to Serpentine Point (2.7m), High Marsh (2.9m), Azalea Meadow (2.9m), Cross Country Boys (3.5m), Potrero (3.9m).
Directions: Bon Tempe Dam — Alpine Pump F.R. to end
Amenities: Outhouses, picnic tables

FEW, IF ANY, Mt. Tamalpais trails provide a better wilderness experience than Kent Trail. Throughout its length, from its early part beside Alpine Lake, to its middle section amidst one of the Mountain's deepest forests, through its upper reaches with sweeping northern vistas, Kent Trail offers solitude, variety, and beauty.

Kent Trail begins from the shore of Alpine Lake, at the base of the fire road down from Bon Tempe Dam. Kent Trail sets off just to the left of the pump station. An MMWD sign indicates that it is 4.2 miles to Potrero Meadow. A line of buoyant orange/red balls stretches across Alpine Lake here, marking a pipeline to a mid-lake pump.

Within 50 yards on Kent, the first of several narrow paths come in from the left. An old pipeline, abandoned in 1956, runs along the route for some two miles.

The Trail arcs around coves of Alpine Lake. At the first, and at several more later, are masses of azaleas, in flower in May and June. Huge Douglas-firs line the shore. The site of Kent Cabin, used by the Kent family for fishing retreats, now sits offshore under Alpine Lake. When the water level drops sufficiently by late summer, Cheda Island emerges. It is named for Virgilio Cheda, an MMWD board director at the time of the building of Alpine Dam. The island was more prominent before Alpine Dam, and thus the lake level, was raised in 1940.

The rolling Trail crosses several streams, some requiring a bit of rock hopping to cross in winter. The biggest stream crossing is of Van Wyck Creek, at 1.1 mile. A bridge was finally added here in 1994. Thirty yards beyond, unsigned and unmaintained Van Wyck Creek Trail sets off sharply left. It can be traced more than a mile along the creek bed up to Stocking Trail.

Kent then encounters a short, steep uphill, and plunges through huckleberry, a common shrub over the next mile. The trunk of a huge Douglas-fir bends toward the Trail, then straightens upward. Just beyond, on the right, is another impressive Douglas-fir, one of the most massive on Tam. Its lowest branch alone is bigger than many sizable trees.

Look, on the right, for the Helen Markt Trail sign. A former Kent shortcut uphill from there has been covered by the MMWD. In another 75 yards is a newer MMWD signpost. Straight ahead, Helen Markt winds 1.75 miles to Cataract Trail and Kent Trail bends left to begin a long, almost unrelenting climb to Potrero Meadow.

The lowest part of the climb was recently improved and widened. The pipeline is still clearly visible embedded in the Trail. Huckleberry narrows the way; their tasty but small black berries are ripest in August or September.

After .3 miles of uphill, you begin to hear the waters of the East Fork of Swede George Creek. Kent arrives directly beside the creek without crossing. At a site now altered by a prominent landslide, a concrete rubble diversion dam on the East Fork was built in 1888. From it, the six-inch steel pipeline was laid to below Lake Lagunitas. Swede George water was an important addition to the County supply, particularly before Alpine Dam was erected in 1919. Swede George himself, who died in 1875, was a woodcutter in the area.

Just above the massive slide, also on the right, is the standing water of Foul Pool. Duck under a huge fallen madrone. Then the Trail enters a magnificent redwood grove, one of the loveliest and quietest spots on Tam. The older giants still show scars from the 1945 fire. Younger redwoods circle the fallen "mother" trees from which they sprouted. Spend some time here (there are great picnic sites) and let the solitude work its wonders.

After just under .9 miles of climbing from Alpine Lake, Kent Trail meets the Stocking and Willow Meadow trails at an intersection presently marked only by logs on the ground. A V-forked madrone, prominent when climbing Kent, is one landmark. Straight ahead, unmarked and barely visible through the tanbark oaks, Willow Meadow rises to higher on Kent. Both Stocking and Kent go left. Then, within 20 yards, Kent veers off right uphill while Stocking continues east to nearby Hidden Lake and beyond.

The climbing gets even steeper; later, wood steps help. In .4 miles from Stocking, just after leaving the tree canopy, a seeming path branches left, quickly to deadend. One hundred yards later, at the rock crest, is an important fork. To the left is a short connector to the vista point of Serpentine Knoll and to routes back to Bon Tempe and Lagunitas lakes. Kent veers right. After a descent, Kent again meets, and crosses, Willow Meadow Trail. To the left is Willow Meadow itself.

Fifteen yards later, Kent Trail crosses the East Fork of Swede George Creek, which flows all year here, over a bridge. One hundred yards later is a four-way intersection. The MMWD added a signpost here in 1993. To the left is Azalea Meadow Trail (not presently signed). Kent continues straight, to Potrero Meadow. To the right is High Marsh Trail, with High Marsh itself .1 mile away.

After another .6 miles of steep uphill, Kent crosses Cross Country Boys Trail. It is within the forest canopy but chaparral is just yards away. Cross Country Boys goes left to Azalea Meadow and drops right to High Marsh.

Kent enters the chaparral. There are splendid views north and west, including of Tomales Bay, the Pacific and the Point Reyes peninsula. After some stone steps, Kent Trail crests at just over 2,000 feet in elevation. The Trail drops a bit as it returns to woodland.

Just beyond, Kent ends at Potrero Camp at the edge of lower Potrero Meadow. Tables, outhouses, a line of azaleas, the meadow, and choice of sun or shade make this a favorite resting spot. The larger, upper Potrero Meadow is .3 miles to the left via Potrero Trail. Just to the right, over the small bridge, unmarked Swede George Trail descends into the woods and a 100-yard connector fire road and path rise to Laurel Dell F.R. by Benstein Trail.

No family name is more closely associated with Mt. Tamalpais than Kent. With wealth derived from their Chicago packing company, Albert Kent (died 1901) and his son William amassed huge land holdings. There was a time when it was possible to walk from the present Kentfield to the ocean at Stinson Beach entirely on their property. William Kent served the region as an independent United States Congressman from 1910-1916. He helped author the legislation to create the National Park Service. He also made many priceless donations to the public on Mt. Tamalpais. These included Muir Woods National Monument, much of Mt. Tamalpais State Park (including Steep Ravine the day before his death in 1928), and the Mountain Theater site. The family remains a benefactor to the County. William's son Thomas Kent, for whom Kent Lake was named, was on the MMWD Board of Directors for 39 years until his death in 1959. In 1988 the family helped save a historic building adjacent to the Adaline Kent School (formerly Kent property), in Kentfield, from the wrecker's ball.

The often realigned Kent Trail first appeared on the 1898 Sanborn map.

LAGOON EXTENSION TRAIL
FROM LAGOON FIRE ROAD TO ROCKY RIDGE FIRE ROAD / .49 miles

Terrain: Wooded; short part in rocky chaparral / MMWD
Elevation: From 1,560' to 1,320' / steep
Intersecting Trails: Van Wyck Creek Trail, .4m
Directions: Bon Tempe Dam — Rocky Ridge F.R. — right on Stocking Trail — left on Kent Trail to connector to Serpentine Point

No TRAIL on Mt. Tamalpais has evoked more confusion over its name than this one. Today's Stocking Trail, which does pass Hidden Lake, was called Swede George Fire Trail on the 1934 Water District map, and Hidden Lake Trail on the W.P.A.-Federal Writer's Project map of three years later. After World War II, that trail was improved to accommodate horses, and the workers renamed it Stocking Trail, to honor Clayton Stocking. Then, through a series of errors, the name Hidden Lake Trail became attached to a then unnamed parallel trail to the south (the one described in this section), which does not pass Hidden Lake. This illogical name appeared on most maps and long caused confusion among visitors to the area. To make matters even worse, there is a second "Lagoon Extension-Hidden Lake" trail, illegally built and not on any map, that runs roughly parallel to, and never more than 100 feet below, the "main" one.

Now a more accurate (but hardly colorful) name, Lagoon Extension Trail, is taking hold; the Trail sets off where Lagoon Fire Road ends. Although the Trail's lower end is nearer a trailhead, the route is described downhill because the lower end is presently very hard to spot.

The short connector from Kent Trail to Serpentine Point (or Knoll) meets the top of Lagoon Extension Trail at the base of Lagoon Fire Road. (In earlier editions of this book, I considered the broad first 250 yards below Serpentine Point as part of Lagoon Fire Road but vegetation has narrowed it to trail width and the MMWD now has a sign marking it as off-limits to bicycles.).

Two paths branch left off Lagoon Extension Trail in those opening 250 yards. The first is a now overgrown route to Kent Trail. The second, just before the route clearly narrows, is the parallel, "alternative" Lagoon Extension Trail. (It immediately bends right, enters deep woodland, crosses a creek in an area where there has been a slide, then rejoins the upper Trail.)

The upper, "true" Trail also now enters deeper woodland. After fording a rivulet, it passes through a haunting stand of fire-scarred, slender redwood trees. The next section is lined with tall manzanita shrubs, which form a canopy over the Trail. Just beyond, look for remnants of an old tree house, occasionally occupied not many years ago. The "alternative" Lagoon Extension Trail comes in from the left.

The Trail continues dropping. It then meets, and crosses, a fork of Van Wyck Creek. Twenty yards above the crossing is a fork. Veer right; left (which appears more obvious) is Van Wyck Creek Trail, which drops to Stocking Trail, then Kent Trail. The remaining route uphill is indistinct. Work your way through a few yards of chaparral and then clamber over the rocks.

Lagoon Extension Trail hits Rocky Ridge F.R. at a small unmarked turnout. Three young Douglas-firs stand by the junction. The west end of No Name Trail is 100 yards to the left. Just beyond it, Stocking Trail (the original Hidden Lake Trail, which passes Hidden Lake) crosses Rocky Ridge. Got it?

LAGOON FIRE ROAD
FROM ROCK SPRING-LAGUNITAS F.R. TO SERPENTINE KNOLL / .64 miles

Terrain: Mostly chaparral / MMWD
Elevation: From 2,040' to 1,560' / very steep
Intersecting Trails: Upper Berry (.1m), Cross Country Boys (.1m), connector to Kent Trail (.6m).
Directions: Lake Lagunitas parking area — Rock Spring-Lagunitas F.R., 1.9 miles

LAGOON FIRE ROAD was carved in the early 1930's as one of several broad fire protection breaks across Water District lands. It ended up playing a key role as a supply route in the battle against the huge fire of 1945. Because Lagoon Fire Road's upper end is easier to locate, and barely farther from a trailhead than the lower end, the trip will be described downhill.

In ascending Rock Spring-Lagunitas F.R. from Lake Lagunitas, Lagoon is the second of two fire roads that drop right (Rocky Ridge F.R. is the first). Lagoon's upper end, 1.6 miles and 1,300 feet in elevation above the lake, is well-signed.

Lagoon descends through woodland. One hundred yards down, Upper Berry Trail crosses. Both left, uphill, and right, downhill, lead back to Rock Spring-Lagunitas F.R. In another 60 yards, Cross Country Boys Trail crosses. To the left is Azalea Meadow; to the right, a union with Upper Berry.

The Fire Road leaves the woods for open views above the chaparral. Lagoon's surface is distinctive; iron-rich red clays mingle with the blue-green serpentine rocks. The prominent large outcropping of Serpentine Knoll (or Point), the Fire Road's destination, is plainly visible. In the 1980's, several pig traps, including perhaps the largest on the Mountain, were placed beside Lagoon. The traps are now gone as the feral pig eradication program seems to have succeeded.

Lagoon hits Serpentine Knoll (Point). The views are outstanding in all directions. At the crest, a short but important connector to Kent Trail departs left. The former 250-yard continuation over the Knoll, narrowed by advancing vegetation and posted as closed to bicycles by the MMWD, is now considered as the top of Lagoon Extension Trail.

There is some debate over which "lagoon" is referred to in the Fire Road's name. Some think it is Hidden Lake, as there once were plans to extend the Fire Road to the lake. Others feel it refers to the seasonally wet area by the Fire Road just south of Cross Country Boys Trail.

LAGUNITAS FIRE TRAIL
FROM LAKE LAGUNITAS TO MIDDLE PEAK FIRE ROAD / 1.5 miles

Terrain: Mixed chaparral and light forest; overgrown; parts with loose rock; un-improved and MARGINAL / MMWD
Elevation: From 800' to 2,250' / extremely steep
Intersecting Trails: Northside (1.2m)
Directions: Lagunitas Dam — Lake Lagunitas F.R., either direction, .8 miles

LAGUNITAS FIRE TRAIL is unsigned, unmaintained (it was abandoned by the MMWD in 1985), extremely steep, and dangerous to take downhill for the loose rock. Yet it remains in occasional use because it is a direct route from Lake Lagunitas to the Mt. Tamalpais summit area, with splendid vistas along the way.

The Lake Lagunitas entrance to the Trail is easy to miss. It lies roughly equidistant from the dam whether circling the lake clockwise or counterclockwise. Clockwise, cross one bridge then follow the straightaway along the south shore. There are two entrances, 20 yards apart, at the first bend left. Counterclockwise, cross two bridges then look right at the first bend.

The Trail rises steeply through a mostly madrone woodland. Lake Lagunitas is visible through the trees. You can also glimpse Pilot Knob across the water. Here Pilot Knob towers above. Keep looking back to gauge your progress; well up, Pilot Knob recedes to a minor hill in the broad panorama. Paths lead back to the lake left and right, but the Trail is reasonably clear.

There are occasional level spots, even short downhills, but the going is definitely up. Irises are abundant in spring. The Trail emerges from the tree canopy into chaparral. The shrubs chamise, chinquapin, yerba santa, chaparral pea and manzanita crowd the route; the latter two are sharp-pointed so don't go sleeveless. The views expand as the Trail climbs the long ridge.

After seemingly endless climbing, Lagunitas Fire Trail hits a prominent clearing. The narrow ridge drops off on both sides. About 35 yards later, the Trail is covered with loose rock, hard to ascend and dangerous to descend. Soon after, the Trail skirts a huge rock outcropping. Carefully clamber up the boulder on a tiny path to enjoy a rest site with great views, and no chance of disturbance.

Less than .1 mile above the rock band, the only intersecting trail, Northside, is crossed. Left leads to East Peak Fire Trail, a "sister" trail on the next ridge east, and to Eldridge Grade. To the right, Northside goes to Colier Spring and Rifle Camp.

Lagunitas Fire Trail is overgrown with manzanita just above the intersection. Then the Trail encounters a second section of loose rock and another prominent boulder. The Trail reenters woodland. A common tree here is California nutmeg, which is not related to the famous spice. Its two-inch needle-leaves end in sharp points. The green fruits are also distinctive. The thin fleshy covering, with a fragrant juice, peels away to reveal the hard seed case.

Some metal and wood fragments maya be visible to the right. They are remnants of a once rather substantial dwelling in these remote woods. A sign labeled the site "Kisban Hermitage," for Ben Kisban, who had a camp here. He was a pharmacist who fled his native Hungary after the 1956 uprising there. Kisban died in a San Rafael nursing home in 1991 at age 89.

The Trail ends when it hits Middle Peak Fire Road. To the left is Ridgecrest Boulevard, near the top of both Old Railroad and Eldridge grades, while right leads to Lakeview Trail and the summit of Middle Peak. This route up the ridge line is an old one. It was widened to a broad fire break, some 200 feet across, by the Civilian Conservation Corps in 1933-34. Advancing vegetation has narrowed it again.

LAKE LAGUNITAS FIRE ROAD
AROUND LAKE LAGUNITAS / 1.58 miles

Terrain: Riparian; tanbark oak-madrone woodland; heavily used / MMWD
Elevation: Around 800' / almost level
Intersecting Trails: Clockwise from east side of dam; Bridle Path F.R. (.1m), Lakeview F.R. (.5m), Lagunitas Fire (.8m), Colier (1.0m), Rock Spring-Lagunitas F.R. (1.4m)
Directions: Lagunitas Dam

THE FIRE ROAD that circles Lake Lagunitas provides one of the most delightful short walks the Mountain has to offer, and is a favorite among families with young children.

To reach Lake Lagunitas, climb the 150-yard connector fire road that rises immediately left of the picnic area at the end of Sky Oaks Road. It passes some interesting sights, including a handsome Port Orford cedar (native to the north, probably introduced here) and a pair of historic buildings. The upper one is now used as the MMWD "sign shop." The connector meets the east end of Lagunitas Dam at a lovely view site; Mt. Tamalpais both rising above the lake and reflected in the water. The loop will be described clockwise from the dam.

Go left up the stone steps. To the left is a private MMWD residence, the home of the lake keeper. In 1877 the first telephone line in Marin County was laid to the lake keeper's residence here. To the right are paths down to the lake's shore. In .1 mile, Bridle Path F.R. comes in on the left. It rises to the start of Pilot Knob Trail, then drops back to the parking area.

The circuit continues, passing paths to the right. They lead onto peninsulas that offer some of the choicest picnic sites in all the Bay Area. There is an outhouse to the left. Beyond, the splendid grassy face of Pilot Knob towers above.

At .5 miles is a fork. Lakeview F.R. goes straight to Eldridge Grade. Lake Lagunitas F.R. veers right to begin a section once known as South Shore Road. The route crosses the East Fork of Lagunitas Creek over a bridge. It is the three forks of this creek, all of which are crossed on the loop, that are impounded to form Lake Lagunitas. Bon Tempe, Alpine, and Kent lakes are also formed by dams lower on Lagunitas Creek's course.

The view across the lake here, with fishermen often lining the far shore, is idyllic. At the end of the straightaway, where the Fire Road bends left, are two entries to the extremely steep, unsigned Lagunitas Fire Trail. It ascends to Middle Peak. This is also the loop's halfway mark.

Just before the next bridge, over the Middle Fork, signed Colier Trail sets off on a precipitous climb to Colier Spring.

After the third bridge (across West Fork), the Fire Road passes a pump station sitting on a pier over the lake. From here, water is pumped all the way up to the radar station atop West Peak. Shortly past, Rock Spring-Lagunitas Fire Road departs sharply left on its long uphill to Potrero Meadow and Ridgecrest Boulevard.

After a couple more bends, there is another fork. Rock Spring-Lagunitas F.R. continues straight down to the parking lot and the loop goes right over Lagunitas Dam. A plaque on the near end of the dam acknowledges the role of the San Francisco Foundation (which then administered the huge Beryl Buck trust fund) in financing restoration work after the storm of 1982. Check the log booms here for turtles sunning themselves. After heavy winter rains, the spillway to the left is often filled with overflow water rushing down to Bon Tempe Lake.

Complete the loop, accurately measured at 1.58 miles, by crossing the dam. There are inviting picnic tables to the left below the dam.

Lake Lagunitas ("lagunitas" means "little lakes" in Spanish) is the oldest and highest in elevation of the five man-made reservoirs on the north side of Mt. Tamalpais. The lake is in one of the wettest areas of Marin; over 90 inches of rain fell in the 1982-83 season. The dam creating the lake was completed in 1873, constructed largely by Chinese laborers working for the fledgling Marin County Water Company, a predecessor to the MMWD. The founder of the company was William T. Coleman, once a prominent San Francisco gold rush-era vigilante. Coleman owned a San Rafael housing tract which received the lake's water. Water also went to San Quentin prison. It was Coleman who planted the eucalyptus trees that lined, for 100 years, the last stretch of paved road before the Lagunitas parking area. All these eucalyptus trees were removed in 1993 to help restore native vegetation.

In 1988, a program began to attempt to make the lake, long a fishing oasis (Coleman released 20,000 trout into the lake as early as 1875), self-sustaining with trout. The pump in the water near the dam oxygenates the water when temperatures rise in summer. There are remnants of the lake's old fish hatchery in the picnic area beside the spillway.

LAKEVIEW FIRE ROAD
FROM LAKE LAGUNITAS FIRE ROAD TO ELDRIDGE GRADE / .78 miles

Terrain: Lightly wooded / MMWD
Elevation: From 800′ to 980′ / lower part almost level, upper part steep
Intersecting Trails: East Peak Fire (.2m), Pilot Knob (.5m)
Directions: Lagunitas Dam — Lake Lagunitas F.R. clockwise, .5 miles

LAKEVIEW Fire Road is well-used as a connection between Lake Lagunitas and Eldridge Grade. To reach its lower end, follow Lake Lagunitas F.R. clockwise from Lagunitas Dam. In a half-mile, at a junction at the easternmost edge of the lake, Lakeview Fire Road continues straight while Lake Lagunitas F.R. loops right. (The MMWD has recently signed the fire road rising from the old Lake Lagunitas parking lot outhouses as the start of Lakeview; I'll stick to the more common designation of Lakeview as only the section above Lake Lagunitas.)

The almost treeless southern face of 1,217-foot Pilot Knob towers above on the left. A meadow opens on the right. Ten feet beyond a closely paired oak and laurel, 300 yards in on Lakeview, barely discernible East Peak Fire Trail sets off to the right.

Lakeview then enters an area until recently dominated by Coulter pines. Coulters, which have the heaviest cones — weighing up to five pounds — of any pine in the world, were originally planted here in the 1930's. They are native to California (the nearest natural stand is on Mt. Diablo), but not to Mt. Tamalpais. The MMWD began cutting the Coulters in 1987 to restore the area's native vegetation after the trees showed signs of disease. A few Coulters still stand here and on nearby trails.

Lakeview bends right and begins climbing steeply. At the start, Pilot Knob Trail, which skirts the Knob's northern flank, departs left at a signed junction.

The Fire Road enters madrone woodland. A path sets off to the left. Lakeview continues gaining elevation until its end at Eldridge Grade. Left on Eldridge is a descent to Phoenix Lake, right a climb to East Peak.

Lakeview Fire Road first appears as a fire trail on the 1925 Northwestern Pacific Railroad map. Trees, both introduced and naturally expanding, have blocked the "lake view" since. There is a completely separate Lakeview Trail on the north side of Middle Peak.

LIBERTY GULCH TRAIL
FROM NORTHERN SHORE OF ALPINE LAKE TO FAIRFAX-BOLINAS ROAD / 1.20 miles

Terrain: Lightly wooded; parts muddy; unmaintained / MMWD
Elevation: From 645' to 940' / gradual
Intersecting Trails: None
Directions: Sky Oaks Road — Bon Tempe Turnoff *OR* Bullfrog F.R.

THIS LITTLE-KNOWN, little-used route rewards hikers with a walk back in time. In 1878, Chinese laborers built Marin's first east-west County Road, from San Rafael to Bolinas. One section ran through the valley now covered by Alpine Lake. Around the turn of the century, when plans for Tamalpais Dam, which would have flooded that part of the road, were proceeding, a bypass was constructed. The bypass is today's Liberty Gulch Trail; slides and vegetation having narrowed it to trail-width most of the way.

To reach the surviving segment of the bypass, take the first right turn off Sky Oaks Road after the ranger station. This dirt road (now called Bon Tempe Road by some because it is the auto access to the dam) is the end of a shortcut, built in 1884, from Ross to the County Road. At the bottom of the downhill, the continuation of the old road is evident across a narrow finger of Alpine Lake. In dry periods, you can walk across. Otherwise, a detour to the right — on Bullfrog F.R., then leaping over the creek, then returning left almost a mile on the path along the shore — is required.

The path passes the concrete foundations for the never-completed Tamalpais Dam. (A larger dam, Alpine, was instead later built downstream.) They are visible on both banks of Alpine and in the lake bed itself when the water level is low.

When opposite the Alpine-Bon Tempe Pump Station across the lake, the Trail begins a steady, gradual ascent. Fragrant yellow madias dot the grasslands in summer and early fall. There are groves of oaks, laurels and Douglas-firs. There are also several short, muddy seeps to be negotiated. Look there for yellow seep-spring monkeyflowers (*Diplacus guttatus*) and sweet-smelling azaleas.

The Trail veers above the arm of Alpine Lake that covers Liberty Gulch. The views are pristine, save for the line of red-orange balls across Alpine to the mid-lake pump. Samuel Vincent Liberty and his wife began operating a dairy ranch in the gulch below in 1876. After the County stage road was built, they opened a roadhouse offering meals. The ranch house burned in 1885, was rebuilt, then abandoned in the 1890's. Later, the Lagunitas Rod and Gun Club had their headquarters there. The building site is now under water.

At one-third mile, the Trail briefly descends. It meets a broad path on the left. This path connects to the shore by a foundation for an old telephone line (removed in 1990) across Alpine.

Soon, ceanothus bushes, a highlight of the Trail in late winter and early spring, begin appearing. Their blue blossoms, and intoxicating fragrance, soon cover the hillside.

Ford a few more seeps and a couple of gullies. You'll begin noticing beer bottles and other debris thoughtlessly tossed down from Fairfax-Bolinas Road above.

The Trail meets a slide. The short remaining passage to the road is quite narrow and sloped. Tred carefully to meet Fairfax-Bolinas Road at a pullout just above milepost sign 4.18. The paved road then follows the original stage route to Bolinas.

LOGGING TRAIL
FROM SHAVER GRADE TO HIDDEN MEADOW / .68 miles

Terrain: Oak woodland; riparian; unmaintained / MMWD
Elevation: From 700' to 230' / very steep
Intersecting Trails: Concrete Pipeline F.R. (.4m), Shaver Grade (.6m)
Directions: Sky Oaks Road — Shaver Grade, .2 miles

AROUND .2 MILES DOWN Shaver Grade from Sky Oaks Road, in the saddle before Shaver's lone rise, two routes branch to the right by a "generic" MMWD trail sign. The upper one, once part of Elliott Trail, is now closed for erosion control. The lower is Logging Trail.

Logging Trail begins through oak-studded grassland. There was a controlled burn here in fall 1997. This is a pleasant, quiet, little-traveled area. Farther along, the stream canyon on the right, a feeder of Phoenix Creek, is lined with laurels, then redwoods.

In just under a half-mile, the Trail meets Concrete Pipeline F.R. at a bend. The unsigned Logging Trail continues across the Fire Road around 20 yards to the left, just beyond the two water pipelines (one with a gaping hole). Logging Trail drops steeply another 250 yards to once again meet Shaver Grade, effectively offering a half-mile shortcut to staying on Shaver. This also unmarked junction is between a laurel and a madrone at a bend in the Grade, at MMWD culvert sign "SG9."

Go 35 yards uphill (left) on Shaver to continue on Logging Trail. The Trail drops steeply again, its route now rocky and eroded. It ends at Hidden Meadow Trail amidst another lovely oak-laden grassland, Hidden Meadow.

Logging Trail actually was the first Shaver Grade, and some call it Old Shaver Grade. In the 1860's, lumber was slid down it from Isaac Shaver's sawmill operation near the present Alpine Dam. The wood was then hauled to Corte Madera Creek at Ross Landing by the junction of today's Sir Francis Drake Boulevard and College Avenue. There it was loaded onto boats, usually bound for San Francisco.

LOWER BERRY TRAIL
FROM BON TEMPE TRAIL TO ROCK SPRING-LAGUNITAS FIRE ROAD / .41 miles

Terrain: Oak-madrone woodland, part grassland; horses permitted / MMWD
Elevation: From 730' to 980' / steep
Intersecting Trails: None
Directions: Lake Lagunitas parking area — Bon Tempe (Shadyside) Trail, .3m

THE HISTORIC Berry Trail was split by the construction of Rock Spring-Lagunitas Fire Road in the mid-1930's. The lower part, now called Lower Berry (or just Berry) Trail, has been restored and signed while the top part, Upper Berry Trail (which see), is also maintained. The middle section, which ran above Rock Spring-Lagunitas F.R., fell into disrepair after water pipelines were laid over it to the Air Force station atop West Peak. It is now heavily overgrown.

Lower Berry rises from Bon Tempe (Shadyside) Trail at the southern tip of Bon Tempe Lake. When entering from the Lake Lagunitas parking area, look for the two Berry trailheads (unsigned in 1998) after the crossing of a rivulet and just before the re-entry into woods.

The uphill is immediately very steep. The lower yards have been heavily eroded. Turn around to get some lovely perspectives of Bon Tempe.

The Trail enters a quiet woodland and climbs steadily in the shade. There are many sizable madrones; one, about 125 yards from the top, has nine full trunks rising from its base.

Lower Berry ends when it hits Rock Spring-Lagunitas Fire Road at a signed junction. Immediately to the right, on the same side of the fire road, is the un-marked No Name Trail. It connects to Rocky Ridge Fire Road.

Berry Trail, perhaps originally an Indian path, was said to have been redis-covered by Mountain veteran S. Lucien Berry around the turn of the century. Berry and his friend Emil Barth then worked on the Trail. Berry's ashes were scattered along the Trail by his widow, his son, and his father, accompanied by Alice Eastwood and John Forbes. Old Freese maps of the Trail carried the words "no berries" to forewarn those seeking edible berries.

MADRONE TRAIL
FROM SKY OAKS-LAGUNITAS TRAIL TO CONCRETE PIPELINE F.R. / .91 miles

Terrain: Madrone woodland; horses permitted (subject to winter closures) / MMWD
Elevation: From 730' to 850' to 500' / steep
Intersecting Trails: Pumpkin Ridge (.2m)
Directions: Sky Oaks Road, .9 miles past Ranger Station

MADRONE TRAIL is perfectly named. For almost its entire length it passes through a woodland dominated by madrones. Madrone is a characteristic tree on much of

Tamalpais — John Thomas Howell pictures a madrone on the frontispiece of his *Marin Flora* — but here, north of Bon Tempe and Lagunitas lakes, they really hold forth. Willis Jepson, whose classic California flora appeared in 1925, said of madrone, "A tree than which none other in the western woods is more marked by sylvan beauty." Madrone's most distinctive feature is its peeling bark, revealing the smooth, cool terra cotta-colored wood beneath. The leaves are thick and leathery, green above, grayer below. The trees bear orange-red fruits in fall.

Madrone Trail sets off from Sky Oaks Road at a horse crossing (marked by white road bumps) on the ranger station side of Bon Tempe Lake's Redwood Cove. This is the same spot where Bon Tempe Shadyside Trail emerges onto the road. This end of Madrone is presently marked only with a "generic" MMWD trail sign.

Madrone immediately veers right, combined with Sky Oaks-Lagunitas Trail. In 30 yards, Madrone splits off left, up the grassy hillside. The .2 miles to the ridge top are narrow and rutted, and muddy in winter.

Madrone Trail crest at the top of Pumpkin Ridge, intersecting Pumpkin Ridge Trail. Both left and right on Pumpkin Ridge Trail lead back to Sky Oaks Road. A few yards right, Madrone Trail, newly signed, continues down on the other side of the ridge.

Switchbacks cut near the top in 1997 take away a bit of Madrone's charm but were necessary for erosion control. Madrone then rolls and winds leisurely down, even occasionally up, through the woodland. This befits such a lovely Tam trail; the joy is the journey, not the destination. Madrones dominate. Deer are never far.

The lower end of the Trail was also reworked in 1997/98. Madrone descends to, and ends at, Concrete Pipeline F.R. by an old sign. Across are a pair of Water District buildings, the Phoenix gate house and pump station. Shaver Grade is one mile to the left, Fish Gulch Trail less than .2 miles to the right.

NO NAME TRAIL
FROM ROCK SPRING-LAGUNITAS F.R. AT LOWER BERRY TRAIL TO ROCKY RIDGE
F.R. / .48 miles

Terrain: Part wooded and riparian, part chaparral over serpentine; unmaintained / MMWD
Elevation: From 980' to 1,260' / steep, parts very steep
Intersecting Trails: None
Directions: Lake Lagunitas parking lot — Rock Spring-Lagunitas F.R., .6 miles

THIS TRAIL, only recently appearing on maps, was dubbed No Name by its few users. It passes through an otherwise untouched part of the Mountain, and has some outstanding view sites. Unmaintained (it is not on MMWD maps), No Name is narrow, unsigned and, in at least one area, tricky to follow.

No Name Trail's start is next to the signpost by the top of Lower Berry Trail at Rock Spring-Lagunitas F.R. No Name appears to be a continuation of Lower Berry, but the now overgrown middle section of Berry actually ran on the other side of the Fire Road. The opening yards of the Trail are particularly narrow, with roots, rocks and a slope down toward the creek also demanding caution. The uphill begins, and is occasionally very steep. The Trail crosses several rivulets then approaches and fords a more sizable stream. This is a lovely area. In winter, the unnamed stream, which meets Bon Tempe Lake at the base of Stocking Trail, cascades down. Later, azaleas bloom here.

No Name then enters an open, rock-strewn area where the route is briefly hard to follow. Go straight up the rocky path. In 25 yards, No Name continues to the right. There are views of the lakes and beyond to the north, and of the summit of Mt. Tamalpais to the south.

No Name passes through another wooded area, then again opens. The Trail ends when it meets Rocky Ridge Fire Road in a level clearing. There used to be a pig trap beside the Trail in these last yards; the battle against the feral pigs seems to have been won, for now. Uphill to the left are a horse trough and hitching post. Stocking Trail is less than .1 mile to the right and Lagoon Extension Trail is 100 yards to the left.

PILOT KNOB TRAIL
FROM LAKE LAGUNITAS TO LAKEVIEW FIRE ROAD / .81 miles

Terrain: Madrone woodland / MMWD
Elevation: From 850' to 1,000' to 900' / gradual
Intersecting Trails: None
Directions: Lake Lagunitas parking lot — Bridle Path F.R., .2 miles

PILOT KNOB is a prominent 1,217-foot hill (1,187' on some maps) on Lake Lagunitas' northeast shore. The Knob's distinctive summit, where its grassy south slope meets the tree-covered north slope in a sharp line, is visible from much of Tam and from many parts of the Ross Valley. Pilot Knob Trail goes near the hill's summit and a side path leads to the very top. The Trail also passes Marin's largest madrone tree.

Two fire roads rise near the outhouses at the Lake Lagunitas parking lot. The connector to the right goes to Lagunitas Dam. The other, once the foot of Pilot Knob Trail but now widened as Bridle Path Fire Road, climbs .2 miles to a crest. From there, Pilot Knob Trail sets off east while Bridle Path drops to Lake Lagunitas.

The early part of Pilot Knob Trail passes through both open and lightly wooded stretches. In the clearings are great views of Tam towering above the lake.

In around one-third mile, in a cleared area to the left, is a massive old madrone. It takes the outstretched arms of five or six people to circle its trunk. Like many other Tam madrones that had their sunlight blocked by redwoods and

Douglas-firs, this tree shows signs of stress. It has received special care by Water District personnel trying to save it. The Window Trail that used to lead to the tree from Sky Oaks Road is now overgrown.

Pilot Knob Trail continues climbing through a mixed woodland. At the route's highest point, a half-mile from the start and before a steady drop down, a steep path goes right. It leads to the top of Pilot Knob itself. Be sure to make this extra 200 yard climb. The open summit is special, a great place to pass a few minutes or a few hours. Lake Lagunitas glistens below, Tam skies above. Pilot Knob's south slope is largely treeless because the direct sun keeps it too dry to support the trees so abundant on the north slope.

Return to Pilot Knob Trail and go right. The Trail descends through the forest. A prominent, massive, double-trunked redwood is known as "Supertree." Madrones, though, remain transcendent.

Pilot Knob Trail ends at a signed junction with Lakeview Fire Road. To the right is Lake Lagunitas and to the left, uphill, is Eldridge Grade.

The Trail was built in 1955 by the Tamalpais Trail Riders. They originally named it Doris Schmiedell Trail, for one of the equestrian group's co-founders, and the MMWD formally recognized the name in 1975. But the Trail has since been closed to horses, and the newest MMWD map shows "Pilot Knob Trail." Schmiedell was descended on her mother's side from a Donner Party survivor, and, on her father's side, from a founder of the San Francisco Stock Exchange. She died in 1993 at age 93. Pilot Knob itself is said to have been named after a similar-looking hill in Vermont.

PUMPKIN RIDGE TRAIL
BETWEEN SKY OAKS ROAD / .72 miles

Terrain: Madrone woodland; horses permitted / MMWD
Elevation: From 730' to 900' to 800' / steep
Intersecting Trails: Madrone (.4m)
Directions: Sky Oaks Road, 1.5 miles past Ranger Station
Spur: To Sky Oaks-Lagunitas Trail, .2 miles

THERE ARE FEW PLACES on Mt. Tamalpais where deer are seen more regularly than on Pumpkin Ridge. A Trail runs atop this madrone-lined ridge. With its lovely views of Bon Tempe Lake and the Mountain, some choice picnic sites, and ease of access, Pumpkin Ridge Trail makes for pleasant hiking. Particularly inviting are the balmy summer evenings the area enjoys (though remember that MMWD lands close to the public around an hour after sunset).

Pumpkin Ridge Trail starts and ends on Sky Oaks Road; I'll describe it from the farther but easier-to-locate trailhead atop Fish Grade. Pumpkin Ridge sets off on the left, when approaching Lake Lagunitas on Sky Oaks Road, just before the road makes its final bend toward the parking area. Formerly, a pair of trails went up the hill; Netting to the right and Pumpkin Ridge to the left. Netting was closed in 1990 and is now almost fully returned to grassland.

Pumpkin Ridge Trail climbs the grassy hill. Steps made from railroad ties were added to this opening section in 1989. At their top, affixed to one of the rocks in the open grassland to the left, is a plaque. It reads:

BRUCE STANTON WAYBUR 1916-1960, WHO LOVED THE HILLS,
THE CREATURES AND HUMANKIND.

Waybur was a University of California graduate, a Rhodes Scholar, and an economist. He died of cancer.

As the Trail crests on the ridge line, look right to see an impressive trio of redwoods. Otherwise, madrones dominate.

A trace of old Netting Trail joins on the right. Then, at a recently signed junction, Madrone Trail crosses the ridge. First, on the right, Madrone descends to Concrete Pipeline F.R. Some 50 feet later, to the left, Madrone drops to Sky Oaks Road.

Pumpkin Ridge Trail continues, fairly level, along the top of Pumpkin Ridge. A few redwoods break the madrone's near-monopoly. Irises are so abundant here in spring that long-time Mountain hike leader and historian Nancy Skinner calls the route "Iris Trail."

You are likely to see or hear deer. The Mountain's natives are mule (black-tail) deer, with a distinctive black-tipped tail. They browse on shrubs, twigs, grass, and flowers, generally in the morning and evening. Mating season is in fall. The males then shed their antlers, soon to begin growing a new set. In early spring, the pregnant does find a secluded site to bear their usually two young. Seeing the spotted, frisky fawns is always a treat.

In .5 miles, the Trail passes an open grassy slope, a nice picnic spot. Here Pumpkin Ridge Trail forks. The option right (arbitrarily called a Spur here) is slightly longer, staying in woodland a bit longer before dropping to Sky Oaks-Lagunitas Trail about 50 yards north of the main Trail.

Pumpkin Ridge Trail descends under an eerie canopy of dead tanbark oaks. It then meets Sky Oaks-Lagunitas Trail, a few feet from Sky Oaks Road, and ends. A small parking turnout and MMWD "Dogs-on-leash" and "No bikes" signs mark the junction.

Doris Vitek, a veteran Mountain equestrienne and wife of long-time MMWD employee and trail builder Jim Vitek, is the "pumpkin" for whom the ridge and Trail are named. Actually, her nickname is "punkin"; "pumpkin" originally appeared as a misspelling on a map. The wood and berries of the madrones actually do add an orange-red, pumpkin hue to the ridge. An earlier name was Nebraska Ridge. The Trail covers an old Water District road across the ridge line.

ROCK SPRING-LAGUNITAS FIRE ROAD
FROM LAKE LAGUNITAS PARKING AREA TO RIDGECREST BOULEVARD / 3.39 miles

Terrain: Half wooded, half chaparral / MMWD
Elevation: From 730' to 2,080' / gradual, lower 1.5 miles very steep
Intersecting Trails: Lake Lagunitas F.R. (.2m-.3m), Lower Berry (.7m), No Name (.7m), Rocky Ridge F.R. (1.2m), Rocky Ridge Trail (1.7m), Upper Berry (1.7m, 2.2m), Lower Northside (1.8m), Lagoon F.R. (1.9m), Azalea Meadow (2.3m), Arturo (2.3m), Northside (2.3m), Potrero (2.3m), Laurel Dell F.R. (2.6m), Benstein (2.9m-3.0m), Mountain Top (3.4m)
Directions: Lake Lagunitas parking area
Amenities: Outhouses, picnic area

Rock Spring-Lagunitas Fire Road (or, occasionally, Lagunitas-Rock Spring F.R.) plays a role in most trips high onto the Mountain from the lakes. Many hardy hikers even use it to reach the Mountain Theater on Mountain Play dates. The Fire Road intersects 15 north side trails and fire roads. It is also one of the few routes that crosses Tamalpais' summit ridge, thereby connecting the north and south faces of the Mountain. Though both the Fire Road's ends are accessible by car, and the views downhill are even better than those going up, it is described uphill be-cause the Lake Lagunitas trailhead is much the more popular starting point.

The Fire Road begins from the far right side (as you drive in) of the Lake Lagunitas parking area, across the bridge over Lagunitas Creek. At the start, to the right, is Bon Tempe (Shadyside) Trail. Rock Spring-Lagunitas F.R. rises to the left, beside Lagunitas Creek. Here is a reminder of how lovely the whole length of the creek, which has been dammed to form Lagunitas, Bon Tempe, Alpine, and Kent lakes, once looked.

At the crest of this first hill is Lake Lagunitas, with the dam to the left. Look carefully at the row of logs in the water and you might see western pond turtles warming in the sunshine.

Rock Spring-Lagunitas F.R. runs together with Lake Lagunitas F.R. for 150 yards before veering right and uphill away from the lake. The next 1.5 miles are very steep. The climb is initially through forest.

In .4 miles above Lagunitas, Lower Berry Trail comes in on the right from Bon Tempe Lake. The Berry Trail once went on to Potrero Meadow before the Fire Road, cutting the route, was built. Berry's middle section on the south side of Rock Spring-Lagunitas F.R. is now overgrown. Also at the Lower Berry junction, unsigned No Name Trail sets off west to Rocky Ridge Fire Road.

The tree cover thins, opening the views. At 1.2 miles, the upper end of Rocky Ridge F.R. joins on the right. It drops to Bon Tempe Dam, and offers a loop possibility back. An old bay here accounts for the name Bay Tree Junction, although Douglas-firs are now the prevalent trees here; one has borne Christmas ornaments in recent Decembers. The climbing begins to ease, but it doesn't end.

At 1.7 miles is a three-way intersection. On the right is the foot of Upper Berry Trail, which parallels the Fire Road up to Rifle Camp. A heavily eroded route on the left (which the MMWD intends to close) marks the bottom of steep Rocky Ridge Trail. It leads to the Lower Northside and Northside trails. A remnant of Berry's overgrown middle section is visible here as well.

One hundred yards beyond, Lower Northside Trail comes in on the left at a series of steps. This extension of Lower Northside was only completed in 1997. Lower Northside runs to Colier Spring.

In another one-sixth mile, back in the Douglas-fir forest, is the upper end of Lagoon Fire Road. It descends to Serpentine Knoll. Six hundred yards beyond, Upper Berry Trail re-enters on the right. (The signpost says it is .5 miles, instead of .05 miles, up to Rifle Camp.) A concrete water tank is to the left.

Shortly beyond, also to the left, is a water trough and, up some stone steps, an old water spigot. The fountain long carried a TCC plaque:

OUR APPRECIATION OF THE KINDNESS OF THE OWNERS OF THIS WONDERLAND IN PERMITTING US TO ENJOY IT, WITHOUT CHARGE, CAN BEST BE SHOWN BY GATHERING ALL PAPER, BOTTLES, AND LITTER AND DEPOSITING SAME IN RECEPTACLES.

Unfortunately, the plaque was removed in 1993; its former place still evident on the rock. Polypody ferns grow beneath.

In a few more yards is historic Rifle Camp, once a hub of several camps in the area. The origin of its name is obscure; one often told story says that a dog named Schneider, owned by Dick Maurer, president of the Down and Outer's Club, dug up a rifle here. It is officially called Rifle Picnic Area now, and there are picnic tables and outhouses. The unusual tree by the farthest table is what may be the Mountain's largest service berry (*Amelanchier pallida*).

Four trails meet the Fire Road at Rifle Camp, a testament to the camp's historic importance. At the base of the camp, on the left, are the lower end of Arturo Trail, which climbs toward West Peak, and the west end of Northside Trail, which connects all the way to Eldridge Grade. Across the Fire Road here is the top of Azalea Meadow Trail, which descends to Kent Trail. At the upper edge of the camp, Potrero Trail sets off across the edge of Potrero Meadow.

A few yards of uphill lead to upper Potrero Meadow, one of the Mountain's treasures. "Potrero" means "pasture" in Spanish, and the meadow was once leased for grazing purposes. Keep off the delicate meadow proper; Potrero Trail is the only permitted route across. Returning visitors will note that the buildings of the Air Force Station, prominent for decades high above on the ridge left, are now gone.

Rock Spring-Lagunitas F.R. continues left around the meadow. In spring, madrones in bloom stand out across the way, lending a yellow tint to the evergreens. A path (the old Potrero Cutoff) goes left back to Arturo Trail. Before leaving the meadow, the Fire Road meets one end of Laurel Dell F.R. There is a second access a few yards beyond.

After a bit more uphill, Rock Spring-Lagunitas F.R. encounters, on the right, Benstein Trail. From this intersection Benstein descends to Laurel Dell Fire Road above Potrero Camp. The Fire Road and Benstein run together for 100 yards, then the latter splits off again, also to the right, up toward Rock Spring.

A crest is reached; there is a glimpse of southern vistas. Paths depart to the right. Then a second crest is hit and, dramatically, even broader southern views open. This is the very divide of the north and south sides of Mt. Tamalpais.

The Fire Road ends as it drops to Ridgecrest Boulevard at a gate across from a Mountain Theater parking lot. An old sign says the Fire Road is a route to Ross. Rock Spring is nearby to the right (west), accounting for the Fire Road's name. The unmarked and unmaintained Mountain Top Trail goes left, up to the former Air Force base site on West Peak, from the same gate.

Rock Spring-Lagunitas Fire Road was built in the 1930's by the Civilian Conservation Corps.

ROCKY RIDGE FIRE ROAD
FROM ALPINE PUMP F.R. TO ROCK SPRING-LAGUNITAS F.R. / 1.78 miles

Terrain: Chaparral; exposed; rocky / MMWD
Elevation: From 720' to 1,410' / steep, parts very steep
Intersecting Trails: Casey Cutoff (.8m), Stocking (1.4m), No Name (1.5m), Lagoon Extension (1.6m)
Directions: Bon Tempe Dam — Alpine Pump F.R., 200 feet

ROCKY RIDGE is a prominent, largely treeless rib on Tam's north side. This Fire Road tops it, offering access from Bon Tempe Lake to several remote north side trails. The exposed terrain can be blustery in winter winds and hot in summer. Outstanding views compensate.

To reach Rocky Ridge, cross Bon Tempe Dam from the parking area, then veer right on Alpine Pump F.R. In 200 feet, Rocky Ridge F.R. sets off uphill to the left. A signpost points the way to Potrero Meadow. Note that the Fire Road is sometimes posted as closed to bicyclists in wet conditions.

The most common Mt. Tamalpais trees — bay, Douglas-fir, madrone, tan-bark oak, live oak, redwood, and buckeye — are all found within Rocky Ridge's first quarter-mile. Higher, the trees, save for a few isolated Douglas-firs, are left behind. The first half mile is much the steepest; the uphill eases higher.

The views are immediately sweeping. Gulls regularly fly overhead on their way to and from Bon Tempe, where they dip in the fresh water. The prominent green, greasy-appearing rocks on the Fire Road are serpentine, designated as California's state rock in 1965. Serpentine, a metamorphic rock thrust up from the deepest levels of the earth's crust, is common on Mt. Tamalpais. Because its soils are heavy in magnesium, and deficient in such essential minerals as calcium, potassium and aluminum, serpentine supports only a specialized, low-growing plant community. The abundant loose rocks and prominent rock outcroppings undoubtedly account for the ridge's name.

In .8 miles, barely noticeable on the left (there is an MMWD sign 15 yards down), is Casey Cutoff Trail. It drops even more steeply, as a shortcut, back to Bon Tempe Dam.

There are actually three brief downhill stretches. At the third, just past a grove of trees, Stocking Trail enters on the left from Bon Tempe Lake. The unmarked junction is all but invisible amidst the rocks and manzanita. The continuation of Stocking, to Hidden Lake, is 75 yards farther up Rocky Ridge on the right. A signpost and line of logs and boulders mark the entrance. This area is ablaze with fragrant, blue ceanothus in early spring.

In another .1 mile there is a clearing on the left. The unsigned No Name Trail sets off through it on its trip to the top of Lower Berry Trail. There is more uphill, then the Fire Road re-enters shade. Four hundred feet above No Name is the unsigned, hard to spot, entry to Lagoon Extension Trail. (It is sometimes marked with a cairn.) Look on the right, at a small turnout before a bend left.

Rocky Ridge Fire Road ends at Rock Spring-Lagunitas Fire Road. The signpost points the way left to Lake Lagunitas, right to Potrero Meadow. The intersection is called Bay Tree Junction for an isolated bay (laurel) that overlooked it; Douglas-firs now dominate. Rocky Ridge itself continues higher, topped by Rock Spring-Lagunitas F.R., then, higher still, by Rocky Ridge Fire Trail (which see) to West Peak.

The route up Rocky Ridge is one of the oldest on Mt. Tamalpais, dating at least to the 1860's. The present Fire Road was built in the early 1930's.

SCOTT TANK FIRE ROAD
FROM SKY OAKS RANGER STATION TO SCOTT WATER TANKS / .25 miles

Terrain: Grassland and oak woodland / MMWD
Elevation: From 700' to 800' / gradual
Intersecting Trails: None
Directions: Across Sky Oaks Road from Ranger Station

BECAUSE IT IS SHORT and deadends at private property, Scott Tank Fire Road is little-used. But it does offer a visit into a pastoral oak woodland and, particularly on the return, outstanding views.

Directly across from Sky Oaks Ranger Station, a few yards before the toll booth, two paved roads depart. One forks right and leads to the private, former Crest Farm. The other leads to a ranger's residence and the gate that marks the start of Scott Tank Fire Road. A sign informs bikers that there is no through access.

The Fire Road rises above Bon Tempe Meadow. Ahead on the left is the private Meadow Club golf course, built in 1926. Deer are a common sight here, particularly in evening. The oak woodland evokes images of an earlier, quieter California. A few invading Douglas-fir trees, which may one day replace the oaks, remind us that even such timeless-looking landscapes change. The land over the ridge to the right (and ahead and to the left as well) is private property. It once was home to the Boy Scout's Camp Lilienthal; the scouts have since moved to Camp Tamarancho about two miles north. (There was also once a Girl Scout camp at Sky Oaks; it is now at Camp Bothin, off Sir Francis Drake just west of Fairfax.)

The Fire Road ends at a pair of green water tanks called the Scott Tanks. The Fire Road was graded to service them. The continuing path is overgrown, and on private property. On the way back, enjoy the excellent view of the north wall of Mt. Tamalpais.

Harry S. Scott built Crest Farm. An avid equestrian, he was a founder and the first president, in 1939, of the Tamalpais Trail Riders.

The Erickson and Olmsted maps label the separate .8-mile route that branches from near the start of Bullfrog Fire Road and runs alongside the north edge of the golf course as Scott Tank Trail. It is not described here because it passes through the private property of the Meadow Club.

SKY OAKS-LAGUNITAS TRAIL
FROM SKY OAKS ROAD OPPOSITE BULLFROG F.R. TO LAKE LAGUNITAS
PARKING LOT / 1.40 miles

Terrain: Mostly grassland, parts wooded; sometimes muddy; horses permitted (seasonal closure) / MMWD
Elevation: Around 750' / almost level, rolling
Intersecting Trails: Shaver Grade (.2m), Elliott (.3m), Pumpkin Ridge Trail and Spur (.5m), Madrone (.8m)
Directions: Sky Oaks Road, .1 mile past Ranger Station

Sky Oaks-Lagunitas Trail (sometimes simply called Sky Oaks Trail) runs alongside Sky Oaks Road, providing an alternative to the pavement. It is popular with horse riders, so is usually muddy in winter. (The initial widened and repaired section of the Trail, to Pumpkin Ridge Trail, has recently been closed to horses during winter.)

The Trail begins about 100 yards past the Sky Oaks toll booth, to the left and just beyond the short deadend road, in an area known as Sky Oaks Meadow. Sky Oaks-Lagunitas Trail bends right, onto the grassy hillside rich with wildflowers (and poison oak!) in spring. Poppies, Chinese-houses, blue and white brodiaeas, larkspurs, cream-cups, and farewell-to-spring are just some of the more colorful blossoms.

The Trail enters shade alongside a creekbed. In one-quarter mile, Sky Oaks Trail crosses the top of Shaver Grade just a few feet below the paved road. Soon after, Sky Oaks-Lagunitas meets what was formerly the top of Elliott Trail — the connection down to Shaver Grade is presently closed by an MMWD "Erosion Control" sign. Continue straight.

Sky Oaks Trail then meets, 50 yards apart, two entrances to Pumpkin Ridge Trail (the first is considered a spur here). The second Pumpkin Ridge access, beside the road, is marked by a generic MMWD sign. The two Pumpkin Ridge options merge above.

In this next open area are striking vistas of Mt. Tamalpais. Also look left up Pumpkin Ridge; it's unusual *not* to see deer grazing on the hillside.

A path connects to the road. The crossing of the road (marked, like other equestrian crossings, by white road bumps) leads to Bon Tempe Trail. Sixty yards beyond, unsigned but clear, Madrone Trail rises left through the grassland. It crosses Pumpkin Ridge then descends to Concrete Pipeline Fire Road. Continue through the baccharis-lined grassland, mindful of the pervasive poison oak.

Sky Oaks-Lagunitas Trail passes a wheelchair-accessible outhouse beneath the huge redwoods of Redwood Cove. The Trail continues up, into woodland, as it rounds the cove. The terrain opens again, with more fine views.

The Trail drops to and crosses Sky Oaks Road, again marked by white road bumps. Three routes fork; a path right to Bon Tempe Trail, a path left through the meadow and, between them, Sky Oaks-Lagunitas' continuation.

The final section is through woodland. There is quickly another fork. Straight leads toward Pine Point peninsula; veer left. Sky Oaks winds through a splendid madrone forest.

The Trail ends at an MMWD "horses" sign at Bon Tempe Trail by the blue array of water valves. They regulate the flow from Bon Tempe Lake through a tunnel (replaced in 1994) to the nearby filter plant. The parking area for Lake Lagunitas is just ahead.

Sky Oaks was the name of the 1930's Civilian Conservation Corps camp by the Trail's start, one of two such camps on Tam (the other was at today's Camp Eastwood). The Sky Oaks name was then attached to the girl scout camp there after World War II and to the present MMWD Ranger Station.

STOCKING TRAIL
FROM BON TEMPE LAKE TO KENT TRAIL / 1.10 miles

Terrain: Lower half lightly wooded and rocky, upper half wooded / MMWD
Elevation: From 730' to 1,250' / lower half very steep, upper half gradual
Intersecting Trails: Rocky Ridge F.R. (.5m), Van Wyck Creek (.7m)
Directions: Lake Lagunitas parking area — Bon Tempe (Shadyside) Trail to first bridge

STOCKING TRAIL has two distinct halves. The lower part, rising from Bon Tempe Lake, is very steep, unmarked and poorly maintained (the Olmsted map no longer even shows it). The upper half west of Rocky Ridge is gentler in slope, well-maintained, and is now signed (maybe, more on this below). Stocking offers a popular route to the deep, quiet forests of northwest Tamalpais, and also passes one of the Mountain's treasures, Hidden Lake.

Stocking begins off Bon Tempe (Shadyside) Trail, .4 miles from the Lake Lagunitas parking lot, on the far side of the first footbridge. Stocking rises to the left, unsigned and indistinct; many potential visitors never find it. A creek, dry in summer, is just to the left.

Climb to the first clearing uphill, a grassy area with boulders on the right. In late summer and early fall it is filled with the sticky, fragrant, yellow flowers of madia. This may have been the site of the turn-of-the-century Camp Handy. Emil Barth named it because is was "handy" to Fairfax and Ross. (Mountain sleuths Phil Frank and Brad Rippe searched this clearing in 1994 and found an intriguing old sign "Camp Bohne," indicating Camp Handy's site may have been lower, possibly now submerged under Bon Tempe Lake.)

The going gets even steeper. Azaleas add color and fragrance in May and June. The Trail emerges from the woodland into serpentine chaparral. Look back to get an excellent vista of Pilot Knob, Bald Hill and the East Bay. There is no clear line through the rocky terrain. Just keep climbing, dodging the manzanita and avoiding twisted ankles, and you will reach Rocky Ridge F.R. No sign marks the intersection.

Stocking continues across Rocky Ridge some yards left (depending where you emerge). The MMWD kept setting wood signposts to mark the entry and someone kept maliciously sawing them down. But the latest sign has stood for some time now, the vandal apparently retired. Good-sized logs and boulders now line the entrance, just in case.

The sharply spiked, six-foot-high shrub chaparral pea lines the early yards. Its lovely rose-purple flowers are in bloom in late spring. Laurels mark Stocking's re-entrance into forest.

In .2 miles from Rocky Ridge, Stocking descends to a new bridge (erected in 1995) across Van Wyck Creek. Twenty yards before the crossing, Van Wyck Creek Trail forks right, to Kent Trail. Ten yards before the bridge, Van Wyck Creek Trail splits left up to Lagoon Extension Trail.

Stocking winds through a delightful forest. Particularly enchanting is a grove of towering redwoods. Stocking passes through a cut in a fallen giant, believed to be the storied Hogan Tree. The plaque which dedicated this redwood grove to veteran Mountain hiker John Hogan, who once had his Camp Hogan here, is said to still be on the tree's underside.

A few yards ahead the Trail skirts a bog marked by a clump of giant chain ferns, the largest ferns on Tam. To the right is Don Richardson Spring; a wooden cover, dated 1933, marks its source. Next to it is a huge burnt, redwood "circle."

Then Stocking suddenly comes upon the treasure of Hidden Lake. Proceed quietly, you never know what unusual animal or animal behavior you'll encounter. Mt. Tamalpais is rich in many things but natural lakes are not among them. This duckweed-covered pond, shrinking in size and drying up in the natural succession of the Mountain's terrain, is unique habitat and the wildlife know it. It was once known as Wildcat Lake; wildcats, or bobcats, still live on Tam. You'll surely want to linger here.

Stocking continues another 100 yards to its junction with Kent Trail. This deep forest is one of the loveliest, quietest parts of Mt. Tamalpais. Redwoods, Douglas-firs, tanbark oaks, and madrones rise high to compete for the sunlight. Unfortunately, this is also one of the Mountain's trickier intersections — here too MMWD signs have been removed. Kent rises left, between a redwood and a huge tanbark oak, to Serpentine Knoll and Potrero Camp. Straight ahead on

Kent, in about 25 feet, is the barely visible, lower end of Willow Meadow Trail. It rises just to the left of a redwood, and into young tanbark oaks. Kent continues down to Alpine Lake.

Clayton Stocking was a long-time employee and foreman for the Marin Municipal Water District. He retired in 1962 and died in 1969. He is also honored by a plaque below the lake keeper's residence, where he lived for 42 years, beside Phoenix Dam. For an explanation of how the whole Trail came to be called Stocking, see the Lagoon Extension Trail. Earlier names included Swede George Fire Trail, Hidden Lake Trail, and, for the part below Rocky Ridge, Camp Handy Trail.

TAYLOR TRAIL
FROM SKY OAKS RANGER STATION TO CONCRETE PIPELINE FIRE ROAD / .52 miles

Terrain: Tanbark oak-madrone woodland; horses permitted / MMWD
Elevation: 700' to 525' / steep
Intersecting Trails: None
Directions: Sky Oaks Ranger Station
Amenities: Fountain

TAYLOR TRAIL OFFERS a pleasant connection between Sky Oaks Ranger Station and Concrete Pipeline Fire Road, avoiding the paved, open-to-cars Sky Oaks Road.

The Trail descends from the fence to the left when facing the newly renovated Sky Oaks Ranger station. There is a water fountain by the building. This was the site, from 1924 to 1941, of a University of California summer camp at which engineering students were taught surveying skills. In the 1930's, the Civilian Conservation Corps housed workers here. During World War II, the area was used by the military. After the war, the Girl Scouts operated their Sky Oaks Camp here.

The attractive, tree-lined Trail drops steadily almost all its length. Particularly appealing is the quiet middle section, dominated by native madrones.

Taylor ends at its junction with Concrete Pipeline Fire Road. To the left, in .6 miles, is Fairfax-Bolinas Road. To the right is the unsigned upper end of Canyon Trail (75 yards) and Five Corners (3/4-miles).

Taylor Trail was built in the early 1930's. It was named for Lawrence B. Taylor, the superintendent of the Civilian Conservation Corps Camp and an avid equestrian. He oversaw many of Tam's major northside trail building projects.

VAN WYCK CREEK TRAIL
FROM LAGOON EXTENSION TRAIL TO KENT TRAIL / 1.1 miles

Terrain: Deep forest, mostly redwoods; riparian; unimproved / MMWD
Elevation: From 1,280′ to 660′ / steep, parts very steep
Intersecting Trails: Stocking, .1m
Directions: Bon Tempe Dam — Rocky Ridge F.R., 1.6 miles — right on Lagoon Extension Trail, .1 mile

It is an old saw among Mountain veterans that if you look hard enough you'll find some sort of trail or path beside all of Tam's creeks. A one-time log skid track beside Van Wyck Creek has recently become worn in as a Trail. The redwood forest it traverses is among the Mountain's loveliest woodland. But, be warned that the Trail is completely unmarked amidst a vast otherwise trail-less swath of Tam, and has several rough patches.

Neither end of Van Wyck Creek Trail is easy to reach; both involve long marches. Since the unmaintained Trail is easier to follow downhill, I'll describe it that way.

To reach the top, take Lagoon Extension Trail (if you can find it!) in from Rocky Ridge Fire Road. At the far edge of the chaparral, and 20 yards before the first creek crossing, Van Wyck Trail forks right. (An easier-to-find access is from Stocking Trail, which lops off the upper 200 yards of Van Wyck.)

Set off down the right bank of Van Wyck Creek (water is on the left), one of the strongest flowing on Tam. This highest section is steep, rocky and narrow. Douglas-firs line the left margin, with chaparral near to the right. The Trail comes to the creek's edge, where mossy boulders abound.

Van Wyck meets Stocking Trail; Stocking's bridge over Van Wyck Creek is 10 yards down to the left. Stocking and Van Wyck are combined for 10 yards to the right, then Van Wyck forks left and down at a big Douglas-fir.

Clumps of native bunchgrasses border the Trail, and laurel is the abundant tree. Some 200 yards below Stocking, Van Wyck Creek Trail makes its lone crossing of the namesake creek it follows. The fording is usually an easy one, even in winter, and the creek will now always be to the right.

Continue ever down. A huge Douglas-fir stands in front of the first Trail-side grove of redwoods and both trees, but mostly the redwoods, dominate the rest of the way. A path comes in from the upper left.

The Trail crosses a small rivulet. The main creek bed nurtures many colorful azalea bushes.

The easy going is broken by a rough section, where fallen trees and slides have obscured the original route. The Trail narrows, steepens, and faces at least two equal-looking forks. In each case, both fork options soon unite. The creek bed should never be more than 100 feet away.

After a short uphill, the Trail goes over, then under, two trunks of a huge downed Douglas-fir. The trunks are still united at the roots. The creek bed is a long, steep drop to the right, so be careful. The Trail goes over a fallen tanbark oak, then passes right through a standing double-trunked one.

The next, very gently downhill section is the most magical of the route, one of the jewels of Tam. Giant, fire-scarred redwoods circle the stumps of their even more massive "parents." Douglas-firs rise just as tall. The creek cascades down strongly. No trail or road is anywhere near. Someone has built a miniature "log cabin" just left of the Trail in a level area once the site of a 19th century logging camp.

All too soon, the bridge over Van Wyck on the Kent Trail comes into view. A huge boulder stands sentinel on the left. Van Wyck Creek Trail ends at its junction with Kent Trail. Rocky Ridge F.R. is 1.5 miles to the right. If you want more of this magical woodland, go left on Kent a half-mile to the Helen Markt Trail junction. Kent then rises through the same forest to meet Stocking Trail.

The Trail has not appeared on maps and has no name but its constant companion, Van Wyck Creek, suggests one. There is, however, a separate Van Wyck Meadow on the south side of Tam.

WILLOW MEADOW TRAIL
FROM KENT-STOCKING TRAIL JUNCTION TO WILLOW MEADOW / .55 miles

Terrain: Deep woods; riparian; unimproved / MMWD
Elevation: From 1,240′ to 1,500′ / steep, short parts extremely steep
Intersecting Trails: Swede George (.4m), Kent (.5m)
Directions: Bon Tempe Dam — Rocky Ridge F.R., 1.4 miles — right on Stocking Trail to end

THIS UNSIGNED TRAIL has only recently appeared on Tam maps. Since one end is at Willow Meadow, I'll use the unofficial name Willow Meadow Trail.

The Trail's lower end, in one of the loveliest woodlands on Tam, is very difficult to spot. From the presently unmarked junction of Kent and Stocking trails (two signs have been sawed down), go downhill on Kent about 15 yards. Willow Meadow Trail starts uphill to the left. The Trail's opening yards are a bit overgrown with young, shrub-like tanbark oaks; the route is then clear to follow. In around 100 yards, just past a huge Douglas-fir, a path branches right.

Willow Meadow Trail rises steadily, with some short extremely steep parts. Because the Trail is little known, and is already in one of the quietest parts of the Mountain, serenity is assured. The East Fork of Swede George Creek becomes audible, then visible, in the deep canyon to the right. The creek runs surprisingly strongly even in late summer.

At a moss-covered, multi-trunked old oak, unmarked Swede George Trail forks right. It crosses the creek (if a fording is possible) and rises to High Marsh Trail and Potrero Camp.

Willow Meadow Trail then meets Swede George Creek for a particularly delightful stretch. Azaleas are abundant. Creekside boulders and logs invite to sit and enjoy.

Willow Meadow Trail hits Kent Trail again at another unmarked junction. Left, Kent heads toward Alpine Lake. To the right, within 15 yards, Kent crosses the East Fork of Swede George over a bridge, then meets High Marsh and Azalea Meadow trails. Willow Meadow Trail continues, less distinctly, across Kent.

In around 100 yards, the Trail ends at Willow Meadow. This large, flat, often wet, meadow is one of Tam's hidden jewels. Willows are found in the moister parts, such as immediately to the right.

Western ridges, from Azalea Hill.

Unusual reverse fog pattern over Bolinas Ridge, from hang glider site #2.

West Ridgecrest Trailhead

West Ridgecrest Trailhead

Directions to West Ridgecrest Boulevard:

Highway 101 — Highway 1 — Panoramic Highway-Southside (Pantoll) Road *OR* Fairfax-Bolinas Road, from either Fairfax (where it is called Bolinas Road) or from Highway 1 at north edge of Bolinas Lagoon

RIDGECREST BOULEVARD (or Road) has long been hailed for its beauty. When it was first opened as a toll road in the late 1920's — $1 per car with two passengers, 25 cents per additional rider — a sign at the northern gate proclaimed it as California's "Most Scenic Drive." It has since become known worldwide as the locale for numerous television commercials, particularly for cars.

The Boulevard runs 6.6 miles along the summit ridge of Tam between Fairfax-Bolinas Road and the East Peak parking area. In this book, it is divided into three trailhead sections: West Ridgecrest, the 3.7 miles between Fairfax-Bolinas Road and Rock Spring; Rock Spring, where Ridgecrest has its lone intersection, with Southside Road; and East Ridgecrest to East Peak.

Ridgecrest Boulevard was built by M.H. Ballou. A toll was collected at the Alpine Toll Gate near the Fairfax-Bolinas Road junction, known as Ridgecrest. A lodge, originally Summit House, later with other names, stood at the junction from 1890 until it burned during the big fire of 1945. Ballou is honored by Ballou Point, a special view sight along the road .8 miles from Rock Spring. There was once a plaque to him there:

M.H. BALLOU, 1858-1926. THESE SURROUNDINGS TYPIFY
THE CHARACTER OF THIS MAN.

West Ridgecrest was not paved until 1939. The military closed the entire boulevard for the duration of World War II. It was then reopened as a free, public road. It is, however, shut each night by gates at Ridgecrest and at Pantoll. The road is also closed during high fire danger days and, rarely, by snowfall; call 499-7191 for a recorded message.

At Fairfax-Bolinas Road, Coastal Trail begins its 9-mile journey across Tam. (Opposite, the 11-mile Bolinas Ridge Fire Road, outside this book's boundary, drops to Olema.) One-and-a-half miles toward Rock Spring, McKennan Trail descends to Bolinas Lagoon. In another .8 miles, Laurel Dell Fire Road departs to the left (east) and Willow Camp Fire Road to the west. Several trails on Tam's north side are reached most easily from the Laurel Dell F.R. trailhead, which has parking for several cars.

Being more directly influenced by the Pacific, Tam's west slope has different weather patterns than the rest of the Mountain. In winter, temperatures are usually warmer. In summer, fog is common, particularly early and late in the day, and temperatures are often 20 degrees or more cooler than on inland trails.

Suggested loops from West Ridgecrest Blvd. (elevation 1,800')
• Laurel Dell F.R., 1.6m, to broad connector to Barth's Retreat — right, .2m, to Mickey O'Brien Trail — right, .7m, to Laurel Dell F.R.-left, .6m, to start **3.1 miles.**
• Laurel Dell F.R., .8m, to Bare Knolls Trail — left, .3m, to High Marsh Trail — right, 1.8m to Cross Country Boys Trail — right, .4m, to Kent Trail — right, .4m, to Potrero Camp — .1m to Laurel Dell F.R. — right, 1.7m, to start **5.5 miles.**
• McKennan Trail, 2.2m, to base — left on Willow Camp F.R., 2.7m to Coastal Trail — left, 1.1m, to start **6.0 miles**

BARE KNOLLS TRAIL
FROM LAUREL DELL FIRE ROAD TO HIGH MARSH TRAIL / .32 miles

Terrain: Mostly grassland / MMWD
Elevation: From 1,690' to 1,750' to 1,700' / steep
Intersecting Trails: None
Directions: West Ridgecrest Boulevard — Laurel Dell F.R., .8m

THIS TRAIL IS TAKEN mostly to visit the "Bare Knolls," a pair of isolated, grassy hilltops with extraordinary views.

From Laurel Dell, follow Laurel Dell F.R. north and uphill for 250 yards. Bare Knolls Trail departs to the left, at fire road-width. The new MMWD sign here notes the route as a "Dead End."

The early yards are through a light Douglas-fir woodland. At a rather sharp demarcation, the broad Trail enters grassland. Immediately, views open.

The route's first crest is in 200 yards. The vistas are outstanding, including a rare look at Kent Lake. The Trail drops to a saddle, from which a path departs, then mounts the second knoll. The views are no less glorious. It would be rare to visit on a sunny weekend day and not find others idling in the grass here.

The remainder of the Trail is barely distinct and steeply downhill. Look across the canyon of Cataract Creek, to the left (west), and note the yellowish tanbark oaks amidst the dark greens of redwoods and Douglas-firs.

Bare Knolls Trail ends at High Marsh Trail at an unsigned junction. Twenty-five yards to the right, High Marsh enters woodland, then winds on to High Marsh itself. To the left, it meets Cataract Trail.

The Trail appears as a deadend fire road on old maps. It is not clear why it was cleared, perhaps solely for the views. The final connection to the later-built High Marsh Trail has been worn in more recently.

COASTAL TRAIL
FROM JUNCTION OF FAIRFAX-BOLINAS AND RIDGECREST ROADS TO HIGHWAY 1, MILEPOST 7.35 / 9.2 miles

Terrain: Mostly grassland with forested sections / MTSP & GGNRA; sections part of Bay Area Ridge Trail
Elevation: From 1,450' to 1,800' to 460' / mostly gradual and rolling, southern part very steep
Intersecting Trails: Old Bolinas-San Rafael (.2m), McKennan (2.1m), Willow Camp F.R. (3.2m), Matt Davis (4.6m-6.2m), Steep Ravine (6.3m), Old Mine (6.3m, 6.6m), Lone Tree Hill F.R. (6.6m), Lone Tree F.R. (6.7m), Dipsea (6.8m), Deer Park F.R. (6.9m), Heather Cutoff (9.0m)
Directions: West Ridgecrest/Fairfax-Bolinas Road junction
Amenities: Bathrooms, fountains, telephone

COASTAL TRAIL is the longest single route in Marin. It stretches, except for short discontinuities, from the Golden Gate Bridge to the Fairfax-Bolinas Road, a distance of over 17 miles. Taking it its full length, or its nine miles over Tam, is one of the Bay Area's special experiences.

The southern part of the route across Tam, from Highway 1 to Pantoll, is a fire road (called Coastal Fire Road here) and open to bicycles. The remainder of the journey to Fairfax-Bolinas Road is at trail-width, and closed to cyclists. Coastal Trail is also called the Coast, and the Pacific Coast, Trail. There is a separate Coast Trail in Point Reyes, between Palomarin and the Limantour Road.

To follow the entire route in the net downhill direction, start at the intersection of the Fairfax-Bolinas and Ridgecrest roads. Tolls were collected near here until World War II. There is parking for a few cars. It was also the site of a lodge, variously called Summit House (for it stood at the highest point on the old San Rafael-Bolinas stage route), Larsen's, Consy's, and Wright's (for successive owners). The lodge was a resting place for stage travelers. It burned in the big 1945 fire, several years after it had been abandoned.

The trailhead sign is inviting, indicating, for example, that it is 15 miles to Tennessee Valley. Also inviting is 11.3-mile-long Bolinas Ridge Fire Road across the pavement. It is a combined use (pedestrian, biker, equestrian) section of the Bay Area Ridge Trail, dropping to Sir Francis Drake Boulevard just above Olema and the Point Reyes National Seashore trail network.

Coastal starts off in a redwood forest beside Ridgecrest Boulevard. This initial mile-long section was once known as Laurel Trail. The route soon drops from the road and crosses a fence through a gate. The fence was erected in 1987 to keep a then growing feral pig population from moving to Point Reyes National Seashore. The hardy pigs were a menace to vegetation, particularly bulbous plants such as the Mountain's orchids. A hunting and trapping program has apparently eliminated them from Tam.

A downhill leads to a haunting forest of laurels. At the base, on the right, Old Bolinas-San Rafael Trail, described in earlier editions of this book, is now posted as closed. The historic trail, perhaps the oldest on the Mountain, likely dates from the 1830's. It connected the mission at San Rafael to the coastal town of Bolinas.

Coastal Trail begins climbing over switchbacks. The Trail then leaves the deep forest into an isolated area of mixed chaparral, grassland, and bay trees. There are ocean views. Pitcher sages are redolent.

Coastal circles back toward Ridgecrest Boulevard. Huge Douglas-firs tower above. The Trail re-crosses the pig fence, then comes to within a few yards of the Boulevard at the head of Morse's Gulch. Just below is an old orchard, which still yields a few apples. The trees were planted by John Wright, who named the grove Fountainhead Orchard, for the spring a few yards to the southwest. Look at the Trail's edge here for some brickwork, remnants of Wright's residence.

Coastal now enters grassland, where it remains for more than four miles. There are almost continuous stunning ocean views. The ocean's warming influence usually keeps at least a few poppies in bloom into December. A path joins on the left. It brings Bay Area Ridge Trail equestrians onto and off Coastal Trail.

The route returns to near the pig fence. You may spot an old bathtub, from the days when the area was grazed. A gate in the fence marks the top of a now overgrown old route. Just ahead, another path rises to Ridgecrest Boulevard.

When the Trail comes closest to the fence, look carefully to spot remnants of the McKennan Gulch Copper Prospect. These include a barren pile of tailings, a change in the color of the Trail itself (from brownish to gray-black), and a depression five yards to the left. The now-filled tunnel entrance is below the fence. All date from a test cut — there was never a working mine — in the 1930's.

Coastal again approaches Ridgecrest Boulevard, this time meeting it. At the junction is the top of McKennan Trail (fire road-width), which drops very steeply to Highway 1 at the southern edge of Bolinas Lagoon. Coastal Trail runs on Ridgecrest for 100 yards then departs from the asphalt to the right (west).

The Trail continues through grassland, then enters a woodland atop Stinson Gulch. Many of the downed trees here fell during a storm in 1990; they took out the bridge as well. The bridge was rebuilt and the plaque on it — IN MEMORY OF MIKE AMOROSO, MILL VALLEY LIONS CLUB 1978 — restored to the far side. Amoroso was a Mill Valley liquor store owner involved in many civic projects.

In another .1 mile is the stone Cook Memorial Bench, one of the Mountain's revered spots. A plaque reads:

ROBERT B. COOK 1959-1979
THIS SCENIC 4.3 MILES SECTION OF PACIFIC COAST TRAIL,
BETWEEN THE MATT DAVIS AND LAUREL TRAILS,
IS DEDICATED TO THE MEMORY OF BOB COOK.
IT WAS CONCEIVED AS HIS EAGLE SCOUT PROJECT AND,
THROUGH HIS PERSISTANCE AND DETERMINATION,
WAS BUILT WITH VOLUNTEER LABOR OVER A TWO YEAR PERIOD.

Cook undertook building the trail soon after the area became open to the public. He then died in an airplane crash on his way to do more trail work, in Idaho. The plaque was unveiled in a ceremony on June 1, 1980. Rest at this special place and enjoy the wonderful view (increasingly blocked by rising Douglas-firs), the serenity, and the sounds of the laurel-lined rivulet just ahead and of the ocean surf.

Coastal rises. Another old cattle drinking tub and a clump of planted lilies are further reminders that the area was privately owned and grazed into the 1970's.

One-quarter-mile from the Cook Bench, Coastal Trail crosses Willow Camp Fire Road. It's a stiff .1 mile uphill to Ridgecrest Boulevard, or a long, steep but gorgeous drop right toward Stinson Beach, where a tough loop can be made with McKennan Trail.

Coastal Trail continues to meander around the gulches of Tam's west face. Several isolated, haunting, groves of laurel trees are passed. A rusted old vehicle lies beneath a laurel, a remaining bald tire perhaps a clue to its arrival here.

Coastal rises to its high point of 1,800 feet. On a fogless day the views from this long, open section are magnificent. Also look for hang gliders, launched from designated sites off Ridgecrest Boulevard, floating toward Stinson Beach.

There is a descent. A sign marks the stretch of Coastal just passed as the Bob Cook Memorial Section, and it has been called Bob Cook Trail. A few yards beyond, just before another laurel grove, Matt Davis Trail drops right on its descent to Stinson Beach.

The Coastal and Matt Davis (which see) trails then run combined for 1.6 fairly level miles, first through grassland, then a mile through a Douglas-fir forest.

The two trails split again when they reach the Panoramic-Pantoll road junction by Pantoll Ranger Station. Coastal Trail veers right (south) down a few steps to enter the Pantoll parking area while Matt Davis continues east.

Through the Pantoll area, Coastal is a paved road. It descends to the right from the ranger station, past the Old Mine and Steep Ravine trails, past some State Park residences, then through the MTSP maintenance yard. At the far end of the yard, Coastal resumes as a dirt fire road.

Coastal passes just above the old mine site that gives Old Mine Trail its name. (Some old maps label this next section of Coastal as Old Mine Fire Road.) Just below, Coastal meets Old Mine Trail at a four-way junction. The unsigned fire road right rises to the top of Lone Tree Hill. Coastal continues downhill.

The Fire Road emerges from the Douglas-fir forest into grassland and one of the Mountain's loveliest and most photographed areas. There are sweeping views, beyond miles of open space, of Mt. Diablo, the downtown San Francisco skyline and of the Pacific.

Coastal passes the top of Lone Tree Fire Road, which descends to Highway 1. One-tenth mile below, Coastal crosses the Dipsea Trail. This junction, the highest point in the Dipsea Race, is known as Cardiac. Dipsea runners love it because it's then basically all downhill to the ocean. The area is also a popular picnic site. A bit more downhill and Coastal meets the western end of Deer Park Fire Road. Deer Park takes the Bay Area Ridge Trail route with it down to Franks Valley.

There is then not another trail intersection for more than two miles. The descent is steep, and glorious. There is little to obstruct the views. Kent Canyon is to the left, Cold Stream Canyon to the right, both marked by a line of trees.

After a brief rise, Coastal passes the remains of a once prominent grove of Monterey pines. The pines were planted in 1959 by then landowner Tony Brazil and his friend Roane Sias. They envisioned growing 5,000 three-to-six-foot Christmas trees, sales of which would finance their children's college educations. The site was called the Brazil-Sias Christmas Tree Farm. But the property was purchased a few years later by the State Park.

In 1979, Hillsborough resident Albert Shansky donated funds for construction of Camp Shansky (or Shansky Backpack Camp) amidst the old tree farm. It was named for his late son, Lee, who had been an avid hiker on Tam. There were four campsites for hikers, including one called "the honeymoon suite." In February 1989, a wind storm decimated the camp and grove. Scores of trees were toppled, others soon after cut down. The camp never reopened. A few years later, remnants of the grove and camp were removed. The area now has a stark appearance but will surely soon be re-covered by vegetation. Many young Monterey pines are sprouting. From behind the old grove, an overgrown ranch road, called Stagecoach Trail by some, descended to Kent Canyon.

After a brief respite, the descent continues, unabated and even steeper than before. No other route crosses this large section of southwestern Tam. The shrub baccharis dominates the treeless terrain, as it often does once grazing ceases on coastal grasslands. Mixed in is gumweed, one of the few flowers still in bloom in mid-summer. It is also recognizable by the creamy, sticky fluid atop it.

At a boundary sign and fence, Coastal F.R. leaves Mount Tamalpais State Park and enters the Golden Gate National Recreation Area, where it basically remains all the way to the Golden Gate Bridge. Heather Cutoff Trail branches left here, descending 21 switchbacks to Franks Valley. (The mileage sign here notes it is 2.3 miles up to Deer Park Fire Road, while the newer sign at Deer Park says the same stretch is 2.0 miles.)

Coastal then runs through the upper reaches of the former Banducci Brothers flower farm (also known as Heather Farm), which supplied Bay Area wholesalers with heather and other flowers since the 1920's. The property became part of the GGNRA in 1980, although the farm continued in operation. But in 1994, the Banduccis lost their right to pump irrigation water from the wells near Redwood Creek — it was considered harmful to the creek's threatened salmon run — and the flower farming essentially ended.

Coastal runs parallel to Highway 1, meets a row of eucalyptus trees, then exits onto Highway 1 across from milepost 7.35. On the ocean side of the highway is a view turnout with a "Dangerous Cliffs" warning sign. There is presently no trail down to Muir Beach, from where the southern journey of Coastal Trail continues.

HELEN MARKT TRAIL
FROM CATARACT TRAIL TO KENT TRAIL / 1.75 miles

Terrain: Coniferous forest / MMWD
Elevation: From 1,080' to 800' / rolling, parts steep
Intersecting Trails: None
Directions: Fairfax-Bolinas Road to milepost 8.09 (six miles west of Sky Oaks Road, .2 miles past Alpine Dam) — Cataract Trail, .6 miles

HELEN MARKT (the "t" is silent) is one of the Mountain's lovelier trails. It winds above the cool, wet, remote southwest shore of Alpine Lake. Since even its shortest loop possibility (with Kent, High Marsh, and Cataract trails) is some eight miles and strenuous, Helen Markt is little-visited. The nearest trailheads are all distant; 2.3 miles from Sky Oaks or from Rock Spring, 1.6 miles from West Ridgecrest Road, or a very steep .6 mile uphill on Cataract Trail from Fairfax-Bolinas Road. I'll describe the latter approach, as it is shortest.

Fairfax-Bolinas Road crosses over the top of Alpine Dam. From the north end (nearer Fairfax), a lovely 4.4-mile fire road, just outside this book's coverage, descends gradually to Kent Lake. At the first bend beyond the dam, where the road begins to rise, is the signed lower end of Cataract Trail. There is some off-road parking.

Climb .6 miles up Cataract Trail to the sizable bridge over Cataract Creek. About 25 yards above the bridge, an MMWD signpost points the way left to the start of Helen Markt Trail. Cataract Trail continues uphill right toward Laurel Dell.

Helen Markt begins downhill. There is a remnant of an older, steeper connection to the Cataract Creek bridge. In 100 yards, the Trail crosses a huge fallen Douglas-fir, cut for easier passage. The downed tree has long been a landmark, and will be for years ahead, though the work of wood-decaying fungi will ultimately prevail. Other stately Douglas-firs still bear clear evidence of the 1945 fire here.

Helen Markt winds and rolls through this relatively unspoiled woodland. Indeed, for a quiet forest walk, Helen Markt has few, if any, equals on Tam. The area above (south) is one of the largest on Tam without a maintained trail.

In one-third mile, at a lovely semi-clearing, there is a fork; veer left (the steeper path down right quickly reconnects). Just beyond where the two options re-merge, in a grove of redwoods after a downhill, look carefully at the left margin of the Trail, and listen, for Broko Spring. It emerges from the ground through the clay as a safe source of cool water most all the year. "Broko" was a nickname for Joe Vitek, brother of the Trail's builder, Jim Vitek, and a volunteer trail worker himself. This is a favorite resting spot. Note the massive redwood stump, nearly encircled by younger root-sprouted "offspring." The stream just ahead cuts through Blake Canyon, named for Arthur H. Blake, a long-time Bay Area hiker and environmentalist who died in 1957.

Beyond are masses of huckleberry shrubs, covered with tasty berries in late summer and fall. At 1.2 miles, the Trail crosses Swede George Creek, one of the strongest streams on the Mountain. The near end of the bridge is secured to a

Douglas-fir, the far end to a redwood, which is now embedding the post. A path right leads to the edge of the creek.

The Trail climbs steeply and hits a short clearing at the edge of chaparral. Look left over the manzanita to see Alpine Dam at the far end of the lake. Helen Markt descends back into the woods. It then touches the shore of Alpine Lake, another fine place to pause. Pacific starflower, with its single pink flower supported on the slenderest of stems, is abundant here in spring.

Helen Markt ends when it meets Kent Trail at an MMWD signpost. (There is an older Helen Markt sign affixed to a tree just ahead, from where a now closed access to Kent arose.) Kent goes straight ahead to Bon Tempe Dam and uphill to Serpentine Knoll, High Marsh and Potrero Camp.

Jim Vitek, who likely knows the north side of Tamalpais better than anyone after 65 years of hiking over it and a career with the MMWD, constructed the Trail in the early 1950's. It was built to provide a new long loop possibility from Bon Tempe. Floating lumber to the remote site of the bridge over Swede George Creek was one of Vitek's trickiest tasks.

Frank and Helen Markt were toll takers on Ridgecrest Boulevard in the 1930's, when a fee was still charged. They lived in a house (destroyed in the 1945 fire) at the junction of Ridgecrest and Fairfax-Bolinas Road. The couple later resided beside Lake Lagunitas, where Frank served as lake keeper from 1940 until his retirement in 1965. Helen died while Vitek was working on this Trail, so it was named in her honor.

HIGH MARSH TRAIL
FROM CATARACT TRAIL TO JUNCTION OF KENT AND AZALEA MEADOW TRAILS
/ 2.21 miles

Terrain: Heavily wooded with some grassland and chaparral / MMWD
Elevation: From 1,700' to 1,520' / gradual and rolling, short parts steep
Intersecting Trails: Bare Knolls (.2m), connector to Laurel Dell F.R. (.6m), Spur of Old Stove (.8m), Music Camp (1.5m), Swede George (twice at 1.8m), Cross Country Boys (2.0m)
Directions: Laurel Dell F.R. — Cataract Trail, .3 miles

IT TAKES AN EFFORT to hike the full length of High Marsh Trail — at least six miles roundtrip, more for a loop — from any place reachable by car. This assures that the Trail, already in one of the remotest parts of the Mountain, will be peaceful and quiet even on the busiest summer weekends. The rolling Trail covers a variety of terrain, has several splendid view sights, and, of course, passes wonderful High Marsh itself.

High Marsh Trail leaves Cataract Trail .3 miles below Laurel Dell. An old bench and new signpost mark the junction. In 50 yards there is a fork; take either option; they quickly join. The Trail then emerges from the forest to a grassy hillside. This is one of the loveliest places on Mt. Tamalpais, with gently contoured hills, wonderful views (including a glimpse of Kent Lake, rarely seen from any Tam trail), and a riot of wildflowers in spring. You'll find orange poppies and fiddlenecks, yellow creamcups and buttercups, white woodland-stars and wild cucumbers, blue-eyed-grass, baby-blue-eyes, and blue lupines, and pink and reds from geraniums and scarlet pimpernels.

As High Marsh Trail crests near the end of the grassland, look right for the somewhat indistinct base of Bare Knolls Trail. It rises to a pair of lovely view knolls and then on to Laurel Dell F.R. Twenty-five yards later, High Marsh Trail reenters woodland.

At the top of the next uphill, a signpost marks a 75-yard connector, a remnant of the old Dead-End Trail, right and uphill to Laurel Dell F.R. High Marsh levels, and passes through a stretch of manzanita.

Atop the next major uphill, the highest point on the Trail and the divide between the drainages of Cataract and Swede George creeks, a spur of Old Stove Trail sets off to the right through manzanita.

Fifty yards later, High Marsh Trail descends steps. There are sweeping views above the chaparral shrubs, to Tomales Bay, Mt. St. Helena and beyond. The Trail returns to a forest canopy then rises to another clearing in the chaparral. A path branches sharply left.

The Trail meets the West Fork of Swede George Creek at an unsigned four-way junction. Music Stand Trail sets off up the creek's left bank toward the Music Camp and Laurel Dell F.R. A path drops left. High Marsh continues across the creek.

Few parts of the Mountain are farther from a road than this next section of High Marsh. The deep forest, in which no signs of civilization are heard or seen, takes the sense of wilderness still further. One of the treasures is a moss-covered "rock garden," just beyond a pair of towering boulders.

The Trail passes through a massive downed Douglas-fir, then crosses a stream. Seventy-five yards later, easy-to-miss Swede George Trail sets off uphill to the right. It connects to Potrero Camp. The two trails runs together for fifty yards, then Swede George Trail forks left down to Willow Meadow Trail. High Marsh veers right, uphill, at this tricky, unmarked intersection.

Finally (or all too quickly) the Trail meets High Marsh itself, somewhat obscured to the left. The marsh, like Hidden Lake a half-mile north, is a drainage-collecting slump that resulted from the huge Potrero landslide (almost two miles long and 3,500 feet wide) of some 1,000 years ago. High Marsh has been noticeably shrinking in recent decades, evolving naturally into a meadow; it already appears as a meadow in summers. It remains an appealing resting place.

At High Marsh itself, Cross Country Boys Trail, newly signed, rises steeply uphill to the right. High Marsh Trail veers left.

It is then a level 200 yards to High Marsh Trail's end at a signed four-way intersection. Kent Trail goes left to Alpine Lake and right to Potrero Camp. The trail directly across is Azalea Meadow (signed "To Lagoon Fire Road"), heading to Rifle Camp.

High Marsh Trail was built almost singlehandedly by Bob Murray in the 1960's. It was originally called Gracie Trail.

LAUREL DELL FIRE ROAD
FROM RIDGECREST BOULEVARD TO POTRERO MEADOW / 2.20 miles

Terrain: Grassland, forest, and chaparral; part riparian / MMWD
Elevation: From 1,920' to 1,640' to 2,020' / gradual, rolling
Intersecting Trails: Connector to Cataract Trail (.3m), Cataract (.6m), Bare Knolls
(.8m), connector to High Marsh Trail (.8m), Old Stove (.9m, 1.3m), connector to
Mickey O'Brien (1.4m), broad connector to Barth's Retreat (1.6m), Music Stand
(1.6m), Potrero Trail (1.7m), Benstein (1.8m)
Directions: Rock Spring — West Ridgecrest Boulevard, 1.4 miles
Amenities: Outhouses, picnic tables

LAUREL DELL Fire Road provides access to some of the famous sites on the north
side of the Mountain, including Laurel Dell itself, Barth's Retreat, the Music
Camp, the two Potrero Meadows, and Rifle Camp. There are also some exceptional vista points.

The Fire Road sets off from West Ridgecrest Boulevard at a gate beside a
parking turnout, 1.4 miles from Rock Spring. Across Ridgecrest here is an entry
to Willow Camp Fire Road.

Fifteen yards in, a sign marks the top of a steep shortcut path down over the
grassland. Laurel Dell F.R. descends in a sweeping arc through the open grassland. It soon enters woodland. In 1/3 mile, a signed connector forks to the right.
It crosses Cataract Creek over Ray Murphy Bridge to meet Cataract Trail. Just
before the Fire Road itself drops to the creek, look left, at the edge of the woodland, for an old fenced enclosure. It was built to protect Laurel Dell's water source
from the cattle that used to graze here.

The Fire Road fords Cataract Creek at the edge of Laurel Dell Meadow,
where Barth's Creek joins. The crossing can be quite wet, even unpassable except
with high boots, after winter rains and there is no easy way to skirt it. One option
is to retreat to Cataract via the Ray Murphy Bridge; Cataract crosses Barth's
Creek a few yards upstream aided by a small bridge. Nearby to the right, Mickey
O'Brien Trail sets off up to Barth's Retreat.

The tree-ringed meadow at Laurel Dell is immensely appealing. Long-time
Tam hikers recall a famous dogwood tree that once stood there. Cataract Trail
comes in through the grassland.

The Laurel Dell picnic area is just ahead on the left. There are two entrances, one on the other side of an incongruous plum tree, the other, with the
famous "Laurel Dell" sign, opposite the outhouses. Laurel Dell has been, justifi-
ably, a favorite destination for generations. Five picnic tables sit beside Cataract
Creek amidst the laurels, but the old water fountain is gone. Cataract Trail, to
High Marsh Trail and Alpine Dam, continues downhill from the picnic area.

Laurel Dell F.R. now heads uphill, into a forest of Douglas-firs. Some 250
yards from Laurel Dell, broad Bare Knolls Trail climbs left to a pair of grassy
crests.

In another couple of hundred feet is a signed, 75-yard-long connector, once part of Dead-End Trail, that also meets High Marsh Trail. Just beyond, at the far end of the big bend, is Old Stove Trail. It begins up over a few wooden steps.

As the route climbs, the tree cover opens. You can look back to the gate at Ridgecrest Boulevard where the Fire Road began. On a level section in the chaparral, Old Stove Trail rejoins Laurel Dell F.R. The junction is directly across from a small clearing which harbors remnants of an old camp site. Beyond, just before the tree line, an unsigned .2-mile connector to Mickey O'Brien Trail leaves to the right.

The Fire Road rises into forest again, then drops back into chaparral. At the bottom of the dip a sign atop a connector fire road points the way right down to Barth's Retreat, where the Simmons and Mickey O'Brien trails meet. The latter offers an easy loop option. To the left is the newly signed top of Music Stand Trail.

Laurel Dell Fire Road crests just ahead. The views to the north are outstanding. On the clearest of winter days, snow-capped mountains, 100 miles away in Mendocino County, may be visible. Closer sights include the Point Reyes peninsula and Alpine Lake.

The Fire Road returns to woodland. It passes a broad connector on the left which drops to Potrero Camp. To the right, signed Benstein Trail begins its journey to Rock Spring.

Part of lower Potrero Meadow is visible to the left. Then the larger upper Potrero Meadow is met. Laurel Dell F.R. bends right. There is an old sign at what used to be a crossing, now closed, of the meadow. A path to Rock Spring-Lagunitas F.R. branches right, then Laurel Dell Fire Road ends when it meets Rock Spring-Lagunitas F.R. itself.

Laurel Dell was earlier known as Old Stove Camp, for a stove once there. It was renamed Laurel Dell by J. H. Cutter, first president of the Tamalpais Conservation Club. Laurel, or bay, is the most common tree on Tamalpais. Laurel Dell Fire Road was built by the Civilian Conservation Corps in the 1930's over parts of Old Stove Trail.

McKENNAN TRAIL
FROM RIDGECREST BOULEVARD TO WILLOW CAMP FIRE ROAD / 1.93 miles

Terrain: Open grassland; views / MTSP
Elevation: From 1,680' to 20' / very steep, parts extremely steep
Intersecting Trails: None
Directions: Rock Spring — West Ridgecrest Blvd., 2.2 miles
Spur: To Highway 1 / .6 miles

McKENNAN TRAIL is long and very steep, one of the toughest uphill grinds on Tam. But since both its ends are accessible by car, a one way, downhill trek with a shuttle is possible and that is how it will be described. A loop with Willow Camp Fire Road and Coastal Trail is another candidate. (Note that the GGNRA designates the route as McKennan Trail, even though it is almost entirely fire road-width, and I follow.)

McKennan sets off to the west from West Ridgecrest Boulevard behind a signed gate. The trailhead is at the northern end of Coastal Trail's short stretch on Ridgecrest, about 1.5 miles from Fairfax-Bolinas Road. Immediately the panorama, which includes the San Francisco skyline, is breathtaking. The ocean is in view nearly the whole way down.

After a relatively level start, the broad Trail — it was once a ranch road — meets a magnificent, old, solitary Douglas-fir. Although battered by lightning and bowed by the wind, it remains alive in the rocky outcrop. The downhill steepens considerably, the first of three such precipitous stretches.

The shrub ceanothus, its blue blossoms intoxicatingly fragrant in late winter and early spring, lines the Trail. There is a brief uphill, then McKennan enters a grove of bay and Douglas-fir. Beyond, the Trail joins an old fence line. Dairy ranches once covered this face of Bolinas Ridge; there are still a few north of Fairfax-Bolinas Road. Past the fence the Trail returns to grassland. The row of trees to the right marks the moister terrain of McKennan Gulch itself. On fog-free days, the posh subdivision of Seadrift comes into ever-sharper focus across Bolinas Lagoon.

At 1.1 miles, there is an ease in the slope and a second Douglas-fir grove. The next downhill is again quite steep.

At a fork, a hiker symbol sign points the way left onto a narrow trail through the baccharis. The .6-mile-long route straight (right) is the original ranch road but is now treated as a Spur of McKennan. Unmaintained but still in good shape, this Spur runs north as it gently descends. In about a half-mile it seems to disappear at a line of goldcup oak trees. Cut left ten yards through the grass to pick it up again. Douglas-firs, which may one day cover the whole hillside now that grazing has ended, become more common. The spur ends at an unsigned gate beside Highway 1 next to milepost 14.06. Morse's Gulch, which forms the northern boundary of this book, then Audubon Canyon Ranch are to the north.

Now back to McKennan Trail. The left turn leads to a wooded canyon, where the Trail bends. There is a short rise. Be cautious of poison oak. Parts of the lower route are also becoming overgrown with French broom.

Two more hikers signs are passed. The long descent ends at Willow Camp Trail, by a barn and cactus patch. Left, Willow Camp rises to Avenida Farralone in Stinson Beach, then up steeply to Coastal Trail (for a loop option). Four hundred feet to the right is a gate, a small parking area, Highway 1 by milepost 13.69 (the town of Stinson Beach is to the south), and the Bolinas-Stinson School.

Hugh McKennan, who came to California from Ireland during the Gold Rush, raised ducks on his ranch here. He shipped up to 1,000 eggs a day from Bolinas to San Francisco by schooner. He also ran the ferry across the lagoon. The Trail appears on the 1898 Sanborn map. Its name has been spelled at least half a dozen ways on maps and park signs over the years since.

MICKEY O'BRIEN TRAIL
FROM LAUREL DELL TO BARTH'S RETREAT / .66 miles

Terrain: Deep woodland; riparian / MMWD
Elevation: From 1,690' to 1,940' / gradual
Intersecting Trails: Connector to Laurel Dell F.R. (.6m)
Directions: Laurel Dell Fire Road trailhead — Laurel Dell F.R., .6m
Amenities: Fountain (untreated), outhouses, picnic tables

THIS IS AN ENCHANTING TRAIL, through deep forest beside a stream, in one of the quietest parts of the Mountain. Since Mickey O'Brien connects two of Tam's landmarks, Laurel Dell and Barth's Retreat, it is part of many north side loop walks.

Follow Laurel Dell Fire Road to Laurel Dell itself; Mickey O'Brien begins to the right at the meadow's southern (near) edge. An alternate, perhaps even more used access is via Cataract Trail from Rock Spring. The Trail's name is misspelled at the trailhead sign.

Mickey O'Brien immediately plunges into woodland. Huckleberry is the common shrub, Douglas-firs and tanbark oaks the main trees. Barth's Creek, which joins Cataract Creek at Laurel Dell, is to the left. It remains a companion the whole way.

In .2 miles the Trail enters its only sizable clearing, at the foot of a grassy, serpentine hillside. At this clearing look left, toward the stream, to see the world's two largest Sargent cypress trees. One is 85 feet high, with a circumference of 10 feet, 2 inches. It has two equally prominent forks splitting from the main trunk about 15 feet up, and many low, now dead branches. An azalea bush stands near its base. The second giant, 96 feet tall but with a smaller circumference, is just downstream.

The Sargent cypress' size and presence here are unusual. They are usually found, stunted and shrublike, on dry, exposed serpentine ridges. And several guides describe the Sargent cypress' height limit as 40 or 50 feet. While the cypress' diagnostic needles and rounded cones are too high to see without binoculars, the trees can be distinguished from surrounding Douglas-firs by the different bark. The preeminence of these giants here was only recognized in 1980, by the late Thomas Harris. Other nearby Sargent cypresses lay fallen, losers in the battle with the Douglas-firs for sunlight.

To the right at the clearing, a quarter-mile up the creek bed, is the surprisingly well-preserved wreckage of a Navy Corsair fighter. It was involved in a two plane collision in 1945. Both pilots parachuted to safety. One of the engines is in Cataract Creek, a few yards upstream from the Ray Murphy Bridge.

There is more uphill on the remainder of Mickey O'Brien. The Trail passes a massive five-trunked oak. Azaleas brush the Trail's left margin.

Mickey O'Brien crosses a pair of rivulets, then squeezes between two boulders. The signpost here used to point to a .2 mile connector (now apparently closed) heading left across Barth's Creek to Laurel Dell Fire Road.

Continue uphill without crossing the creek. A marked path leads up right to an outhouse. The Trail terminates at a bridge over Barth's Creek. The bridge is dedicated to the memory of veteran Mountain worker and hiker Harold Atkinson, who helped build Mickey O'Brien Trail in 1930 and rerouted it in 1971. Few people ever worked harder on the Mountain's trails.

From the bridge's near side, Simmons Trail begins its journey to Rock Spring. Across the bridge is Barth's Retreat (see Simmons Trail) and a connector fire road. Halfway up the road is Lincoln Fairley Trail and atop it is Laurel Dell F.R.

Michael Francis "Mickey" O'Brien was a native San Franciscan who devoted himself to the Mountain. He was a charter member of the Tamalpais Conservation Club, served as its president in 1925-26, edited its newsletter, *California Out Of Doors*, for eight years, and was on the executive committee for 30 years. In 1947, at age 69, he suffered a heart attack after a session of working on Hoo-Koo-E-Koo Trail. Returning to the Mountain just three weeks later to continue his work, he collapsed again and died at Alpine Lodge, beside Panoramic Highway. It was the perfect way to go for a Mountain veteran. This Trail, once called Barth's Creek Trail, then K.C. Trail, was dedicated to him in 1948.

OLD STOVE TRAIL
BETWEEN LAUREL DELL FIRE ROAD / .33 miles

Terrain: Mostly chaparral; unmaintained / MMWD
Elevation: From 1,780' to 1,960' / steep
Intersecting Trails: None
Directions: West Ridgecrest Blvd. — Laurel Dell F.R., .9 miles
Spur: To High Marsh Trail / .1 mile

TODAY's Old Stove Trail is a remnant of a once long and well-used route that is now largely covered by the later-built Laurel Dell Fire Road. To reach the trailhead, descend Laurel Dell Fire Road from Ridgecrest Boulevard. Two-hundred-fifty yards beyond Laurel Dell itself, the Fire Road makes a sweeping bend, from which three trails set off to the left. The first is Bare Knolls Trail, the second a connector to High Marsh Trail, and the third is Old Stove. Look for the wooden steps.

On one visit, on a November morning as fog was lifting after a night of rain, I saw 500 or more spider webs densely packed over Old Stove's opening yards. The Trail quickly rises out of the forest and into chaparral, where it remains.

In .1 mile, a later-built Spur of Old Stove branches left. It descends 200 yards, through manzanita and then into light woodland, to High Marsh Trail. The Spur's High Marsh junction may also be hard to spot; it is at a crest on High Marsh Trail, .2 miles east of the signed "75-Yard" connector to Laurel Dell F.R. and 50 yards west of the wood steps.

Back on the main Old Stove, there are glorious views to the north from this high knoll. Old Stove continues snaking through the shrubs. Chamise replaces manzanita as the dominant shrub.

Laurel Dell F.R. comes into sight and Old Stove Trail ends when it meets it. Across the fire road is a fairly prominent clearing in the trees; it was an old camp site, remnants of which are still occasionally unearthed. Barth's Retreat and Music Stand Trail are to the left.

Old Stove Trail dates to around 1910 as a connection from Laurel Dell to Potrero Meadow. Laurel Dell was originally called Old Stove Camp, for an old stove there. (Using a metal detector, and with permission from the Water District, Phil Frank recently uncovered what appears to be that stove.) There was also an Old Stove Extension, which ran from Laurel Dell across Cataract Creek up to Bolinas Ridge. Already faint, it was all but obliterated after a storm in December 1987.

WILLOW CAMP FIRE ROAD
FROM WEST RIDGECREST BOULEVARD TO HIGHWAY 1 / 2.82 miles

Terrain: Coastal scrub and grassland / MTSP
Elevation: From 1,900' to 10' / very steep
Intersecting Trails: Coastal (.1m), McKennan (2.7m)
Directions: Rock Spring — West Ridgecrest Blvd., 1.4 miles

WILLOW CAMP Fire Road (GGNRA signs call it Willow Camp Trail, although it's almost entirely fire road-width and open to bicycles) offers an unrelentingly steep connection between Bolinas Ridge and the coast. There are open, sweeping ocean views all the way. For those taking it as part of a loop, it is worth noting that Willow Camp is a bit less precipitous than its neighbor to the north, McKennan Trail, and steeper than Matt Davis Trail to the south. A one-way, downhill shuttle is also possible, as both ends of Willow Camp (and even an intermediate point) are accessible by car.

There are three entrances to Willow Camp from Ridgecrest Boulevard, all just south of, and across the pavement from, the top of Laurel Dell F.R., 1.4 miles from Rock Spring. There is some shoulder parking on both sides of the road. Directly across Laurel Dell F.R. is the newest, signed entrance. One hundred yards to the south, behind a white gate, is the start of the Fire Road and a parallel trail.

At the top, 1,900 feet in elevation, the views are broadest but they remain no less lovely all the way down (except, of course, in the coastal fog common in summer). After 150 yards, the entrance from opposite Laurel Dell F.R. joins on the right. Just below, the parallel trail joins the Fire Road at an important intersection. To the left here, Coastal Trail departs toward Matt Davis Trail and Pantoll. Twenty more yards down, Coastal separates right to McKennan Trail and Fairfax-Bolinas Road. Continue downhill toward Stinson Beach.

At .4 miles, the Fire Road enters a haunting grove of bays, oaks, and massive, lichen-covered Douglas-firs. The Douglas irises found in the woodland here are a different species from the ground irises abounding on the grasslands just a few yards ahead, offering an opportunity to distinguish between them. Douglas iris is taller, with stems of eight inches or more. Their arching leaves are shiny above, dull below. Ground iris grows close to the ground, has similar upper and lower leaf surfaces, and a lovely fragrance. Just before leaving the forest, on the right, is a magnificent dead Douglas-fir; its huge low branches hint that it may have been the first in the grove.

Beyond the grove, back in grassland, there are few obvious landmarks; a string of underground telephone cable markers, a seep, some Douglas-firs. Since there's no getting lost here, just enjoy the views. They can extend from the western half of San Francisco to Point Reyes and out to the Farallon Islands. Check out the trail pattern visible below to avoid possible confusion later.

The roar of the surf at Stinson will become audible part way down. Baccharis is much the most common shrub lining the Fire Road, at times narrowing it to trail-width. Also common, lower, is wild cucumber, or manroot.

Just beneath the level of the prominent water tanks, a four-way junction is reached. To the right is the start of the former Stinson Gulch Trail, a now overgrown water pipeline route which deadends in a canyon. The path to its left, marked by a hiker's sign and a water pipeline, offers a quarter-mile shortcut in the descent of Willow Camp F.R. Continue left. In 25 yards there is another fork; the short fire road to the left goes up to the water tanks.

It's then some 300 yards downhill to a large "Willow Camp Trail" sign. A sign warns that you've just made it through mountain lion habitat. To the right and left is a GGNRA service road. Beyond the gate is a small parking area at the end of Avenida Farralone in Stinson Beach. Veer right to continue.

Willow Camp now drops much more gently. It meets the bottom of the shortcut path. It then descends through a cool wooded stretch. Non-native ivy covers much of the vegetation. The route cuts through an old ranch, now on parkland; please respect the few remaining residents' privacy. A connector fire road to the right leads to a water tank. Continue straight.

At a marked junction, beside a huge clump of cacti and an old barn, McKennan Trail sets off to the right on its extremely steep climb back up to Ridgecrest Boulevard. Take McKennan, then go 1.1 miles south on Coast Trail, to complete a loop.

The remaining 400 feet to the gate beside Highway 1 at milepost sign 13.69 can be called part of either Willow Camp F.R. (which I do for measurement purposes) or McKennan. There is some off-road parking here. Bolinas Lagoon, one of the finest birdwatching spots in the Bay Area, is across the road. Bolinas-Stinson School borders on the right and central Stinson Beach is 1.2 miles to the left.

Willow Camp was the original name of Stinson Beach. The town was renamed in 1920 for Nathan Stinson, who had bought land in the area in 1870 and then developed the summer resort. Willows still line Easkoot Creek beside the main entry into the popular beach. There was a Willow Camp Trail on the 1898 Mt. Tam Sanborn map; it appears as a fire road on post-World War II maps.

Falls on West Fork of Fern Creek, Miller Trail.

Key Junctions

THERE ARE MANY important multiple trail junctions on Mt. Tamalpais. Most of those accessible by car are designated as trailheads. Other key off-road junctions, where four or more trails meet, are presented below to avoid repetition in the text. The elevation of the junction, and the nearest trailhead(s), are also given.

BOY SCOUT JUNCTION, 380' (*Deer Park*)

This big junction has seven spokes. Clockwise from Deer Park Fire Road, with your back to Deer Park, they are: Bald Hill Trail to Six Points, Deer Park F.R. rising to Five Corners, a connector fire road dropping to Canyon Trail, Moore Trail briefly combined with Ridge Trail, Junction Trail, and Deer Park F.R. downhill. The name arose from the Boy Scouts' Camp Lilienthal, once a half-mile to the west. The scouts have since moved to Camp Tamarancho on the slopes of White's Hill.

CAMP ALICE EASTWOOD, 600' (*Mountain Home, Muir Woods*)

This historic area was the site of the first Muir Woods Inn, from 1907 to 1913, and of a Civilian Conservation Corps camp in the 1930's. Alice Eastwood was curator of botany at the California Academy of Sciences for 56 years and a life-long hiker and naturalist on the Mountain. She was present when the current group camp was named in her honor in 1949, on her 90th birthday. Meeting the paved, level clearing of the camp, clockwise with your back to the asphalt section of Camp Eastwood Road, are: Fern Canyon Trail to Muir Woods, Plevin Cut Trail, Camp Eastwood Road descending to Muir Woods, Sierra Trail rising to Panoramic Highway, and paved Camp Eastwood Road to Mountain Home.

FIVE CORNERS, 520' (*Phoenix Lake, Deer Park*)

There are actually six options at Five Corners; a short, connector fire road was added after the junction's name was well established. The six choices, clockwise from the top of Deer Park F.R. with your back to Deer Park, are: a broad .1-mile connector to Bald Hill Trail, the combined Shaver Grade and Concrete Pipeline F.R. going downhill, Elliott Trail, Shaver Grade going uphill, and Concrete Pipeline F.R. toward Fairfax-Bolinas Road. In 1989, Harrison Ford and Sean Connery were at Five Corners filming a chase scene for the film "Indiana Jones and the Last Crusade."

MOUNTAIN THEATER, 1,990' (*Rock Spring*)

The Mountain Theater, formally called the Sidney B. Cushing Memorial Theater, is one of Tamalpais' star attractions. The first Mountain Play was presented there in 1913, and the stone seats added in the 1930's. Five trail options directly meet the theater. They are: Rock Spring, across the upper row of seats, heading west to Ridgecrest Boulevard and east to West Point; Bootjack and Easy Grade trails coming in from the south; and Mountain Theater Trail going west to Old Mine Trail.

PHOENIX JUNCTION, 200' (*Phoenix Lake*)

Four fire roads and a trail meet at this important junction at the western tip of Phoenix Lake. They are, clockwise from Phoenix Lake Fire Road with your back to the lake: Eldridge Grade beginning its climb to the top of Tam; Fish Grade to Sky Oaks Road; Fish Gulch Trail, and Shaver Grade to Five Corners.

RIFLE CAMP, 2,000' (*East Ridgecrest Road*)

Rifle Camp (now formally Rifle Picnic Area), at the eastern edge of upper Potrero Meadow, is an historic gathering and resting spot and trail junction. It has outhouses and picnic tables, even a place to hang packs. It supposedly got its name after a dog dug up a rifle at the site. The intersecting trails and fire roads are: Potrero Trail crossing the meadow; Rock Spring-Lagunitas F.R. going north and south; the lower end of Arturo Trail; the west end of Northside Trail; and the upper end of Azalea Meadow Trail.

SIX POINTS, 550' (*Deer Park, Phoenix Lake*)

There are presently only five options at Six Points as the old sixth path climbing higher up Bald Hill is now overgrown. The choices, clockwise from Yolanda Trail with your back to Phoenix Lake, are: Hidden Meadow Trail; Bald Hill Trail toward Five Corners; Six Points Trail down to Deer Park F.R.; and Yolanda continuing to Worn Spring F.R.

WEST POINT, 1,780' (*East Ridgecrest Road, Pantoll*)

West Point refers to the westernmost point of the Mt. Tamalpais & Muir Woods Railway, "The Crookedest Railroad in the World." The West Point Inn, still standing and still offering accommodations (by reservation only), was built at the site in 1904. From here, travelers could rest before transferring to or from the Bolinas stagecoach. West Point, with its splendid views, picnic tables, fountain, and inn offering light refreshments and bathrooms, remains a favorite stopping place for Mountain visitors. The intersecting trails and fire roads, clockwise from Old Railroad Grade with your back facing downhill, are: Nora Trail dropping to Matt Davis Trail; West Point Trail also dropping to Matt Davis; Old Stage Road to Pantoll; Rock Spring Trail to the Mountain Theater; and Old Railroad Grade continuing around the inn to the summit.

Rocks

THE GEOLOGICAL HISTORY of Mt. Tamalpais is a tangled one and far from completely understood. Some authorities show the Tam region as under water as recently as a couple of million years ago, as most of the rest of the Bay Area clearly was. Others point to Tam's absence of marine fossils, which are found on other Bay Area hills, as evidence that the Mountain has been above water, perhaps as an island (as believed in native Coast Miwok lore), for tens of millions of years.

To better comprehend what is known about Tam geologically, some background on plate tectonics is in order. The Earth's crust is composed of plates, which are in slow but steady motion. These movements have split continents and built mountain ranges. Mt. Tamalpais lies at the western edge of the North American Plate. Just to its west, across the San Andreas Fault (over which Bolinas Lagoon lies), is the Pacific Plate, on which the Pt. Reyes peninsula sits. At one time another plate, the Farallon, lay between the North American and Pacific plates. The Pacific Plate is creeping northwest along the fault at an average rate of nearly two inches a year. The movement is occasionally more dramatic — 20 feet in seconds during the 1906 earthquake.

The rocks that comprise Mt. Tamalpais are mostly 80-150 million years old. They largely formed from sediments that were eroded off the predecessor of today's Sierra Nevada to the ocean basin that covered western California. These sediments were deposited atop volcanic rock that lay beneath the sea. Some of this volcanic rock intruded upward. The North American plate then rode over the Farallon plate, scraping off, jumbling, and thrusting upward these rocks as today's Coast Range, of which Tamalpais is a part. This mixture of rocks, whose chronology is so difficult to unravel, is called the Franciscan Complex (or Assemblage or Formation). Thus, though some its rocks are of volcanic origin, Tamalpais itself was never a volcano.

Erosion then began its relentless task. Less resistant rock was washed away, and the combination of earthquakes and water-logged soil helped trigger landslides. Salem Rice, who has studied the geology of the Mountain more closely than anyone, speculates that Tam has been roughly its present height for millions of years, that today's three-peaked profile became recognizable around 100-150,000 years ago, and that further erosion and slides will someday turn the highly resistant rock core of East Peak into more of a spire.

All three of the basic rock classes — igneous, metamorphic, and sedimentary — are represented on Mt. Tamalpais, with sedimentary rocks much the most common. Some of the more abundant rock types, which account for over 95% of the Mountain, are described below.

SANDSTONE, MUDSTONE, SHALE

These sedimentary rocks form the bulk of Mt. Tamalpais. Sandstone, mudstone, and shale are composed of, in decreasing order of particle size, compressed and bound sand, mud, and clay. They were compressed into rock about 80 to 150 million years ago. Graywacke is a dark-gray compact type of sandstone dominant on the Mountain. It is made up of medium-sized, angular sand grains between which are mud and clay-sized particles. Because these rocks readily weather to soil, which is in turn covered by vegetation, they are not generally seen exposed. Much of the sandstone, mudstone, and shale has been well fractured and sheared, forming, with other rocks, what is called "melange."

GREENSTONE
Greenstone is an igneous basalt rock of volcanic origin; occasionally pieces can be found showing the holes, called vesicles, from which gases escaped as the lava cooled. It is green, from the presence of the mineral chlorite, only when fresh. Though highly resistant, when fractured greenstone weathers to a thick, iron-rich soil which oxidizes to a reddish brown. This soil holds moisture well and supports both forests and grasslands. Bolinas Ridge, on the western side of Tamalpais and the most coherent rock mass on the Mountain, is greenstone basalt. Pilot Knob and most of Bald Hill are also blocks of greenstone.

SERPENTINE
Serpentine (also called serpentinite) is the best known and most distinctive rock on Mt. Tamalpais. Its varying gray-green-bluish boulders cover sections of trails such as Rock Spring, Rocky Ridge and Eastwood. Serpentine is a metamorphic rock formed deep in the earth, below the floor of the Pacific, from peridotite, the most abundant rock of the earth's mantle. Because serpentine lacks aluminum, a main ingredient of clay soils, it does not weather to soil and thus remains largely exposed. It is also deficient in the important plant nutrients calcium, potassium and sodium, and has a very high level of magnesium, toxic to some plants. It thus supports a plant life that is quite distinctive; some plants grow only on serpentine, others take different forms or exist out of their normal ranges on it. The seats of the Mountain Theater are blocks of serpentine, most of which were hauled to the site from elsewhere on Tam. Serpentine is the state rock of California.

CHERT
Chert is a very hard (harder than steel) sedimentary rock. It is composed almost 100 percent of the mineral quartz, which is crystallized silica (silicon dioxide). Chert is formed by the precipitation of silica, originally from microscopic marine protozoans called radiolaria, in sea water. Use a good hand lens to see the embedded skeletal radiolaria. Chert often appears in uniform 1-3" layered beds. Because chert resists erosion, and appears in several colors (white is common on Tam), its few outcropppings stand out.

QUARTZ TOURMALINE
This rather rare metamorphic rock is found in only a few places on Tam. It is highly resistant to erosion. East Peak is a block of quartz tourmaline. Quartz tourmaline boulders that fell from the peak are found on trails below.

Creeks

SCORES OF CREEKS lace Mt. Tamalpais. A few flow year-round, many dry up in summer before being replenished by fall rains. Some of the larger creeks on the Mountain, all crossed by trails, are described below. Note that creeks have an unambiguous right and left bank, as determined by facing downstream (the direction the water flows).

BILL WILLIAMS CREEK

Fed by several forks (all crossed by Tucker Trail), Bill Williams Creek flows through Bill Williams Gulch into Phoenix Lake. It, and Phoenix Creek (beside lower Shaver Grade), are the lake's major sources. A still evident dam on Bill Williams Creek, dating back over 100 years, provided an early water source for the Ross Valley. Bill Williams, reputedly a deserter from the Confederate army, lived by the creek in the 1860's.

CATARACT CREEK

Cataract Creek starts just east of Rock Spring, at around 2,000 feet in elevation. The creek, followed for just about its whole length by Cataract Trail, descends relatively gently to Laurel Dell. Then it begins dropping precipitously. The creek's strong flow and numerous waterfalls make it a favorite of Mountain visitors. Cataract Creek once met Lagunitas Creek just above the present Alpine Dam. Today it flows into Alpine Lake.

CORTE MADERA CREEK

This Corte Madera Creek, not to be confused with one of the same name that runs through the Ross Valley, flows down Tamalpais' southeast flank. Its highest feeder is near 2,000 feet, east of East Peak. Track of the Mt. Tamalpais Railway followed the creek upstream two miles from downtown Mill Valley. Corte Madera Creek empties into Richardson Bay near Tamalpais High School. Corte Madera means "cut wood" in Spanish; the redwoods along the creek's drainage were important sources of lumber in Gold Rush days.

FERN CREEK

The higher of Fern Creek's two forks starts from near the top of Old Railroad Grade, at just over 2,200 feet. Fern Creek drops some 2,000 feet down the Mountain's south side to Redwood Creek in Muir Woods National Monument. Fern Creek Trail passes beside its upper reaches, Fern Canyon Trail beside its lower course. Fern Creek was once tapped as a water source for Mill Valley, Tiburon, and Belvedere. Remnants of the pipeline and intakes are still evident.

LAGUNITAS CREEK

Lagunitas is the most important creek in Marin County. Four dams have been placed along its course to store much of the county's water supply. The creek forms from three forks high on the Mountain's north face, the East Fork being the highest at near 2,300 feet. These three forks now merge in Lake Lagunitas (elevation 784'). Lower in elevation along Lagunitas Creek are the dams impounding Bon Tempe Lake, Alpine Lake, and, just outside this book's boundary, Kent Lake. Lagunitas Creek then continues through Samuel P. Taylor State Park, where it is sometimes called Papermill Creek. Beyond, it flows to the town of Point Reyes Station, then empties into Tomales Bay. The creek still supports salmon and steelhead trout — the largest silver salmon, 22 pounds, ever caught in California was taken in its waters — but at a fraction of historic levels.

LARKSPUR CREEK

The headwaters of Larkspur Creek, on the Mountain's east slope, are below Blithedale Ridge. Two feeders meet at Dawn Falls, below which the creek flows through Baltimore Canyon. After crossing under Larkspur's Magnolia Avenue the creek meanders towards Corte Madera Creek. Larkspur is a common Tamalpais wildflower.

REDWOOD CREEK

Redwood Creek flows down Redwood Canyon and through the heart of the virgin redwoods of Muir Woods National Monument. It then winds through Franks Valley and meets the ocean at Muir Beach. Redwood Creek also still supports a salmon and steelhead run (it too sharply reduced). The adult salmon struggle upstream in winter to lay and fertilize their eggs, then die. The young swim downstream to the ocean after the fall rains, there to spend several years before returning to Redwood Creek to complete their life cycle.

SWEDE GEORGE CREEK

Swede George Creek has three strong-flowing forks that descend the Mountain's deeply wooded northwest face starting from around the 2,000-foot level. High Marsh Trail crosses all three forks. The three forks unite just before flowing into Alpine Lake. Swede George Creek was used as a water source until the 1950's; the pipeline is still visible along Kent Trail. Swede George (his full name not given even in his obituary) was a woodcutter who lived on the Mountain in the 1860's. He then suffered paralysis and lived as a ward of the County until his death in San Rafael at "about 40 years of age."

VAN WYCK CREEK

Van Wyck Creek lies between the drainages of Swede George Creek to the west and Lagunitas Creek to the east. Its headwaters are at around 1,600 feet. Several trails (Kent, Lagoon Extension, Stocking, Van Wyck Creek Trail) cross the creek before it empties into Alpine Lake. Sidney Van Wyck was a lawyer who volunteered his services to the Tamalpais Conservation Club during their legal battles in the 1920's to create Mt. Tamalpais State Park.

WEBB CREEK

Webb Creek starts above Panoramic Highway, west of Pantoll, and flows to the ocean. Its course is down lovely Steep Ravine, with the Steep Ravine Trail crossing it eight times and the Dipsea Trail once. The creek flows under Highway 1 to end at the Pacific a few yards north of the Steep Ravine (Rocky Point) cabins. The mouth of the creek is by a hot spring, now accessible only during minus tides in fall. Jonathan Webb was president of the Tamalpais Conservation Club in 1915-16 and long an aide to William Kent, who once owned the creek's entire drainage. Webb died in 1944.

OTHERS
There are many other important, named creeks on Mt. Tamalpais. They are grouped below by drainage area, with approximate origin and outlet.

South Slope: Cascade (from Old Plane Trail to Old Mill Creek); Galena (from Temelpa Trail to Corte Madera Creek); Laguna (from West Point to Redwood Creek); Old Mill (from Gravity Car Fire Road to Richardson Bay); Rattlesnake (from Rock Spring Trail to Redwood Creek); and Spike Buck (also from Rock Spring Trail to Redwood Creek).
North Slope: Bon Tempe (from Meadow Club to Alpine Lake); Deer (from Six Points to San Anselmo Creek); and Phoenix (from Five Corners to Phoenix Lake).
West-Southwest Slopes: Cold Stream (Coastal Trail to the Pacific); Easkoot (Dipsea Trail to the Pacific); Kent (Dipsea Trail to Redwood Creek); Lone Tree Creek (Cardiac Hill to the Pacific); and Table (Coastal Trail to the Pacific).
East Slope: Tamalpais (Windy Ridge to Corte Madera Creek); and Warner (Corte Madera Ridge to Richardson Bay).

Lakes

THERE ARE FIVE man-made lakes — Alpine, Bon Tempe, Kent, Lagunitas, and Phoenix — within the Mt. Tamalpais watershed. All are on the Mountain's north side, all were dammed for reservoirs, and all but Phoenix are on the drainage of Lagunitas Creek. Fishing is permitted (license required for those over 16) in all the lakes, which are periodically stocked. Boating, permitted before World War II, is now prohibited, as is swimming. Other natural sites on Tam that carry the designation "lake, "such as Hidden Lake and Lily Lake, are quite small and shallow.

KENT LAKE

Kent (just outside the area detailed in this book) is much the largest of the Tamalpais watershed lakes. Its storage capacity of 32,900 acre feet is nearly four times that of the next largest reservoir, Alpine. Kent Lake (elevation 400 feet) was formed by the erection of Peters Dam in 1953. Peters Dam can be reached by a short walk up from Shafter Bridge, on Sir Francis Drake Boulevard just west of the town of Lagunitas. There is no access to Kent Lake from the west; the steep, wooded slope between Kent and Bolinas Ridge is the largest trackless area on Tamalpais. Kent Lake can be reached from the northeast off Pine Mountain Ridge or via a level 4.4-mile fire road that sets off on the north side of Alpine Dam.

ALPINE LAKE

Alpine Lake, at elevation 646 feet, has a storage capacity of 2.9 billion gallons, a surface area of 219 acres, a shoreline of 10.4 miles, and a mean depth of 103 feet. Alpine was formed in 1919 upon completion of Alpine Dam, at the site of the former Alpine Bridge over Lagunitas Creek. The dam, crossed by Fairfax-Bolinas Road, was raised eight feet in 1924 and 30 additional feet in 1941. When Alpine overflows, a mighty waterfall cascades down the dam's west face. Water from Alpine is pumped up into Bon Tempe or flows down to Kent Lake. The Kent and Helen Markt trails traverse the lake's south shore but there are no all-trail loop options.

BON TEMPE LAKE

Bon Tempe Lake, at 718 feet above sea level, was created in 1949 by Bon Tempe Dam. The lake flooded part of the old Swiss Bautunpi (of which Bon Tempe is a corruption) Brothers' dairy ranch. The lake has a capacity of 1.3 billion gallons and a surface area of 144 acres. Water from the lake flows directly to the nearby Bon Tempe treatment plant, then is distributed to southern Marin County customers via the Southern Marin Line. The lake is readily accessible from Sky Oaks Road. A four-mile trail circles Bon Tempe's shore.

LAKE LAGUNITAS

Lagunitas was the first of the Mountain's man-made lakes, dating from 1873. The dam forming it was then the third largest on all the West Coast. Lake Lagunitas (sometimes called Lagunitas Lake) is the highest of Tam's reservoir lakes, at 784 feet, and the smallest, with a capacity of 127 million gallons and a surface area of 23 acres. The lake was originally used by developer William Coleman to supply water to his new housing tract in San Rafael and to San Quentin Prison. Water flows from Lagunitas to Bon Tempe. Lagunitas was drained in 1986 as part of the preparation (so far not fully successful) to make it self-sustaining with trout. Lagunitas is just uphill from the parking and picnic area at the end of Sky Oaks Road. A 1.6-mile fire road circles the lake.

PHOENIX LAKE
Phoenix Lake has long been the most visited of the lakes, as it is the closest to population centers. Both because Phoenix is so popular as a recreation destination and because its surface, at 183 feet, is several hundred feet lower in elevation than the nearest MMWD treatment plant, its water is pumped up and distributed only in emergencies, as during the drought of 1975-76. The prominent pump now in the center of the lake was placed in 1989 to prepare for a then emerging shortage. Otherwise, overflow above Phoenix' 172 million gallon capacity passes out of the reservoir system. Phoenix Dam was erected in 1905 and raised in 1907. Phoenix Lake was drained in 1984, when its wooden spillway, deemed unsafe, was replaced by a concrete one. Phoenix is reached through Ross' Natalie Coffin Greene Park at the end of Lagunitas Road. A well-used 2.33-mile loop, half trail and half fire road, circles its 25-acre surface area.

Weather

MOUNT TAMALPAIS, along with most of coastal California, has a Mediterranean climate characterized by mild temperatures, dry summers with cool evenings, and winter rains. There are four other such Mediterranean climatic zones in the world; the coast of Chile, the west coasts of Australia and South Africa, and the Mediterranean basin itself. While there is rarely a day when the sun doesn't shine somewhere on Tam, fog and rain are key components of the Mountain's weather.

Fog is a common occurrence, particularly on the Mountain's western and southern slopes from May into September. The summer fog cycle begins with prevailing winds that flow parallel to the northern California coast. They push surface water of the Pacific southward and, ultimately, away from the land. The surface water is replaced by upwelling water, 10 to 15 degrees cooler, from deeper in the ocean. This cold water is well known to anyone trying to swim off the Northern California coast. Inshore winds, moisture-laden after a long trip over the ocean, come into contact with the cold coastal waters. Cooler air holds less moisture so the excess water condenses, much of it on salt spray particles, as fog. When hot inland air rises, as it does most every summer afternoon, it forms a low pressure area that "sucks" in this coastal fog bank.

The Mountain's west slope, nearest the ocean, is naturally most affected by summer fog. August average temperatures are among the coolest in North America. Fog can be an almost daily occurrence; Point Reyes, just northwest of Tam, is many years the foggiest place in the lower 48 states. Usually, though, the warming mid-day sun burns the fog off for a few hours. Fog also penetrates to Tam's southern flanks through the gaps of Franks and Tennessee valleys. The eastern slopes are less affected, though fog drawn into San Francisco Bay may cover the area early and late during summer days. The north side, protected by the wall of Tamalpais, is virtually fog-free in summer, with sunny skies daily and temperatures usually surpassing 80 or 90 degrees. The sight of Tam's summit ridge blocking the advancing fog is a common, but always dramatic, summer spectacle.

By September, the lowering sun cuts the difference between inland and offshore temperatures sufficiently to turn off the main fog-producing mechanism. The entire Mountain is generally sunny all day and, without the fog's cooling influence, temperatures are often warmer than in mid-summer.

By mid to late October, the Pacific High, a vast high-pressure air mass, has retreated far enough south, with the jet stream following, to open the Tam region to storms moving across the ocean. The first rains may be warm ones from off Mexico. Later, generally by the end of November, the winter rain pattern begins, with storms blown in from off Hawaii or Alaska.

In winter, a different type of fog, known as "radiation" fog, occasionally covers parts of the Mountain, particularly on the north side. Air near the ground absorbs moisture from the damp earth. In early morning, temperatures have dropped so low, sometimes below freezing in the valleys, that the moisture condenses as fog. Hilltops may be sunny. This fog usually burns off by mid-morning.

The occasional, much publicized, weather phenomenon known as "El Nino" alters Tam's weather patterns. Dramatic effects include warm, winter rain deluges, such as the storm that wreaked havoc on communities surrounding Tam in early January, 1982.

Annual rainfall has averaged 52 inches at Lake Lagunitas (and 40 inches in Muir Woods) over the past 100 years; more than double the average for San Francisco. January is usually the wettest month followed, in roughly equal pairs, by December-February, November-March, and October-April. But exceptions are commonplace; December of 1989 had no rain at all, a first for at least 100 years. The highest annual rainfall was 109 inches in 1889-90 and the lowest was 20 inches in 1923-24. A major drought occurred in 1975-77, when there were consecutive years with under 25 inches of rain. The almost 90 inches that fell in the "El Nino" year of 1982 was the 20th century high. Kentfield has been among the wettest populated weather stations in the country.

Warmer, spring-like days are often commonplace by February. Indeed, more than 100 Tamalpais plant species usually bloom in January. The grasslands generally appear greenest in March. The Pacific High then begins drifting back north, blocking the rains. The rainless period may last up to five or six months, from May through October. By early June, the grasses are brown and become a major fire danger on Tam. The fog cycle is born anew.

The upper part of the Mountain often has its own weather. Winds reached 107 miles per hour on December 1, 1951. The all-time Tam low temperature of 19 degrees, dating from January 19, 1922, was apparently shattered on both December 22 and 24, 1990, when Sky Oaks Ranger Station recorded 4 degrees. On May 14, 1921, the aurora borealis, or northern lights, was plainly visible. (A few old-timers still recall it.) There is, every few years, enough snow to cross-country ski. The largest snowstorm in modern times was in January, 1922; a poster of Tam blanketed in white has been widely distributed. There was a separate weather station near East Peak from 1898 into the 1920's.

Another weather factor worth noting is the existence of "micro-climates" on Tam. The shape of the valleys and ridges creates pockets differing in rain, fog, and temperature conditions. "Banana belts" nest amidst fog-bound areas. Redwood trees, which require abundant year-round moisture, grow yards away from dry chaparral shrubs like chamise. To paraphrase an old expression, "If you don't like the weather on Tam, just keep walking!"

Flora

JOHN THOMAS HOWELL, in his definitive book, *Marin Flora*, described some 1,400 species of vascular plants (the most evolutionarily advanced plants, from ferns through those producing flowers), more than 800 of which are found on Mt. Tamalpais. Clearly, only a sampling of the Mountain's rich flora can be presented here. A familiarity with these species, representing most of the plants regularly encountered, should serve the needs of most Tamalpais visitors, or form a base for further study.

Beside each plant's common name is the botanical (scientific) name. These may appear intimidating at first, but are essential. Many plants have no, or several, common names, and some common names are applied to more than one species. Besides, the botanic names are often lovely and descriptive in their own right. Botanic names are given in the trail descriptions only for those plants not described below.

Please do not pick or otherwise disturb the Mountain's native flora. It is unlawful, disrupts Tam's ecosystem, and deprives later visitors. Besides, many common plants contain toxic foliage, flowers, fruits, and/or seeds.

Plant Communities

The Mountain's flora forms several plant communities, or associations. For simplicity, these communities are grouped into four basic ones that are cited frequently in the text. (For greater detail, refer to Howell or to the California Native Plant Society's *Plant Communities of Marin County* by W. David Shuford and Irene Timossi.) These associations serve only as guides. Disparate communities such as redwood forest and chaparral are frequently found just yards apart, the communities' boundaries and makeup are themselves in transition, and many plants can be found in more than one habitat.

REDWOOD/DOUGLAS-FIR (CONIFEROUS) FOREST

Redwoods and Douglas-firs, in pure stands and intermingled with one another and with other trees, form the Mountain's tallest and deepest forests. Both are conifers; the seeds are borne in cones. Pines, also conifers, are not naturally found on the Mountain.

Redwoods were once more common on Tamalpais and throughout the Bay Area. Logging in Marin began in the 18th century — the Mexican land grant that included Mill Valley and most of Mt. Tam was called "Corte Madera del Presidio," "cut wood for the Presidio," the fort in San Francisco dating from 1776. John Reed erected the sawmill that gave Mill Valley its name (and which still stands, reconstructed, in Old Mill Park), in the 1830's. But most of Tam's virgin stands of redwoods and Douglas-firs were cut to supply San Francisco's building frenzy in the gold rush years from 1849. Muir Woods reminds us of the treasures we have lost.

Second-growth redwoods, many now over 100 years old and reaching the 200-foot heights of the original monarchs, are now found on many of the wettest parts of the Mountain. Redwoods require year-round moisture so favor stream

canyons in the summer fog belt (which provides water during the rainless summers). The correlation between redwoods and creek canyons soon becomes obvious to anyone traversing the Mountain's trails.

Competing directly for sunlight with the redwoods, and therefore often just
as tall, are Douglas-firs. They are vigorous colonizers, and have successfully invaded Tam's hardwood forests and grasslands over the last several decades.

BROAD-LEAVED (HARDWOOD) FOREST

The other type of woodland on Mt. Tamalpais consists of non-conifers (also
called hardwoods) which have broad leaves (as opposed to conifers' needles).
Five trees — laurel (bay), madrone, tanbark oak, coast live oak, and buckeye —
make up most of this forest on Mt. Tamalpais. Of the five, all but the buckeye
retain their leaves throughout the year. This forest tends to occur between the
wetter redwood forests and the drier chaparral and grasslands. There is, however,
much intermingling. Excellent examples of this woodland occur around Lake
Lagunitas and Phoenix Lake.

CHAPARRAL

Howell says, "It is the chaparral that gives to Mt. Tamalpais its distinctive
texture . . . From a distance, there is a velvety quality that characterizes it and
gives depth to the blues and purples that pervade the slopes; from near at hand
there is still that seeming smoothness and a lawnlike quality that belie the tough
and rugged character of the plant cover. Up steep slopes, over rolling summits,
and across broad flats spreads the unbroken array of shrubs, dense, erect stiff —
the pile in the fabric of the mountain's mantle."

Chaparral is distinctive of coastal California and of the world's four other
Mediterranean climates (coastal Chile, the west coasts of South Africa and Australia, and the Mediterranean Basin). Largely treeless, it is dominated by shrubs,
whose impenetrable nature becomes known to every Mt. Tamalpais visitor won-
dering off trail. Chaparral covers the Mountain's drier, exposed slopes and ridges,
where the shallower soils lack humus or the rocks don't hold soil. Early pictures,
for example, of the upper 1,500 feet or more of the south side of Mt. Tamalpais
show all but unbroken chaparral. Subsequent tree plantings and expansion by
native trees in the absence of fire has altered that image somewhat, but chaparral
remains dominant. Near the ocean, a different type of chaparral cover prevails,
called coastal scrub here. It is dominated by shrubs such as lupine, sage, baccharis,
poison oak, and blackberry.

GRASSLAND

The Mountain's grasslands are now comprised largely of non-native grasses.
The native perennial bunchgrasses invariably lost in competition with the more
vigorous introduced annual grasses. These Old World grasses were imported both
deliberately, as livestock feed, and accidentally, such as on hooves of cattle and
horses. A few native grasses, which do not brown as quickly in summer as the
alien grasses, retain footholds on Tam, particularly amidst light woodlands.

The Mountain's grasslands are presently shrinking as control of fire and elimination of grazing has permitted invasion by bracken fern, the shrub baccharis (coyote brush), and Douglas-fir. Large expanses remain, among other places, along Bolinas Ridge, on Bald Hill, and in the Potrero Meadows.

Ferns

Ferns differ from the evolutionarily more advanced flowering plants in that they reproduce by spores, not seeds, and have two distinct, alternate generations. The sporophyte generation, the one commonly seen, bears and drops the spores. The spores germinate into the smaller gametophyte generation, which produces sperm and egg cells. Sperm, dependent on moisture for mobility, fertilize the eggs, which then develop into the sporophytes. There are some 20 species of ferns on Mt. Tamalpais, the commonest of which are listed below.

BRACKEN FERN (*Pteridium aquilinum*)

Bracken, one of the more widely distributed plants in the world, may be the most abundant fern on Tamalpais. It is found in many habitats but is most prominent when it is colonizing grasslands, as along the Hogsback section of the Dipsea. Bracken's young, still rounded shoots are considered a delicacy (called "fiddleneck") in the Orient, but mature fronds have been known to poison cattle.

WESTERN SWORD FERN (*Polystichum munitum*)

This large fern is so named because its leaflets have serrated edges and hilt-like bases. It is very common in redwood forests, such as in Steep Ravine, and other deep woodlands.

WESTERN (GIANT) CHAIN FERN (*Woodwardia fimbriata*)

Woodwardias are the largest ferns found on the Mountain, sometimes rising to six feet or more in height. They are found only in wet places — in seeps and along stream beds. Howell cites the stand on Stocking Trail at Van Wyck Creek as containing "the largest and most luxurious specimens."

GOLDBACK FERN (*Pityrogramma triangularis*)

Goldbacks are found in shaded areas somewhat drier than those favored by the above two species. The leaflets curl up and dry in summer. This fern is well known for leaving a tracing of golden-green powder when its underside is pressed against a dark object.

MAIDENHAIR FERN (*Adiantum jordani*)

The much admired maidenhair, with its delicate, rounded segments, is common in shaded, rocky canyons. A close relative, A. *pedatum*, with divided stalks, is known as five-finger fern.

Trees

While there are more than a million trees on Mt. Tamalpais, five or six species account for perhaps 90% of them, and another handful most all of the rest. Thus, even infrequent visitors to Tam can learn to distinguish the trees and

gain a richer understanding and appreciation of the natural history of the Mountain. The trees are presented here in, very roughly (based on my own observa-
tions, not on any scientific census), descending order of their abundance on Mt.
Tamalpais.

CALIFORNIA LAUREL (*Umbellularia californica*)

Laurel (interchangeably called "bay" in this book) is likely the most common tree on the Mountain. Its evergreen leaves—elliptical, 2-5" long, and shiny
dark green above — are unmistakeable for their pleasing, pungent fragrance. The
leaf's oils are so much more potent than the bay-leaf of commerce that some
recipes call for using it in a strength of 1 part to 10, and the definitive *Jepson
Manual* notes it "may produce TOXIC effects in some people."

The laurel's shape varies according to environmental conditions, ranging
from thick-trunked, 80-foot-tall, fully-crowned specimens in protected valleys to
thin, bent, 6-foot survivors on the windiest, exposed ridges. Bays often grow in
circles, root sprouting from a dead "mother" tree. It is also common to see multiple shoots sent straight up from a fallen or bent tree.

Laurel nuts were eaten, after roasting, by local Indians. The tree is commonly called "pepperwood" and "Oregon myrtle" to the north, where many prod-
ucts from it are crafted. The tree is in the same family as the true Mediterranean
laurel (of the laurel wreath), but a different genus.

DOUGLAS-FIR (*Pseudotsuga menziesii*)

It would be difficult to even occasionally visit Mt. Tamalpais and not come
away with respect for the Douglas-firs, perhaps, in total biomass, the most abundant living thing on the Mountain. They grow to huge heights and girth, rival-
ling, and sometimes surpassing, the redwoods, with whom they often compete for
sunlight. For years the ancient Kent Tree, a Douglas-fir still standing in Muir
Woods, was the tallest tree in Marin.

Douglas-firs are found along most all trails, and are often dominant. They
are actively colonizing areas of the Mountain's grasslands, converting them to
forests. A dramatic example is at Lone Tree Hill. Where just a single tree, a
redwood, stood on its south facing slope early in this century, it is today covered
with Douglas-firs.

Pseudotsuga means "false hemlock," as the trees display some characteristics
of hemlocks and some of the true firs. The cones, 2" to 3-1/2", are distinctive for
their three pointed bracts. The flexible evergreen needles—singly in rows, not in
sheathed bundles like the pines—are 3/4" to 1-1/2" long. Douglas-firs have thick,
deeply furrowed bark that feels harder to the touch than redwood's. The trunks
can be branchless for great heights or, when the tree originally grew without
competition for sunlight, may be circled with low branches. Such low-branched
old trees are sometimes known as "wolf trees," as they were thought to kill (by
blocking sunlight) understory vegetation.

REDWOOD (*Sequoia sempervirens*)

Redwoods are the tallest trees in the world, with specimens more than 360 feet high in Humboldt County and over 250 feet on Mt. Tamalpais. They are also among the longest living of all things, some more than 2,000 years old. And, of course, redwoods are among the world's best loved trees, attracting more than 1.5 million visitors annually to Muir Woods, which has the Mountain's finest stands.

Also distinctive is the very thick, reddish-brown bark. Redwoods often survive fires because of this thick bark and its lack of flammable resins. Scientists have unraveled much of the fire history of Tam by studying redwoods. The bark is also resistant to insect and fungus infestation.

The tree's short evergreen needles may vary in appearance between lower and topmost branches. The cones are remarkably small for so large a tree, 1/2" to 1-1/8". They hold the tiny redwood seeds which, though they weigh only 1/8,000th of an ounce, contain all the genetic information needed to sustain the tree for centuries. Most reproduction is, however, vegetative. Younger trees, sprouting from the "mother" tree's surprisingly shallow roots, commonly encircle dead monarchs.

Redwoods were once wide ranging over the Pacific Rim but global climatic changes have reduced them to a narrow coastal band from just south of Big Sur to southernmost Oregon. They were more widespread on Mt. Tamalpais as well before virtually all were logged.

Also on the Mountain are many dense groves of thin, relatively short redwoods, as along Sierra Trail. Some of these stands sprang up after fires and have not yet thinned out; others represent mature redwoods struggling at the limits of their range.

The coast, or California, redwood is related to, but a different genus from, the more massive in girth giant sequoia (*Sequoiadendron giganteum*), which grows in a few groves in the Sierra. (There is a planted grove alongside Morse's Gulch Trail.)

MADRONE (*Arbutus menziesii*)

The madrone is well known to Mountain visitors for its highly distinctive bark, which peels back in strong light to reveal the smooth reddish wood. This wood remains cool to the touch on the hottest of summer days. The trunk and branches are often twisted. The 2" to 6" long evergreen leaves are thick and leathery, elliptic in shape, dark green and shiny above.

Madrones lend a distinctive feel to areas they dominate, such as the ridges north of Lakes Lagunitas and Bon Tempe. There, alongside the Pilot Knob and Madrone trails, are to be found Marin's largest madrones.

W. L. Jepson, author of the landmark *Manual of the Flowering Plants of California*, wrote of the madrone, "No other of our trees . . . makes so strong an appeal to man's imagination — to his love of color, of joyful bearing, of sense of magic, of surprise and change." Howell adds "(madrone's) flowers and fruits (are) beyond compare — the former like sculptured ivory urns, the latter like etched carnelian globes."

The madrone is in the same family (heath) as the shrub manzanita. Both can display peeling bark, and a small madrone can be the same size as a large manzanita. The bigger leaves of madrone are a distinguishing feature. Local Indians ate the madrone's fruits both heated and raw.

TANBARK OAK (*Lithocarpus densiflorus*)

Though in the same beech family as the oaks, the tanbark oak, or tanoak, is not a true oak (genus *Quercus*). One difference is that the male flowers are in erect catkins, as opposed to the drooping catkins of oaks.

Though rarely dominant in any one area of Mt. Tamalpais, tanbark oaks are nonetheless widespread and abundant, as on the south shore of Lake Lagunitas and on Old Mine Trail above Pantoll. Tanbark oaks are generally associated with madrones at the drier borders of redwood forests. They range in size from over 100 feet, as by the junction of Simmons and Kent trails, to shrubs at the edge of chaparral.

Tanbark leaves are distinctive; oblong, thick, leathery, light green above and lighter below, with wavy toothed borders. The leaves vary significantly in length, from 2 to 8 inches depending on habitat.

The acorns of tanbark oaks were a principal source of flour for Marin's native Americans. Later, the bark was the main source in California of tannin, used for tanning leather, dyeing, and for making ink. Indeed, tanoaks were once commercially harvested on Mt. Tamalpais.

There have been significant, as yet unexplained, tanbark oak die-offs in recent years, such as in Baltimore Canyon.

OAK (*Quercus* spp.)

There are some 10 species of oak growing on Mt. Tamalpais. The oaks are not always easy to tell apart, as they often have different leaves on the same tree and hybridize with one another. All have alternate leaves, separate male and female flowers on the same twig, and hard-shelled acorns.

Coast live oak (*Q. agrifolia*) may be the Mountain's most common oak tree. Its leaves are convex above, and the midribs on the lower side have small hairs. Canyon live, or goldcup, oaks (*Q. chrysolepis*) have a golden (turning to gray) pubescence on the underside of their young leaves. They are found on the upper slopes, such as the Mountain Theater area. The large, usually 7-lobed deciduous leaves of the black oak (*Q. kelloggii*) are distinctive. One shrubby oak, *Q. parvula* var. *tamalpaisenis*, was only recently identified.

Oak seedlings are a favorite food of deer, whose unchecked population on the Mountain may have adversely effected oak's ability to compete.

CALIFORNIA BUCKEYE (*Aesculus californica*)

While most of the Mountain's trees are deciduous and relatively unchanging in appearance over the year, buckeyes alter greatly. In winter their smooth, light gray branches are bare. In early spring, fresh, distinctive 5-parted palmate leaves emerge. In late spring, pinkish, fragrant candle-like flower clusters rise. In summer, the pear-like fruit capsules (buckeyes) form. The leaves begin yellowing and dropping. In fall the capsules darken, and linger on otherwise bare limbs into winter.

Buckeye seeds are poisonous. Local Indians leeched out the toxin (which they used to stupefy fish), then turned the residue to flour. The buckeyes' nectar and pollen are said to be poisonous to bees. Buckeyes are found throughout

Tamalpais; there is a Buckeye Trail on the northwest slope of Bald Hill.

Our species, a member of the horse chestnut family, is different from the buckeye that is the state tree of Ohio.

TOYON (*Heteromeles arbutifolia*)

This member of the rose family may either be a shrub or small tree (to 15 feet) on Tamalpais, depending on growing conditions. Its shiny, evergreen leaves are sharply saw-toothed. Also distinctive are the clusters of small red berries, similar to the Christmas berries of the eastern holly, that mature in fall and persist through winter.

CALIFORNIA NUTMEG (*Torreya californica*)

The California nutmeg is fairly common high on the Mountain's north side, as along Northside Trail. The sharp-pointed needles, with two whitish lines below, are diagnostic; accidentally squeeze a row and you'll not soon forget the nutmeg. The tree and seeds are aromatic. Male and female reproductive parts are found on separate trees. Nutmeg bears an elliptical fruit with a fleshy outer green layer (aril) around a hard-shelled seed.

Though nutmegs are often little more than shrub height, Howell reported an 86-footer fallen in Cataract Creek. Marin's nutmegs are botanically unrelated to the true nutmegs from which the spice is made; the name arose because the fruits look somewhat similar.

SARGENT CYPRESS (*Cupressus sargentii*)

Sargent cypress forms striking stands high on the Mountain, almost always on exposed serpentine rock. Distinctive are the small round cones, sectioned into 6 or 8 parts. Also, the short, scalelike leaves differ from those of the other conifers on Tam. Sargent cypresses are often stunted, with twisted trunks. However, the two largest Sargent cypresses in the world (the tree only grows in California) are on the Mickey O'Brien Trail. One is 96 feet tall, the other 85 feet. Still, a recent edition of The Audubon Society's *Field Guide to North American Trees* listed the species height limit as 50 feet!

Howell may have been contemplating the cypress stand on Simmons Trail when he wrote, "These gray-green trees blend with the gray-green rock of the serpentine barrens to form a picturesque and memorable part of the Mt. Tamalpais scene."

BIG-LEAF MAPLE (*Acer macrophyllum*)

This is an aptly named tree; it has among the largest leaves of any of the world's some 125 species of maples. Most people recognize the deeply lobed, 5-parted maple leaf. The leaves add fall color to the Mountain as they turn yellow before dropping. Single seeds are found in each of the paired "wings" of the fruit, called a samara. Look for the maples along streams, such as Corte Madera Creek on the lower part of Old Railroad Grade.

ALDER (*Alnus* spp.)

There are two species of alder on the Mountain, white alder (A. *rhombifolia*) and red alder (A. *rubra*). The latter is found only near the coast, and has the edge of its leaf rolled inward. Alders grow almost exclusively along stream banks, where they can be fairly abundant, as on the lower part of the Steep Ravine Trail. Howell writes of the white alder, "To see the green-gold of their blossoming crowns in January is one of the floral treats of the year."

CHINQUAPIN (*Castanopsis chrysophylla*)

Though often shrub-like, chinquapins can reach over 50 feet tall, as on Benstein Trail. Most distinctive are the spiny, bur-like fruit capsules, often abundant on the ground beneath the trees. The folded, lance-shaped leaves, shiny green above and yellow below, are also diagnostic. Chinquapins are in the same beech family as the oaks, but are of a different genus, and bear erect catkins.

WILLOW (*Salix* spp.)

Several species of willow grow naturally on Tam. The arroyo willow (S. *lasiolepis*) is perhaps most abundant. Willows may be found high on the Mountain in wet soils, such as at Willow Meadow, but are more abundant along coastal streams.

CALIFORNIA WAX MYRTLE (*Myrica californica*)

The wax myrtle, or bayberry, is often shrubby on the Mountain, but a tree when protected. Its elongated, saw-toothed, spotted, aromatic leaves are broadest near the pointed tips. The fruits are in berry-like clusters, with a waxy coating.

INTRODUCED TREES

There are no pines native to Mt. Tamalpais but at least four, **Monterey** (*Pinus radiata*), **coulter** (*P. coulteri*), **knobcone** (*P. attenuata*), and **bishop** (*P. muricata*), have been planted and become locally naturalized.

Monterey has needles in clusters of 3 and closed cones whorled around the limbs and trunk. Many were planted along the old rail line, such as at Mesa Station, West Point, and today's East Peak parking lot. Coulters, which have the heaviest pine cones in the world, up to 5 pounds, were planted in the Bon Tempe and Lake Lagunitas area around 1930. They are now gradually being removed by the MMWD, as along Lakeview Fire Road. Bishop pines also have closed cones in rings or whorls, but with needles in bunches of 2. They are native on the west side of the San Andreas Fault, though with some natural stands on the east side, just north of Tam. There is a large, planted row on Old Plane (Vic Haun) Trail. Knobcones have slender cones and 3 needles per bunch. Stands are on Laurel Dell Fire Road, between Laurel Dell and Potrero Meadow.

Eucalyptus and acacia are two Australian natives that were introduced to Tamalpais. They are being removed in some areas — the distinctive, 100-year-old row of eucalyptus on Sky Oaks Road near the Lake Lagunitas parking lot was cut down in 1992—to help restore native vegetation and to minimize fire danger (both are high in flammable resins). Acacias are found abundantly near Mountain Home on Panoramic Trail and Gravity Car Grade.

Shrubs

Shrubs are generally considered to be plants with woody stems, less than 10 feet tall, and without a single main axis or trunk. There is, however, overlapping, and several species appear on Mt. Tamalpais as both trees and shrubs, depending on growing conditions. Sargent cypress, for example, is a tree that grows 90 feet high on Mickey O'Brien Trail but a shrub-like two feet by the intersection of Northside and Rocky Ridge trails.

Shrubs are an important component of the flora of Mt. Tamalpais, dominating huge areas, notably the chaparral. As with the trees, though less dramatically, fewer than 25 species account for most of the shrubs on the Mountain.

Below are the most common of Mt. Tamalpais's shrubs. They are grouped, alpabetically by common name, within the plant community in which they are most likely to be found.

Chaparral
CALIFORNIA SAGEBRUSH (*Artemesia californica*)
The shrub's gray foliage has a distinctive sage fragrance. The leaves are divided into thread-like segments. It is abundant in coastal scrub.

CEANOTHUS, CALIFORNIA LILAC (*Ceanothus* spp.)
There are some 50 species of ceanothus in California, at least six on Mt. Tamalpais. Blue-blossom (*C. thyrsiflorus*) is the most common here. Its branchlets are ridged and its glossy leaves are prominently 3-veined. But most distinctive is the sweet, pervasive fragrance exuded from its clusters of blue flowers in early spring. Indigo-brush (*C. foliosus*), buckbrush (*C. cuneatus*), and muskbrush (*C. jepsonii*) of the high serpentine are other common Tamalpais ceanothus species.

CHAMISE (*Adenostoma fasciculatum*)
This member of the rose family rivals poison oak as perhaps the single most common shrub species on the Mountain, particularly on the drier slopes. Its short evergreen needles are in bunches (fascicles). The stems are stiff. Chamise's cream-colored, stalkless flowers bloom in crowded, pyramidal clusters in late spring. They linger and turn purplish, giving Tamalpais' south face its characteristic tint in fall. The plant is also known as greasewood.

CHAPARRAL PEA (*Pickeringia montana*)
This shrub has lovely pink-purple, pea-like flowers, which linger into September. It also has sharp, spiny stem tips that can be painful to the unwary.

GOLDEN-FLEECE (*Ericameria arborescens*)
The branches of this sunflower family shrub rise erect and closely bunched. In late spring, the rich green foliage stands out in the chaparral. The shrub is later crowned with clusters of yellow flowers, colorful into early fall.

MANZANITA (*Arctostaphylos* spp.)
Manzanita is abundant on Tam and throughout California's chaparral. There

are dozens of species in the state, some six on the Mountain. "Manzanita" means "little apple" in Spanish for the appearance of the fruit. The pinkish-tinged, delicate, urn-shaped flowers are a common sight in late winter and early spring and fallen blossoms sometimes cover sections of trails. Also distinctive is the bark, which peels, like that of the related madrone, to reveal a reddish trunk. Two of the manzanita species have fire resistant burls at their bases. Another, *A. hookeri* ssp. *montana*, or Tamalpais manzanita, is found only in Marin County, on serpentine, and was originally named by Alice Eastwood for Tamalpais. It is the latest blooming of Tam's manzanitas.

OAKS (*Quercus spp.*)

Oaks are generally trees but one variety of the interior live oak, (*Q. wislizenii* var. *frutescens*) and one species, leather oak, (*Q. durata*), are important shrubs on Tamalpais. The former, more common, has plane (uncurved) leaves. The latter has tough leaves that are convex above, with the margins rolled inward. Leather oak is restricted to serpentine outcrops.

STICKY (BUSH) MONKEYFLOWER (*Mimulus aurantiacus*)

Most Tam visitors recognize the funnel-shaped, orange-buff flowers of this widespread shrub. It is in bloom from February through August, often later. The bottom sides of the opposite leaves have a sticky-to-the-touch coating, hence the common name.

TREE (BUSH) POPPY (*Dendromecon rigida*)

Though not as abundant as other shrubs listed here, tree poppies stand out when their large, four-petaled, bright yellow flowers are abloom in late spring.

YERBA SANTA (*Eriodictyon californicum*)

The leathery, willow-shaped leaves of yerba santa are sticky above, woolly below. They are sometimes spotted with a black mold. Yerba santa has purplish-white, trumpet-shaped flowers. The leaves were used, either smoked or as a tea, by local Indians and early settlers to ease respiratory ailments.

Grassland

BACCHARIS (*Baccharis pilularis*)

Baccharis, also called coyote brush and chaparral broom, is abundant alongside most all Tamalpais grassland trails. It is quick to colonize grassland after livestock grazing ceases, as is evident on Tam's western slopes. Each shrub contains either male or female flowers. In winter, the seeds are dispersed by white tufts of hair, which top the seeds, and give the female shrubs another common name, fuzzy-wuzzy.

LUPINE (*Lupinus spp.*)

There are some ten lupine species on Mt. Tamalpais, several of them shrubs and not easy to tell apart. Lupines are in the pea family and have their characteristic flowers, usually blue, and seed pods. Their palmate leaves are also distinctive. Howell calls the low growing, grayish-leaved Tamalpais lupine (*L. albifrons* var. *douglasii*) "one of the most beautiful flowering shrubs."

Woodland

CALIFORNIA HAZEL (*Corylus cornuta* var. *californica*)

Hazel is a large shrub, occasionally a small tree. It is common along streamside trails throughout the Mountain. Its round leaves are very soft to the touch. The drooping male catkins begin appearing in January; the tiny, female catkins, with bright red stigmas, are separate and erect. The nuts, which squirrels and chipmunks usually harvest before hikers can find them, resemble the related filberts of the east coast. They were eaten by local Indians.

HUCKLEBERRY (*Vaccinium ovatum*)

Huckleberries line long sections of many forest trails, such as Sierra, Kent and, of course, Huckleberry. The berries are small, but sweet and tasty when black and ripe at the end of summer. The alternate leaves are shiny above, with saw-toothed margins. The pinkish-white flowers are urn-shaped like the manzanita's and madrone's; all are members of the heath family.

WESTERN AZALEA (*Rhododendron occidentale*)

Azaleas are found in wet areas; stream banks, springs, and marshes. Their showy, fragrant, creamy-white flowers make them one of the Mountain's favorites. Azaleas are usually in peak bloom in June. The smooth green leaves sprout anew each spring. Azaleas are perhaps most abundant on Tam along the East Fork of Swede George Creek, which includes Azalea Meadow.

ELK CLOVER (*Aralia californica*)

Elk clover (also called spikenard) is found in wet places, its roots always near flowing water. The huge leaves, as large as any to be found on the Mountain, are diagnostic. Amazingly, they die back each year, to grow anew full size in the spring. One of the last shrubs to blossom, elk clover sends up clusters of tiny white flowers in mid-summer. They produce purple-black berries (not edible) in fall.

CALIFORNIA HONEYSUCKLE (*Lonicera hispidula*)

Honeysuckle is a vine that entwines itself around other plants, and is often seen overhanging woodland trails. The uppermost of the opposite leaves are fused around the stem. It produces pinkish flowers in spring and red berries in late summer. Other berry-producing members of the honeysuckle family on Tamalpais are red and blue elderberry, two species of snowberry, and twinberry.

COFFEEBERRY (*Rhamnus californica*)

In fall, the black berries of this shrub resemble coffee beans in appearance, hence the name. Coffeeberry, commonly 3-5 feet tall, is found in both light woodland and grassland margins.

Multi-Habitat

POISON OAK (*Toxicodendron diversilobum*)

Unfortunately, what may be the Mountain's most common shrub, poison oak, is, in the words of the *Jepson Manual*, "one of the most hazardous plants in California." Anyone who has had a case of the itchy rash learns to identify the plant's distinctive lobed, triple-leaf clusters. But the plant assumes radically different appearances, hence the species name, "diverse-leaved." (The genus name is Latin for "poisonous tree.") Poison oak can be an isolated plant a few inches high, grow as mats on coastal hills, form thickets several feet tall, climb high as a vine or even appear to be a small tree. In summer, the leaves turn from green to red; this red colors many a hillside. It is related to poison ivy and poison sumac but not to the true oaks.

FRENCH AND SCOTCH BROOM

Brooms, not native to Marin, form thick borders to many trail and road cuts, in grassland and light woodland, particularly on the east side of the Mountain. Indeed, they have completely overrun and obscured several old routes. Because brooms are so invasive and hardy, with abundant, long-lived seeds, they crowd out native flowers (to the detriment of native understory animals as well). Broom is also considered a serious fire menace. Many groups and individuals pull broom. The MMWD has launched a ten-year "Broom Free By 2003" program, which organizes volunteers in regular broom pulls.

Brooms bear striking yellow blossoms through much of the year. On hot summer days, seeds are literally exploded outward, expanding the plant's range.

Contrary to what is often said, French broom (*Genista monspessulanus*) is the more common broom on Tam. Scotch broom (*Cytisus scoparius*) has larger flowers and smaller, almost needle-like leaves. French broom is native to southern France; its specific name, "*monspessulanus*," means "of Montpelier." It was widely planted as a garden ornamental, then moved onto Tam. Howell said of it, in his *Marin Flora* of 1948, "(French broom is) . . . a pernicious shrub weed exhibiting an aggressive vigor that the native vegetation cannot withstand."

Wildflowers

Mt. Tamalpais is exceptionally rich in wildflowers, with some 700 native and introduced species, in more than 400 genera and some 100 families, having been identified. Many species grow here at either their northern or southern geographic limit. Also, there are several species (called endemics) that grow only on or near the Mountain, and nowhere else on Earth.

There is floral color on Tam all year. Alice Eastwood, the grand lady of the Mountain's flora, once said, "There have been years when a hundred native plants could be found in bloom on and around Mt. Tamalpais in early January," (*California Out Of Doors*, 1915). Star lilies sometimes appear in December, just as the last California fuchsias and tarweeds are departing. The season is generally at its peak from mid-March to mid-May.

Presented below is a selection of 50 of the Mountain's most abundant or showiest native species. They are grouped by color of the floral leaves — the petals and sepals. Be aware that color can vary among flowers of the same species and that nature's colors rarely fit neatly into groupings. For each flower, both the common and scientific name is given. There is then a brief description. This is followed by the flower's principal habitat, its peak blossoming months, and its family. (The *Asteraceae*, or sunflower family, has the most representatives on Tam.) Habitat and period of bloom are only guides and approximations. The peak bloom, for example, depends on weather, the flower's location on the Mountain, and other factors; expect to find representatives of all the species a bit before and after the months given.

Remember, do not pick any flowers. It is not only illegal, it robs others of the chance to enjoy them and prevents the plants from forming seeds for next year's flowers. Also, some species are very rare and local. Further, picked wildflowers generally wither quite quickly.

White
Soap-plant (*Chlorogalum pomeridianum*)
The spider-like flowers stay tightly shut through the day, opening only in late afternoon to attract vespertine (evening active) insects. The up to two-foot-long, wavy-edged, narrow leaves, clustered around the base, are distinctive any time of the day. The name arises from a lather-producing substance in the bulbs, used by native Americans in washing.
Grassland • May-June • Lily family

Western trillium, Wake-robin (*Trillium ovatum*)
Trillium is closely associated with redwoods. It has three broad, pointed leaves, whorled around the stem. The single white, tri-petaled flower atop the stalk (pedicel) fades to pink/purple. A second Mountain trillium species, giant wake-robin (*T. chloropetalum*), is stalkless.
Redwoods • February-March • Lily family

Fairy-bells (*Disporum hookeri*) and Fairy-lanterns (*D. smithii*)
These similar species both have drooping flowers and orange-red berries that are only visible when the terminal leaves are lifted. Fairy-bells, with pale green petals, are more common than the whiter fairy-lanterns of deep woodlands.
Coniferous forest • March-April • Lily family

Fat (*Smilacina racemosa*) and Slim (*S. stellata*) Solomon's-seal
Both species have clusters of tiny six-petaled flowers. Fat Solomon's-seal has broader leaves, which clasp the stem, and scarlet berries; Slim Solomon's has red-striped green berries.
Coniferous forest • February-March • Lily family

Miner's-lettuce (*Claytonia perfoliata*)
This well known plant is identified by the round, leafy disk that clasps a

stalk of tiny flowers. These fleshy leaves were a source of greens for local Indians and early settlers. It is found in wet places.
Woodland • February-April • Purslane family

California strawberry (*Fragaria californica*)
    The small but tasty berries are unmistakeable. Also distinctive are the serrated, three-parted leaves.
Woodland borders • May-June • Rose family

Milk-maids (*Cardamine californica*)
    These very common flowers are often the first, or close to first, to bloom on the Mountain. They can almost always be found in January, then persist into June. The four small petals frequently have a pinkish tinge.
Broad-leaved forest • January-March • Mustard family

Morning-glory (*Calystegia purpurata*)
    This is the most common of several morning-glory species on Tam. The plant's long stem trails along the ground, or entwines around shrubs. The outer edge of the united petals usually have a pinkish, then later purplish, tinge.
Coastal grassland • April-June • Morning-glory family

Yerba buena (*Satureja douglasii*)
    Yerba buena trails low on the ground in woodlands. It has one small, five-petaled, two-lipped flower at each leaf. Its fragrant glossy leaves have long been used in teas. San Francisco's first name was Yerba Buena, "good herb."
Broad-leaved forest • May-June • Mint family

Woodland-star (*Lithophragma affine*)
    There are two similar *Lithophragma* species on the Mountain. They are not as abundant as some of the other flowers here but the five white petals, each cleft into three parts at the top, are quite showy and distinctive.
Forest and Grassland • March-April • Saxifrage family

Wild cucumber, Manroot (*Marah fabaceus*)
    The five-petaled flowers grow along entangling vines that can reach 30 feet in length. The roots are huge, accounting for the common name "manroot." The large 5-7 pointed leaves have a U-shaped base. The globe-shaped fruits, each containing four seeds, are covered with spines. A second species grows along the coast.
Grassland • March-May • Gourd family

Yarrow (*Achillea millefolium*)
    The small white flowers are found in flat-topped clusters above 1-3 foot stalks. The "thousand leaves" of the species name refers to the fine divisions. It was named for Achilles, in myth the first of many to use it medicinally.
Grassland • April-June • Sunflower family

Rosinweed (*Calycadenia multiglandulosa*)
The small irregular flowers stand out because they bloom in late summer and fall. The roughly one-foot-tall stems have short leaves covered with a sticky, fragrant, glandular secretion.
Grassland • August-October • Sunflower family

Yellow-Cream
Star lily (*Zigadenus fremontii*)
These are among the first "spring" bloomers, sometimes showing color in late December. The 6 cream-colored flower segments form a star pattern.
All but deep forest • January-March • Lily family

Yellow mariposa-lily, Gold-nuggets (*Calochortus luteus*)
This is a striking flower, its three brilliant yellow petals marked with red-brown blotches on their inner surfaces. They are often found with poppies on grassy hillsides. There are several other showy *Calochortus* species on Tam as well.
Grassland • May-June • Lily family

California-buttercup (*Ranunculus californicus*)
This well-known flower has many petals-9 to 16-with shiny upper surfaces. Local Indians boiled the otherwise poisonous seeds and roots before eating them. "Ranunculus" means "little frog," both enjoy wet places.
Moist areas • February-May • Buttercup family

Cream-cups (*Platystemon californicus*)
Each of the 6 cream-colored petals has a yellow spot at the base. The long single stem, 3-12 inches tall, is very hairy.
All but deep forest • March-April • Poppy family

Redwood violet (*Viola sempervirens*)
The lower three of the five asymmetrical petals have purple veins; the lowest a V-shaped point. The rounded, evergreen ("sempervirens" means "evergreen") leaves rise from creeping stalks. These violets are found under redwood trees. There are other violet species on the Mountain.
Redwoods • March-April • Violet family

Footsteps-of-spring (*Sanicula arctopoides*)
The flat rosette of three-parted, toothed leaves is yellowish, as are the clusters of tiny flowers. It is indeed a harbinger of spring. There are several other common sanicles on Tam.
Grassland • February-March • Parsley family

False lupine (*Thermopsis macrophylla*)
Can be told from true lupines by the 3 palmate leaflets; lupines have 4 or more leaflets. The hairy stalks rise to 3 feet. Often found in dense clusters.
Grassland • March-April • Legume family

Narrow-leaved mule-ears (*Wyethia angustifolia*)

The long, lance-shaped basal leaves resemble mules' ears. The flower heads look like the true sunflowers. A second Tamalpais species is found in more shaded areas.

Grassland • March-April • Sunflower family

Tarweed (*Hemizonia lutescens*)

One of the latest flowers to bloom, tarweed provides yellow color and a pleasing, characteristic fragrance to otherwise dry grasslands in late summer and fall. The 2-4 foot stalks are hairy and sticky. There are other Tamalpais tarweeds, in both the Hemizonia and Madia genera.

Grassland • July-November • Sunflower family

Gumweed (*Grindelia hirsutula*)

This is a rather unmistakeable plant for the milky, gummy resinous fluid exuded at the top of the buds. The showy flower heads brighten brown grasslands.

Grassland • May-June • Sunflower family

Goldfields (*Lasthenia californica*)

Goldfields' golden-yellow flower heads appear as carpets, coloring grasslands. The hairy stems can be 1-10 inches tall.

Grassland • February-May • Sunflower family

Orange

California poppy (*Eschscholzia californica*)

This is the state flower of California. It is actually not a true poppy (in the genus *Papaver*, of which there is one species on the Mountain, blooming only after fires). The petals close in the evening. Poppies can be found in flower into fall. Howell says, "No poet has yet sung the full beauty of our poppy, no painter has successfully portrayed the satiny sheen of its lustrous petals, no scientist has satisfactorily diagnosed the vagaries of its variations and adaptability. In its abundance, this colorful plant should not be slighted: Cherish it and be ever thankful that so rare a flower is common!"

Grassland • March-April • Poppy family

Brown, Green

Mission-bells, Checker-lily (*Fritillaria affinis*)

The brown, mottled, nodding, bowl-shaped flowers are often missed in deep woodland, but when one is spotted, their abundance becomes clear. Mission-bells send up large leaves their first year to gather the energy stores needed for blossoming the following spring. The plant was first discovered on Mt. Tamalpais.

Woodland • March-April • Lily family

Fetid-adder's-tongue, Slink-pod (*Scoliopus bigelovii*)

In January, the paired, large, mottled, glossy leaves of slink-pod appear abundantly in redwood forests. The three-petaled, purple-striped flowers are harder to see; they have a "fetid" odor. The slender, sinewy flower stalks droop to the ground after fertilization, self-planting the seeds.

Coniferous forest • *January-February* • *Lily family*

Red-Pink
Red clintonia (*Clintonia andrewsiana*)
The plant's huge, glossy, basal leaves stand out in redwood forests. They finally send up a rosy clusters of flowers. After fertilization, clintonia produces blue berries.

Redwoods • *April-May* • *Lily family*

Calypso orchid (*Calypso bulbosa*)
Though not common on Tam, the calypso cannot be omitted. Each plant has a single oval leaf and flower, the slipper-like lower sixth petal of which is speckled. They are generally found only beneath Douglas-firs. There are several other orchids (perhaps the largest plant family in the world) on Tam; all are rare.

Douglas-fir forest • *March-May* • *Orchid family*

California fuchsia, Zauschneria (*Epilobium canum*)-
Fuchsias are quite noticeable because they provide vivid color in fall. The woody plants have red tube-shaped flowers — a favorite of hummingbirds — beyond which the stamens and pistils extend.

Chaparral • *August-October* • *Evening primrose family*

Indian-pink (*Silene californica*)
Indian-pink is uncommon, but a visual treat when seen. Each of the flower's scarlet red petals are lobed into 4 parts. Opposite leaves clasp the 6-18 inch stalks.

Woodland margins • *May-July* • *Pink family*

Starflower (*Trientalis latifolia*)
The starflower's stalk (pedicel) is remarkably thin and delicate. It supports pink, star-shaped flowers. The number of petals, although usually 6, can vary.

Woodland • *April-May* • *Primrose family*

Indian warrior (*Pedicularis densiflora*)
Indian warrior is a root parasite, taking nutrients from other plants. The finely cut, fern-like leaves are tinged red-purple. The tubular flowers have an upper beak and a shorter lower lip. It is one of the earliest bloomers.

Chaparral • *January-March* • *Figwort family*

Indian paintbrush (*Castilleja subinclusa*)
Paintbrush is a very distinctive plant, with brilliant red tubular flowers projecting at right angles from atop 2-foot-tall stems. Each flower has two protruding yellow, joined petals.

Woodland, Chaparral • *February-April* • *Figwort family*

Farewell-to-spring (*Clarkia amoena*)

The four, showy pink-red petals display a darker red blotch in the center. The plant is one to three feet tall. It blooms as spring ends, hence the name. There are some five other clarkias on Tamalpais. Perhaps most striking is red-ribbons, or lovely clarkia (*C. concinna*). Three of its four petals point up, one down, and each is three-lobed. Helen Sharsmith, in her *Spring Wildflowers of the San Francisco Bay Region*, says of it, "flowers of bizarre beauty."

Grassland • *April-May* • *Evening primrose family*

Wild buckwheat (*Eriogonum nudum* and *E. luteolum*)

Though the tiny, clustered flowers are hardly showy, the buckwheats are noticeable because they are in bloom in summer and fall.

Chaparral • *July-September* • *Buckwheat family*

Redwood sorrel (*Oxalis oregana*)

This abundant plant of the redwood forests has three-part leaves, which fold over in excessive heat. Each 4-7 inch stalk produces a single, funnel-shaped flower, which ages from white to pink.

Redwoods • *February-March* • *Pink family*

Checkerbloom (*Sidalcea malvaeflora*)

These large, colorful flowers stand out atop their 1-2 foot stalks in grass-lands. The species produces two types of flowers; a larger, pale mauve one that has pistils and stamens, and a smaller, deep rose one that has only female parts.

Grassland • *March-May* • *Mallow family*

Columbine (*Aquilegia formosa*)

Columbine is one of the Mountain's more striking flowers, always a treat to discover. The 5 scarlet petals form nectar tubes, yellow on the inside, that project upward on the nodding stalk.

Woodland • *March-May* • *Buttercup family*

California milkwort (*Polygala californica*)

Although not showy or abundant, milkwort is noticeable because it provides late season color in woodland areas. The flowers are usually a pale rose.

Woodland • *May-June* • *Milkwort family*

Venus (Red) thistle (*Cirsium occidentale*)

This is one of Tamalpais' native thistles; several rapidly expanding introduced thistle species, such as yellow star, are now considered as problems. The reddish to purplish flowers project high among white, cobweb-like hairs. The plant stands 1 to 4 feet tall.

Chaparral • *May-June* • *Sunflower family*

Blue-Purple
Shooting-star (*Dodecatheon hendersonii*)
Shooting-stars are very distinctive, much admired, early bloomers in light woodland. The 4 petals, usually purplish, are bent downward. They are separated from the dark, pointed anther tube by a white to yellow band.
Woodland • *February-March* • *Primrose family*

Mount Tamalpais jewelflower (*Streptanthus glandulosus ssp. pulchellus*)
This sub-species grows only on Tam, and nowhere else. It is found high on the Mountain, generally in serpentine. The flask-shaped flower has 4 purple petals overhanging the purple sepals. The 1-2 foot stem is hairy.
Chaparral • *May-June* • *Mustard family*

Hound's-tongue (*Cynoglossum grande*)
This is always one of the first Tam wildflowers to bloom each year. Some plants already display round, prickled, fruits by March. The large, long stalked leaves give the plant its name. The blue flowers are coiled on the 1-3 foot stem. They have a white ring in their center, as do the very similar, but smaller leaved, forget-me-nots. Forget-me-nots, introduced from Europe, are now naturalized on Tam.
Broad-leaved woodland • *January-February* • *Borage family*

Douglas iris (*Iris douglasiana*)
The iris, with the poppy, may be the best loved of the Mountain's flowers. It displays an infinite variety of shadings. Indeed, "iris" means rainbow in Greek. It has a 3-parted, petal-like style that can be lifted to reveal the hidden stamens. All parts of the iris are poisonous. A second species, ground iris (*I. macrosiphon*), is shorter and has a fragrance.
Woodland margins • *February-May* • *Iris family*

Blue-eyed-grass (*Sisyrinchium bellum*)
The common name is misleading; the "eyes" (stamens and pistil) in the center are yellow and it is not a grass (although found abundantly in grassland). "Sisyrinchium" means "pig snout," as pigs dig for the woody roots. The specific name "bellum" (beautiful) seems more appropriate.
Grassland • *February-May* • *Iris family*

Blue dicks (*Dichelostemma capitatum*)
One of some seven similar Tam species, once all grouped in the *Brodiaea* genus. All have leafless stems and underground bulbs. Blue dicks are among the first to bloom, with a tight cluster of flowers. The later blooming Ithuriel's-spear, or grass-nut, has flowers on longer stalks that spread at the tips. Later blossoming still, into July, is harvest brodiaea. It has 3 stamens, unlike the 6 of the previous two species.
Grassland • *February-March* • *Lily family*

Baby-blue-eyes (*Nemophila menziesii*)

Howell says, "Certainly this is one of the most beautiful and best-loved wildflowers of the spring, a high favorite with everyone." The 5 united petals, above a sprawling stem, are generally a sky blue, though the color can vary. Also common is *N. heterophylla*, with smaller, paler, bowl-shaped flowers. It is found more in shaded areas.

Grassland • February-March • Waterleaf family

Western larkspur (*Delphinium hesperium*)

The spurred upper sepal makes larkspurs distinctive. There are 5 small petals. The town on the Mountain's east slope was named (apparently in error) for this flower. Red larkspur (*D. nudicaule*) is also common, in more shaded areas.

Grassland • May-June • Buttercup family

Sky lupine (*Lupinus nanus*)

There are some ten lupine species, not always easy to distinguish from one another, on Mt. Tamalpais. Some are shrubs. Of the annual, sky lupine, Howell writes, "It is this lupine which in the spring obscures the green of grassy hils and valleys with mantles and sheets of blue . . ."

Grassland • March-April • Legume family

Fauna

MT. TAMALPAIS is also home to a richly diversified animal world. Presented below are some of the birds, mammals, reptiles, amphibians, and fish (and even a famous mollusk) to be found by the patient Tam observer.

Mollusk

There are, of course, many "lower" animals on Tam — thousands of species of insects alone — too numerous to describe. One common animal without backbone worth noting is the beloved banana slug (*Ariolomax dolichophalus*). Slugs are members of the phylum Mollusca, class Gastropoda (with snails). Banana slugs, which in 1977 came within a governor's signature of becoming the official California State mollusk, are found gliding over their own mucus trails in wet forests. They have two eye stalks and, below, two feelers. Banana slugs are hermaphroditic, meaning each slug has both male and female organs.

Birds

More than 300 species of birds have been seen on or above Mt. Tamalpais, or along its shores. More than 70 species breed on the Mountain. Some birds spend their whole lives on the Mountain, many just the winters, a smaller number only summers, and a sizable number just pass through during migration. For example, the raptor (bird of prey) migration south over Tam each fall is one of the more spectacular of its kind in the United States. Described below, in standard ornithological order, are some of the more numerous birds that reside on Mt. Tamalpais all year.

Double-crested cormorant (*Phalacrocorax auritus*)

Cormorants are common on the north side lakes, where they compete with anglers (invariably more successfully, so thus a source of some annoyance) for fish. They have a long, dark, slender body with an orange throat pouch. Look for them on log booms in the lakes, drying their outstretched wings.

Great blue heron (*Ardea herodias*)

Great blue herons are tall (4-5 feet), graceful, gray-blue birds. They stand motionless in shallow water, patiently waiting to spear fish and crustaceans. Great blues nest on Tam in redwood trees at Audubon Canyon Ranch. The nesting season, enjoyed by many thousands of visitors each year, begins in late January.

Great egret (*Casmerodius albus*)

These all-white plumaged birds, with yellow bills and black legs, also nest at Audubon Canyon Ranch. They start arriving in March, then proceed to outnumber the neighboring great blue herons. A smaller, also all-white, egret, the snowy (*Egretta thula*), with a black bill and yellow legs, has also recently begun to nest at the Ranch. The great egret was long the symbol of the National Audubon Society, one of whose initial missions was to stop their slaughter for the plumes (aigrettes) used in women's hats.

Mallard (*Anas platyrhynchos*)

Thousands of ducks, representing at least ten species, regularly winter on the Mountain's lakes. Most are migrants that breed farther north. Only the mallard consistently breeds here. Male mallards have a glossy green head, white collar, and chestnut breast. The females, as with many ducks, are plainer; a mottled brown.

Gulls (*Larus* spp.)

The most numerous local gull species are California (*L. californicus*), ring-billed (*L. delawarensis*), and western (*L. occidentalis*). The latter is the only gull common the year around. Of the three, westerns are the largest, ring-billeds the smallest. Gulls take three to four years to reach unmottled, full adult plumage. Adult westerns have pink legs, California gulls have greenish-yellow legs, and ring-billeds, yellowish legs. Ring-billed gulls bear a black ring near the tip of their bill.

Turkey vulture (*Cathartes aura*)

With a wing span of nearly six feet, turkey vultures are the largest birds seen on Tam, save for the rare eagle and roughly equal sized ospreys. They are a familiar sight as they soar silently on the thermals, rarely flapping their wings, in search of carrion. If you come across a turkey vulture rising from the ground, there's likely to be a dead deer or other mammal nearby. Turkey vultures, the region's only vulture, are distinguishable from hawks by the black and white pattern under their wings, the V-shape (dihedral) in which they hold their wings, and their small, naked, red head. Turkey vultures nest on the Mountain in hollow stumps and rotting logs.

Red-tailed hawk (*Buteo jamaicensis*)

The piercing, descending cry of the red-tailed hawk, described as "keeeer-r-r," is one of the most vivid of the wild sounds on Tamalpais. The call is sometimes well imitated, though always a trifle feebly, by Steller's jays. Red-tails are commonly seen soaring, circling, and sometimes "stilling"—floating motionless against the wind—in search of rodents and other small mammals. They are the largest resident hawk, with a wing span of more than four feet. The diagnostic dark brown head is seen in all ages but only the adults have the distinctive red tail.

Osprey (*Pandion haliaetus*)

Ospreys can be found circling above the north side lakes as they hunt for fish. Osprey have whiter underparts and heads than the more abundant red-tailed hawks, and a bend in their outretched wings. Ospreys build huge nests atop Douglar-fir snags at Kent Lake. That area had rebounded by the early 1990's, after years of DDT insecticide-induced declines, to become the largest oprey breeding colony in California.

American kestrel (*Falco sparverius*)

Kestrels are the smallest of the area's falcons, a family of fast-flying raptors distinguished by their long, narrow, pointed wings. Kestrels are often seen hovering over a single spot as they seek reptiles, small mammals and insects. Two larger falcons, the merlin (*F. columbarius*) and peregrine (*F. peregrinus*), are much rarer.

California quail (*Callipepla californica*)

This is the state bird of California. Quail are often heard giving their distinctive "chi-ca-go" call or rustling through brush, or seen scurrying across trails. In summer, adults may have 10 or more young trailing behind. The plume atop the head is diagnostic.

Mourning dove (*Zenaida macroura*)

Mourning doves are ground feeders who rise with an explosive start when startled. Their pointed tails have white outer feathers. The dove's "mournful" cooing can sometimes be mistaken for an owl's call. They are the most abundant and widespread of America's doves. In the same family are band-tailed pigeons (*Columba fasciata*), found in flocks atop trees in Tam's woodlands.

Great horned owl (*Bubo virginianus*)

Owls, nocturnal and well camouflaged when they perch in trees by day, are not readily seen. The great horned owl is the likeliest to be noticed, particularly if it is being "mobbed" by smaller birds trying to force its departure. The great horned's large size (to 25 inches in length), ear tufts and its distinctive hoots are characteristic. Like all owls, they fly silently as they hunt prey and have immobile eyes.

Anna's hummingbird (*Calypte anna*)

The Anna's is the only hummingbird to winter on the Mountain. They go into a torpor at nights to reduce body heat loss. Anna's have all-green backs. In summer, they are joined by Allen's (*Selasphorus sasin*) and the uncommon rufous (*S. rufus*) hummingbirds; mature males of both these species have a rufous color on their back. The males of all three species do splendid mating flights; arcing, climbing, then ending with a rapid dive that produces a distinctive sound with their tail feathers.

Acorn woodpecker (*Melanerpes formicivorus*)

The acorn woodpecker, with its red cap, white forehead and cheeks, black chin, and white wing patches, is quite noticeable. These gregarious woodpeckers store acorns in tight fitting holes, often in Douglas-firs, so that squirrels cannot pry them out. Downy (*Picoides pubescens*), hairy (*P. villosus*) and Nuttall's (*P. nuttallii*) are three other black-backed woodpeckers. They too hammer away at trees searching for insects, building nests, or signaling territorial claims.

Northern flicker (*Colaptes auratus*)

Flickers are large (12-14 inches) woodpeckers that are just as likely to be found feeding on the ground (if they haven't been startled first) as in a tree. The white rump is quite prominent, and diagnostic, in flight on the otherwise barred back.

Scrub jay (*Aphelocoma coerulescens*)

There are two species of jays present, if not seemingly omnipresent, on Mt. Tamalpais; scrub and Steller's (*Cyanocitta stelleri*). Both are blue but of different species from the blue jay of the east. Scrub jays are more common in the Mountain's drier chaparral and oak woodland regions. Steller's, distinguished by their black crests, are more likely found in the cool, coniferous forests. A famous old sign at Van Wyck Meadow says that three "Stellar" jays live there.

Common raven (*Corvus corax*)

Ravens are considered perhaps the most intelligent of all birds, and are one of the widest ranging. They figured prominently in the mythology of the native Miwoks, and still hold a special appeal as they soar over the wildest places. Ravens are larger than Tamalpais' other large all-black bird, the American crow (*Corvus brachyrhynchos*). Ravens have a wedge shaped tail, as opposed to the fan shape of the crow, and a more nasal call.

Chestnut-backed chickadee (*Parus rufescens*)

These tiny, 4-3/4" birds are among the most approachable on the Mountain; they often come within a foot or two as they dart among tree limbs. Their black cap and throat, white cheeks, and rufous back, plus the call that sounds like "chick-a-dee," also identify them.

Bushtit (*Psaltriparus minimus*)

Often associated with chickadees, but even smaller, are the plain, gray, bushtits. Indeed, they are Tam's smallest birds outside the hummingbirds. Bushtits usually are found in small flocks flitting between shrubs.

Wrentit (*Chamaea fasciata*)

The call of the male wrentit — accelerating, single-pitched stacatto notes ending with a descending trill (the trill is absent from females' calls) — is heard throughout the year in Tam's chaparral. Spotting the common, 6-1/2", brown bird in the thick shrubbery is less easy. Wrentits may spend their whole lives in a single acre or two.

American robin (*Turdus migratorius*)

The robin needs no introduction. There are several other members of the thrush family on Tamalpais. The varied thrush (*Ixoreus naevius*), similar in appearance to the robin but with a dark "necklace" across its breast, winters in mixed woodlands. Hermit thrushes (*Catharus guttatus*) have spotted breasts, white eye rings, and a lovely, flutelike song. Swainson's thrushes (*C. ustulatus*) are summer nesters that head for Central and South America in winter.

Western bluebird (*Sialia mexicana*)

Bluebirds are always a pleasing sight. The males are a deep blue-purple on the head, throat, and wings. Both males and females have chestnut breasts. They dart for insects in open areas.

Western meadowlark (*Sturnella neglecta*)

Meadowlarks wear a distinctive V-shaped black "necklace" across their yellow breasts and have white outer tail feathers. They sing a flute-like, gurgling song. They are found most commonly in grassland.

Red-winged blackbird (*Agelaius phoeniceus*)

Among the most abundant birds in America, red-winged blackbirds are found in marshes and boggy grasslands on Tamalpais, as on the Dipsea Trail above Stinson Beach. The red on the adult male's black wing, when caught in the right light, is particularly brilliant. The males of the just as abundant Brewer's blackbird (*Euphagus cyanocephalus*) are all black, with a purplish gloss on the head and neck.

Pine siskin (*Carduelis pinus*)

Pine siskins are finches, a family of sparrow-sized, thick-billed seedeaters that have a characteristic undulating flight. Siskins can be found in most Tam habitats, but usually in coniferous woodland or atop thistles. When flying, often in large groups, siskins display yellow in their tail and wings on otherwise brown, streaked bodies. Other common Tamalpais finches include: purple finch (*Carpodacus purpureus*), a woodland denizen that is actually rose-red; house finch (*C. mexicanus*), a native of the west that was introduced to the east coast in the 1940's; and the bright yellow, black and white-patterned American (*Carduelis tristis*) and lesser (*C. psaltria*) goldfinches, commonly seen darting among thistles.

California towhee (*Pipilo fuscus*)

Two species of towhees live and breed on Tamalpais. Both have long tails and forage on the ground, scratching up food with their feet. The California (formerly the Brown) towhee is notable for its very lack of distinguishing marks; it is plain brown, rusty beneath the tail. The rufous-sided towhee (*P. erythrophtalmus*), on the other hand, is strikingly patterned. Its black wings have white spots and its black tail white outer edges. The white belly is bordered with rufous, and the eyes are red.

Dark-eyed junco (*Junco hyemalis*)

Juncos may be the most common birds on Mt. Tamalpais; it would be an unusual walk in which a few aren't seen. They are sparrow-size with a dark head, white belly, and white outer tail feathers which are visible in flight. Juncos forage on the ground, and build nests on the forest floor.

White-crowned sparrow (*Zonotrichia leucophrys*)

White-crowned sparrows migrate, but many are present all year on Tam. Adults have white and black-striped caps. They are seen scratching for food on trails, then darting into shrubs or grassland when approached. Their songs display dialects, and experts can distinguish where a particular white-crowned was raised. Golden-crowned sparrows (*Z. atricapilla*), found from October to April, are similar in appearance and habit.

Song sparrow (*Melospiza melodia*)
        Song sparrows are often seen perching, and singing, atop shrubs. They have a distinctive brown spot on the upper-center of their streaked breasts. Their specific name, "melodia," is accurate; they have a lovely song.

Fish

Coho salmon (*Oncorhynchys kisutch*)
        Coho (also called silver) salmon still spawn in Muir Woods' Redwood Creek. The 18-30 inch long, silver to brick-red adults swim upstream from the Pacific after the onset of winter rains. Females deposit 2,000-3,500 eggs each in shallow depressions at the creek's edges. Males, although exhausted, sometimes need to fight for the privilege to fertilize these eggs. The females then cover the eggs. All the adults die soon after.
        In 40-60 days, the young emerge and spend the summer in the creek. The first significant fall rains allow Redwood Creek to breach the sandbar that forms each summer at its mouth by Muir Beach. The young fingerlings, around 2-1/2 inches long, can then complete their downstream migration. They reach the ocean, adapting to the salt water. After one to three years (usually two) in the open water, they gather once again offshore outside Redwood Creek. Only some six salmon out of every 10,000 eggs laid complete the full life cycle.
        Redwood Creek's coho run has been steadily declining, even more sharply since 1984. In 1994, only ten adults were counted along with a few juveniles.

Steelhead trout (*Oncorhynchys mykiss*)
        Steelhead have a life cycle similar to the closely related coho (silver) salmon. (In 1989, biologists reclassified steelhead into the same genus as salmon.) Adults swim up Redwood and Lagunitas creeks each winter to spawn and the young head to the ocean each fall. A significant difference is that some steelhead adults are able to survive the spawning season, swim back to the Pacific, and return to spawn again. The 26-inch-long adults develop a red lateral band in fresh water. In 1997, steelhead throughout the central California coast were classified as "threatened" under the Endangered Species Act.

Amphibians

SALAMANDERS
        The **Pacific giant salamander** (*Dicamptodon ensatus*) is found near Tam's creeks and lakes. Individuals can reach 12 inches in length, although half that size is more typical. **Ensatina** (*Ensatina eschscholtzi*) are salamanders with reddish-orange spots on their dark upper surface. **California slender salamanders** (*Batrachoseps attenuata*) are indeed slender, almost worm-like, and have short limbs.
        Tam's two **newts, rough-skinned** (*Taricha granulosa*) and **California** (*T. torosa*), are similar in appearance. Both are brown with orange undersides. They spend much of the year lumbering slowly over land, then, in winter, seek calm water to breed.

FROGS, TOADS

The **western toad** (*Bufo boreas*) is Tam's common toad. It breeds in water in spring.

The **Pacific treefrog** (*Pseudacris regilla*) can climb trees but spends most of its time at ground-level. Their loud, duck-like quack belies their small (under two inches) size.

The **red-legged frog** (*Rana aurora*), the west's largest native frog (around five inches), and the **yellow-legged frog** (*R. boylei*) are both declining in numbers throughout their range. The earth's thinning ozone layer has been blamed for lowering reproductive success in several frog species.

Bullfrogs (*R. catesbeiana*) were introduced to California and Mt. Tamalpais only this century. They can be up to eight inches in length.

Reptiles

LIZARDS

It would be hard to take a walk on Tam and not spot lizards scurrying afoot. The common Tam species have regenerative tails.

Western fence lizards (*Sceloporus occidentalis*) are often seen basking in the sun atop rocks, logs, or fence posts. Males have blue throat patches and blue on the underside of the belly; a common name is "blue-belly." **Western skinks** (*Eumeces skiltonianus*) are sleeker and shinier, more snake-like. They have a brown stripe, edged with light and black stripes, down their backs. Skinks hunt insects under leaves, logs, and rocks. Juveniles have striking blue tails. **Alligator lizards** (*Elgaria multicarinata* and *E. coerulea*) spend much time under rocks and logs, but are also good climbers. Befitting their name, they do bite.

SNAKES

Several species of snakes live on Mt. Tamalpais and coming across one is not uncommon. Only the rattlesnake is any danger to man, and even rattlesnake bites are very rare with apparently no fatalities ever on Tam.

Tam's **rattlesnake**, the western (*Crotalus viridis*), is two-to-five feet in length. Rattlers are distinguished by their broad, triangular head and the rattles at the tip of the tail. A rattle segment is added each time the snake sheds its skin, which can be 3-4 times annually for young snakes, once a year or less for older rattlers. Rodents comprise much of their diet. Rattlers are most active in hot weather.

The **rubber boa** (*Charina bottae*) is shiny, plain brown above, lighter below. The tail is shaped somewhat like its head. They are 14-29 inches in length, and prefer moist, wooded areas. They kill by constriction.

The **gophersnake** (*Pituophis melanoleucus*) can grow to eight feet in length. It resembles the rattlesnake in appearance and behavior; when aroused, they sometimes hiss, flatten their head, and vibrate their tail. Gophersnakes kill rodents, rabbits, and birds by constriction.

The **common**, or **California, kingsnake** (*Lampropeltis getulus*) is also large, three-to-seven feet in length. The alternating bands of black or brown with white or yellow are distinctive. They too can hiss and vibrate their tail like the rattlesnake, but actually eat rattlers, along with other snakes and lizards.

The **western racer** (*Coluber constrictor*) can reach six feet in length. They are sleek, have large eyes, and are gray-green in color. Racers are good climbers.

Gartersnakes (*Thamnophis* spp.) are the most aquatic of local snakes. They are slender, around 2-3 feet long, and are stiped on the back and sides.

The two-foot-long **ringneck snake** (*Diadophis punctatus*) usually has a diagnostic orange neck ring. The belly and underside of the tail are also orange-red, with the bright side of the tail flashed when the snake is alarmed.

Mammals

Seeing a mammal (other than *Homo sapiens!*) in the wild is always a special experience. More than 35 species—ten of them bats—are regular residents on Tam. Some of the largest are presented below.

MULE (BLACK-TAILED) DEER (*Odocoileus hemionus*)

The black-tailed is the native, and only, deer species on Mt. Tamalpais. With several of their predators gone, and hunting long forbidden, deer are now abundant on Tam.

In fall, male bucks spar with their antlers of hardened cartilage for mating rights. After breeding, the antlers are shed. A new set, likely larger than the previous year's, begins to form in winter. In spring the antlers are covered with short hairs, "velvet," which are then scraped off.

Females (does) seek hidden shelters to bear their usually two fawns in spring. The young, spotted fawns, a joyous Mountain sight in spring, are able to walk within minutes of birth.

Deer are most active in early morning and during dusk, their favorite times for browsing on shrubs, berries, sprouting trees, and other plants. They have an average lifespan in the wild of around 16 years.

SQUIRREL, CHIPMUNK

Western gray squirrels (*Scirius grisius*) are a familiar sight on the Mountain as they scurry up trees and leap across branches. Gray squirrels make barking sounds, deeper than birds' calls. They feed mainly on acorns; many are stored and never found again. They nest in trees and bear a litter of 3-5 young in spring. Gray squirrels were almost wiped off the Mountain in the 1930's by a rabies epidemic.

California ground squirrels (*Citellus beecheyi*) are less common on Tam. Ground squirrels build long burrows in grassland. They lack the gray squirrel's light underbelly, have a dark patch between their shoulders, and a less bushy tail. They can have two litters a year.

Sonoma chipmunks (*Eutamias sonomae*) dart among rocks and shrubs high on the Mountain. They jerk their tail each time they chirp. They pack their fur-lined cheek pouches with seeds, often burying them to be re-dug later. The light striping on the back provides excellent comouflage. These chipmunks nest around logs, and give birth to 4-6 young. Tam's chipmunk was once regarded as a separate species.

RABBIT, HARE

Its long ears make the **black-tailed hare** (*Lepus californicus*), or jackrabbit, unmistakeable. They startle potential predators by using their long hind limbs to make a sudden, initial leap, then bound and zig-zag at up to 35 miles per hour. Females scrape the barest of nests, or none at all, and give birth to 1-3 litters a year, each with from 2-4 furry young.

Brush rabbits (*Sylvilagus bachmani*), or cottontails, are smaller and less swift than jackrabbits. They stick to dense vegetative cover to avoid predators. Their young, like all true rabbits, are born blind, without fur, and helpless; the young of hares are born fully furred and capable of hopping.

BOBCAT (*Lynx rufus*)

Bobcats, though not rare on the Mountain, are seen only infrequently because they are largely nocturnal and their fur provides excellent camouflage. They can be mistaken for an escaped house cat but are bigger (15 to 30 pounds), have tufted ears, and, most diagnostic, a short, bobbed tail. The usually two young are born in spring and are cared for by the mother until fall. As with all cats, they leave no claw marks on their tracks. Bobcats capture rodents, rabbits, and birds, and sometimes eat carrion.

SKUNK

There are two species of skunk found on Mt. Tamalpais, the **striped** (*Mephitis mephitis*), and the **spotted** (*Spilogale putorius*). Striped skunks have two white stripes lining their black backs. They reside in deeper woods. The smaller spotted skunks have four broken stripes and a white-tipped tail.

Skunks are omnivorous, feeding on insects, berries, rodents, eggs, or carrion. Their powerful scent gland spray keeps them relatively free of natural enemies. In spring, 2-6 young are born. They remain in the mother's care, often trailing single file, through the summer. Skunks are usually nocturnal; if you see one roaming during the day it may well be rabid and should be given an even wider berth than usual.

RACCOON (*Procyon lotor*)

Raccoons also are nocturnal and omnivorous. Raccoons have extremely agile and sensitive fingers, believed to contain more sensory nerves than found on any other mammal. Raccoons tend to dunk their food in water before eating. Litters are usually 2-7, reared by the female. Raccoon scat is common atop rocks along Tam's fire roads and trails. Raccoons are fearless night raiders of trash containers alongside homes on the Mountain's slopes.

GRAY FOX (*Urocyon cinereoargenteus*)

You have to be sharp, and lucky, to see a fox on Mt. Tamalpais, as they are nocturnal, wary, and blend in with chaparral. (A possibly rabid one once growled at me, bared its teeth and chased me off Easy Grade Trail in mid-day.) Gray foxes have a light reddish-brown underside and a black-tipped tail. They are omnivorous, eating rodents, insects, grasses, berries, and other plants and can climb trees when seeking birds' eggs. Gray foxes mate in winter, then both parents share in raising the 2-5 young born in spring.

The non-native **red fox** of east of the Sierra (*Vulpes vulpes*) has recently established a breeding population as well.

LONG-TAILED WEASEL (*Mustela frenata*)

Though rarely seen, weasels are not uncommon, particularly on Tam's grassy west slopes. The slender weasel—nine inches in body length, plus a 3-6 inch tail, but weighing only about eight ounces—invades mouse and rat burrows. Weasels are golden-brown above, whitish-yellow below. They raise a single litter of 4-8 young a year out of dens dug under rock slides and woodpiles.

RARE, LARGER MAMMALS

Mountain lions (*Felis concolor*) are also known as cougars and pumas. They were regular Tam residents (although never in large numbers; they require sizable hunting territories) before the arrival of European settlers, then were completely, or almost completely, extirpated. During the last few decades, Marin had a small resident mountain lion population on the Point Reyes peninsula, but verified Tam sightings were extremely rare. In 1994, there began a rash of reliable, publicized Tam sightings. The GGNRA and MMWD now post mountain lion warnings. Still, chances of an encounter are negligible. Mountain lions, unless provoked or guarding young, are secretive, wary animals.

Coyotes (*Canis latrans*), also long absent, have drifted back onto Tam from Sonoma County and west Marin ranch lands during the past decade. Indeed, at press time, regional sheep ranchers are clamoring for more effective ways to control coyote depredations on their flocks. Coyotes are also wary and more Tam naturalists have heard their evening calls than have seen them.

Black bear (*Ursus americanus*), and their larger cousins, grizzlies (*U. arctos*), long roamed Tam until the last black bear was trapped in Muir Woods around 1880. There was a verified black bear Tam sighting, presumably a single stray from Sonoma County, in 1993.

Feral pigs (*Sus scrofa*) are descendants of pigs introduced for hunting and of escaped domestics. Their burgeoning numbers on Tam, perhaps 200 at the peak, made them a major problem in the mid-1980's. The pigs uprooted bulbs and other vegetation, and threatened to increase still further. Traps were set, professional hunters brought in and a fence was built along Coastal Trail to keep pigs from roaming down into Point Reyes. These measures have sharply reduced, if not eliminated, Tam's feral pig population. One captured boar was six feet, seven inches from tail to snout and weighed 330 pounds.

Jurisdictions

FOR THE SEVERAL MILLENNIA that Coast Miwoks were the sole inhabitants of the Mt. Tamalpais area, there were no ownership claims, in the modern sense, on the Mountain. When Francis Drake landed in Marin in 1579, the first European to do so, he laid claim to the land in behalf of the British throne, and called it Nova Albion. But today's Marin County was generally recognized as part of Spain's New World Empire, which stretched to the tip of South America, for the several centuries following the voyages of discovery of Columbus and their other early explorers.

Spain ignored today's California, establishing no settlements whatsoever, for centuries. But when threats to its California sovereignty began arising late in the 18th century, from the Russians, British, French, and the new United States, Spain began building a chain of missions, presidios (forts), and pueblos across the State.

In 1817, Mission San Rafael Arcangel, the first European settlement in Marin, was opened. The local Coast Miwok population was almost immediately decimated by disease. Unfenced Mission livestock began roaming on Tamalpais.

By 1822, control of California passed to the new nation of Mexico, which had just rebelled from Spain. In the 1830's, Mexico divided all of Marin into huge land grants. Most of Tamalpais was awarded to two men, John Reed and William Richardson. When effective control of California passed to the United States in 1846, the status of these land grants was called into question and they remained in a legal limbo for decades. Reed died in 1843 but his heirs managed to hold on to most of the grant lands. Richardson died in 1856 and his 19,000 acre rancho, which included the largest chunk of Tam, passed to Samuel Throckmorton.

Mt. Tamalpais remained completely privately owned — mostly carved into dairy ranches, but with logging operations, hunting, mining, and other ventures as well — into the 20th century. Then, in 1908, to save one of the last stands of uncut redwood trees in the Bay Area, William Kent donated the initial acreage of Muir Woods National Monument to the federal government. That marked the start of a trend that has continued to this day, and most of Mt. Tamalpais is now publicly owned. The principal managers of Mountain lands are described below.

Marin Municipal Water District (MMWD)

The Marin Municipal Water District (abbreviated throughout this book as MMWD) manages the largest part of Mt. Tamalpais. The MMWD was created in a County-wide election in 1912 as the first public water district in California. It supplanted private water companies already operating on the Mountain.

The MMWD manages virtually all the north side of Mt. Tamalpais. Its holdings continue north across the Fairfax-Bolinas Road (this book's boundary) onto Pine Mountain and San Geronimo Ridge. On the Mountain's south face — which is no longer tapped as a source of water — MMWD boundaries cut through Rock Spring, the Mountain Theater, Panoramic Highway and Mountain Home. To the east, the MMWD extends to Old Railroad Grade, Blithedale Ridge, and Windy Ridge. On the west, the MMWD boundary runs along the spine of Bolinas Ridge.

The MMWD provides water to more than 55,000 service connections, 90% of them residences, in southern and central Marin. It maintains seven reservoirs (four — Alpine, Bon Tempe, Lagunitas, and Phoenix — entirely within this book's boundaries) with a total storage capacity of 26 billion gallons, 822 miles of pipeline, 139 storage tanks, 107 pump stations, and two water treatment plants. These reservoirs and structures are now prominent features of the Mountain.

The Water District has another role beyond providing and protecting the County's water supply; managing watershed lands as public open space. One of their recent visitor's brochures states, "Mount Tamalpais holds a spiritual significance for the San Francisco Bay Area. It is a beacon for the community; a guardian of things that are wild and wonderful; a friend; an experience . . . it is truly a place to be revered and respected. Marin Municipal Water District is steward of this land, protecting it for water supply and preserving it for future generations. Enjoy the watershed experience. It is a legacy that we pass to our children."

The MMWD maintains a ranger station at Sky Oaks, on Sky Oaks Road off Fairfax' Bolinas Road. The phone number is 459-5267. There are MMWD ranger residences on the Mountain near there, and at lakes Lagunitas, Alpine and Phoenix. All district lands are open to the public from sunrise to sunset, without charge, except for a motor vehicle fee (presently $3 daily, $4 on summer weekends, or $30 for an annual pass) to use Sky Oaks Road. Group activites with more than 19 participants require special permits. No overnight camping or use is allowed. The administrative headquarters of the Marin Municipal Water District is at 220 Nellen Avenue in Corte Madera (924-4600).

Mount Tamalpais State Park (MTSP)

Mount Tamalpais State Park (abbreviated MTSP) is the second largest land unit (6,400 acres) on the Mountain. The park comprises much of the south side of Tamalpais, south of the MMWD lands (but excluding Muir Woods) to Highway 1. On the west, the park extends to the Pacific, between Golden Gate National Recreation Area lands to the south (near Muir Beach) and north (Stinson Beach). To the east, Panoramic Highway marks the park's boundary.

William Kent and others had hoped to create a Tamalpais park since at least 1900. In the 1920's, the imminent building of a road between Mountain Home and Stinson Beach (today's Panoramic Highway) stirred the Tampalpais Conservation Club and other outdoors groups into action. They feared the road would lead to development of the private 500+ acre Newlands-Magee property, which lay between Mountain Home and Bootjack. A California legislative bill authorized the state to contribute $1 for every $2 collected to buy the parcel. When James Newlands and William Magee refused to sell, condemnation proceedings fixed the value of their land at $52,000. The money was raised and the purchase completed in 1928. The Newlands-Magee property, plus 138 acres south of it to Muir Woods and 200+ acres in Steep Ravine, the latter two parcels donated by William Kent, became the initial nucleus of Mount Tamalpais State Park. It was the second (after Big Basin) in what is now a 285-unit State Park system.

Today, the park draws more than one million visitors annually. Park head-quarters are at the Pantoll ranger station (388-2070), where there are several employee residences. The park operates four overnight fee campgrounds, the only ones on Mt. Tamalpais (see Recreation section). Mount Tamalpais State Park is open every day without charge although, beginning in 1991, a $5 parking fee was instituted at the Bootjack, Pantoll, and East Peak lots, and, in 1998, at Rock Spring.

Note that many State Park trail signs indicate the trail name on top, in smaller letters, and the destination below, in larger letters.

Golden Gate National Recreation Area (GGNRA)

The Golden Gate National Recreation Area (GGNRA) was created in 1970, partly in response to a public outcry over plans to develop a huge residential tract (Marincello) in the Marin Headlands just south of Mt. Tamalpais. Today, with holdings in three counties (San Mateo, San Francisco and Marin), it is the most visited national recreation area in the United States.

The GGNRA administers almost all the considerable public land in Marin south of Mt. Tamalpais as well as parcels to the Mountain's north and west. On Tam itself, its lands include Muir Woods (see below), West Peak (under lease from the Water District until the year 2005), the southwest corner of the Mountain, and tracts on the northwest slope of Bolinas Ridge. Also, the beach at Stinson, formerly a State park (and earlier a County park), is GGNRA-managed.

The GGNRA is headquartered in San Francisco's Fort Mason. The Stinson Beach office phone number is 868-0942. The Golden Gate National Park Association (556-2236) is a largely volunteer organization that assists the park in many ways, including fundraising and management of GGNRA bookstores.

Muir Woods National Monument (MWNM)

Muir Woods (now part of the GGNRA, but with its own administrative staff) is the most visited part of Mt. Tamalpais, drawing some 1.6 million visitors annually from around the world. Most of these tourists see little more of the Monument than the narrow, level stretch along Redwood Creek north of the main entrance. Actually, the Monument covers 560 acres, north and west of the main entrance, and rises to 1,300 feet in elevation at Cardiac Hill near the crest of the Dipsea Trail. Another boot-shaped parcel lies south of Muir Woods Road.

The preservation of Muir Woods from logging, development, and a dam was a key event in Marin Country's then fledgling environmental movement. Towering stands of virgin redwoods once lined many Bay Area creek canyons before they were felled to provide the wood used in the post-Gold Rush building boom. By 1900, few uncut groves remained. A 1903 meeting at the Lagunitas County Club in Ross resulted in organization of a Tamalpais National Park Association. This helped prompt William Kent to purchase, two years later, 295 acres of uncut redwoods along Redwood Creek. The seller, Lovell White, reportedly had offers of over twice the $45,000 price, but knew that Kent, who already owned huge tracts of the Mountain, would protect the land. In 1908, partly to thwart an attempt by the North Coast Water Company to condemn 57 acres and build a dam on Redwood Creek, Kent donated the whole parcel to the federal government. Kent later donated more than 180 additional acres to the monument.

Muir Woods is open daily from 8 a.m. to sunset. A $2 admission fee was inaugurated in 1997. The Monument phone number is 388-2595.

Marin County Open Space District (MCOSD)

The Marin County Open Space District (MCOSD) was formed as a tax-supported public agency in the general election of 1972. One percent of County property taxes go to the District. Their more than 1,000 acres of Tamalpais acquisitions since then have been concentrated on the Mountain's east side, in the Baltimore Canyon area, on King Mountain, and along Blithedale and Corte Madera ridges. The District has been the most active agency in recent years in purchasing additional Tamalpais land, helped in part because it also administers open space funds donated by the sizable Marin Community (Buck) Foundation.

MCOSD preserves on Tamalpais usually do not have water fountains, toilets, or other amenities. Parking at access points is often very limited. Many of the trails and fire roads are not signed and few are named. Rangers do patrol the lands, and, in 1997, were given authority to issue citations. The District's headquarters are at the Marin County Civic Center in San Rafael. The phone number is 499-6387.

Audubon Canyon Ranch (ACR)

Audubon Canyon Ranch occupies a sizable parcel on the northwest corner of Mt. Tamalpais, north from Volunteer Canyon and west of Bolinas Ridge. The Ranch was founded in the early 1970's as a joint effort of the Golden Gate and Redwood chapters of the Audubon Society to protect a nesting site for great blue herons and great egrets. The Ranch has become an important nature preserve and education center. Because ACR lands are open to the public only on weekends during the nesting season of March to mid-July, none of the several trails through the Ranch are included in this book. Permission to enter at other times should be obtained from Audubon Canyon Ranch, 4900 Shoreline Highway, Stinson Beach, Ca. 94970 (868-9244).

Private

Though one of the criteria used in selecting trails to include in this book was that they be on public land, a handful presented do pass through private property. They are included because they have long been traveled without hindrance, or because there is a public easement through the land, or because only a small fraction of the trail's total length is private. I urge the reader to be particularly courteous when passing through or beside any of these private sections, not only because it is proper, but because future access could someday be denied.

Bay Area Ridge Trail

The approximately 400-mile long Bay Area Ridge Trail was originally scheduled to be completed by 1998. The goal is to provide pedestrians, bikers, and equestrians with a public access route around San Francisco Bay. Some parts of the Ridge Trail will accommodate all three types of user; in other areas there will be parallel routes.

The first of the Tam sections of the Ridge Trail were dedicated on September 23, 1989. New blue signs were placed. Trails and fire roads that are part of the Bay Area Ridge Trail are noted as such in the text.

The Ridge Trail enters Mt. Tampalpais from the south via Miwok Trail — this 8-mile connection from the Golden Gate Bridge was dedicated on October 17, 1994. At press-time, only the hikers' route across Tam had been completely finalized. It follows Miwok Trail (with a short stretch on Dias Ridge Fire Road) to Redwood Creek Trail. It then crosses paved Muir Woods Road and climbs Deer Park Fire Road to Coastal Fire Road. A right leads to Pantoll Ranger Station and a crossing of Panoramic Highway. Hikers then take Matt Davis Trail and Coastal Trail to Fairfax-Bolinas Road.

Note that the Bay Area Ridge Trail is not a separate jurisdiction and has no management authority; rules of the land managers through which it passes prevail. The Bay Area Ridge Trail Council office is at 311 California Street, Suite 510, San Francisco, CA 94104. The phone number is (415) 391-0697.

A completely separate shorter and flatter Bay Trail, which will pass the eastern base of Tam as it circles San Francisco Bay, is also envisioned.

Recreation

Hiking

Hiking was the original "raison d'etre" for visiting Mt. Tamalpais. Summit registers atop the Mountain began filling with hikers' signatures from the late 1800's. (Some copies are preserved in the Mill Valley Library History Room.) That anyone can, at any time and without any reservation or fee, take a walk through the beautiful, varied, and vast open spaces of the Mountain is a privilege long cherished and zealously guarded.

No group has organized more hikes on the Mountain, literally thousands, than the Sierra Club. Their first Tam hike was in 1902, ten years after the club was founded by John Muir here in the Bay Area. Hikes are open to members and non-members alike without charge. Membership information, and the club's Activities Schedule, can be obtained from the Bay Chapter office at 6014 College Avenue, Oakland 94618 (510/658-7470), or from the Sierra Club's national headquarters at 85 Second Street, San Francisco 94105 (415/977-5500). There is an active Marin chapter.

The Mt. Tamalpais Interpretive Association (MTIA), a dynamic, all-volunteer group formed in 1983 to support the State Park in the wake of Proposition 13 budgets cutbacks, has also developed an extensive, free hiking program. Interpretive walks are offered from various State Park trailheads every Saturday and Sunday morning. Schedules are posted on trailhead information boards, such as at Pantoll, Bootjack, and Mountain Home. Association volunteers also staff the East Peak Visitor Center, which they have refurbished. The association can be reached at Box 3318, San Rafael, CA 94912 (388-2070).

In spring, during the egret and heron nesting season, docents lead walks through Audubon Canyon Ranch. The Ranch is at 4900 State Route (Highway) 1, just north of Stinson Beach. The phone number is 868-9244.

The Tamalpais Conservation Club (TCC), whose motto is "Guardian of the Mountain," has been active in trail maintenance and hiking issues since 1912. They can be reached at Room 562, 870 Market Street, San Francisco 94102. The newer Trails Preservation Council (388-5347) advocates hikers rights.

Many other other hiking and social clubs have been associated with Mt. Tamalpais. Some, such as the Tourist Club and the California Alpine Club, both of which have clubhouses on the Mountain, and the Contra Costa Hills Club, are still active. Others, such as the Cross Country Boys Club and the Down & Outer's Club, have passed into Mountain lore.

Several Marin community recreation departments also offer walking classes on Tam.

Running

Running has a long and colorful history on the Mountain. The Dipsea Race, now the oldest cross country race in America and one of the most famous trail runs in the world, was first held in 1905. High school cross-country meets have been contested on Tam for decades. A hardy band of runners has gathered at Mountain Home every Saturday morning since the 1960's to begin their long runs. Virtually every local distance runner trains on the Mountain.

To some runners, no trail is too steep, narrow or rocky. However, trails noted as "very steep," "extremely steep," "rocky" or "marginal" in the text headings will prove unrunnable for most people. Some trails, shared with horses, can be quite muddy after rains, and are so noted. Otherwise, Mt. Tamalpais' fire roads and trails offer some of the best running to be found anywhere in the world.

Much the largest running club in Marin is the Tamalpa Runners. Membership information can be obtained by writing them at P.O. Box 701, Corte Madera 94925.

Mountain Biking

Mountain bikes were literally invented in the shadow of Mt. Tamalpais, in small shops near the San Anselmo-Fairfax border in the 1970's. The pioneers first tested their fat-tired, multi-geared, durable bikes on Tam. Even the "mountain" in "mountain bike" refers to Tamalpais. The popularity of these off-road bikes has proved phenomenal, spreading throughout the world.

Presently, in all regional jurisdictions, biking is permitted on all Tamalpais' paved roads and fire roads, and is not permitted on any trails. I specifically labelled each route in this book as either a trail or a fire road (or a grade, the same as a fire road for biking purposes) to make this distinction clear. Speed limits are 15 miles per hour, 5 on curves or when passing. CHECK SIGNS AND THE LATEST JURISDICTION REGULATIONS because all rules are subject to change. The Bicycle Trails Council of Marin (P.O. Box 494, Fairfax, CA 94978; 456-7512) represents many mountain cyclists on local issues.

Horse Riding

Riding horses remains a popular activity on Tam, as it has been since the arrival of the first European settlers. Horses (and donkeys) were rented to Tam tourists beginning in the 1890's. Horse-drawn stagecoaches plied routes across the Mountain for decades until motor vehicles rendered them obsolete.

Horses are permitted on the Mountain's fire roads and on some trails. Trails open to horses are noted with "horses permitted" in their heading description. Trails in Mt. Tamalpais State Park, except for Riding and Hiking and Heather Cutoff, are closed to horses. Tam trails through Marin County Open Space District and Golden Gate National Recreation Area lands are open to horses, unless posted otherwise. Marin Municipal Water District trails, a mixed lot regarding horse access, are usually well-signed. Horses are not permitted inside Muir Woods National Monument. Remember that SIGNS AT TRAILHEADS, AND THE CURRENT REGULATIONS OF THE JURISDICTION MANAGERS, TAKE PRECEDENCE.

Three important stables (none of which offer rentals) on the Mountain are: Marin Stables (on leased MMWD land) at 139 Wood Lane, Fairfax (459-9455); Sky Ranch at 106 Crest Road, Fairfax (459-9925); and Golden Gate Stables in Muir Beach. The nearest stables offering hourly rentals are Miwok Livery at Tennessee Valley, south of the Mountain off Highway 1, and at Five Brooks, also off Highway 1, north of Stinson Beach.

The Tamalpais Trail Riders, founded in 1939, represent many Mountain riders on local issues. Their address is P.O. Box 63, San Anselmo, California, 94960.

Camping

Overnight camping on Tamalpais was once all but unrestricted. Hundreds of people spent weekends, and some lived full-time, in popular camp sites or in their own remote nooks. Sharp-eyed visitors can still find stashes of cooking utensils and other remnants of those camps. After the depression years of the 1930's, when camping on Tamalpais peaked, and particularly after the 1960's, when a new generation rediscovered living on the Mountain, restrictions against camping tightened. Today, overnight camping is permitted on Tam at only a handful of designated sites.

These campgrounds, all in Mt. Tamalpais State Park, are:

Alice Eastwood Group Campground — Camp Eastwood Road. Open only to larger (up to 75 people) groups. Reservations are required. Has water, outhouses, campfire area.

Pantoll — Junction of Panoramic Highway and Pantoll Road. Sixteen wooded campsites all within a short walk of the parking area. First come, first served; usually filled early in summer. Presently $15 per campsite ($16 on weekends, $2 less for seniors, and $3 for walk-in site #3). Firewood is sold. There is a telephone, and restrooms with flush toilets. The Pantoll phone number is 388-2070.

Steep Ravine (Rocky Point) Environmental Campground — Base of Rocky Point Road below Highway 1. Six campsites (and ten rustic cabins) on bluff above the ocean. There are outhouses, water, and a telephone. No pets allowed. Reservations are required; call 1-800-444-PARK (number subject to change) well in advance. The campsites are booked at Pantoll. If daily demand exceeds supply, a lottery is held — names are drawn from a ranger's hat — at 2 p.m.

Franks Valley Group Horse Camp — Muir Woods Road at Santos Meadow near base of Heather Cutoff Trail. The newest campground, opened in 1990. Overnight stays for groups with two to twelve horses. Reservations required, call Pantoll at 388-2070.

Camping is also allowed, by advance permit only, on lands of the Marin County Open Space District.

Nature Study

Muir Woods National Monument, the Golden Gate National Recreation Area, and the Marin County Open Space District all offer ranger-led natural/cultural history walks over their lands. Other contacts include:

California Native Plant Society — Concentrates on plant study and preservation of the native flora. Information on the Marin chapter can be obtained from Wilma Follette, 1 Harrison Avenue, Sausalito 94965.

College of Marin — Marin's community college regularly offers courses on area geology, wildlife (including marine life), plants, weather, etc. at its two campuses. Most classes are open to adults of any age who register and pay the nominal fees. Catalogs can be obtained from COM, College Avenue, Kentfield 94904. The admissions office phone number is 485-9412.

Audubon Society of Marin — Conducts scores of birdwatching walks annually. The local Redwood chapter's phone number is 383-1770.

Terwilliger Nature Education Society — Outings are geared to younger people, but adults enjoy "tripping with Terwilliger" as well. Beloved founder Elizabeth Terwilliger still occasionally comes along. The address is 76 Albert Park Lane, San Rafael 94901; phone number, 456-7283.

Fishing

Lake Lagunitas was stocked with fish soon after it was filled in 1873, and angling has been a popular pastime on Tam ever since. The old fish hatchery beneath Lagunitas Dam is still visible. Fishing is permitted, and popular, at all MMWD lakes (Alpine, Bon Tempe, Kent, Lagunitas, and Phoenix) in the Tamalpais watershed. Bass and trout are periodically stocked.

Beginning in the late 1980's, Lake Lagunitas has been managed as a self-sustaining trout fishery. The lake was drained, all the bass were removed, an aerator to provide oxygen during the hot summer months was installed, 8,000 Shasta strain rainbow trout were planted and new regulations — fishing only with artificial lures and a single barbless hook and a catch limit of two fish under 14 inches — were initiated. At Phoenix, some 1,700 tires were placed on the lake bed after it was last drained in the mid-1980's to serve as breeding places for large-mouth bass.

Fishing is subject to the California Fish and Game Code and all anglers over age 16 need a valid fishing license. Be sure to check and observe posted regulations. The MMWD offers a fishing hotline (459-0888), which includes information on when the lakes were last stocked.

Dogs

Each of the Mountain's jurisdictions has its own regulations regarding dogs. Basically, dogs are not permitted at all in Muir Woods National Monument, other federal (Golden Gate National Recreation Area) lands on the Mountain, and in Mount Tamalpais State Park. They are allowed on leash on maintained Marin Municipal Water District fire roads and trails, unless otherwise posted. In 1997, the Marin County Open Space District, which had the most liberal policy regarding dogs among Tam's land managers, began requiring dogs to be leashed while on trails. Voice control remains the standard on MCOSD fire roads. Designated wilderness areas are off limits to dogs.

Rules change; trail signs and published regulations prevail.

Hang Gliding

While all Tam jurisdictions discourage non-passive recreational activities, hang-gliding has long been permitted from designated sites off West Ridgecrest Boulevard near Rock Spring.

Some Cautions

Almost all who spend time on Mt. Tamalpais come to view it as a friend, even as a protector. Still, there are some potential problems that call for caution.

Ticks Ticks are eight-legged, blood-sucking arachnids (not insects) that have long been a nuisance on the Mountain. There is a danger of infection if they become embedded in the skin. Ticks, attracted to the warmth of mammals, brush off from foliage. They quickly and firmly attach themselves, then penetrate the skin with their head.

The tick problem has gotten more serious in recent years because of the spread, though it is still rare, of Lyme disease. The disease is caused by a bacterial spirochete (*Borrelia burgdorferi*), only discovered in 1983, carried by some ticks. If left untreated, Lyme disease (named for Old Lyme, Connecticut, where the disease was first described in 1975) can be debilitating, causing arthritis and heart and nerve problems. Our Lyme disease-carrying tick is the western black-legged (*Ixodes pacificus*), active just about all year. It is tiny (only 1/8-inch long) and visible only upon close examination.

Check yourself, or have a friend check, for ticks after trips, particularly if you went cross-country in grassland. If you find a tick, one long-time self-remedy is to dab olive oil or petroleum jelly (Vaseline) on the tick to smother it, wait 15-30 minutes, gently pull the tick straight out with sterile tweezers, then thoroughly clean the area. If the head remains embedded, if the tick has been lodged for a while, if the area shows any sign of infection, or if a circular, reddish rash has formed around the bite (often a diagnostic symptom of Lyme disease), see a physician. Early treatment of Lyme disease with antibiotics is usually successful.

Poison oak Contact with the oily sap of poison oak causes a dermatitis in most people, though the resulting degree of inflammation and itching varies widely. To compound the problem, poison oak may be the most abundant shrub on Mt. Tamalpais, common in many habitats. It also takes on a variety of appearances. It may be short or tall, single stalked or branching, a vine, or even a short tree. The three-lobed leaves, which turn reddish in late summer, are diagnostic (the old axiom is "leaves of three, let it be ") and all Mountain visitors soon learn to recognize it at a distance. Even without its leaves in winter, poison oak can still be toxic. If you know, or think, you've touched the plant, shower soon after using a strong soap such as Fels naphtha. Tecnu Cleanser is a relatively new, very effective, and now widely available product to apply after poison oak exposure.

Giardiasis Through 1997, there have apparently been no documented cases of giardiasis, an intestinal ailment caused by the protozoan *Giardia lamblia*, resulting from drinking Mt. Tamalpais water. Still, to be safe, the Marin Municipal Water District has, on their lands, posted formerly commonly used but untreated water sources as "non-potable." Readers must choose for themselves whether to drink untreated water. It is always wise, however, to TAKE AN ADEQUATE SUPPLY OF DRINKING WATER ON ANY TRIP ON THE MOUNTAIN.

Yellowjackets, Bees Yellowjackets (genus *Vespula*), wasps with an uncanny ability to sense picnickers' lunches, can be a nuisance during summer months. Female worker yellowjackets are the culprits, increasing in numbers and aggressiveness as the season progresses. Keeping food well sealed is one meager defense. These yellow and black-banded insects also congregate around water fountains, such as at Deer Park and East Peak. Stings are usually only mildly painful but can cause severe reactions in some people, requiring emergency medical attention. Prompt removal of the venom (through vacuum devices contained in many sting kits) and application of Benadryl or hydrocortisone cream are helpful. Swelling and itching commonly lasts 2-4 days.

Bees (with wasps and ants, members of the huge order *Hymenoptera*) are represented by many species on Tam. Disturbing a colony — a danger even in winter when some species are hibernating in soil and logs — can produce unpleasant consequences. Females alone are capable of stinging, injecting a protein/enzyme mix to which human reactions vary. Again, sensitive individuals may require swift medical attention. Others might try the same topical antihistamines (such as hydrocortisone and Benadryl) to relieve swelling and itching.

Rattlesnakes Rattlesnakes live and breed on Mt. Tamalpais, but bites are extremely rare and fatal encounters nil. The Mountain's variety of the Western rattlesnake (*Crotalus viridus*) is usually 2-4 feet long. It has the characteristic broad, triangular head, and rattles, a segment of which is added each time the snake sheds its skin. Give a rattlesnake, even a dead one, a wide berth to avoid any problems. Gophersnakes, also found on the Mountain, bear some resemblance to rattlers, including a vibrating tail when aroused. They, and all other Mountain snake species, are harmless.

Mushrooms Mushrooms are fungi, a separate kingdom from plants and animals, that produce a fleshy, fruiting body. Hundreds of mushroom species grow on Mt. Tamalpais, particularly in forests during the rainy season. Take a walk on any woodland trail after a rain and be dazzled by the numbers and variety. Mushroom collecting on Tam, once unregulated, is now controlled. Check with the managing land authority for current rules.

Some local mushroom species, are, of course, highly toxic and it is not uncommon to hear of fatalities each season somewhere in the Bay Area. The *Amanita* family is particularly dangerous; deadly poisonous members bear such names as "death cap" (*A. phalloides*) and "destroying angel" (*A. ocreata*). Needless to say, only experienced mycologists should consider sampling wild mushrooms.

Mountain lions In 1994, a 150-pound mountain lion killed a runner in the Sierra foothills. Within months there were several confirmed mountain lion sightings on Tam, after decades of almost none, and fears mounted. There are now mountain lion warnings at several Tam trailheads. But chances of a meeting a mountain lion are so remote that no one need alter in any way their behavior on the Mountain. The standard GGNRA warning sign reads:

"Remain calm — do not run.
Pick up small children immediately.
Stand upright — maintain eye contact.
Back away slowly.
Be assertive — if approached, wave your arms, speak firmly or shout, and throw sticks or rocks.
If attacked, fight back aggressively. "

Homo sapiens   In 1979-80, David Carpenter, the so-called "Trailside Killer," murdered several hikers on Mt. Tamalpais and on other Bay Area trails. An unprecedented fear gripped the Mountain. Carpenter was caught in 1980, then tried, convicted, and given a death sentence.

The fact is that the Mountain has always been a safe place, and remains so. Crimes of any sort on Tam are rare. There are occasional car break-ins — don't leave valuables in cars parked at trailheads — but if you lose an item on a trail it will more likely than not be returned to you. Those wary to venture alone on the Mountain can always find companions from the groups listed above. Report suspicious activities to a ranger.

Fire   Fires have always been a part of Mt. Tamalpais, even before the arrival of settlers. In historic times, a fire in 1859 reportedly burned for three months. In 1881, another scorched 65,000 acres. In 1904, 14,000 acres burned. In 1929, a fire destroyed 117 homes in Mill Valley, lit up the night sky of San Francisco, and was visible in Santa Cruz. The last major Tam conflagration was in 1945, clearing 17,000 acres on the north side. Since lightning is rare in Marin, modern-era fires are usually man-made.

There has considerable debate over the issue of fire management on Tam. While most experts and land managers now favor controlled burns to diminish potential fuel sources, others argue against any interference. There have also been proposals to clear long, broad fire breaks.

At all times, but particularly during the hot, rainless months of summer and fall, Mountain visitors must exercise exceptional caution regarding potential fire-causing activities. Smoking is now prohibited entirely on MMWD lands, in summer (April 1 through November 30) on MCOSD trails. Several times a year, when high temperatures combine with dry air, land managers close trails, with heavy fines for violators. During fire season, the Marin County Fire Department maintains an information line, 499-7191, for daily updates on fire conditions, including Mt. Tamalpais trail and road closures.

Chronological History

150,000 years ago — Erosion of less resistant rock leaves Mt. Tamalpais with a profile somewhat resembling today's shape.

18,000 years ago — The global ice age peaks; so much of the earth's water is tied up as ice that sea level is 30 miles west of Mt. Tamalpais.

7,000 years ago — Coast Miwok Indians, migrants from Siberia, begin living along the ocean and bay margins of Mt. Tamalpais.

3,000 years ago — The Potrero Landslide, almost two miles long and nearly 3,500 feet wide, drops a huge chunk off the north side of Tamalpais.

1,200 years ago — The oldest known living redwood tree on Mt. Tamalpais sprouts.

1542 — The Spanish explorer Juan Cabrillo sails past Tamalpais and may have been the first European to see it.

1792 — British navigator George Vancouver produces the first map of the San Francisco Bay Area that has Mt. Tamalpais distinctly identified, though not named.

1793 — Spaniards in Lt. Felipe de Goycoechea's overland expedition are believed to be the first Europeans to walk on the Mountain; it is unknown if they ascended to the summit.

1817 — Mission San Rafael Arcangel is established, beginning European settlement in Marin County. Cattle grazing is introduced to Mt. Tamalpais shortly after, substantially altering the vegetation. The native Indian population is decimated within a few decades, mostly by European diseases.

1822 — Control of California passes from Spain to the new nation of Mexico.

1826 — British Captain Frederick Beechey prepares a detailed nautical map of the Bay Area and gives the name "Table Mountain," which persists for decades, to Mt. Tamalpais. He may have been the first European to reach the summit.

1834 — The Mexican government makes the first of its Marin County land grants, which includes the eastern slope of Mt. Tamalpais, to Irish-born John Reed. Two years later, Reed builds an adobe house and a sawmill in what is now Mill Valley.

1835 — The southern and western flanks of Mt. Tamalpais are included in a 19,000 acre land grant to William Richardson.

1846 — Possession of Alta California passes from Mexico to the United States. California becomes a state in 1850.

1848 — The discovery of gold in the Sierra foothills sets off a boom in hitherto sleepy San Francisco. The demand for lumber accelerates commercial logging on Tam, which is soon cleared of virtually all its first growth redwoods.

1873 — Lagunitas Creek is dammed to form Lake Lagunitas as a reliable source of drinking water for a growing San Rafael. Dams forming Phoenix (1905), Alpine (1919), Bon Tempe (1949), and Kent (1954) lakes follow.

1880 — The apparently last bear resident on Mt. Tam is trapped in Redwood Canyon.

1884 — Eldridge Grade, the first stage road up the Mountain, opens.

1893 — A rough wagon road into Redwood Canyon (Muir Woods) is graded, bringing the first rush of tourists.

1896 — The Mt. Tamalpais Railway lays 8.5 miles of track from Mill Valley to near East Peak and begins bringing passengers up on its steam-powered trains. A spur to Muir Woods opens in 1907. The railway ceases operations, and the track is torn up, in 1930.

1898 — The first trail map of the Mountain is published by Sanborn and Knapp.

1901 — A marine observatory is built atop East Peak. It was rebuilt in 1937 and now serves as a fire lookout.

1904 — West Point Inn is built.

1905 — The first Dipsea Race is run.

1906 — The devastating San Francisco earthquake and fire begins another rush of development to Marin and the Mountain's slopes.

1908 — William Kent donates Muir Woods to the United States Government. It is the first public park land on Mt. Tamalpais.

1912 — The Marin Municipal Water District, which now manages most of Mt. Tamalpais, is created by a public referendum. It replaced earlier private water companies holding Mountain lands.

The Tamalpais Conservation Club is formed and organizes the first of its trail maintenance days, which continue to this day. The Tamalpais branch of the Tourist Club is founded the same year, and the California Alpine Club in 1914. Both still have clubhouses on the Mountain.

The original Mountain Home Inn opens.

1913 — The first Mountain Play, "Abraham and Isaac," is performed.

1917 — Mt. Tamalpais Game Refuge is established.

1918 — The first of five annual Women's Dipsea Hikes, pioneering events in women's sports in America, is held.

1925 — Ridgecrest Boulevard, from Fairfax-Bolinas Road to near East Peak, is built as a toll road.

1928 — Mt. Tamalpais State Park, one of the first in the California system, is created. Subsequent additions enlarge it from 500 to more than 6,000 acres.

1929 — Panoramic Highway, across the Mountain, opens. The connection to Ridgecrest Boulevard (between Pantoll and Rock Spring) was finished the following year.

A devastating fire sweeps the Mountain's south side, destroying 117 Mill Valley homes.

1933 — The depression-inspired Civilian Conservation Corps sets up two camps on the Mountain and begins a variety of major building projects, including fire roads and the Mountain Theater.

1937 — The opening of the Golden Gate Bridge creates still another wave of construction around the Mountain.

1941 — The Army closes off significant parts of the upper Mountain for military purposes.

1944 — Eight servicemen die when a Navy seaplane crashes into the southeast face of the Mountain.

1945 — One of the largest fires in the county's history burns out of control for a week on Tamalpais' north side.

1951 — The Mill Valley Air Force Station is built atop West Peak on land leased from the Marin Municipal Water District. The summit, then the Mountain's highest, is bulldozed from 2,604 feet to 2,567 feet, making it lower than East Peak. The property was declared surplus in 1983, and the lease transferred to the Golden Gate National Recreation Area. In 1986, the first buildings were torn down by volunteers.

1962 — The Marin and Golden Gate Audubon Society chapters join to help establish Audubon Canyon Ranch. The Ranch later expands its Tamalpais acreage.

1971 — The Golden Gate National Recreation Area, now with extensive holdings on the south and west of the Mountain, is created.

1972 — The Marin County Open Space District, which subsequently acquires sizable parcels on the east side of the Mountain, is formed by a general election.

1974 — The first "mountain" bikes, direct forebears of today's machines, are tested on the north side of Mt. Tam.

1980 — David Carpenter creates an unprecedented atmosphere of fear on the Mountain by murdering several hikers. He was captured, then found guilty and sentenced to death.

The Mt. Tamalpais History Project, headed by Lincoln Fairley, is organized.

1989 — In recognition of its importance as a world resource, Mt. Tamalpais is named by the United Nations as an International Biosphere Reserve, one of just 250 on the planet.

Further Study

History Collections

Lucretia Little History Room — This room, in the basement of the Mill Valley Public Library, houses perhaps the most extensive collection of Mt. Tamalpais literature, maps, photographs, and artifacts. It is open, staffed by volunteers, generally four to six hours a day, Tuesday through Saturday. The library is at 375 Throckmorton Avenue; the phone number is 389-4292.

Anne Kent California History Room — Kent is the family name most closely associated with Tamalpais. This splendid collection is part of the Marin County Free Library, in the Civic Center in San Rafael, and is open during regular library hours. The phone number is 499-7419.

Marin County Historical Society — The Society's headquarters, repository for a broad range of books, photographs and artifacts, are in the historic Boyd Gate House Museum at 1125 B Street in San Rafael. The phone number is 454-8538.

There are also important Tam-related collections in the Jack Mason Museum in Inverness, the Bancroft Library at the University of California in Berkeley, and at public libraries in the communities that surround Mt. Tamalpais.

Recommended Maps

Trails of Mt. Tamalpais and the Marin Headlands, published by the Olmsted Bros. Map Co., Berkeley. This handsome, full-colored map features forty-foot contour intervals, historical references, and covers Marin from Pine Mountain to the Golden Gate. Many of the map's mileage figures were taken from this book. The 7th edition appeared in 1996.

Erickson's Mount Tamalpais Trail Map, published by Eureka Cartography, Berkeley. This is the updated successor to the classic, Freese Bros. Tam maps.

Mount Tamalpais State Park Map, published by the State. Includes adjacent Water District and GGNRA trails. Available at Pantoll and at Marin District Headquarters (7665 Redwood Boulevard, Novato).

Mt. Tamalpais Watershed Map, published by the Marin Municipal Water District. It too was updated in 1994. It covers MMWD lands on Tam, and west to Kent Lake. It is sold for $2 at Sky Oaks and at MMWD headquarters (220 Nellen Avenue, Corte Madera).

Marin County Open Space District, Southern Preserves, published by the MCOSD in 1997. The *Southern Preserves* brochure, one of four covering MCOSD lands, includes Mt. Tam. Available for $2 each at the MCOSD Office (Room 417, Marin County Civic Center).

Books In Print

Among many Mt. Tam-related books, the following are presently, or were recently, in print:

Mount Tamalpais, A History, by Lincoln Fairley (Scottwall Associates, San Francisco, 1987). A handsome book, with superb photos, lovingly researched by Fairley.

The Crookedest Railroad in the World, by Ted Wurm and Al Graves (Trans-Anglo Books, Glendale, Ca., 1983). The definitive work on the Mt. Tamalpais & Muir Woods Railway.

Marin Flora, by John Thomas Howell (University Of California, Berkeley, second edition 1970). The authoritative compilation of the Mountain's trees, shrubs, wildflowers, and ferns.

Dipsea, The Greatest Race, by Barry Spitz (Potrero Meadow Publishing Co., San Anselmo, Ca., 1993). The story of the nation's second oldest footrace, run over Mt. Tam since 1905.

Mill Valley, The Early Years, by Barry Spitz (Potrero Meadow Publishing Co., San Anselmo, Ca., 1997). The story of the town that has long served as the gateway to Tam.

Dreams of Tamalpais, by Sharon Skolnick (Last Gasp, San Francisco, 1989). Explores the Mountain's spiritual significance.

Muir Woods, by James Morley (Smith-Morley, San Francisco, 1991). Features more than 100 stunning color photographs.

Muir Woods, Redwood Refuge, by John Hart (Golden Gate National Park Association, San Francisco, 1991). An attractive and informative guide.

Web of Water, by Maya Khosla (Golden Gate National Park Association, San Francisco, 1997). A guide to Redwood Creek, which flows through Muir Woods.

Organizations

Several volunteer organizations are devoted to Mt. Tamalpais. They include, in alphabetical order:

Golden Gate National Park Association (GGNPA) — This very active non-profit group supports the staff of the Golden Gate National Recreation Area, which administers Muir Woods and much of Tamalpais' western slope. Membership information can be obtained through GGNPA, Fort Mason, Building 201, San Francisco 94123; 776-0693.

Health & Habitat — Headquartered on Tam, Health & Habitat works to preserve and restore native species and habitats. Founder Sandra Ross can be reached at: Health & Habitat, 76 Lee Street, Mill Valley, CA 94941.

Mt. Tamalpais History Project (MTHP) — The group promotes historical research, restoration and preservation, and dissemination of information. The project can be reached through Fred Sandrock at 21 South Green, Larkspur, CA 94939.

Mt. Tamalpais Interpretive Association (MTIA) — Founded in the early 1980's, the MTIA supports State Park staff by leading hikes, operating the Mt. Tam Visitor Center near East Peak, and fundraising. Their motto is, "If you love the Mountain, there's a place for you." The MTIA can be contacted at Box 3318, San Rafael, CA 94912; 388-2070.

Tamalpais Conservation Club (TCC) — The TCC was founded in 1912 after hikers saw a hunter butchering a deer near Rock Spring. The TCC played a major role in establishing Mt. Tamalpais State Park. The TCC, long known as "Guardian of the Mountain," is active in trail maintenance, conservation issues, and helping to finance public land acquisitions. The address is 870 Market Street, Room 562, San Francisco 94102; 391-8021.

Appendix

Trail	Miles*	Trailhead	Page
Alpine	.35	Pantoll	138
Alpine Pump F.R.	.50	Sky Oaks	184
Arturo	.49	East Ridgecrest	20
Azalea Hill	.85	Sky Oaks	185
Azalea Meadow	.85	East Ridgecrest	21
Bald Hill	.71	Deer Park	10
Barbara Spring	.34	Old Highway 101	118
Bare Knolls	.32	West Ridgecrest	226
Ben Johnson	1.27	Muir Woods	100
Benstein**	1.16	Rock Spring	168
Bill Williams	.64	Phoenix Lake	152
Blithedale Ridge F.R.	2.33	Mill Valley	52
Bon Tempe	3.96	Sky Oaks	186
Bootjack**	2.77	Muir Woods	101
Bridle Path F.R.	.27	Sky Oaks	188
Buckeye	.25	Deer Park	11
Bullfrog F.R.	.83	Sky Oaks	189
Camino Alto F.R.	1.19	Old Highway 101	119
Camp Eastwood Road	2.25	Mountain Home	82
Canyon	.69	Deer Park	11
Casey Cutoff	.51	Sky Oaks	190
Cataract	2.89	Rock Spring	169
Cedar F.R.	.72	Old Highway 101	120
Coastal	9.2	West Ridgecrest	227
Colier	1.5	Sky Oaks	190
Concrete Pipeline F.R.	2.78	Sky Oaks	192
Corte Madera Ridge F.R.	1.69	Old Highway 101	121
Corte Madera	.37	Mill Valley	54
Cross Country Boys	1.00	Sky Oaks	193
Cypress	1.56	Mill Valley	55
Dawn Falls	1.84	Old Highway 101	123
Deer Park F.R.	1.13	Deer Park	12
Deer Park F.R. (#2)	2.39	Muir Woods	104
Deer Park Trail	.84	Deer Park	13
Dias Ridge F.R.	2.18	Highway One	40
Dias Trail	.93	Highway One	41
Dipsea	6.8	Mill Valley	56
East Peak Fire	1.2	Sky Oaks	194
Eastwood	.50	East Ridgecrest	22
Easy Grade	.60	Pantoll	139
Eldridge Grade	5.46	Phoenix Lake	153
Elliott	.48	Deer Park	13
Escalon-Lower Summit F.R.	1.26	Old Highway 101	125

Fern Canyon	1.03	Muir Woods	105
Fern Creek	.74	East Ridgecrest	23
Filter Plant Road	1.00	Sky Oaks	196
Fish Grade	.76	Phoenix Lake	154
Fish Gulch	.57	Phoenix Lake	155
Garden Pump	.38	Mill Valley	61
Glen F.R.	.87	Mill Valley	62
Gravity Car Grade	.97	Mountain Home	84
H-Line F.R.	.89	Mill Valley	62
Harry Allen	1.15	Phoenix Lake	156
Heather Cutoff	1.46	Muir Woods	107
Helen Markt	1.75	West Ridgecrest	231
Hidden Cove	.33	Sky Oaks	197
Hidden Meadow	.77	Phoenix Lake	157
High Marsh	2.21	West Ridgecrest	232
Hill 640 F.R.	.30	Pantoll	140
Hillside	.70	Muir Woods	108
Hogback F.R.	.61	Mountain Home	85
Hoo-Koo-E-Koo	4.04	Old Highway 101	126
Horseshoe F.R.	.28	Mill Valley	63
Huckleberry	.61	Old Highway 101	128
Indian F.R.	1.33	Old Highway 101	129
International	.52	East Ridgecrest	24
Junction	.25	Deer Park	14
Kent Canyon	.5	Muir Woods	109
Kent F.R.	.67	Old Highway 101	130
Kent Trail	3.85	Sky Oaks	197
King Mountain Loop**	1.95	Old Highway 101	131
Ladybug	.46	Old Highway 101	133
Lagoon Extension	.35	Sky Oaks	200
Lagoon F.R.	.78	Sky Oaks	201
Lagunitas Fire	1.5	Sky Oaks	202
Lake Lagunitas F.R.	1.58	Sky Oaks	203
Lakeview F.R.	.78	Sky Oaks	205
Lakeview Trail	.25	East Ridgecrest	25
Laurel Dell F.R.	2.20	West Ridgecrest	234
Liberty Gulch	1.20	Sky Oaks	206
Logging	.68	Sky Oaks	207
Lone Tree	1.68	Highway One	42
Lone Tree Hill F.R.	.27	Pantoll	141
Lost	.52	Muir Woods	110
Lower Berry	.41	Sky Oaks	208
Lower Northside	.91	East Ridgecrest	26

Rocky Ridge Fire Trail	.8	East Ridgecrest	33
Ross	.66	Phoenix Lake	159
Scott Tank F.R.	.25	Sky Oaks	216
Shaver Grade	1.69	Phoenix Lake	160
Sierra	1.05	Mountain Home	93
Simmons	.95	Rock Spring	178
Six Points	.57	Deer Park	16
Sky Oaks-Lagunitas	1.40	Sky Oaks	217
Southern Marin Line F.R.	2.78	Old Highway 101	134
Stapelveldt	1.02	Pantoll	144
Steep Ravine	2.12	Pantoll	145
Stocking	1.10	Sky Oaks	218
Sun	.69	Mountain Home	94
Swede George	.86	Rock Spring	180
Tavern Pump	.33	East Ridgecrest	34
Taylor	.52	Sky Oaks	220
TCC	1.80	Pantoll	147
Telephone	.6	Mill Valley	71
Temelpa	1.5	Mill Valley	72
Tenderfoot	1.09	Mill Valley	74
Three Wells	.27	Mill Valley	75
Troop 80**	1.48	Mountain Home	95
Tucker	1.65	Phoenix Lake	161
Tucker Cutoff	.26	Old Highway 101	135
Upper Berry	.45	East Ridgecrest	35
Van Wyck Creek	1.1	Sky Oaks	221
Verna Dunshee	.68	East Ridgecrest	36
Warner Canyon F.R.	1.19	Mill Valley	76
Warner Falls	.48	Mill Valley	77
West Point	.65	Pantoll	148
Wheeler	.53	Mill Valley	78
Willow Camp	2.82	West Ridgecrest	239
Willow Meadow	.55	Sky Oaks	222
Worn Spring F.R.	2.51	Phoenix Lake	162
Yolanda**	2.23	Phoenix Lake	164
Zig-Zag	.50	Mill Valley	79

TOTAL MILEAGE   **209.4**

* When mileage is shown to two decimal places (hundredths of a mile), distance was measured with a surveyor's wheel.

** Trails containing a spur; distance of all spurs (total of 2.0 miles) not included.

BARRY SPITZ has been exploring Mt. Tamalpais for more than 25 years. He has served as president of the Mt. Tamalpais History Project, been on the boards of directors of the Tamalpais Conservation Club, Marin Discoveries, and Golden Gate Audubon Society, and been a member of the Marin County Trails Committee and the San Anselmo Parks and Recreation Commission. Spitz has led interpretive trips on Tam for the College of Marin, California

The author with wife Pamela and daughters Lily (l) and Sally, at Bullfrog Road.

Native Plant Society, Marin Discoveries, San Anselmo Parks and Recreation, Golden Gate Audubon Society, and other groups. Spitz lives in San Anselmo with his wife Pamela and daughters Sally and Lily.

Also By The Author

MILL VALLEY, THE EARLY YEARS

The first published history of Mill Valley, long the principal access to Mount Tamalpais. Explores the town's colorful past, from Coast Miwok and Spanish-Mexican rancho days to World War II. Chapters on the railway up Mount Tamalpais, Muir Woods, Mount Tamalpais State Park. 272 pages, 175 historic photographs. Indexed. Cloth.

DIPSEA, THE GREATEST RACE

The story of the fabled Dipsea, the oldest cross country race in America, run over Mt. Tamalpais from Mill Valley to Stinson Beach since 1905. Includes accounts of every race, a removable, four-color map of the Dipsea Trail, 65 photographs, biographies of all champions, and full statistical tables. Chapters on the pioneering Women's Dipsea Hikes of 1918-1922, the Double Dipsea, and Quadruple Dipsea. 240 pages. Indexed. Cloth and paperback.

Copies of *Tamalpais Trails* may be ordered by mail for $18.95 each (plus sales tax of $1.37); of *Mill Valley, The Early Years* for $35 (tax, $2.54); and of *Dipsea, The Greatest Race* for $27.95 for hardbound (tax, $2.03) and $18.95 for paperback (tax, $1.37). Postage will be paid by the publisher. Phone inquiries to: (415) 454-2769. Send check or money order, payable to Potrero Meadow Pub. Co., to:

Potrero Meadow Publishing Co.
P.O. Box 3007
San Anselmo, CA 94979

The author will be be happy to honor requests for autographs or personal inscriptions.